Sustainable Development Goals Series

"This is a fascinating, informative and brilliantly argued two-volume book project that puts forward a convincing case for *communication for all* as an additional goal for the 2030 Agenda for Development, also known as the Sustainable Development Goals (SDGs). Expert scholars and researchers, led by renowned Jan Servaes & Muhammad Jameel Yusha', collectively take a stand for the purpose of revisiting and updating the agenda, collectively agreed by 193 countries in 2015. From several perspectives and regions, book takes head on the challenge of unpicking the Sustainable Development and the SDGs is accompanied by a clear call for including communication and culture in it. The volume makes it clear that if adopted by the 2030 Agenda for as the 18 SDG, it could create a framework that could leverage the role of communication and culture in achieving the SDGs. The unprecedented book provides evidenced and an unmissable voiced that uphold the right to communicate as a bedrock for democracy, development, and social change. The call to action is supported by evidence that is both fascinating and relevant. From several perspectives, including the capability, multiplicity and participatory approaches, communication and culture for all, as an SDG, could become the rallying point for inclusive social change and development. It is a legacy project that rises to the challenge. The book is not just urgent, it is a must read for all."
—Winston Mano, *Reader/Associate Professor, School of Media and Communication, University of Westminster, UK*

"The Sustainable Development Goals have given the nations and peoples of the world non-authoritarian guidelines and signposts that each can apply in their own context, to increase our capacity to care for the planet, its human inhabitants and the wider web of life. This can only be done by widely sharing knowledge and communication. This book is an exemplary knowledge commons. Through this approach, we can all learn, in the whole world, but locally contextualized, how we can communicate the experiences of positive change for human health. Any improvement anywhere becomes a shared experience everywhere. I would recommend this approach for every single domain of development."
—Michel Bauwens, *Founder and Director of the P2P Foundation*

"This book offers a much-appreciated counterweight to the relegation of communication to a secondary role. Instead, it demonstrates communication's centrality to development and humanity. The chapters, each in their own ways, mobilize justified support for the democratization of communication and an intensified respect for communication rights, which promise to offer increased opportunities for a global understanding through dialogue, grounded in a radical acknowledgement of diversity."

—Nico Carpentier, *President, International Association for Media and Communication Research (IAMCR)*

"Jan Servaes and Muhammad Jameel Yusha'u have elevated the discussion about the Sustainable Development Goals by drawing attention to the missing link in SDGs. Researchers and policy makers would find this book invaluable in the effort to ensure that no one is left behind in the realization of the 2030 Agenda for Development."

—Abdalla Uba Adamu, *Professor, Department of Information and Media Studies, Bayero University, Kano, Nigeria*

The **Sustainable Development Goals Series** is Springer Nature's inaugural cross-imprint book series that addresses and supports the United Nations' seventeen Sustainable Development Goals. The series fosters comprehensive research focused on these global targets and endeavours to address some of society's greatest grand challenges. The SDGs are inherently multidisciplinary, and they bring people working across different fields together and working towards a common goal. In this spirit, the Sustainable Development Goals series is the first at Springer Nature to publish books under both the Springer and Palgrave Macmillan imprints, bringing the strengths of our imprints together.

The Sustainable Development Goals Series is organized into eighteen subseries: one subseries based around each of the seventeen respective Sustainable Development Goals, and an eighteenth subseries, "Connecting the Goals," which serves as a home for volumes addressing multiple goals or studying the SDGs as a whole. Each subseries is guided by an expert Subseries Advisor with years or decades of experience studying and addressing core components of their respective Goal.

The SDG Series has a remit as broad as the SDGs themselves, and contributions are welcome from scientists, academics, policymakers, and researchers working in fields related to any of the seventeen goals. If you are interested in contributing a monograph or curated volume to the series, please contact the Publishers: Zachary Romano [Springer; zachary.romano@springer.com] and Rachael Ballard [Palgrave Macmillan; rachael.ballard@palgrave.com].

Jan Servaes • Muhammad Jameel Yusha'u
Editors

SDG18 Communication for All, Volume 1

The Missing Link between SDGs and Global Agendas

Editors
Jan Servaes
KU Leuven
Leuven, Belgium

Muhammad Jameel Yusha'u
Harvard Kennedy School
Cambridge, MA, USA

ISSN 2523-3084   ISSN 2523-3092   (electronic)
Sustainable Development Goals Series
ISBN 978-3-031-19141-1   ISBN 978-3-031-19142-8   (eBook)
https://doi.org/10.1007/978-3-031-19142-8

This Palgrave Macmillan imprint is published by the registered company Springer Nature Switzerland AG.
The registered company address is: Gewerbestrasse 11, 6330 Cham, Switzerland

To the millions of people who strive for a sustainable future that is just and equitable, whilst living within the limits of supporting ecosystems.
To Patchanee, Fiona, Lisa, and extended families...
To Hauwa, Asma and Aishah for the blessing of having you as a family

PREFACE AND OVERVIEW OF THE BOOKS

Serendipity still exists. Even in corona times!

In September 2020 we were informed by Mala Sanghera-Warren, Commissioning Editor of Journalism, Media and Communication, and Molly Beck, coordinator of the advisory boards for Humanities subject areas at the Palgrave Macmillan office in London, that Palgrave was creating a new cross-disciplinary series dedicated to the Sustainable Development Goals (SDGs). The Palgrave Sustainable Development Goals series will span Palgrave's entire publishing portfolio, from Humanities subject areas (Media Studies, Cultural Studies, Literature, History, and Philosophy) to Politics, the Social Sciences, and Business and Finance.

They inquired whether I'd be interested in joining the advisory board for this new series. During the pursuing exchanges I did accept not only the board's membership but also the challenge to coordinate the editing of two volumes, of what we initially called "the missing SDG".

A Call for Chapters and Abstracts was distributed widely with a deadline set for 10 June 2021. Authors whose abstract met the high-quality criteria were contacted by 10 July 2021. Full chapters were expected by 1 November 2021. A total of 36 chapters were submitted. They all went through a two-tier peer-review process. This review and selection process was not always easy. We had to disappoint a number of people who were eager to contribute. After revisions, 21 manuscripts were selected for publication. They are split over the two volumes as follows:

Overview of Volume 1: The Missing Link Between SDGs and Global Agendas

This volume contains 11 chapters.

In the introductory chapter, Jan Servaes and Muhammad Jameel Yusha'u position the need for an 18th Sustainable Development Goal—Communication for All.

Chapter 2, by Laurenzo Vargas and Philip Lee, explores the intersections between the United Nations Sustainable Development Goals (Agenda 2030) and communication and information issues. Taking a communication rights-based approach that emphasizes the need to address communication and information poverty in order to achieve sustainable development, the authors examine the four goals (5, 9, 16, and 17) where communication and information issues feature most prominently and make the case for the inclusion of an 18th goal—Communication for All—in order to address a range of communication and information deficits, such as digital exclusion and undemocratic media landscapes, that impede meaningful and transformational sustainable development.

Chapter 3, by Chi Kit Chan and Paul Siu Nam Lee, explicates the significance of communication to the promotion and practices of Sustainable Development Goals (SDGs). The chapter highlights how communication could contribute, and is indispensable, to the grand project of (re)setting global agendas for the sustainable goals.

In other words, communication is a much-needed jigsaw puzzle to complete the global momentum to (re)set SDGs as our universal goals. It plugs the strategic gap of shaping the world as well as local opinion, scrutinizes the cultural issues of introducing SDGs to different societies, and ushers in constructive and constitutive dialogues among various disciplines, contributing to social development for all.

In *Chap. 4*, Víctor M. Marí Sáez presents two primary theoretical challenges: the analysis of the basic characteristics of the current socio-political context of extractive capitalism and the ability to consider communication as an alternative post-capitalist horizon. He argues that a conception of (material and social) goods and communication as a commons implies a radically alternative worldview and political horizon. This approach includes a perspective of the economy, environment, and communication which encounters in the formulation of the commons a very useful theoretical template for constructing alternatives to extractive capitalism.

In *Chap. 5*, Andrea Ricci argues that six forces shape contemporary information and communication eco-systems. The first force is the logarithmic growth of information, particularly, but not only in the social media landscape. The second force is produced by the phenomena of the reflectivity of information and the impacts of reverb tails. The third force comes from the presumed recipients of information which have increasingly inconstant and insufficient attention. The fourth force is played by competition which disaggregates communities, including those of media and intelligence practitioners. The fifth force is brought by propaganda which dominates in a time erroneously considered as peaceful. The sixth force is introduced by oblivion and its growing black whole, the edges of which seem to start just after real-time experiences.

The six forces strike at the very core the metabolism of development: fostering the growth of cultures which hamper progress; limiting the understanding of "what works" to an elite of nomads with little capacity or willingness to coalesce; even endangering—with intelligence failures or ineffective risk analysis—the survival of individuals, companies, and State organizations. The sequence of strategic intelligence failures since 9/11, the incapacity to stop climate change, the unfolding of the COVID pandemic, the challenges brought by globalization and social media to companies' growth and individuals can all be analyzed under the lens of epistemic and cultural disservices induced by the influence of the six forces. The forces have in the past already challenged society. Today the energy behind the forces is dangerous: in stark contrast with the amount of information and communication at our disposal, basic certainties seem unknowable, weak, and questionable. Acts of governance are necessary to inverse the polarity at each of these six levels, truly supporting all other SDGs.

Chapter 6, by Naíde Müller, argues that strategic communication is a determining factor for social mobilization in the achievement of legitimacy and participatory and democratic adhesion. However, several areas of strategic communication, namely public relations, have long failed to recognize activism-related activities as an integral part of discipline and practice.

In this chapter, a case study which builds on an ethnographic approach at UMAR, a feminist NGO based in Portugal, and the consultation of communication experts is presented to illustrate the areas where public relations and activism intersect and to show how these intersections could be better understood and debated if SDG18 were included in the 2030 Agenda.

In *Chap. 7*, Valentina Bau discusses the importance of media literacy among groups who have experienced conflict, with particular focus on the youth. Drawing on the essential competencies of the digital and media literacy framework, the chapter analyzes the role that communication for development (C4D) projects implemented in conflict-affected realities can play when media literacy is placed at the center.

While discussing how these interventions can be built to have a positive impact on young people living in conflict-affected realities, this chapter reveals how targeting media literacy through a communication-specific goal is essential for development.

Chapter 8, by Jude William Genilo and Kamolrat Intaratat, investigated the initiatives and undertakings of the top ranked universities in the THE Impact Rankings 2021 toward Communicating the SDGs. The top ranked universities included (1) University of Manchester, (2) University of Sydney, (3) RMIT University, (4) La Trobe University, and (5) Queen's University. The findings indicated that these universities allocated a lot of time, energy, and resources in communicating the SDGs—through their teaching (degree programs); research (books, book chapters, and research papers); stewardship (websites, student-run media, and campus-based platforms); and community outreach (social media accounts, news articles, blogs, podcasts, video recordings, and opinion pieces). Based on their endeavors, the chapter recommends performance metrics and indicators for possible inclusion in future THE Impact Rankings.

Chapter 9, by Rachel E. Khan and Yvonne Chua, assesses disinformation or the so-called fake news which causes public confusion and risky behavior. They argue that misinformation undermines one of the underlying goals of communication for all: the formation of an informed and critical citizenry so essential to democracy and development.

Using the COVID-19 pandemic as a take-off point, this chapter discusses the ecology of false information and a scoping review of its effects on SDG goals. The chapter also discusses the processes by which disinformation is spread from the obscurity of the internet to the sphere of public and private communication platforms. As important, it explores multistakeholder efforts in countering fake news, and simple, appropriate tools and responses that citizens can use to safeguard spaces for communication.

In *Chap. 10*, Sol Sanguinetti-Cordero argues that the COVID pandemic presents us with a key opportunity to explore alternative ways in which the SDGs could be more inclusively applied. The first step should be to create a SDG18 in order to foster the realization of each of the 17

SDGs earlier agreed upon by the UN, thus promoting development and social change. Although the technology, knowhow, and all the necessary tools we need for a more developed, inclusive, healthy, and sustainable society already exist, SDG18 should be the means through which these reach the people who need them the most.

This chapter critically analyzes and explores what available routes of actions already exist and are not being exploited thoroughly, and which could be expeditiously developed or put to use in order to foster a more integrated communication system for development and social change within the SDG framework.

A summary with conclusions is being presented in the concluding *Chap. 11*.

Overview of Volume 2: Regional Perspectives and Special Cases

This volume contains ten chapters.

The introductory chapter by Jan Servaes and Muhammad Jameel Yusha'u summarizes the highlights from Volume 1 and elaborates on the Sustainable Competitiveness Framework.

In *Chap. 2*, Charles C. Okigbo and Jude Ogbodo start by noticing that the global landscape for development communication and social change has changed radically in the new millennium. Among the most significant of these changes is the international consensus on the importance of setting transnational targets for socio-economic developments across the globe. However, what was glaringly missing in this commitment was the recognition that communication is the catalyst and engine that drives positive socio-economic changes locally, regionally, and globally.

This has necessitated the call for "Communication for All" to stress the centrality and urgency of communication in serious development and social change enterprises.

The authors provide a short background on the MDGs and SDGs, as a backdrop for explaining Communication for All before arguing why it matters, especially in the African development context. They argue that Communication for All should have been the 18th SDG, but now that it is not the case, strategic communication deserves to be a clear component of all the 17 SDGs. The binding constraints of African development present perplexing and multifactorial challenges that deserve more attention than they get now from within the continent. More than any other world region, Africa needs "Communication for All" to pervade all aspects of human engagement on the continent.

Chapter 3, by Edgardo Luis Carniglia, argues that systematic, deep, and persistent inequalities are considered the main dilemma of development communication theory and practice in Latin America, the most unequal subcontinent in the twenty-first century.

Dilemmas related to social class, income, well-being, ethnicity, gender, and territory inequalities pose a serious threat for the future of development communication research and practice in a heterogeneous Latin American space, which at present is more vulnerable as a result of the COVID-19 pandemic.

Chapter 4, by Paul Clemens Murschetz, Franzisca Weder, Eduard Frantz, and Timo Meynhardt, explores the role of Public Service Media (PSM) in supporting SDG18, from facilitating dialogue within the community to acting as a critical watchdog over business and government. They look to issues of public value theory and performance measurement with a view to strengthening PSM's role toward remaining strong arbiters of SDG18.

Critical debates into public value theory and performance management practice can help improve our understanding of the challenges of PSM trying to add value to programming output and service quality as perceived by audiences. In their view, the Public Value Scorecard (PVSC) model, which measures public value from an audience perspective, is an effective framework to generate valuable insights into the needs of increased audience engagement of public value creation for PSM.

In *Chapter 5*, Holly Randell-Moon focuses on First Nations voices in the Australian media landscape, as it has been well established that Australian news reporting has been harmful to First Nations. Misinformation about First Nations continues through deficit discourse and the framing of First Nations through statistics as deprived in comparison to non-Indigenous socio-economic standards. The sustainability of First Nations is inextricably connected to the accessibility, contestation, and creation of communication platforms that center First Nations information, perspectives, and goals.

An SDG18 Communication for All would not only support the important role of First Nations to the global communications environment; it would create a policy framework and information literacy imperative to ensure First Nations sovereign communication.

Chapter 6, by Bashir Sa'ad Abdullahi and Habeeb Idris Pindiga, compares traditional mass media to social media platforms from the perspective of educating the public about the SDGs and thereby help achieve social and behavioral changes needed to attain the goals.

This chapter tracks the major and recurring disinformation trends about SDGs on social media platforms and how COVID-19 exacerbated the trends of disinformation on SDGs. Studies have shown that development issues, in particular those pertaining to SDG3 (Health) and SDG13 (Climate action), are prone to disinformation. Using sampled social media posts from Twitter, along with insights from documented cases around the world, the chapter highlights the impact of disinformation on the attainment of the SDGs, arguing that such disinformation is undermining the implementation of the SDGs. The chapter further makes recommendations on how effective communication by all stakeholders can help tackle the damage disinformation is doing to the journey toward attaining the SDGs.

In *Chap. 7*, Sharynne McLeod, Sarah Verdon, and Kathryn Crowe contend that if SDG18 truly stands for "Communication for All", then we must listen to and advocate for people whose voices are rarely heard despite their right to "freedom of opinion and expression" being articulated as in the Universal Declaration of Human Rights and subsequent conventions and declarations.

This chapter focuses on three groups of people whose voices are particularly marginalized: (1) people with communication disabilities, (2) children, and (3) people who do not speak/understand/read/write the dominant language of their community. These three groups make up a large portion of the world's population but are unheard due to their invisible disability. The intersectionality between these three groups is a particular focus of this chapter leading to a call for multilingual children with communication disability to be supported to take their place as communicators in society, to fulfill their potential as multilingual speakers, and to realize their communication rights.

Chapter 8, by Satarupa Dasgupta, argues that women's equality is an integral aspect of inclusive and sustainable development. Therefore, the success of all SDGs depends on the achievement of Goal 5—the attainment of gender equality. Unfortunately, the targeted elimination of many of the structural barriers that restrict women's rights in private and public spheres has halted due to the COVID-19 pandemic.

Intimate partner violence (IPV) is of serious national concern that has the potential to be exacerbated in scope and impact by the COVID-19 pandemic. The chapter incorporates a conceptual framework of intersectionality, which recognizes that women of color experience life and negotiate a pandemic through multiple systems of oppression. The effects of the COVID-19 pandemic can reverse the limited progress made on gender equality and women's rights globally.

The chapter adds to research on a proposed SDG18 which will create a framework of accessible communication strategies for all. The proposed SDG18 can play an important role in overcoming barriers toward the attainment of Goal 5 among immigrant women (in the US), by highlighting on intersecting issues of displacement and marginalization during and after the pandemic.

In *Chap. 9*, Nurcan Törenli and Zafer Kıyan review the crisis communication model adopted by the Turkish Ministry of Health. The study argues that an effective crisis communication strategy, required during the COVID-19 pandemic, could not be adopted due to the communication problems across the social stakeholders in Turkey. This miscommunication stemmed from the Ministry of Health's flawed strategy and the value paradox due to the neglect of social reaction, demands, concerns, and requirements.

The Ministry of Health did not provide accurate, adequate, and timely information to its citizens, leading to the interruption of mutual and solidaristic communication between the ruler and the ruled. The Turkish COVID-19 experience presented in the study is a significant example that demonstrated how the provision of Sustainable Development Goals, especially the elimination of poverty (SGD1), hunger (SGD2), health and welfare (SGD3), and gender equality (SGD5), could be interrupted, and how the disruption of communication during the crisis could complicate normalization for social stakeholders in the absence of an accurate and realistic communication strategy.

A summary with conclusions is being presented in the concluding *Chap. 10*.

Leuven, Belgium   Jan Servaes
Cambridge, MA   Muhammad Jameel Yusha'u

ACKNOWLEDGMENTS

We would like to acknowledge several people for their assistance in the preparation of these volumes.

In the first place, of course, all authors who contributed a chapter. Their expertise is self-evidenced across all contributions. We shouldn't forget other authors who expressed a sincere interest in the subject matter, some even submitted an abstract and chapter, but got selected out during the final review process.

The reviewers should be thanked for their assistance with the selection and peer review of the abstracts and manuscripts. The nature of their work requires that they remain anonymous.

At the publisher's level, apart from Mala Sanghera-Warren and Molly Beck, also Lauriane Piette, Associate Editor, and Arunaa Devi, the Book Project Coordinator and her production team, should be singled out.

Jan Servaes, Diest, Belgium
Muhammad Jameel Yusha'u, Jeddah, Saudi Arabia
21 May 2022, Eat more Fruits and Vegetables Day

CONTENTS

1   Introduction: The Need for an 18th Sustainable
    Development Goal—Communication for All   1
    Jan Servaes and Muhammad Jameel Yusha'u

2   Communication and Information Poverty in the Context
    of the Sustainable Development Goals (SDGs): A Case
    for SDG 18—Communication for All   25
    Lorenzo Vargas and Philip Lee

3   Significance of Communication Studies to SDGs:
    (Re)setting Global Agendas   61
    Chi Kit Chan and Paul S. N. Lee

4   Sustainable Development Goals and Communication as a
    Commons in the Context of Extractive Capitalism:
    Tensions and Possibilities   85
    Víctor Manuel Marí Sáez

5   Six Information and Communication Dynamics That
    Call for the Adoption of an 18th Sustainable
    Development Goal   107
    Andrea Ricci

6   The Role of Strategic Communication in Gender Equality
    Activism and Collective Action: Illustrating the Need for
    SDG18   149
    Naíde Müller

7   Media Literacy and Conflict: Understanding Mediated
    Communication for the Achievement of Peace and
    Development   177
    Valentina Baú

8   Creating Safe Communication Spaces Amidst the
    Disinformation Quandary   199
    Yvonne T. Chua and Rachel E. Khan

9   Communicating the SDGs: Formulating Performance
    Metrics for Higher Education Institutions   235
    Jude William Genilo and Kamolrat Intaratat

10 SDG-18 Communication for All: The Tool We Need for
    Real Development and Social Change   265
    Sol Sanguinetti-Cordero

11 Conclusion: SDG18—The Soul of An Ambitious
    Agenda—Communication and the Match Towards
    Sustainability in the COVID-19 Century   283
    Muhammad Jameel Yusha'u and Jan Servaes

Index   295

NOTES ON CONTRIBUTORS

Valentina Baú, PhD works as a senior lecturer and researcher at the University of Western Sydney (Australia). Both as a practitioner and as an academic, her work has focused on the use of the media and communication in international development. She has completed a PhD at Macquarie University on the role of participatory media in conflict transformation and reconciliation after civil violence. Her present research explores different approaches and evaluation methodologies in the area of Communication for Development in Peacebuilding. In the past, Valentina has collaborated with international NGOs, the United Nations, and the Italian Development Cooperation, while working in different areas of the Global South. Her work has been published in established academic journals as well as on renowned online platforms.

Chi Kit Chan (PhD, The Chinese University of Hong Kong, 2014) is an associate professor in the School of Communication at the Hang Seng University of Hong Kong. He works mainly in journalism, media studies, and political communication. His scholarly articles are seen *in Journalism, Chinese Journal of Communication, China Perspectives*, and *Global Media and China*. His most recent publication is *Hong Kong Media: Interaction Between Media, State and Civil Society* (Palgrave Macmillan, 2022).

Yvonne T. Chua is Associate Professor of Journalism at the University of the Philippines, College of Mass Communication (UP-CMC) in Diliman, Quezon City, Philippines. She holds a master's degree in public management from the University of the Philippines. A journalist for four decades,

Yvonne has been associated with several fact-checking initiatives in the Philippines, including Vera Files Fact Check, Tsek.ph, FactRakers, and the Philippine Fact-Checker Incubator. She is a member of the Philippine Commission on Higher Education's Technical Committee on Journalism, which monitors and proposes policies and standards in journalism education at the tertiary level. Yvonne has produced award-winning investigative reports, including a book-length investigation on corruption in public Philippine education that received the National Book Award for Journalism. Her current research interests include information disorders and fact-checking, journalism ethics and standards, and media and democracy.

Jude William Genilo, PhD is the head of the Media Studies and Journalism Department, University of Liberal Arts Bangladesh (ULAB). He is also the director of ULAB's Institutional Quality Assurance Cell (IQAC). He obtained his Doctor of Philosophy and Master's in Communication from the University of the Philippines-Diliman. He has undergraduate degrees in Economics and Management from De La Salle University-Manila. Before joining ULAB, he headed the postgraduate program of a prestigious public relations school in Jakarta and served as a research fellow at the Kasetsart University Research and Development Institute (KURDI) in Bangkok. He is co-editor (with Brian Shoesmith) of the anthology, *Bangladesh's Changing Mediascape: From State Control to Market Forces* (2013).

Kamolrat Intaratat, PhD is currently working as an associate professor at the School of Communication Arts, Sukhothai Thammathirat Open University (STOU), Thailand. She is also the chair of the International Master in Communication Arts for ASEAN and the founder and director of the Research Center of Communication and Development Knowledge Management. She worked as the dean of the Faculty of Communication Arts and a board member of the e-Society policy program of the Ministry of Information Communication and Technology, Thailand. She obtained her PhD under the University Consortium Program (SEARCA) from the University of the Philippines, Los Banos, in Development Communication and Development Management and from University of Queensland, Australia, in Agricultural Extension and Community Development.

Rachel E. Khan, PhD, DPA is Professor of Journalism at the University of the Philippines College of Mass Communication (UP-CMC) in

Diliman, Quezon City, Philippines. She is also the editor of the *Asian Congress for Media and Communication (ACMC) Journal*, an open-access academic journal of the ACMC, a professional organization of media and communication professionals and academics. She is the associate dean of UP-CMC and concurrent chair of the Department of Journalism. Previously, she served as research and publications director of the Asian Media Information and Communication Centre and as deputy director of the Centre for Media Freedom and Responsibility. She holds a master's degree in journalism from the Columbia University under the Fulbright program and a doctorate in Public Administration at the University of the Philippines. She has written and edited several textbooks on journalism and media literacy. Her research interests include social media and online journalism, media literacy, and ethics.

Paul S. N. Lee, PhD is a professor at the School of Communication, Hang Seng University, Hong Kong. He received his PhD in Communication from the University of Michigan. His research interests include international and intercultural communication, information and communication technologies, telecommunications policy, social media, and political communication.

Before joining Hang Seng University, he had taught at the School of Journalism and Communication, the Chinese University of Hong Kong, for about three decades. He served as school director (1998–2005) and dean of Social Science (2005–2014) in the period. Professor Lee has published more than 100 papers and book chapters, in addition to 14 authored and edited books. His works were published at major international venues including *Journal of Communication, Telematics and Informatics, Telecommunication Policy, Media, Culture & Society*, and *Asian Journal of Communication*. Professor Lee was the founding editor of the *Chinese Journal of Communication*.

Philip Lee is general secretary of the World Association for Christian Communication (WACC) and editor of its journal *Media Development*. His publications include *Communication for All: New World Information and Communication Order* (1985); *The Democratization of Communication* (ed.) (1995); *Many Voices, One Vision: The Right to Communicate in Practice* (ed.) (2004); *Public Memory, Public Media, and the Politics of Justice* (ed. with Pradip N. Thomas) (2012); *Global and Local Televangelism* (ed. with Pradip N. Thomas) (2012), and *Expanding Shrinking Communication Spaces* (ed. with Lorenzo Vargas) (2020).

Víctor Manuel Marí Sáez, PhD is a tenured professor at the University of Cadiz, Spain. With a BA in Information Sciences from the Complutense University of Madrid (Spain) and a PhD in Journalism from the University of Seville, Marí Sáez has completed research stays at a number of universities including those of Coimbra (Portugal), Roskilde (Denmark), Temuco (Chile), Lyon 2 and Bordeaux-Montaigne (France), among others.

He is the leader of the research group "Comunicación y Ciudadanía Digital" and the principal investigator of the project "Digital Solidarity Communication. Analysis of the Imaginaries, discourses and communicative practices of NGDOs in the horizon of the Agenda 2030" (2020–2023) (PID2019-106632GB-I00 (https://digicom2030.uca.es/)), funded by the Agencia Estatal de Investigación de España (AEI).

A specialist in communication, education, social movements, and information and communication technologies (ICTs), Mari Saez has worked as a communication consultant for different Spanish organizations and has participated in national and international research projects in this regard.

With over 25 years of experience as a researcher, Marí Sáez has authored a large number of scientific and informative papers, books, and book chapters on communication, ICTs, solidarity and social change, in some of the most important international communication journals, including *Communication Theory, International Communication Gazette*, and *TripleC*. Some of his books form part of the bibliographies of the curricula of undergraduate and postgraduate degree programs in Spain and Latin America, like, for example, *Globalización, nuevas tecnologías y Comunicación* (Madrid, Ediciones de la Torre, 1999) and *Comunicar para transformar, transformar para comunicar* (Madrid, Editorial Popular, 2011). In 2020, he contributed to Jan Servaes' *Handbook of Communication for Development and Social Change* (Springer).

Naíde Müller is a PhD candidate in Communication Sciences, grantee of the Portuguese Foundation for Science and Technology (FCT), and researcher at the Center for Communication and Culture Studies (CECC) at the Faculty of Human Sciences, Catholic University of Portugal (UCP), where she also teaches for the master's degree program in Communication Sciences. She is a visiting scholar at the College of Communication & Information, Kent State University (OH, US), with an R&D@PhD scholarship 2021 by Luso-American Development Foundation (FLAD). She graduated in Business Communication and Public Relations by Escola Superior de Comunicação Social and obtained Master's in Integrated Communication by Instituto Superior de Novas Profissões. She has more than ten years of professional experience as a communication consultant and public relations advisor in corporate, nonprofit, and political projects. She investigates and publishes in the areas of strategic communication, human rights activism, and media relations.

Andrea Ricci, PhD is currently the EEAS Senior Expert in Risk Analysis at the European Union in Brussels. He started his EU career dealing with the emergence of the WWW and the international aspects of the information society, notably in developing countries and the Mediterranean region. He has spent more than 20 years in EU External relations dealing with Open Source Intelligence, Crisis Management, Security Policy, Field Security, Conflict Prevention, Peace Building, Turkey and the Migratory Crisis. He set up and led the first Crisis Room in the EU institutions, has co-led the EUSITROOM in the EEAS, and helped set up early warning capabilities in various international organisations (Arab League, OAS, Caricom). A graduate in Political Science (Rome), he holds an MA in European Studies (College of Europe) and a PhD in Information and Communication Sciences (ULB). His current research interests focus on intelligence analysis, early warning, strategic foresight, risk analysis, and their impact on crisis management performance.

Sol Sanguinetti-Cordero works at the Environment & Technology Institute (ETI) of the Pontificia Universidad Catolica del Peru, Lima (Peru). He is a practitioner with over twenty years of solid hands-on experience on Public Policy, Sustainable Development and Communications, both at international and national levels, working with international organizations, public sector, civil society, and academia. Currently, his work and research focus on bridging the project and research divide through finding practical applications and exploring how good practices are implemented on the field.

Jan Servaes, PhD has been UNESCO Chair in Communication for Sustainable Social Change. He has taught International Communication and Communication for Social Change in Australia, Belgium, China, Hong Kong, the United States, the Netherlands, and Thailand, in addition to several teaching stints at about 120 universities in 55 countries. Servaes is editor of the Lexington Book Series *Communication, Globalization and Cultural Identity* (https://rowman.com/Action/SERIES/LEX/LEXCGC) and the Springer Book Series *Communication, Culture and Change in Asia* (http://www.springer.com/series/13565) and was editor-in-chief of the Elsevier journal *Telematics and Informatics: An Interdisciplinary Journal on the Social Impacts of New Technologies.*

Servaes has undertaken research, development, and advisory work around the world and is the author of more than 500 journal articles and 30 books on such topics as international and development communication, ICT and media policies, intercultural communication, participation and social change, and human rights and conflict management. He is known for his "multiplicity paradigm" in *Communication for Development. One World, Multiple Cultures* (1999).

Lorenzo Vargas is a communication for development specialist and researcher on citizens' media. He directs the Communication for Social Change Program of the World Association for Christian Communication (WACC), supporting community media initiatives in the Global South. He holds degrees in international development and communication from York University and McGill University and is pursuing a PhD in Communication and Culture at Ryerson University, where he is affiliated with the Global Communication Governance Lab. He has also pursued studies on media policy at the University of Brasilia and the University of Oxford. His publications include *Citizen's Media as a Tool for the Local Construction of Peace in Colombia: Opportunities for Youth* (2013); *Indigenous Community Media Aid Reconciliation in Canada* (2015); and *Expanding Shrinking Communication Spaces* (ed. with Philip Lee) (2020).

Muhammad Jameel Yusha'u, PhD is Editor-in-Chief of Africa Policy Journal and Edward S. Mason Fellow in Public Policy and Management, and Mid-Career candidate in the master program in Public Administration at John F. Kennedy School of Government, Harvard University. He works as the Division Manager for Outreach & Communication at the Islamic Development Bank. He is the author of *Regional Parallelism and Corruption Scandals in Nigeria* (2018) and co-editor of The Palgrave Handbook of International Communication and Sustainable Development (2021). He has worked as a journalist with the BBC World Service, London. During his stint at the BBC, he has contributed content/punditry to BBC World Today, BBC Focus on Africa, BBC World Have Your

Say, BBC Arabic and more. He coordinated the first multimedia election desk and represented the Africa Service in reporting the royal wedding of the Duke and Duchess of Cambridge for the BBC. Prior to joining the BBC, he was British Correspondent for Deutsche Welle (Hausa Service). He has served as a Senior Lecturer in Media and Politics and Program Leader for the master's program in mass communication/business at Northumbria University, Newcastle upon Tyne, UK; Associate Lecturer in Global Journalism at the University of Sheffield; as well as a Lecturer in Mass Communication at Bayero University, Kano, Nigeria. He holds a PhD in Journalism Studies and M.A. in Political Communication from the University of Sheffield, UK, and an MBA from IE Business School, Madrid, Spain. Jameel is an alumnus of the Executive Education Program in Innovation and Entrepreneurship: Policy Considerations, JF Kennedy School of Government, Harvard University, and the Silicon Valley Executive Education Program in Innovation and Entrepreneurship, Haas School of Business, University of California, Berkeley. His research has been published in leading journals such as Global Media and Communication, African Journalism Studies, Journal of African Media Studies and the Journal of Arab and Muslim Media Research. He has published several book chapters on online journalism, corruption and the media, critical discourse analysis, and representation of Muslims in the media.

ABBREVIATIONS

ACCE	African Council for Communication Education
ACMC	Asian Congress for Media and Communication
AI	Artificial Intelligence
AIBD	Asian Institute for Broadcasting Development
AIDS	Acquired Immune Deficiency Syndrome
AMIC	Asian Media Information and Communication Centre
ASEAN	Association of Southeast Asian Nations
BCC	Behavior Change Communication
CCMS	Centre for Communication, Media and Society
CCSDG	Communication/Culture and the Sustainable Development Goals
CDSC	Communication for Development and Social Change
CfD or C4D	Communication for Development
CFPD	Communication for Participatory Development
CIA	Central Intelligence Agency
CIESPAL	International Center for Higher Communication Studies in Latin America
CODESRIA	Council for the Development of Social Science Research in Africa
CS	Corporate Sustainability
CSC	Communication for Social Change
CSD	Commission on Sustainable Development
CSO	Civil Society Organization
CSR	Corporate Social Responsibility
CSSC	Communication for Sustainable Social Change
CSSC&D	Communication for Sustainable Social Change and Development
CTCs	Community Technology Centers

DevCom	Development Communication
DSC	Development Support Communication
EC	European Commission
ECA	Ethnographic Content Analysis
EIA	Environmental Impact Assessment
EU	European Union
FAO	Food and Agriculture Organization
FGD	Focus Group Discussions
GAID	Global Alliance for ICT and Development
GATS	General Agreement on Trade in Services
GDI	Gender Development Index
GDP	Gross Domestic Product
GEM	Gender Equity Measure
GFATM	Global Fund to Fight AIDS, Tuberculosis, and Malaria
GLTB	Gay, Lesbian, Transgender, and Bisexual
GNH	Gross National Happiness
GNI	Gross National Income
GNP	Gross National Product
HDI	Human Development Index
HIV	Human Immunodeficiency Virus
HIV/AIDS	Human Immunodeficiency Virus/Acquired Immune Deficiency Syndrome
HPI	Human Poverty Index
IAMCR	International Association for Media and Communication Research
ICA	International Communication Association
ICT4D	ICTs for Development
ICTD	Information and Communication Technologies for Development
ICTs	Information and Communication Technologies
ILO	International Labour Organisation
IMF	International Monetary Fund
INEXSK	Infrastructure, Experience, Skills, Knowledge
IPDC	International Programme for the Development of Communication
IPS	Inter Press Service
ISCED	International Standard Classification of Education
IT	Information Technology
ITU	International Telecommunications Union
IUCN	International Union for Conservation of Nature
KAP	Knowledge, Attitude, and Behavior
LDCs	Least Developed Countries
M&E	Monitoring and Evaluation
MDGs	Millennium Development Goals

MOOCs	Massive Online Open Courses
NAM	Non-Aligned Movement
NGO	Non-Governmental Organization
NICTs	New Information and Communication Technologies
NITI	National Institution for Transforming India
NTIA	US National Telecommunications and Information Administration
NWICO	New World Information and Communication Order
OECD	Organisation for Economic Co-operation and Development
OPEC	Organization of Petroleum Exporting Countries
OU	Open University
PAR	Participatory Action Research
PBS	Public Broadcasting Service
PCR	Participatory Communication Research
PCRN	Participatory Communication Research Section/Network
PDR	People's Democratic Republic
PFA	Press Foundation of Asia
PPE	Personal protective equipment
PPP	Public-Private Partnership
PR	Public Relations
PSA	Public Service Advertisement
PSB	Public Service Broadcasting
PSM	Public Service Media
PV	Participatory Video
PVE	Perceived Value of Exchange
PVU	Perceived Value of Use
R&D	Research and Development
RME	Research, Monitoring, and Evaluation
RNTC	Radio Netherlands Training Center
RTC	Right to Communicate
SAARC	South Asian Association for Regional Cooperation
SD	Sustainable Development
SDGs	Sustainable Development Goals
SE	Sufficiency Economy
SEs	Social Enterprises
SEZ	Special Economic Zone
SITE	Satellite Instructional Television Experiment
SME	Small and Medium Enterprise
SMS	Short Message Service
STI	Sexually Transmitted Infections
TAM	Technology Acceptance Model
UDHR	Universal Declaration of Human Rights

UGC	User-generated content
UK	United Kingdom
UN	United Nations
UNAIDS	Joint United Nations Programme on HIV/AIDS
UNCDP	United Nations Capital Development Programme
UNCED	United Nations Conference on Environment and Development
UNCSD	United Nations Conference on Sustainable Development
UNCSTD	United Nations Commission on Science and Technology for Development
UNCTAD	United Nations Conference on Trade and Development
UNDG	UN Development Group
UNDP	United Nations Development Programme
UNEP	United Nations Environment Programme
UNESCO	United Nations Educational, Scientific, and Cultural Organization
UNFCCC	United Nations Framework Convention on Climate Change
UNFPA	United Nations Population Fund
UNICEF	United Nations Children's Fund
UNIFEM	United Nations Development Fund for Women
UNSC	United Nations Statistical Commission
US	United States
USAID	United States Agency for International Development
USSR	Union of Soviet Socialist Republics
WB	World Bank
WCC	World Council of Churches
WCED	World Commission on Environment and Development
WFTO	World Fair Trade Organization
WHO	World Health Organization
WMO	World Meteorological Organization
WSIS	World Summit on the Information Society
WTO	World Trade Organization
WWF	World Wildlife Fund

LIST OF FIGURES

Fig. 6.1   Visual representation of the connections between respondents
and response categories (NVivo software)   164
Fig. 7.1   Design framework of C4D interventions aimed at developing
media literacy during conflict (drawing on Hobbs' 2010 Media
Literacy Essential Competencies)   187
Fig. 8.1   Information disorder model, Wardle (2020)   204
Fig. 8.2   Lasswell's process of communication model (1948)   206
Fig. 8.3   Proposed model of combatting disinformation   218
Fig. 9.1   Tag Cloud Visualizing Keywords of RMIT searches on
communicating the SDGs   250

LIST OF TABLES

Table 1.1	Sustainable Development Goals (SDGs) adopted by UN Member States	3
Table 4.1	Four types and dimensions of digital commons	97
Table 6.1	List of interviewees, institutions, and expertise	160
Table 7.1	Essential Competencies of Media Literacy, from Hobbs, 2010, p. 19	186
Table 9.1	Study framework showing ToC aspects and their indicators	246
Table 9.2	Top ranked universities included in the study	247
Table 9.3	Communication-related undergraduate programs in the top five ranked universities	248
Table 9.4	Communication-related graduate programs in the top five ranked universities	248
Table 9.5	Sustainability programs and policies featured in Queen's University website	251
Table 9.6	USYD campus-based media platforms	252
Table 9.7	Number of followers in digital platforms of the top ranked universities (as of 27 October 2021)	254
Table 9.8	Joining date in various social media accounts of the top ranked universities	254
Table 9.9	Number of tweets, posts and views of various social media accounts of the top ranked universities (as of 27 October 2021)	254
Table 9.10	Website news content on SDGs at UOM from 16 September to 15 October 2021	255
Table 9.11	Select LTU ideas and society events relating to SDGs (2018 to 2021)	256

Table 9.12   Recommended teaching performance metrics for
                   communicating the SDGs in the THE Impact Rankings   257
Table 9.13   Recommended research performance metrics for
                   communicating the SDGs in the THE Impact Rankings   258
Table 9.14   Recommended stewardship performance metrics for
                   communicating the SDGs in the THE Impact Rankings   258
Table 9.15   Recommended community outreach performance metrics
                   for communicating the SDGs in the THE Impact Rankings   259

Introduction: The Need for an 18th Sustainable Development Goal— Communication for All

Jan Servaes and Muhammad Jameel Yusha'u

Abstract The 2030 Agenda for Development or what is known as the Sustainable Development Goals (SDGs) is perhaps the most ambitious agenda collectively agreed by 193 countries in human history. In 2015, the UN Member States adopted the 17 SDGs as a framework that would help address the challenges being faced by humanity: from eradicating poverty, ending hunger, providing universal access to healthcare and education, addressing climate change to the partnering of individuals, philanthropists, and nation states to achieve the global goals.

Yet, the framers of the 2030 Agenda for Development, comprising key stakeholders from all sectors of life, forgot to dedicate one goal to the role of communication and culture in achieving the SDGs.

J. Servaes (✉)
KULeuven, Belgium

M. J. Yusha'u
Harvard Kennedy School, Cambridge, USA

J. Servaes, M. J. Yusha'u (eds.), *SDG18 Communication for All, Volume 1*, Sustainable Development Goals Series, https://doi.org/10.1007/978-3-031-19142-8_1

1

Such an oversight has attracted the attention of media and communication scholars, academics, and policy makers who understand that it is nearly impossible to achieve the SDGs without the articulation and embrace of the role of communication for development. The challenge for us is to revisit and reposition the field of Sustainable Development and the SDGs, and include communication and culture in it.

Keywords MDG • SDG • Communication for all • Sustainability

From MDGs to SDGs

The Millennium Development Goals (MDGs) were scaled-up to the Sustainable Development Goals (SDGs) in 2015. The MDG initiative followed decades of debate over how nations might collaborate on long-term strategies for a global social agenda. Wealthy countries were asked to increase development aid, relieve the debt burden on poor countries, and give them fair access to markets and technology.

On the 25th of September 2015, during the 70th session of the United Nations General Assembly in New York, 193 nations committed to the SDGs, which set out a transformative agenda that links human health and prosperity to environmental health and equity. Some argue that the Sustainable Development Goals (SDGs) are just a sequel to the Millennial Development Goals (MDGs), while others consider them a major reboot (Servaes, 2017, 2021; Vandemoortele, 2015).

The SDGs are obviously more comprehensive than the MDGs and resulted from an extensive and participatory process. As a consequence, considerably more targets (169 versus 18) and more words (about 5000 versus about 300) were needed to spell out the SDGs. While the Millennial Development Goals (MDGs) (https://www.un.org/millenniumgoals/) were comprised of eight goals and 21 targets expected to be reached by December 2015, the post-2015 development agenda was outlined in the form of 17 Sustainable Development Goals (SDGs), 169 associated targets, and 304 indicators (https://sdgs.un.org/goals, SDSN 2015) (see Table 1.1).

The new 2030 Agenda for Sustainable Development "is a plan of action for people, planet and prosperity. It also seeks to strengthen universal peace in larger freedom. We recognize that eradicating poverty in all its forms and dimensions, including extreme poverty, is the greatest global

Table 1.1   Sustainable Development Goals (SDGs) adopted by UN Member States

SDG	Goal	Official wording
1	End poverty in all its forms everywhere.	No poverty
2	End hunger, achieve food security and improved nutrition, and promote sustainable agriculture.	Zero hunger
3	Ensure healthy lives and promote well-being for all at all ages.	Good health and well-being
4	Ensure inclusive and equitable quality education and promote lifelong learning opportunities for all.	Quality education
5	Achieve gender equality and empower all women and girls.	Gender equality
6	Ensure availability and sustainable management of water and sanitation for all.	Clean water and sanitation
7	Ensure access to affordable, reliable, sustainable, and modern energy for all.	Affordable and clean energy
8	Promote sustained, inclusive and sustainable economic growth, full and productive employment and decent work for all.	Decent work and economic growth
9	Build resilient infrastructure, promote inclusive and sustainable industrialization, and foster innovation.	Industry, innovation, and infrastructure
10	Reduce inequality within and among countries.	Reduced inequalities
11	Make cities and human settlements inclusive, safe, resilient, and sustainable.	Sustainable cities and communities
12	Ensure sustainable consumption and production patterns.	Responsible consumption and production
13	Take urgent action to combat climate change and its impacts.	Climate action
14	Conserve and sustainably use the oceans, seas, and marine resources for sustainable development.	Life below water
15	Protect, restore, and promote sustainable use of terrestrial ecosystems, sustainably manage forests, combat desertification, and halt and reverse land degradation and halt biodiversity loss.	Life on land
16	Promote peaceful and inclusive societies for sustainable development, provide access to justice for all and build effective, accountable, and inclusive institutions at all levels.	Peace, justice, and strong institutions
17	Strengthen the means of implementation and revitalize the global partnership for sustainable development.	Partnerships for the goals

Source: https://sdgs.un.org/goals, Sustainable Development Goals (2021)

challenge and an indispensable requirement for sustainable development" (https://sustainabledevelopment.un.org/post2015/transformin gourworld).

THE PRE-HISTORY

The discussion about MDGs and SDGs has a long history, as documented by Lee and Vargas (2020), Servaes (2017), Weder et al. (2021), XXX (2020), and others. It dates back to the emergence of the Non-Aligned Movement in the fifties and sixties, the discussion about the New International Information Order (NIIO) debate in the seventies, and the so-called MacBride (1980) report, which resulted in the advocacy of the "Right to Communicate" to be accepted as a fundamental human right (CRIS, 2005; Hamelink, 1994; Servaes, 2017b).

The principle of the *right to communicate* contained both the passive and active right of the communicator/receiver to inform and be informed. This principle first appeared in 1969 in an article by Jean D'Arcy, the then director of the UN information bureau in New York. D'Arcy (1969, p. 14) wrote that "the time will come when the Universal Declaration of Human Rights will have to encompass a more extensive right than man's right to inform, first laid down twenty-one years ago in Article 19. This is the right of man to communicate". Only in 1974, this principle made its entrance in the UNESCO discourse. Both individual and social rights and duties are included in this right to communicate. This right has become basic for the search for a public or participatory oriented view on communication issues.

At the same time, another and related shift took place in the discussions on communication rights and responsibilities, that is, from the so-called maintenance duty of the government toward the media to the emphasis on the government's duty to take care of and to *create the conditions and infrastructure* in which the freedom of communication can be realized and stimulated as a fundamental social right. These rights embody the duty of the state and all social organizations to place people's collective interests before national and individual interests. At the same time, there is the related recognition that individual rights under international law are linked with the notion that individuals have duties and obligations as well (Hamelink, 1994).

The right to communication as a fundamental human right clearly indicates that another communication model necessitates participatory democratization and thus a redistribution of the power at all levels. The point of departure is not an elitist position, but development from the grassroots. Therefore the MacBride Report suggests that the right to communicate "promises to advance the democratization of communication on all levels—international, national, local, individual" (MacBride, 1980, p. 171).

Fundamental here is the other vision of the role of the authorities in processes of social change. Unlike the confidence in and respect for the role of the state, which is characteristic of the modernization and dependency paradigms, the third *multiplicity paradigm* (see Servaes, 1999; Servaes & Malikhao, 2020) has a rather reserved attitude toward the authorities. Policies therefore should be built on *more selective participation strategies* of dissociation and association.

COMMUNICATION AND CULTURE STILL MISSING

Notwithstanding this expressed emphasis on the importance of communication and culture in international policies, these principles remain largely absent in the MDG- and SDG-debate. We wondered very early on where communication and culture issues were in all of this (Servaes, 2007a, 2007b, 2008, see also Byrne, 2011; Vandemoortele, 2011, 2016). Also Silvio Waisbord (2006, p. 3) "cannot help but notice that communication goals are absent... While everyone seems to think that communication is important, apparently it is not crucial enough to make it into the (MDG) list".

This absence of cultural rights, communication freedoms, and democracy was even confirmed by policymakers within the UN-agency system. For instance, on 25 June 2007, the Director of UNESCO's Bureau of Strategic Planning urged the Director of the UN Development Group Office (UNDG) in a letter that "while Communication for Development remains critical to achieving the MDGs, it has not been adequately recognized as an essential element in development planning within UN programming exercises in general and CCA/UNDAF in particular. Participants expressed the need to rectify this deficiency and to make it a policy to integrate Communication for Development at field level throughout the planning, implementation and evaluation phases of UN assistance programmes" (quoted in Servaes, 2017a, p. 6).

Though the SDGs have formed the key theme for several conferences by the United Nations (UN) and were the key subjects during the annual meetings of multilateral development, banks and governments prioritized the implementation of the SDGs in one way or another in their national development programs; yet, a key pillar that would strengthen the realization of these ambitious goals—that is, the role of communication in its holistic sense—was missing. There were only few passing targets in the SDGs, especially in SDG 16 (UN, 2020a), that addressed this key function that drives human activity especially in the twenty-first century.

Despite this major omission, even officials of the United Nations have acknowledged that massive awareness is required to achieve the 2030 Agenda for Development. The former UN Under-Secretary-General for communications and public information, Cristina Gallach, stated in 2017 that communicating the SDGs is key to achieving global development targets. In her words, "the more we communicate about the SDGs and make people aware of the agenda, the more the governments will be accountable and will ensure that it is implemented" (UN News, 2017).

Notwithstanding this acknowledgement at the highest level of the UN, an explicit role for communication as a dedicated goal with clear targets in the SDGs remained conspicuously absent. Nothing exposed this oversight more than the outbreak of the COVID-19 pandemic.

Due to the coronavirus outbreak most countries around the world imposed a lockdown in order to suppress the spread of the virus. Vital economic activities were halted. The airline industry came to an abrupt stop. Universities around the world had to suspend lectures physically and resorted to online teaching. Online shopping skyrocketed. Major meetings by different stakeholders and policymakers, including preparatory meetings by G20 leaders, had to be conducted online. Global conglomerates, corporate organizations, top IT giants all closed their offices.

Just 10–20 years ago, this would have been a global catastrophe. Yet the global community survived mainly on the communication infrastructure available. The world survived on the most important SDG that the framers of the 2030 Agenda for Development had missed.

OTHER GAPS AND OMISSIONS

The role and place of communication and culture were not the only major oversight. Notwithstanding their relevance, the SDGs also contain the following major omissions and gaps:

- sustainable development and resiliency;
- human and indigenous rights;
- the need for digital inclusion; and
- the SDGs beyond the COVID-19 pandemic.

Once again, our criticism does not mean that the SDGs have no worth. However, their practical relevance requires that we dig deeper and position the issue in a more contextual and complex setting.

Sustainable Development

Sustainability and resilience are two of the many concepts currently popular in the academic community, especially with regard to how we understand processes of lasting social change. Indeed, although there is no formal definition of "sustainability", it continues to remain popular in various political, social, and economic discourses, particularly those of environmental groups as a call to action to raise awareness around the current depletion of finite natural resources (for recent overviews, see Agyeman, 2013, Farley & Smith, 2014, Foster, 2015, Servaes, 2013, Servaes & Malikhao, 2017, UN, 2013).

Sustainable development is seen as a means of enhancing decision-making so that it provides a more comprehensive assessment of the many multi-dimensional problems society faces. What is required is an evaluation framework for categorizing programs, projects, policies, and/or decisions as having sustainability potential.

Communication and Culture

Communication and culture are both keys to sustainable development, at the same time as being development goals in themselves. To date, development has mostly focused on poverty and education but the rapid advancement of Information Communication Technologies (ICTs) is changing that. People can now communicate any time and from any place, catalyzing a wider array of opportunities to the development sector. The world today is interconnected and interdependent.

Within this framework, communication and information play a strategic and fundamental role by (a) contributing to the interplay of different development factors, (b) improving the sharing of knowledge and information, and (c) encouraging the participation of all concerned. By promoting the free flow of ideas, as is the case in UNESCO's mandate, a truly transformative environment can be enabled through the advancement of communication. Disadvantaged groups can now actively participate in their own community's development.

Digital Inclusion

In addition, while the digital age is disrupting social systems and driving transformations at a scale and pace unparalleled in history, the SDGs remain quite silent on this topic (UN News, 2020). Indeed, today digital technologies are shaping what we read and consume, our votes, and how we interact with each other and the world around us. Many risks and uncertainties are emerging, including threats to individual rights, social equity, and democracy, all amplified by "the digital divide"—the differential rate of internet penetration and access to digital technologies around the world.

Therefore, also Amy Luers (2020) pleads for an *18th SDG: Sustainability in the Digital Age* (https://sustainabilitydigitalage.org/montreal-statement/). This statement calls on society to recognize that tackling the climate crisis, building a sustainable world, and working toward a just and equitable digital future are inherently interconnected agendas.

The Montreal Statement on Sustainability in the Digital Age (https://sustainabilitydigitalage.org/montreal-statement/) outlines five immediate actions needed to overcome profound risks of the digital age and leverage its transformative capabilities to build a climate-safe, sustainable, and equitable world. These include the need to:

- build a new social contract for the digital age, which addresses individual rights, justice and equity, inclusive access, and environmental sustainability;
- ensure open and transparent access to data and knowledge critical to achieving sustainability and equity;
- foster public and private collaborations to develop and manage Artificial Intelligence (AI) and other technologies in support of sustainability and equity;
- promote research and innovation to steer digital transformations toward sustainability and equity; and
- support targeted communication, engagement, and education to advance the social contract.

Human and Indigenous Rights

It is increasingly recognized that human rights are essential to achieve sustainable development. However, "international human rights treaties are notably absent from the SDGs" (Macchi, 2020). And, furthermore, which "human rights" are we talking about?

The MDGs served as a proxy for certain economic and social rights but ignored important human right linkages of the so-called third generation: group and collective rights, the right to self-determination, the right to economic and social development, the right to a healthy environment, the right to natural resources, the right to communicate and communication rights, the right to participation in cultural heritage, and the rights to intergenerational equity and sustainability (Gupta, 2020; Macklem, 2015; Servaes, 2017b) (https://www.coe.int/en/web/compass/the-evolution-of-human-rights). Today, in addition to these solidarity rights, one starts speaking of a fourth generation of human rights: the right to exist digitally, the right to digital reputation, and the right to digital identity (https://www.thalesgroup.com/en/dis/government/magazine/digital-inclusion-human-right-have-identity).

It is fair to say that gradually more human rights principles and standards become reflected in the new global development framework of the 2030 Agenda for Sustainable Development (https://sdg.human-rights.dk/).

For instance, Indigenous peoples have a higher profile in the SDG document—they are directly mentioned several times within the text—more than they did in the MDGs. However, "Indigenous Peoples' visions of development were not included in the SDGs and their collective rights were not given sufficient recognition ... The SDGs also do not affirm the collective rights of Indigenous Peoples to their lands, territories, and resources" (Kumar, 2020, p. 118).

Non-discrimination and non-exclusion are cornerstones to the successful application of the 2030 Sustainable Development Agenda. According to current development rhetoric, these must be realized as universal values, which are at the heart of a functioning, stable, and peaceful global society (Maclean, 2015).

Therefore, we notice that most of the *SDGs remain focused on social and economic rights*, rather than the cultural and people's rights listed in the third and fourth generation of human rights. In our opinion, a bottom-up perspective on sustainable development would argue in favor of empowerment: the ability of people to influence the wider system and take control of their lives. Therefore, this perspective argues that a communication rights-based approach needs to be explicitly built into development plans and social change projects to ensure that a mutual sharing/learning process is facilitated. Such communicative sharing is deemed the best guarantee for creating successful transformations. Because all human rights are "local" (Servaes, 2017b).

THE SDGS BEYOND THE COVID-19 PANDEMIC, THE UKRAINE "WAR OF ATTRITION", AND INCREASING INEQUALITY

Since 2019 the COVID-19 pandemic has shown why communication is essential to human survival. A major lesson that comes out of the COVID-19 pandemic is the role of communication in providing support for the survival of the global economy and society as a whole. The global community became more attached to the traditional and social media in order to understand the nature of the virus, how it spreads, and measures needed to curtail the spread of the infection. The pandemic, which started as a health crisis and later metamorphosed into a full-blown economic crisis, is now having a direct and indirect impact on the possibility of achieving each of the SDGs (Servaes & Yusha'u, 2021).

The COVID-19 crisis has made people more aware of the vulnerability of global supply chains (World Bank, 2020a, 2020b). The failure of China's zero-COVID strategy and the drastic lockdowns in Shenzhen and Shanghai indicate that, two years after the outbreak of the pandemic, the risk of disruption to global supply chains has still not been eliminated. If parts from the Far East are missing, assembly lines in Europe come to a standstill. The paradigm shift away from efficiency ("just in time") to greater resilience ("just in case") is accelerating the hidden trend toward deglobalization under way for some time.

Following the global lockdown, the resilience needed to survive the pandemic largely rested on the shoulders of the available communication infrastructure. *Zoom*, which had an average of 19 million daily users in December 2019, now averages 300 million users per day. *Teams*, developed as a tool for remote work, had 145 million daily users, as confirmed by Microsoft CEO Satya Nadella in April 2021 (Goodison, 2021).

A study by the World Health Organization shows rapid increase in remote consultation in the healthcare industry, especially in UK, France, Malta, Germany, Poland, Luxemburg, and Austria.

The pandemic also exposed major development challenges such as digital inequality (UN World Social Report, 2020; Whiting, 2020; World Social Report, 2020). Suddenly, the issue of inequality, which is the premise of SDG10, became even more apparent. According to the UN, COVID-19 has forced the closure of schools in 191 countries affecting 1.5 billion students and 63 million primary and secondary school teachers. Many developing countries do not have the digital infrastructure to move from teaching physically to online tutoring thereby bringing to the fore the question of the digital divide (Yusha'u, 2020). Without communication infrastructure, addressing the digital divide would be a mirage. The leaders of the Agence Universitaire de la Francophonie (AUF), the Association of Commonwealth Universities (ACU), and the International Association of Universities (IAU), representing more than 2000 universities worldwide, agreed during the United Nations High-Level Political Forum (HLPF) 2020 that international collaboration in higher education is needed to solve the world's pressing challenges and achieve sustainable development (O'Malley, 2020).

However, while one of the major findings of the 2020 Sustainable Development Report (SDR, 2021; Lafortune et al., 2020) was that before the COVID-19 outbreak, the world was making progress toward the SDGs, this optimism has since evaporated. Although no country was on track to achieve the SDGs, the evolution of the SDG Index scores (included in the Sustainable Development Report) between 2010 and 2019 suggests some convergence, with regions and income groups that had lower SDG Index scores in 2010 progressing faster. Due to time lags in data generation and reporting, these results represent the situation before COVID-19. In particular, areas of the Global South, including sub-Saharan Africa, Latin America, and the Caribbean, made significant progress during the MDGs period (2000–2015) and also showed progress on the SDGs. Of all UN regions, East and South Asia demonstrated the most progress on the SDGs (Salsiah Alisjahbana et al., 2020).

The report also highlighted significant disparities in progress across the goals and countries. For example, Côte d'Ivoire, Burkina Faso, and Cambodia improved the most on the SDGs, while Venezuela, Zimbabwe, and the Republic of the Congo regressed the most (Sachs et al., 2020).

In an analysis, published in the authoritative *World Development*, Moyer and Hedden (2020) also question how feasible the SDGs are under the current circumstances. They highlight difficulties for some SDG indicators (access to safe sanitation, high school completion, and underweight children) that will not be resolved without a significant shift in domestic and international aid policies and prioritization.

In addition, Moyer and Hedden cite 28 particularly vulnerable countries that are not expected to meet any of the nine human development targets. These most vulnerable countries should be able to count on international aid and therefore financial support.

Also the discussion about globalization has emerged again with some arguing that "nation states" have remained important in the corona crisis. While globalization facilitates the rapid spread of viruses around the world, concerted national action by governments, the private sector, civil society, and the scientific community has led to different solutions and strategies at national rather than supranational or global levels.

In addition, Marc Saxer (2022), head of the Asia Department at the Friedrich Ebert Stiftung, argues that Russia's invasion of Ukraine has upended the world order—and with it the energy, production, distribution, and finance systems. It is "a war of attrition that each side believes it will win, but that both sides will lose" (Sachs, 2022). *It is also a serious setback in the realization of SDGs 16 andSDG17* (UN, 2020a; UNCCD 2017; UNDP, 2020b, 2020c; UNEP, 2020).

The current crisis, including hostilities among major powers like China and Russia versus the US, raises the *fear of global conflict instead of global cooperation*. Some do also see other trends emerging: "The traditional powers of the west are neither as strong economically, nor as confident of their social and organizational superiority. China, along with developing countries in Asia and Africa that have better weathered COVID storm, will likely increase their global footprint at a much faster rate than they have been doing in the past decades" (Khan & Khan, 2020; UNESCO, 2020). These trends have only intensified since the "war" in Ukraine and the related "deglobalization" (Gresh, 2022).

Implementation needs to start with each country selecting and adapting those aspects of the SDGs that are most relevant to their national context. This is often dismissed as cherry-picking through a non-participatory process. However, in our opinion, besides government, such selection and adaptation need to include civil society, academics, think tanks, trade unions employers federations, and the people at large (Servaes,

2007b, 2008, 2017a; Vandemoortele, 2018). The question should also be how global targets make a difference at national and sub-national levels? Because, as Bali Swain and Yang-Wallentin argue: "Resources are limited and SDGs are fraught with trade-offs and inconsistencies. Therefore, strategic policy focus on socio-economic development in the developing countries may be a successful short-run policy to achieve sustainable development. Developed countries' results, however, suggest a greater propensity to achieve sustainable development by focus on the environmental and social factors" (Bali, 2020, p. 105; see also Nilsson et al., 2018).

Sustainable lifestyle concepts that are grounded in a mechanistic paradigm are no longer useful, and are preventing an effective response to our complex and dynamic world. Therefore, Böhme et al. (2022) argue that a new relational framing is needed, a new conceptual approach that has the potential to transform research, policy, and practice.

We will expand this argument further in the introductory article of Volume 2 with a focus on the *Global Sustainable Competitiveness Index (GSCI)*.

SDG18-Communication for All

Building on the works of Lee and Vargas (2020), Servaes (2020), and Yusha'u and Servaes (2021), we see SDG18 (Communication for all) as inevitable in achieving the 2030 Agenda for Development.

Philip Lee and Lorenzo Vargas (2020), referring to the so-called MacBride report (1980), argue that "it is all the more astonishing that communication and media were not made part and parcel of every SDG or subject to an SDG of their own, since none of the SDGs can be achieved unless people are able to communicate their dreams, concerns and needs—locally, nationally, regionally, globally. The obstacles are many: social, cultural, political, ideological, yet communication can help overcome them all" (Lee & Vargas, 2020, p. 4). They therefore propose another SDG to the list: *SDG 18: Communication for All*, with the goal to "expand and strengthen public civic spaces through equitable and affordable access to communication technologies and platforms, media pluralism, and media diversity" (ibid., p. 5).

According to Lee and Vargas, "no matter the issue—poverty, conflict resolution, self-determination, migration, health, land, housing, the climate crisis—little can be done without effective communication" (Lee & Vargas, 2020, p. 2). They were particularly critical of the failure of the

SDGs to appreciate the relevance of free expression as a goal of development and a means to development.

Therefore, for them SDG18 should be one of the SDGs with the following as a goal and targets:

Goal: Expand and strengthen public civic spaces through equitable and affordable access to communication technologies and platforms, media pluralism, and media diversity.

Target 1.1 By 2030, ensure the existence of spaces and resources for men and women, in particular the poor and vulnerable, to engage in transparent, informed, and democratic public dialogue and debate.

Target 1.2 By 2030, ensure the existence of regimes where creative ideas and knowledge are encouraged, can be communicated widely and freely to advance social justice and sustainable development.

Target 1.3 By 2030, ensure protection for the dignity and security of people in relation to communication processes, especially concerning data privacy and freedom from surveillance.

Target 1.4 By 2030, ensure communication spaces for diverse cultures, cultural forms, and identities at the individual and social levels (Lee & Vargas, 2020, p. 5).

Chapter 2 in this volume shares the proposition of Lee and Vargas (2020). We propose additional targets for SDG18.

1.5   Ensure the use of communication as a tool for economic empowerment and community development by governments, private sector, and civil society.

1.6   Use media and communications in promoting accountability, tackling misinformation, strengthening good governance, and effective citizen engagement in public affairs.

1.7   Provide communication and technological infrastructure for all to support remote access for citizens in health, education, and all public services and economic activities during emergencies.

Crucial Factors

In our view, the realization of the 2030 agenda can only be achieved on the basis of the following three factors.

Finance

The first is financing. The critical question that is posed in various forums about the SDGs invariably ends with the question: who is going to fund it? Where will the money come from? How can low- and middle-income countries generate sufficient resources to finance the 2030 development agenda (The Global Goals, 2020).

Although each country has its own priorities, paying the bills for the SDGs remains a delicate matter. The Asia-Europe Foundation calculated (2020, p. 6) that "the total investment costs to achieve the SDGs by 2030 are between USD 5 and USD 7 trillion per year at the global level and between a total of USD 3.3 and USD 4.5 trillion per year in developing countries.

This implies an average investment need of USD 2.5 trillion per year in developing countries. To better understand the real financial needs of the SDGs, these countries should prepare their own estimates, at least for their priority objectives".

In one in five developing countries, GDP per capita will not return to 2019 levels by the end of 2023, even before absorbing the impacts of the Ukraine war. "The war in Ukraine and rise in arms spending undermine development aid to the World's poor", observes Thalif Deen (2022a), IPS United Nations bureau chief and regional director for North America.

A significant effort must be made through the private sector and philanthropists. While governments and ordinary people have been hit hard by the health and economic impact of COVID-19, in a way it has been good news for billionaires, many of whom have seen their wealth grow astronomically. "Billionaires' wealth has risen more in the first 24 months of COVID-19 than in 23 years combined. The total wealth of the world's billionaires is now equivalent to 13.9 percent of global GDP. This is a three-fold increase (up from 4.4 percent) in 2000", according to the latest Oxfam International report (https://www.oxfam.org/en/research/profiting-pain), titled "Profiting from Pain" (Deen, 2022b).

A report from the Washington-based Institute of Policy Studies (IPS) shows that US billionaires have seen their wealth grow by $1 trillion between March and November 2020. Amazon's owner Jeff Bezos' net worth increased 61 percent between March and November 2020, from $113 billion to $182.4 billion. The report added that just four years ago, there was not a single multi-billionaire, that is, a person with a net worth of more than $100 billion. Since November 2020, at the height of the COVID-19 pandemic, there are now at least five multi-billionaires, namely Jeff Bezos of Amazon; Bernard Arnault, president of Louis Vuitton; Bill

Gates, founder of Microsoft; Mark Zuckerberg of Facebook; and Elon Musk of Tesla (Huffington Post, 2020).

These billionaires, along with the more than 2000 billionaires from around the world, are wealthy enough to help make substantial progress on some of the SDGs.

Political Will

The second important factor that can help achieve the SDGs is political will. Many countries have drawn up ambitious national development plans that look great on paper. How many of those plans end up being realized? (Vorisek & Yu, 2020; UN, 2020b).

When one sees that the fortunes of a country have been successfully changed through the effective implementation of national plans, one cannot separate such achievements from the strong political will of the leaders. The example of China speaks for itself.

The crucial question to be asked is whether that political will is there. UN Secretary-General, Antonio Guterres, responded to a mid-term review of the Sustainable Development Goals (UN, 2020a): "It is inevitable that one crucial ingredient is still missing. Political will. Without political will, neither the public opinion, nor the stakeholders take sufficient action". This is where the challenge to achieve the SDGs lies, that is, a real political will.

Communication for Development

The third factor is the need for robust communication for development and social change, so that political will can be conveyed to all stakeholders. Leaders who inspire change do so with the communication tools available in their time.

While the digital age disrupts social systems and drives transformation at a scale and pace unparalleled in history, the SDGs remain quite silent on the subject. Indeed, today digital technologies determine what we read and consume, how we vote, and how we interact with each other and the world around us.

Many risks and uncertainties are emerging, including threats to individual rights, social justice, and democracy, all amplified by "the digital divide"—the differential speed of internet penetration and access to digital technologies around the world.

Communications for social change in the era of COVID-19 must also consider the challenge of misinformation when initiating communication strategies. Therefore, the communication strategies of the World Bank, UNICEF, or WHO are not comprehensive enough.

First, they failed to take into account the challenges of infodemics and fake news in addressing the COVID-19 pandemic. The second shortcoming is that the strategies contain little scientific communication to make the public aware of how health professionals make decisions and advise the public about its safety. Disinformation is a critical factor that exacerbates the challenges that communication for development and social change must address. Technology, social change, and human behavior are interconnected, but their impact remains complex (Walther, 2021).

ANOTHER TIMEFRAME AND MAIN OBJECTIVE NEEDED

For all these reasons, the UN and the rest of the international community need to be realistic and review the 2030 Agenda for Development by shifting the timeline from 2030 to 2050.

Some regional organizations, such as the African Union, go even further. They have already postponed the date for achieving their development goals to 2063 (https://au.int/en/agenda2063/sdgs).

Furthermore, the SDGs should be prioritized with SDG1 on the eradication of extreme poverty as the *main objective* for the next 10 years. Eradicating extreme poverty is likely to have implications for other SDGs also, in particular SDGs 2, 3, 4, 5, and 6.

Efforts to eradicate extreme poverty should not be based on slogans, but should be supported by governments, funding agencies, donors, and philanthropists seen as the best chance to save humanity. Intellectual errors and policies imposed on low- and middle-income countries, which plunge them further into the abyss of underdevelopment, must be avoided.

Serious thought should be accorded to the post-COVID-19 world due to the impact of the lockdown on the global economy. Some governments, multinational institutions, and private sector are hastening to institutionalize remote work before the pandemic ends.

As an interim measure, working from home has contributed significantly in reducing the impact of the pandemic, but what is the impact of working from home on the future of work in a post-COVID-19 world?

Will the closure of offices, firms, and other businesses for remote work accelerate or reduce the chances of achieving the SDGs? Is there sufficient data to back the policy decisions on a permanent remote work culture? How does this affect the employability of low and unskilled workers?

These are the questions that policy makers must think through. The SDGs are meant to promote social inclusion and reduce inequality, not to save money and increase profitability.

Setting the timeline for the achievement of the SDGs to 2050 will allow sufficient time to re-evaluate progress made so far, complete missing objectives, such as SDG 18 on communication for all, and bridge the lost ground of the SDGs.

It will also give the global community ample time to strategize on how to deal with the potential rise of right-wing, populist, and nationalist governments, which may impose limits on the SDGs through their disdain for multilateralism. And plans must also be made in advance to mitigate the next disasters that could impair the achievement of the SDGs.

Conclusion

The magnitude of COVID-19 and the current fear of global conflict instead of global cooperation are forcing us to re-think our strategies and approaches. The pandemic draws attention to the fact that, in order to support those who are hit hardest and enhance their resilience for the future, our development interventions should be multidimensional (Horton, 2020).

An additional goal—SDG18: Communication for All—is necessary if we are to witness a world that is free from poverty, inequality, and where issues of climate change and environmental degradation are addressed.

Therefore, "we need a revolution in policy mind-set and practice. Inclusive and accountable governance systems, adaptive institutions with resilience to future shocks, universal social protection and health insurance and stronger digital infrastructure are part of the transformations needed" (Salsiah Alisjahbana et al., 2020).

References

Agyeman, J. (2013). *Introducing just sustainabilities. Policy, planning and practice.* Zed Books.

Asia-Europe Foundation. (2020). *Who will pay for the Sustainable Development Goals?* Retrieved May 12, 2020, from https://www.asef.org/images/docs/ ASEF%20-%20Who%20Will%20Pay%20for%20the%20Sustainable%20 Development%20Goals_9Dec_v7%20HIGHRES.pdf

Bali Swain, R., & Yang-Wallentin, F. (2020). Achieving sustainable development goals: Predicaments and startegies, International Journal of Sustainable Development & World. *Ecology, 27*(2), 96–106. https://doi.org/10.108 0/13504509.2019.1692316

Böhme, J., Walsh, Z., & Wamsler, C. (2022). *Sustainable lifestyles: Towards a relational approach.* Sustainability Science https://doi.org/10.1007/s11625-022-01117-y

Byrne, E., Nicholson, B., & Salem, F. (2011). Information communication technologies and the millennium development goals. *Information Technology for Development, 17*(1), 1–3.

CRIS. (2005). *Assessing communication rights: A handbook.* Communication Rights in the Information Society. WACC.

d'Arcy, J. (1969). Direct broadcast satellites and the right to communicate. *EBU Review, 118*(1969), 14–18.

Deen, T. (2022a). *War in Ukraine & Rise in Arms Spending Undermine Development Aid to the World's Poor.* IPS News. https://www.ipsnews.net/2022/04/war-ukraine-rise-arms-spending-undermine-development-aid-worlds-poor/

Deen, T. (2022b). *Covid-19: Rise of the super rich & fall of the world's poor.* IPS News. Retrieved May 23, 2022, from https://www.ipsnews.net/2022/05/covid-19-rise-super-rich-fall-worlds-poor/

Farley, H., & Smith, Z. (2014). *Sustainability. If it's everything, is it nothing?* Routledge.

Foster, J. (2015). *After sustainability. Denial, hope, retrieval.* Routledge/Earthscan.

Goodison, D. (2021). *Microsoft CEO Satya Nadella's plan to unlock 'Trillions of Dollars' in partner opportunity.* CRN. Retrieved April 12, 2021, from https://www.crn.com/news/cloud/microsoft-ceo-satya-nadella-s-plan-to-unlock-trillions-of-dollars-in-partner-opportunity

Gresh, A. (2022). *Quand le Sud refuse de s'aligner sur l'Occident en Ukraine.* Le Monde Diplomatique, Mai 2022. https://www.monde-diplomatique.fr/2022/05/GRESH/64659

Gupta, V. (2020). *A simple plan for repairing our society: We need new human rights, and this is how we get them,* Medium, June 3. https://medium.com/@vinay_12336/a-simple-plan-for-repairing-our-society-we-need-new-human-rights-and-this-is-how-we-get-them-cee5d6ededa9

Hamelink, C. J. (1994). *The politics of world communication. A human rights perspective.* Sage.

Horton, R. (2020). *The COVID-19 Catastrophe. What's gone wrong and how to stop it happening again.* Polity Press. 133 p.

Huffington Post. (2020). *US Billionaires grow wealth by over $1 Trillion Since Pandemic Began: Report.* Retrieved May 12, 2020, from https://www.huff-

post.com/entry/billionaires-wealth-grows-coronavirus-pandemic_n_5fbeb24dc5b61d04bfa69373?guccounter=1&guce_referrer=a
HR0cHM6Ly93d3cuZ29vZ2xlLmNvbS8&guce_referrer_
sig=AQAAAIu1QrngitY9ff8f0yLccB_X9UKi1PuB-iMSrAUNnOkbl5tXOoTd
su6YJMSye5VOaDRaxI5RorAa6WteIHNFDqF109axsyh33RAaDQ112WsJ3
YyrN39n-ekP5Sdb-BEffr_zH2a1d7PES4NJALLZEbIloYrr1BYG-
bisPzIvI7OiC
Khan, D., & Khan, L. Y. (2020). *Will COVID-19 change the global balance of power?*.
IPSnews. http://www.ipsnews.net/2020/10/will-covid-19-change-global-
balance-power/?utm_source=English+-+SDGs&utm_campaign=0a2c7878c2-
EMAIL_CAMPAIGN_2020_10_05_08_29_COPY_01&utm_
medium=email&utm_term=0_08b3cf317b-0a2c7878c2-4622673
Kumar, S. D. (2020). What do the SDGs mean for the world's Indigenous peoples?. In P. Lee & L. Vargas (Eds.), *Expanding shrinking communication spaces*
(pp. 115–123). Southbound, Penang.
Lafortune, G., Woelm, F., Fuller, G., & Marks, A. (2020). *The SDGs, COVID-19
and the global South: Insights from the sustainable development report 2020*.
IPSnews.net. Retrieved July 23, 2020, from http://www.ipsnews.net/
2020/07/sdgs-covid-19-global-south-insights-sustainable-development-
report-2020/?utm_source=English%20-%20SDGs&utm_campaign=
e756da33e1-E
Lee, P., & Vargas, L. (Eds.). (2020). *Expanding shrinking communication spaces*.
Southbound.
Luers, A. (2020). *The missing SDG: Ensure the digital age supports people, planet,
prosperity & peace*. https://www.globalissues.org/news/2020/07/06/26585
MacBride, S. (Ed.). (1980). *Many voices, one world. Communication and society.
Today and tomorrow*. UNESCO.
Macchi, C. (2020). *The SDGs and the urgency of human rights in times of crisis*.
Blog. Retrieved May 18, 2020, from https://www.globalstudies.ugent.be/
the-sdgs-and-the-urgency-of-human-rights-in-times-of-crisis/
Macklem, P. (2015). Human rights in international law: Three generations or one?
London Review of International Law, 3(1), 61–92. https://doi.org/10.1093/
lril/lrv001
Maclean, K. (2015). *Cultural hybridity and the environment. Strategies to celebrate
local and Indigenous knowledge*. Springer.
Moyer, J. D., & Hedden, S. (2020). Are we on the right path to achieve the sustainable development goals? *World Development, 127*, Article ID: 104749.
https://doi.org/10.1016/j.worlddev.2019.104749
Nilsson, M., Chisholm, E., Griggs, D. et al. (2018). Mapping interactions between
the sustainable development goals: Lessons learned and ways forward. *Sustain
Sci, 13*, 1489–1503. https://doi.org/10.1007/s11625-018-0604-z.

O'Malley, B (2020). *Universities are key to achieving sustainable development.* https://www.universityworldnews.com/post.php?story=2020071109 4917938

Sachs, J. (2022, May 10). *Ending the war of attrition in Ukraine.* https://www.project-syndicate.org/commentary/only-negotiation-can-end-ukraine-war-of-attrition-by-jeffrey-d-sachs-2022-05

Sachs, J., Schmidt-Traub, G., & Lafortune, G. (2020). SDGs: Affordable and more essential now. *Nature, 584,* 344.

Salsiah Alisjahbana, A., Wignaraja, K., & Susantono, B. (2020). *Fast-tracking the SDGs: Driving Asia Pacific transformations.* United Nations (ESCAP), the Asian Development Bank (ADB) and the United Nations Development Programme (UNDP), Bangkok. https://doi.org/10.22617/SPR200149-2

Saxer, M. (2022, May 5). *The coming world order.* https://socialeurope.eu/the-coming-world-order

SDSN (Sustainable Development Solutions Network). (2015, June 22). *Indicators and a monitoring framework for the sustainable development goals. Launching a data revolution for the SDGs.* In A report by the Leadership Council of the Sustainable Development Solutions Network. Revised working draft.

Servaes, J. (1999). *Communication for development. One world, multiple cultures.* Hampton Press.

Servaes, J. (Ed.). (2007b). *Communication for development. Making a difference.* Background paper for the World Congress on Communication for Development, Rome, 25–27 October 2006.

Servaes, J. (Ed.). (2013). *Sustainability, participation and culture in communication. Theory and Praxis.* Intellect-University of Chicago Press.

Servaes, J. (2017). *Introduction: From MDGs to SDGs.* In J. Servaes (Ed.), *Sustainable development goals in the Asian context* (pp. 1–22). Springer.

Servaes, J. (Ed.). (2020). *Handbook on communication for development and social change* (Vols. 1+2). Springer (@1506pp.). https://link.springer.com/referencework/10.1007/978-981-10-7035-8#toc

Servaes, J. (2021). The sustainable development goals: A major reboot or just another acronym? In M. J. Yusha'u & J. Servaes (Eds.), *The Palgrave handbook of international communication and sustainable development.* Palgrave Macmillan. https://doi.org/10.1007/978-3-030-69770-9_2

Servaes, J., & Malikhao, P. (2017). The role and place of Communication for Sustainable Social Change (CSSC), International Social Science Journal, Wiley & UNESCO, vol. LXV, 217/218, September–December 2014, pp. 171–184. ISSN: 0020-8701.

Servaes, J., & Malikhao, P. (2020). Communication for development and social change: three development paradigms, two communication models, and many applications and approaches. In J. Servaes (Ed.), *Handbook of communication for development and social change.* Springer.

Servaes J., & Yusha'u, M. J. (2021, July 30). *Are UN's sustainable development goals in the Doldrums due to the Corona Virus?* IIPS News and Views from the Global South. http://www.ipsnews.net/2021/07/uns-sustainable-development-goals-doldrums-due-corona-virus/

Servaes, J. (2007a). Harnessing the UN system into a common approach on Communication for Development. *The International Communication Gazette, 69*(6), 483–507. http://gaz.sagepub.com

Servaes, J. (2008). Confusion about MDGs and participatory diffusion. *Global Journal Communication for Development and Social Change, 2*(3).

Servaes, J. (Ed.). (2017a). *The sustainable development goals in an Asian context.* Springer. 174pp. ISBN 978-981-10-2814-4 http://www.springer.com/in/book/9789811028144

Servaes, J. (2017b). All human rights are local. The resiliency of social change. In H. Tumber & S. Waisbord (Eds.), *The Routledge companion to media and human rights* (pp. 136–146). Routledge.

Sustainable Development Goals. (2020). *Goal 17: Revitalize the global partnerships for sustainable development.* Retrieved November 3, 2020, from https://www.un.org/sustainabledevelopment/globalpartnerships/

Sustainable Development Report. (2021). https://www.sustainabledevelopment.report/reports/sustainable-development-report-2021/

The Global Goals. (2020). *9-Industry, innovation and infrastructure.* Retrieved October 30, 2020, from https://www.globalgoals.org/9-industry-innovation-and-infrastructure

UN. (2013). *A new global partnership: Eradicate poverty and transform economies through sustainable development.* The Report of the High-Level Panel of Eminent Persons on the Post-2015 Development Agenda. United Nations.

UN. (2020a). *Goal 16: Peace, justice and strong institutions.* Retrieved November 3, 2020, from https://sdgs.un.org/goals/goal16

UN. (2020b). *With political will, smart policy choices, 'Tremendous' gains possible over coming decade, secretary-general says, pointing to transformative moment for change.* Retrieved December 5, 2020, from https://www.un.org/pressTechnological

UN News. (2017). *Communicating SDGs key to achieving global development targets.* Retrieved May 29, 2020, from https://news.un.org/en/story/2017/03/552532-communicating-sdgs-key-achieving-global-development-targets-senior-un-official

UN News. (2020). *Startling disparities in digital learning emerge as COVID-19 spreads: UN education agency.* Retrieved May 1, 2021, from https://news.un.org/en/story/2020/04/1062232

UN World Social Report. (2020). https://www.un.org/en/desa/world-social-report-2020

UNCCD. (2017). *GOAL 15: Life on land-facts and figures, targets, why it matters.* Retrieved November 3, 2020, from https://knowledge.unccd.int/publications/goal-15-life-land-facts-and-figures-targets-why-it-matters retrieved

UNDP. (2020b). *Goal 6: Clean water and sanitation.* Retrieved October 28, 2020, from https://www.undp.org/content/undp/en/home/sustainable-development-goals/goal-6-clean-water-and-sanitation.html

UNDP. (2020c). *Goal 12 targets.* Retrieved November 12, 2020, from https://www.undp.org/content/undp/en/home/sustainable-development-goals/goal-12-responsible-consumption-and-production/targets.html

UNEP. (2020). *Goal 7: Affordable and clean energy.* Retrieved October 28, 2020, from https://www.unenvironment.org/explore-topics/sustainable-development-goals/why-do-sustainable-development-goals-matter/goal-7

UNESCO. (2020). *COVID-19: At least a third of the world's school children unable to access remote learning during school closures, new report says.* Retrieved October 15, 2020, from https://www.unicef.org/press-releases/covid-19-least-third-worlds-schoolchildren-unable-access-remote-learning-during

Vandemoortele, J. (2015). *Are the SDGs a major reboot or a sequel to the MDGs?*

Vandemoortele, J. (2016). *SDGs: The tyranny of an acronym?* https://impakter.com/sdgs-tyranny-acronym/

Vandemoortele, J. (2018). From simple-minded MDGs to muddle-headed SDGs. *Development Studies Research, 5*(1), 83–89. https://doi.org/10.1080/21665095.2018.1479647

Vandemoortele, J. (2011). If not the millennium development goals, then what? *Third World Quarterly, 32*(1), 9–25.

Vorisek, D., & Yu, S. (2020). Understanding the cost of achieving the sustainable development goals. *Policy Research Working Paper.* The World Bank Group. Retrieved October 14, 2020, from http://documents1.worldbank.org/curated/en/744701582827333101/pdf/Understanding-the-Cost-of-Achieving-the-Sustainable-Development-Goals.pdf

Waisbord, S. (2006). Where is Communication in the Millennium Development Goals? *Media Development, LIII*(3), 3–6.

Walther, C. (2021). *Technology, social change, and human behavior. Influence for impact.* Palgrave Macmillan.

Weder, F., Krainer, L., & Karmasin, M. (Eds.), (2021). *The sustainability communication reader.* Springer. https://doi.org/10.1007/978-3-658-31883-3

Whiting, K. (2020). *5 shocking facts about inequality, according to Oxfam's latest report.* Retrieved November 1, 2020, from https://www.weforum.org/agenda/2020/01/5-shocking-facts-about-inequality-according-to-oxfam-s-latest-report/

World Bank. (2020a). *COVID-19 to add as many as 150 million extreme poor by 2021.* Retrieved October 14, 2020, from https://www.worldbank.org/en/

news/press-release/2020/10/07/covid-19-to-add-as-many-as-150-million-extreme-poor-by-2021

World Bank. (2020b). COVID19: *Remittances to shrink by 14 % by 2021*. Retrieved November 3, 2020, from https://www.worldbank.org/en/news/press-release/2020/10/29/covid-19-remittance-flows-to-shrink-14-by-2021#:~:text=Remittance%20flows%20to%20low%20and,to%20%24470%20billion%20in%202021

World Social Report. (2020). *Inequality in a rapidly changing world*. Retrieved November 1, 2020, from https://www.un.org/development/desa/dspd/wp-content/uploads/sites/22/2020/01/World-Social-Report-2020-FullReport.pdf

XXX. (2020). *Blog series: Debating the SDGs*. https://www.globalstudies.ugent.be/blog-series-debating-the-sdgs/

Yusha'u, M. J. (2020). COVID-19, digital divide and the rise of online education. *SDGs Digest* (11), p. 18. Retrieved May 29, 2020, from https://books.isdb.org/view/383020/18/

Yusha'u, M. J., & Servaes, J. (Eds.). (2021). *The Palgrave handbook of international communication and sustainable development* (p. 2021). Cham.

Communication and Information Poverty in the Context of the Sustainable Development Goals (SDGs): A Case for SDG 18—Communication for All

Lorenzo Vargas and Philip Lee

Abstract This chapter explores the intersections between the United Nation's Sustainable Development Goals (Agenda 2030) and communication and information issues. Taking a communication rights-based approach that emphasizes the need to address communication and information poverty in order to achieve sustainable development, the authors examine the four goals (5, 9, 16, and 17) where communication and information issues feature most prominently and make the case for the

The authors gratefully acknowledge the teamwork that led to the crafting of this chapter, with valuable inputs from a number of sources including present and former colleagues, researchers, and WACC project partners.

L. Vargas (✉) • P. Lee
World Association for Christian Communication (WACC), Toronto, Canada
e-mail: LV@waccglobal.org; PL@waccglobal.org

25

J. Servaes, M. J. Yusha'u (eds.), *SDG18 Communication for All, Volume 1*, Sustainable Development Goals Series, https://doi.org/10.1007/978-3-031-19142-8_2

inclusion of an 18th goal: Communication for All, in order to address a range of communication and information deficits, such as digital exclusion and undemocratic media landscapes, that impede meaningful and transformational sustainable development.

Keywords Communication rights • Sustainable development • Communication for social change • Media democracy • Sustainable Development Goals

INTRODUCTION

Millions of people on every continent lack access to communication platforms, are underrepresented or misrepresented in the media, have limited familiarity with media literacy, have restricted access to relevant and accurate information and knowledge, are excluded from participation in decision-making processes, or live in contexts with little media freedom. These issues can be summed up as communication and information poverty, a form of poverty that contributes to people's sense of powerlessness and inability to make themselves heard, one of the most prevalent manifestations of poverty according to a landmark World Bank study (Narayan et al., 2000). As such, communication and information poverty is a critical dimension of poverty in all its forms.

Addressing these types of communication and information deficits is critical to achieving the vision of the United Nations' 2030 Agenda for Sustainable Development and its 17 Sustainable Development Goals (SDGs). This is because they impede full participation in development processes, especially for the poorest and most marginalized people in society. This belief echoes the findings of a report published by the UN Development Group on the post-2015 development agenda, which found that people want to have a public voice in decisions concerning development and called for "putting people—their rights, aspirations, and opportunities—at the center of development" (United Nations Development Group, 2013).

Unfortunately, tackling communication and information poverty does not always form part of development agendas set by donors, international institutions, and national governments. Equitable access to communication and information, despite being the backbone of democratic societies, is often taken for granted by those who set development priorities. This can partly be attributed to the fact that communication and information issues are often less tangible than other development priorities, such as food security or access to life-saving medication. But it also results from the inherently political nature of communication: the configuration of the information and communication ecosystem of any given society (Whose voices are heard? Who has the ability to set the public agenda? Whose stories are being ignored?) reflects power dynamics and responds to the economic and political interests of dominant groups.

This means that official development discourse, so used to portraying development as a technical rather than a political problem, is often unwilling to tackle an issue that may provoke resistance or pushback from states and economic elites. For example, it is hard to imagine entities such as the UK's Foreign, Commonwealth & Development Office (FCDO), formerly the Department for International Development (DfID), or USAID financing a development intervention seeking to democratize the media sector in a country like Brazil, where the fact that politicians and local economic elites are involved in media businesses and just four TV stations have 70% of the national audience means that there exist very narrow avenues for marginalized communities to shape public opinion (Reporters Without Borders, 2018).

Nevertheless, information and communication considerations must be part of development agendas since political and social change—and with them sustainable development—depend on unfettered access to communications. Furthermore, tackling communication and information issues helps enable the achievement of a range of other objectives, and can enhance the long-term sustainability of some development outcomes, such as health-related behavioral change.

The United Nation's 2030 Agenda does bring in several communication and information issues, which is very encouraging. For example, SDG 5 highlights the importance of Information and Communication Technologies (ICTs) as tools for women's empowerment, while SDG 9 promotes universal internet access. ICTs are also mentioned in SDG 4 and SDG 17. SDG 16 calls attention to the importance of access to public information legislation and to the imperative of protecting journalists, trade unionists, and human rights defenders.

Despite this progress, and as is explored below, more detailed integration of communication and information issues into the SDGs and its targets would have strengthened the vision and outcomes of Agenda 2030.

This chapter[1] explores the relationship between communication and information issues and the 2030 Agenda. It also presents a series of recommendations for donor governments, international institutions, national governments, and other stakeholders to address communication and information poverty as part of development interventions guided by SDG 5 (gender equality), SDG 9 (industry, innovation, and infrastructure), SDG 16 (peace, justice, and strong institutions), and SDG 17 (partnerships for goals). Lastly, it makes a case for the recognition of an 18th SDG: Communication for All.

Equally importantly, these recommendations reflect the position that taking a rights-based approach to communication and information is the most ethical way to address the issues listed above. This is because of the existence of widely accepted rights frameworks around communication and information, such as the right to freedom of expression, the right to access information, and linguistic rights, all of which draw on principles of equality, accessibility, affordability, and inclusion.

The overriding concept that emerged during the consultation process that led to this chapter is that of communication and information poverty. This is understood as a form of poverty that goes hand-in-hand with economic and social poverty and needs to be addressed in order to achieve sustainable development. Communication and information are "essential conditions for development and affect every aspect of life. [Therefore], communication and information poverty, despite being only one dimension of poverty, affects all other dimensions" (Barja Daza & Gigler, 2007).

---

[1] This chapter is the result of a process that involved face-to-face and online consultations with some 90 grassroots communication activists around the world. Most of these activists are representatives of civil society organizations working on communication rights issues around the world with the technical and financial support of WACC. For the full list of activists, see Annex. WACC staff carried out focus groups, structured interviews, and informal conversations with these activists during in-person events in Hong Kong, New York, and San Jose, Costa Rica, as well as online. These findings were subsequently presented to different academic fora, including the 2018 IAMCR conference, in order to solicit feedback.

Key Manifestations of Communication and Information Poverty

- Lack of access to platforms meaningfully to raise concerns about issues that affect one's life
- Under/misrepresentation in media content
- Low levels of media literacy
- Limited access to relevant information, including public information
- Exclusion from decision-making processes
- Restrictions on freedom of expression, association, and assembly
- Absence of a free, independent, inclusive, and pluralistic media sector
- Prevalence of negative stereotypes about marginalized groups
- Social and cultural factors preventing genuine participation (e.g., discrimination because of gender, race, ethnicity, social class, etc.)
- Media concentration in the hands of the powerful
- Inaccessibility of information and communication (e.g., linguistic barriers)
- Breaches of privacy, especially in relation to digital communication
- Limited opportunities to participate in decision-making processes related to the regulation and governance of communication ecosystems

COMMUNICATION AND DEVELOPMENT

Since the inception of international development as a global project in the 1950s, development practitioners and researchers have highlighted the potential of communication in supporting development processes (Melkote, 2000; Servaes, 1999). Over the years, this led to the emergence of greatly varying practices within the field of communication for development, such as communication strategies for agricultural extension, technology transfer, behavioral change, and participatory communication (Colle, 2008). As a result, a plethora of labels has emerged to describe the field, such as communication for social change, development communication, development support communication, communication for development, participatory communication, media development, development media, social communication, and behavioral change communication (Manyozo, 2011).

Two main approaches have historically shaped the role of communication in development. On the one hand is an understanding of communication as "a linear process of information *transmission* that causes social change in terms of knowledge, attitudes and behaviors". This understanding is typically connected to the view of development as modernization, which emphasizes the replication of Western paths to progress. An example would be early models of agricultural extension, which provided farmers in the Global South with information about new farming practices often without taking into account the local context. The transmission approach generally tends to overlook issues such as local culture, local access to media, and farmers' ability to participate in decision-making, all of which are related to communication and information poverty.

On the other hand, there is the view that "communication is a complex *process* that is linked to culture, and that is connected to global and local economic, political, and ideological structures". This idea is conceptually linked to views of development as empowering marginalized communities and challenging unequal power relationships (Melkote & Steeves, 2001; Servaes, 2006.) An example is the use of community-based theatre as a mechanism to generate debate, explore cultural identities, and build consensus around common problems. This approach tends to understand communication and information from a rights-based perspective and addresses key communication and information poverty issues such as the existence of platforms for genuine participation, media literacy, and cultural and linguistic relevance.

The field has also been shaped by regional concepts of communication, with some regions of the world having a strong tradition in participatory dialogue-based communication and others having historically focused on media structures or on media content for development (Manyozo, 2012).

Today, there is growing consensus that communication-based development interventions should abide by principles such as consultation, inclusion, locally driven needs, gender equality, community empowerment, participation, and respect for human rights. There is also increased recognition that all of the approaches to communication for development can contribute to processes of social change, depending on the local context, the issue at hand, and the appropriateness of tools used (mass media, community media, community dialogue, public art, etc.).

The notion of communication as a cyclical or two-way process of exchange embedded in culture is also a defining feature of interventions that view communication as one of the building blocks of sustainable development. This evolving understanding of communication reaffirms the idea that integrating communication and information issues into development is more about a holistic approach that addresses communication and information poverty than about simply providing people with information or access to communication technologies.

A RIGHTS-BASED VIEW OF COMMUNICATION

Addressing communication and information poverty through development interventions should be done from a rights-based perspective. This is because, in addition to drawing on existing and widely accepted rights frameworks, a rights-based approach provides development practitioners with a lens with which to view, understand, and address communication and information issues.

The right to freedom of expression, enshrined in Article 19 of the Universal Declaration of Human Rights, is the starting point for taking a rights-based approach to communication and information. "It is regarded as a central pillar of democracy, protecting the right to call our rulers to account, vital to preventing censorship, an indispensable condition of effective and free media" (CRIS Campaign, 2005). However, in any given society communication power both enables and limits access to information and communication, which in some cases may undermine freedom of expression. For example:

> A poor person seeking to highlight injustice in their lives and a powerful media mogul each have, before the law, precisely the same protection for their right to freely express their views. In practice, however, the former lacks a means to have her/his voice heard, while the latter can powerfully amplify her/his message and ensure it is widely heard. (ibid.)

As a result, the right to freedom of expression is best guaranteed when promoted *alongside* a number of other rights. This is particularly important today as communication ecosystems are becoming increasingly complex due to rapid technological change, different levels of access to platforms, multi-layered and often transnational media governance processes, growing dependence on digital technology, and the emergence of digital media as key spaces with the potential to advance inclusion and social change (Couldry & Rodriguez, 2015).

Other rights that help "construct the environment in which freedom of expression may be fully consummated" include "a right to participate in one's own culture and language, to enjoy the benefits of science, to information, to education, to participation in governance, to privacy, to peaceful assembly, to the protection of one's reputation" (CRIS Campaign, 2005) all of which are part of the International Bill of Rights. Further crucial elements include diversity of media content and ownership, press freedom, diverse and independent media, and democratic access to media (ibid.) More recently, documents such as the Charter of Digital Rights promoted by the civil society network European Digital Rights (EDRi) have put the spotlight on new important dimensions of this equation such as data protection, transparent governance, and freedom from surveillance (European Digital Rights, 2014).

The following are some of the key rights already recognized in international human rights documents that help enable access to information, communication, and participation at all levels:

- Freedom of expression, including the right of the media to operate freely (Universal Declaration of Human Rights (UDHR) 18, 19, 21, International Covenant on Civil and Political Rights (ICCPR) 19)
- Access to information from public and private sources that pertains to the public interest (UDHR 19, ICCPR 19)
- A diverse and plural media, in terms of sources, content, views, and means of transmission (UDHR 19, ICCPR 19)
- Universal access to the media necessary to engage with the public sphere, including direct communication and a right to assembly (UDHR 19, ICCPR 19, 21, 22)
- The right to literacy and to a basic education (UDHR 26, International Covenant on Economic, Social and Cultural Rights (CESCR) 13)
- Affordable and equitable access to the means and media for knowledge-sharing (UDHR 19, 27, ICCPR 19, 27)
- Communicate in one's mother tongue in key spheres such as politics and media (ICCPR 10f, 27)
- Privacy of personal communication (ICCPR 17)

HOW COMMUNICATION AND INFORMATION POVERTY UNDERMINES THE VISION OF THE SUSTAINABLE DEVELOPMENT GOALS (SDGs)

"Transforming our World: Agenda 2030 for Sustainable Development" is the United Nations' framework for development between 2015 and 2030. It is a *universal* agenda, including both developed and developing countries, that seeks to balance economic growth, environmental sustainability, peace, and human development in order to bring about genuine social progress. Agenda 2030 is grounded in human rights frameworks and reaffirms the outcomes of other global processes such as the Declaration on the Right to Development (1986), the Rio Declaration on Environment and Development (1992), the United Nations Framework Convention on Climate Change (1992), and the Beijing Platform for Action (1995), among others.

Agenda 2030 sets 17 Sustainable Development Goals (SDGs), which are "integrated and indivisible, global in nature and universally applicable, taking into account different national realities, capacities and levels of development and respecting national policies and priorities". Each goal contains several targets in order to guide implementation, although these targets remain "aspirational and global" (United Nations, 2015).

While the implementation of the SDGs is the responsibility of national governments, Agenda 2030 foresees a Global Partnership between governments, civil society, the private sector, UN agencies, and other stakeholders in order to mobilize the resources and knowledge needed to implement the vision of Agenda 2030.

However, it seems obvious that this vision *cannot* be fully realized unless communication and information ecosystems enable people to participate in decision-making related to their sustainable development needs. To illustrate this point, the paragraphs below examine the four SDGs where communication and information issues feature most prominently: SDGs 5 (gender equality), 9 (industry, innovation, and infrastructure), 16 (peace, justice, and strong institutions), and 17 (partnerships for the goals). Thinking and recommendations around these SDGs are also explored.

SDG 5: GENDER EQUALITY

Agenda 2030 recognizes the importance of addressing gender inequality as a central component of bringing about sustainable development. Goal 5 seeks to achieve gender equality and empower all women and girls. Its nine targets and 14 indicators address critical gender issues such as discrimination against women and girls, violence against women and girls, harmful practices such as early and forced marriage and female genital mutilation (FGM), women's unpaid work, women's access to economic resources, and access to sexual and reproductive health, among others.

Gender inequality is a key dimension of communication and information poverty because gender issues affect how women and girls are represented in the media, have access to media platforms, and gain information and knowledge. Gender inequality also undermines the ability of women and girls to exercise their right to freedom of expression, which in turn prevents them from fully participating in decision-making processes about matters that affect their lives. In this sense, communication and information poverty perpetuates gender inequality in a broader sense and undermines sustainable development.

Under Goal 5, four targets in particular highlight the relationship between communication and information poverty and gender equality. The first is *Target 5.1. End all forms of discrimination against all women and girls everywhere.* As research has shown (Macharia et al., 2015), women are under- and misrepresented in media content, a form of discrimination that exacerbates, perpetuates, and normalizes other forms of discrimination against women and girls.

The second target under Goal 5 is *Target 5.2. Eliminate all forms of violence against all women and girls in the public sphere, including trafficking and other types of exploitation.* Many women and girls around the world face violence when exercising their right to freedom of expression. This is particularly the case for women journalists, as many encounter gender-based violence at work according to a survey by the IFJ (International Federation of Journalists, 2017). The issue has also repeatedly come up in the context of online communications.

The third target under Goal 5 is *Target 5.5: Ensure women's full and effective participation and equal opportunities for leadership at all levels of decision-making in political, economic, and public life.* The link to communication and information issues is self-evident as women need to have access to communication platforms and to information in order to enjoy full and effective participation. The reference to equal opportunities for leadership, reflected in indicator 5.5.2, is also important as it reinforces the need to promote women's leadership within the media sector.

The fourth target under Goal 5 is *Target 5.B: Enhance the use of enabling technology, in particular information and communications technology, to promote the empowerment of women.* As mentioned above, one of the key manifestations of communication and information poverty is limited access to communication platforms and resources. Having greater access to affordable mobile telephony, as Indicator 5.B.1 for this target suggests, would certainly help address a number of communication and information needs for many women.

Working toward these targets is critical to helping address communication and information poverty as experienced by women and girls. Nevertheless, there is significant work to be done to promote gender equality in communications. For example, the 2020 Global Media Monitoring Project (GMMP) reports statistical evidence pointing to a loss of traction in narrowing media gender disparities over the past decade and regression on some indicators (Macharia et al., 2020). This means that, despite considerable effort by activists, allies in the media, media training institutions, and others, achieving gender equality in and through the media remains a formidable task.

At the same time, public awareness about the relationship between communication, gender, and development has grown in recent years, as has the number of initiatives by UN agencies, stakeholder networks, and civil society organizations. For example, the UNESCO-led Global Alliance for Media and Gender (GAMAG) was founded in 2013 to accelerate the implementation of recommendations on "Women and the Media" contained in "Section J" of the 1995 Beijing Platform for Action. Similarly, in 2016 UN women launched the Step It Up for Gender Equality Media Compact to urge media organizations to play their part in advancing gender equality and women's rights within the Post-2015 Development Framework. These issues continue to be explored in spaces such as the Generation Equality Forum, convened by UN Women in 2020 to take stock of progress on gender equality. Such developments reaffirm the imperative of considering communication issues both from a gender justice and from a human rights perspective.

RECOMMENDATIONS TO ADDRESS COMMUNICATION AND INFORMATION POVERTY FROM A GENDER PERSPECTIVE IN THE CONTEXT OF AGENDA 2030

Donor governments, national governments, international institutions, and civil society need to:

- Recognize that gender inequality has an impact on the way people access communication and information, which in turn limits their ability to improve their lives. For example, while gender disparities in relation to communication and information vary widely depending on context, men tend to have greater access to information than women, which in turn excludes many women and girls from participating in decision-making.
- Support initiatives to enable and enhance women and girls' ability to participate in development processes, including access to media platforms where they can raise concerns about issues that affect their lives and opportunities for women's groups to establish their own media.
- Strengthen research and advocacy related to the representation of women and girls in media content.
- Promote women and girls' access to learning opportunities about media literacy, particularly in relation SDG 4 (quality education).
- Promote wide access to public information, particularly in ways that take into account the gendered dimension of access to information.
- Support efforts to make all media outlets "safe spaces" for women and girls. This can take the form of internal dialogue, the development of ethical standards, awareness-raising, and specially crafted content. Community media, a form of media that is supposed to reflect values such as inclusion, diversity, and equality, should take the lead in guiding commercial and public media toward greater gender equality.
- Promote and strengthen networks of media professionals working for gender equality.
- Encourage and recognize the work of women through public communication via traditional and digital media platforms. This can take the form of advocacy, awareness-raising, and specialized content.
- Support efforts to tackle patriarchal cultural practices and social norms at all levels, particularly at the grassroots level. Moreover, support communication and education processes that can help to raise

awareness about the impact of patriarchy on society and help change behaviors in matters related to gender issues. This should also include working with community and religious leaders that reinforce patriarchy.

- Build the capacity of women and women's rights organizations at all levels, particularly at the grassroots level to articulate the ways in which women experience gender inequality.
- Support media training of women to help enable their participation in the media sector as journalists, editors, and managers.

A declaration was issued following a consultation in New York in 2017, which offered additional recommendations, some of which are:

- Help eliminate gender stereotypes and hate speech from public media, and continually promote gender equality in the media.
- Incorporate gender-sensitivity, local history, and cultural diversity in the education and training of professionals in the field of communications in order to increase gender sensitivity of reporting and to eliminate sexist and misogynist media content.
- Ensure freedom of expression for women and lesbian, gay, bisexual, and transgender groups.
- Strengthen the visibility of women and girls from minority and marginalized groups, rural women, women with disabilities, migrants, refugees, displaced women, and their equal access to media to be part of content production, news making, and speaking about their experiences.
- Developing and promoting media tools for gender-sensitive reporting (gender-sensitive language, databases of experts, journalist codes) but also continually monitoring their implementation in media content, in the community of journalists and their associations (WACC Project Partners, 2018).

SDG 9: Industry, Innovation, and Infrastructure and SDG 17: Partnerships for the Goals

In the United Nation's 2030 Agenda, SDGs 9 and 17 recognize the need to enable people everywhere to benefit from access to the internet and to mobile telephony. This represents undeniable progress from a communication and information perspective as increased access to relevant technology and platforms can help equip people with the tools to participate in the information society, have their voices heard, and contribute to the production and dissemination of knowledge. This is especially relevant as it is estimated that about three billion people lack access to the internet and about two billion do not have access to a mobile phone (Global Digital Report, 2018).

Goal 9 (industry, innovation, and infrastructure) highlights the issue of access to Information and Communication Technologies (ICTs) and the internet under Target 9.C: *Significantly increase access to information and communications technology and strive to provide universal and affordable access to the internet in least developed countries by 2020.* For national governments, this goal reinforces their obligation to provide universal access to basic telecommunication services to their citizens, including those living in remote areas. It also creates an opportunity to promote more democratic models for the development and ownership of communication infrastructure, as exemplified by community-managed telecommunication company *Telecomunicaciones Indígenas Comunitarias* (TIC) in Oaxaca, Mexico (Lakhani, 2016; Ó Siochrú, 2017).

Goal 17 (Partnerships for the Goals) focuses on the finance, technology, capacity, trade, effectiveness, monitoring issues related to the implementation of Agenda 2030. Under the "technology" area of this SDG, two targets focus on internet access: Target 17.6 *Enhance North-South, South-South and triangular regional and international cooperation on and access to science, technology and innovation,* Indicator 17.6.2 *Fixed internet broadband subscriptions per 100 inhabitants, by speed;* and Target 17.8 *Fully operationalize the technology bank and science, technology and innovation capacity-building mechanism for least developed countries by 2017 and enhance the use of enabling technology, in particular information and communications technology,* Indicator 17.8.1 *Proportion of individuals using the internet.* Increased access to the internet can have a significant impact on communication and information needs, especially at the grassroots level (Rey-Moreno, 2017) particularly as access to services in many parts of the world is increasingly internet-mediated.

The focus on access to ICTs and internet services in Agenda 2030 is commendable. Nevertheless, at a time when digital communication is becoming increasingly prevalent and policymakers in many countries are developing the digital infrastructure and digital governance models of the future, it is critical to move beyond the celebration of access in order to address more structural issues. Questions about ownership, regulation, privacy, data-mining, and illegal surveillance of civil society actors must be central elements of the conversation about ICTs in development. Some of these issues were raised by the United Nations Special Rapporteur on the Promotion and Protection of the Right to Freedom of Opinion and Expression, David Kaye, in his office's 2015, 2016, and 2017 reports (Office of the High Commissioner for Human Rights).

Agenda 2030 is an opportunity to advance transparency and accountability in relation to the digital infrastructure of the twenty-first century. Failure to address these issues will raise political and ethical concerns ranging from the subversion of democracy to intrusion into and control over peoples' lives through surveillance and artificial intelligence (AI). This may ultimately undermine the credibility and legitimacy of digital platforms, as the scandal around privacy practices at Facebook in 2018 demonstrated (Sich et al., 2018).

Greater access to the internet and digital platforms is insufficient. It is essential to promote the use of these new tools in such a way that those communities most often excluded achieve greater participation and that helps create the political will to implement public policies which contribute to greater equality and inclusion. This use of digital platforms must occur within a framework of rights that helps generate genuine opportunities for free and informed participation to promote truly sustainable development.

RECOMMENDATIONS TO LEVERAGE INCREASED ACCESS TO ICTS AND TO THE INTERNET IN ORDER TO ADDRESS COMMUNICATION AND INFORMATION POVERTY

Despite the existence of several problematic aspects in the field of digital communications, such platforms continue to be vital tools for marginalized communities in that they can, when used strategically, help influence the media and public policy agendas in favor of their interests, help their communities organize for change, and encourage active citizenship. Donor governments, national governments, international institutions, and/or civil society are called on to:

- Establish regulatory bodies, operating within legislated guidelines, that represent the public interest and take content moderation and platform governance out of the exclusive preserve of private sector companies in order to improve democratic expression on the internet. Civil society organizations would need to play important roles on these bodies to facilitate independent oversight and to prevent these spaces from being co-opted by either state or private sector actors. In order to be relevant, these bodies would need to have a functioning mechanism "with teeth" to address complaints, resolve disputes, and remove hateful content.

- Explore creating public or non-profit alternatives to existing private digital platforms. These would be platforms that, much like public service media, would have to operate outside the logics of the market and exist primarily to promote democratic debate, ensure transparent access to information, and guarantee freedom of expression.
- Take steps to reduce the concentration of digital power (i.e., ownership, control, and monopolistic practices) in a handful of private tech companies and work toward creating greater competition in the technology sector.
- Support community-initiated efforts to develop and/or manage telecommunications infrastructure in order to increase access to mobile telephony and internet services.
- Promote initiatives that link established community media platforms to ICTs, especially in ways that promote interactivity and participation. The community media sector has a wealth of expertise and experience in participatory and democratic participation. Combining community media with ICT can serve to turn increased access to ICTs into community-level participation.
- Facilitate the formation of networks of citizen communicators and journalists belonging to marginalized communities and social movements so that they can use digital communication platforms in their advocacy work on issues that affect their communities.
- Advance research about the relationship between access to ICTs, community participation, and development.
- Promote inter-sectoral partnerships to address violations of human rights online, such as online violence and illegal surveillance.
- Build digital media production training for marginalized and excluded communities, including women and girls.
- Support digital media literacy among marginalized and excluded communities, including women and girls.

- Build the capacity of marginalized and excluded communities, including women and girls, to develop and use open-source software.
- Build the capacity of civil society organizations to participate in policy making processes related to communication infrastructure, policy, and digital rights.
- Promote digital solutions that help enable community participation in decision-making.

SDG 16: Peace, Justice, and Strong Institutions

The 2030 Agenda, within the framework of Goal 16 (peace, justice, and strong institutions), recognizes that democracy, good governance, and the rule of law play a fundamental role in achieving sustainable development. Open and democratic access to communication and information underpins the achievement of all these objectives as it can help promote social inclusion, peaceful conflict resolution, advance the rule of law, shed light on corruption, promote trust in institutions, and enable participation. There is also a direct link to fundamental freedoms such as freedom of expression and freedom of association. A number of targets within this goal have a direct link to communication and information issues.

Target 16.1 *Significantly reduce all forms of violence and related death rates everywhere* is strongly linked to media and communication issues. Open and trust-based communication has the potential to help ameliorate conflict situations, promote a culture of dialogue, and advance non-violent conflict resolution. Peace-oriented media can also create spaces for meaningful exchange among perceived adversaries. Responsible and ethical media coverage of conflict can help counter hate speech, change perceptions and behaviors, and ensure access to information on conflict prevention.

Target 16.3 *Promote the rule of law at the national and international levels and ensure equal access to justice for all* is intimately linked to information and communication issues. Media freedom, access to information, and freedom of expression are essential to keep institutions in check, as well as to promote trust in the justice system.

Target 16.5 *Substantially reduce corruption and bribery in all their forms* has a strong relationship to media freedom issues, as media outlets and investigative journalists need protection and safeguards to ensure they can carry out their work effectively. It would be difficult to reduce corruption when the media are concentrated in a few hands and journalists do not have the freedom to investigate cases of corruption.

In relation to Target 16.6 *Develop effective, accountable, and transparent institutions at all levels*, it is clear that freedom of information and other communication rights are essential to promote transparency and accountability within public institutions. The media ought to reflect the views of all sectors of society, especially those of the most disadvantaged people, in order to achieve greater transparency and diversity within public institutions.

Target 16.7 *Ensure responsive, inclusive, participatory, and representative decision-making at all levels* has multiple connections to communication and information issues. An essential element of exercising communication rights is the opportunity for people to participate in decision-making, especially in relation to issues that directly affect their lives. This requires access to information, particularly public information. People must also be able to exercise their right to freedom of expression, have access to relevant means of communication, and be guaranteed a right of reply and redress. People also have the right to participate in the "formulation and governance of the communication sphere… at the national level, but also in the context of international relations" (CRIS Campaign, 2005).

Target 16.10 *Ensure public access to information and protect fundamental freedoms, in accordance with national legislation and international agreements* has numerous connections to communication and information issues. The two indicators under this target reflect this: Indicator 16.10.1 *Number of verified cases of killing, kidnapping, enforced disappearance, arbitrary detention and torture of journalists, associated media personnel, trade unionists and human rights advocates in the previous 12 months* and Indicator 16.10.2 *Number of countries that adopt and implement constitutional, statutory, and/or policy guarantees for public access to information.* The inclusion of this target and indicators in Agenda 2030 is commendable. While an indicator related to freedom of expression would have strengthened this target, especially in relation to the reference to "fundamental freedoms", this target is still central for all those working on addressing communication and information poverty.

Target 16.B. *Promote and enforce non-discriminatory laws and policies for sustainable development* can also be examined from a communication and information perspective. Numerous groups in society face discrimination and other barriers in relation to communication and information. For example, many Indigenous people are unable to access public information in their language, preventing them from participating in society.

In sum, the explicit references to communication and information issues within Goal 16 are limited to access to public information and to the protection of journalists and other human rights defenders. In this sense, the goal fails to reference pivotal issues such as freedom of expression, linguistic rights, digital convergence, and media ownership and control that are inextricably related to peace, justice, and strong democratic institutions. Nevertheless, the many instances in which communication and information issues implicitly intersect with the targets of SDG 16, as listed above, represent valuable opportunities for those tackling communication and information poverty. These intersections allow groups working in fields such as community media, media monitoring, advocacy on access to information, participatory communication, and citizen journalism to make direct links to specific SDGs in order to highlight the importance of their work and to gain broader support for it.

Recommendations to Address Communication and Information Poverty in the Context of SDG 16

Donors, national governments, international institutions, and civil society are called upon:

- At the national level, to support an audit of existing communication and information laws and regulations in order to identify systemic policy and legal issues that undermine the rule of law, the struggle against corruption, trust-based relationships between citizens and institutions, participatory decision-making, fundamental freedoms, and the fight against discrimination.
- At the national level, to convene a summit of key stakeholders (civil society, public sector, media, and communication organizations) to discuss communication and information poverty issues based on the national audit described above.
- To develop awareness-raising campaigns about the ways in which communication and information poverty undermines peace, justice, and strong institutions.

- To work toward a Communication Rights Charter as a way to galvanize support around the need to address communication and information poverty.
- To support community media, particularly community radio, as it can be an effective communication platform to enable individuals and communities to participate in decision-making and access relevant information, particularly when strategically linked to social media platforms or SMS systems. Community media outlets that actively facilitate listeners' groups and are linked to people's organizations should be prioritized. This support should include extensive capacity building and efforts to link community stations with one another in order to share knowledge and technical expertise.
- To protect journalists and media workers linked to community media outlets, most of whom lack the support of established media organizations.
- To support and strengthen the role of independent public service media as one of the cornerstones of diverse and pluralistic media systems.
- To support the integration of media literacy into education systems, including adult education initiatives, in order to equip people with the knowledge and skills to demand transparent and accountable media institutions and to participate in decision-making.
- To support interpersonal communication efforts. Peace, access to justice, and more productive relationships between citizens and institutions can be greatly advanced through interpersonal communication processes, such as community dialogue, public forums, public art, and so on. These are spaces where ideas can be discussed and shared. Communication processes must be consultative and non-hierarchical in order to lead to meaningful change.
- To highlight the experience of marginalized communities in public communication from a pluralistic perspective. This can help to strengthen institutions and to create spaces for new issues to be discussed. It can take the form of media content, especially when produced by communities themselves, which sheds light on the stories of those communities in order to promote awareness and international solidarity. This can help to address under- and misrepresentation, a phenomenon that undermines peaceful coexistence, fair treatment, and social cohesion.

- To build the strategic communications capacity of civil society organizations in order to enable them better to effect change. This also
  entails access to communication technologies and resources.
- To promote a diverse, open, free, accountable, and democratic
  media system.
- To defend the rights of freedom of assembly and association, including in online spaces, in order to enable people to participate in
  decision-making, hold institutions and decision-makers to account,
  and guarantee human rights.
- To build the capacity of civil society organizations to participate in
  policy-making processes, particularly in relation to communication
  and information issues.

SDG 18: Communication for All

The sections above explored four SDGs with strong links to communication and information issues and called for greater attention to be paid to
communication and information poverty issues that undermine broader
sustainable development. In this light and since communication clearly
underpins genuinely sustainable development and requires equitable
access to information and knowledge, to information and communication
technologies, as well as plurality and diversity in the media, the authors of
this chapter have identified what should have been UN Sustainable
Development Goal 18: Communication for All. Its purpose is
self-evident:

Goal: Expand and strengthen public civic spaces through equitable and
affordable access to communication technologies and platforms, media
pluralism, and media diversity.

Target 1.1 By 2030, ensure the existence of spaces and resources for men
and women, in particular the poor and vulnerable, to engage in transparent, informed, and democratic public dialogue and debate.

Target 1.2 By 2030, ensure the existence of regimes where creative ideas
and knowledge are encouraged, can be communicated widely and freely
to advance social justice and sustainable development.

Target 1.3 By 2030, ensure protection for the dignity and security of people in relation to communication processes, especially concerning data
privacy and freedom from surveillance.

Target 1.4 By 2030, ensure communication spaces for diverse cultures, cultural forms, and identities at the individual and social levels.

The indicators for these four targets remain to be determined, although to some extent, they can be found in existing indices of political and social freedoms, such as the Social Progress Index, UNESCO's Media Development Indicators, Reporters Without Borders' World Press Freedom Index, and WACC's Global Media Monitoring Project (GMMP).

To illustrate how SDG 18 might directly influence outcomes, the sections below examine key information and communication issues, such as undemocratic communication systems, digital illiteracy, and the ongoing exclusion of historically marginalized communities that undermine broader sustainable development.

DEMOCRATIZING COMMUNICATION AND INFORMATION ECOSYSTEMS

Many of the structures that perpetuate information and communication poverty are linked to the legislative and policy frameworks that govern media and information systems, which in turn reflect power dynamics in society that exclude certain groups from media landscapes. UNESCO's Media Development Indicators, which are widely accepted around the world as the main framework to assess media development (UNESCO, 2008), exemplify the work needed to make media systems more inclusive, transparent, and pluralistic from a policy perspective. Work by UNESCO to develop Internet Universality Indicators in order to promote a more open, rights-based, and inclusive internet (UNESCO, 2017) is also critical, and will become more significant as digital and internet-based communication innovations emerge.

Civil society needs to be an active participant in the development of legislative and policy frameworks to democratize communication, media, and information ecosystems. There is much to be learnt from the experience of a number of civil society organizations from Latin America which over the past 15 years have advocated more democratic communication, media, and information ecosystems in their national contexts. During the first two decades of the twenty-first century, governments of several Latin American countries, in most cases with the support of civil society actors, developed new laws and public policy frameworks that sought to democratize access to the media. Some examples among others are the Organic Law of Communication in Ecuador; the General Law of Telecommunications, Information and Communication Technologies in Bolivia; the Audio-visual Communication Services Law in Argentina; and the Media Law in Uruguay.

These new policies have elements in common. For example, they promoted the equitable distribution of licenses between clearly defined sectors: public, private or commercial, and community. In some cases, there is also a fourth sector: the Indigenous communication sector. Another element in common is the existence of rules to prevent and/or discourage the concentration of media in a few hands, especially in the hands of foreign or domestic capital conglomerates whose influence in other sectors of the country's economy is too great. In general, these policies have also included the establishment of regulatory agencies with the ability to impose sanctions to enforce the new rules.

Many of the new media regulation frameworks have faced considerable obstacles. On the one hand, the private and commercial sectors, accustomed to a much more favorable regime, have opposed the implementation of new policies, arguing that they constitute attacks on press freedom and freedom of expression. On the other hand, in many cases these new regulations have occurred in highly politicized environments and have been seen as tools for the governments of the day to promote their political agendas. This politicization in many cases has reduced the legitimacy of these processes and has made them vulnerable to electoral change, as in the case of Argentina from 2015 onwards.

In addition, there have been many failures in the implementation of these new frameworks, such as a lack of concrete and sustainable mechanisms to strengthen the community broadcasting sector, on which production quotas were often imposed that were difficult to meet. However, despite such problems, it is undeniable that these processes of democratization of the media represent a step forward for communication rights.

Civil society played a central role in the development of these new media regulation frameworks, in many cases openly supporting and promoting them. Many civil society actors have tried to maintain an independent position, especially in contexts where the issue of media regulation has been politicized, while other actors have decided to align themselves more closely with clearer political positions. In some cases, this dynamic led to deep divisions within civil society in those countries.

New models for media regulation seen in places such as Uruguay and Ecuador contrast with the models of countries such as Mexico, Colombia, Brazil, Chile, and Peru, and most countries of Central America and the Caribbean, which have not undergone major changes in recent years. Most of these countries have legal frameworks for the regulation of media that in one way or another try to discourage the concentration of media, but the reality is that a market logic prevails in the field of communication in these countries. In some cases, the community media sector is recognized, as in Colombia and El Salvador, but in others, such as Mexico, Costa Rica, Guatemala, and Peru, the sector is either not recognized or faces great difficulties in order to operate legally. Cuba is an exception to the rule because, although the private sector does not play any role in the country's media, the state sector covers most of the media, in many cases excluding the community sector.

In addition to public advocacy to democratize access to the media, coalitions of civil society organizations in several Latin American countries have also contributed to the development of legal frameworks and public policies on other issues related to communication. For example, during the past 15 years several coalitions have emerged that contributed to changes in access to public information, as in the case of Brazil and Mexico, and to changes in legal frameworks that criminalized contempt and certain forms of public expression, such as in the case of Chile and Guatemala (Segura & Waisbord, 2016).

Recommendations to Promote Civil Society Participation in Policymaking About Communication and Information

The central recommendation is *to support the development of civil society coalitions at the national level interested in promoting concrete changes to communication and information legislation and policy, related to issues such as access to information, Internet governance, and media regulation.* This recommendation is based on the belief that civil society is a crucial actor in the struggle for more open, inclusive, and democratic media ecosystems.

Such coalitions must be diverse, inclusive, and open spaces for dialogue with different actors, but they must also have the capacity to develop clear common agendas and objectives. This type of coalition must also have the tools to produce and disseminate knowledge, interact with state agencies, establish alliances with sectors of civil society that have not traditionally been involved in communication activism, and influence public opinion in favor of the democratization of communication. It is also essential that they be participatory coalitions so that they are truly legitimate.

Support for the development of these coalitions on the part of external development stakeholders should be a medium-term project in order to lay the foundations of movements that can monitor the implementation of any communication policy, and that can be mobilized when there are setbacks. These coalitions must start from the following common principles:

- Communication is a human right that allows for the defense and promotion of other rights.
- The right to freedom of expression is an essential part of the right to communication.
- Cultural diversity is fundamental to achieve a more democratic communication system. The existence of a regulatory framework that promotes cultural expression, including those of marginalized groups, is necessary to guarantee cultural diversity.
- The electromagnetic spectrum is a common good and must be democratized. For this, there must be clear and equitable rules on the ownership and concentration of the means of communication to avoid concentration of power in a few hands.
- Citizens have the right to participate in governance processes and decision-making on communication policies.
- Community and citizen media are expressions of the right to communication and should be supported.
- Efficient and equitable access to public information must be guaranteed.

Donors, governments, international institutions, and other development stakeholders are called upon to support the formation of these coalitions through capacity building, technical expertise, access to financial resources, and opportunities to advance their agendas at regional and international forums.

INVESTING IN MEDIA LITERACY FOR THE DIGITAL AGE

Another key issue is the urgent need to deal with online disinformation and misinformation. The emergence of numerous digital communication platforms such as social networks and smartphones over the last decade has been accompanied by the hope that these platforms would help democratize communication ecosystems and help bring about social change. For instance, citizen journalism offered great potential as a counterweight to mainstream news media as it represented an opportunity for the mobilization of marginalized communities in addition to broadening access to information and knowledge.

However, despite the fact that in many cases these digital platforms have helped generate greater awareness of various social problems, there is a growing sense of caution concerning the risks that these new platforms present to society. For instance, the explosion of "fake news" has shown that digital platforms can be used to manipulate and influence media agendas unscrupulously and to attack democratic processes.

Today, media ecosystems are characterized by a convergence of digital and traditional media, a fragmentation of audiences, issues of privacy, and a lack of transparency about how decisions governing communication and information flows are made. Despite these new realities, in their curricula many educational systems have failed to reflect the need for students to acquire the necessary knowledge and skills to navigate a world that is increasingly mediated and digitized. This need is especially relevant in the context of SDG 4: quality education.

Donors, governments, international institutions, and other development stakeholders are called upon to support the inclusion of comprehensive and information and media literacy programs in the education systems of countries around the world.

MARGINALIZED AND HISTORICALLY EXCLUDED COMMUNITIES

Even if Agenda 2030 were to better integrate communication and information issues, special efforts would have to be made in order to address the communication and information needs of certain communities. This entails recognizing that there are groups in society whose communication and information needs are routinely ignored in the context of development. This can be the result of issues such as language barriers, prejudice, geographical distance, or differences in access to media platforms. Some of the groups whose communication and information needs are rarely addressed include people living with disabilities, migrants, ethno-cultural minorities, and people from the LGBTQ communities, among others. One of the groups whose communication and information needs have most often been overlooked around the world by policymakers and decision-makers is Indigenous peoples.

Indigenous peoples are distinctive through their particular way of life, beliefs, and relationship to the environment. Many have left their traditional life for towns and cities, or work for wages part of the time and return to the land at other times. Indigenous people often practice mixed livelihoods, but in most cases, a subsistence economy is the basis of how they make their living. For Indigenous peoples, "traditional environmental knowledge" is at the heart of their identity and culture—understood as the actual living of life rather than just the knowledge of how to live. Indigenous peoples are the custodians of unique languages, knowledge systems, and beliefs and they possess invaluable knowledge of practices in the sustainable management of natural resources.

In 2007, the United Nations General Assembly adopted the Declaration on the Rights of Indigenous Peoples (UNDRIP), reflecting global concern that Indigenous peoples continue to suffer from historical injustices that prevent them from exercising their rights. The declaration acknowledged the fact that Indigenous peoples are organizing for political, economic, social, and cultural development and that they have the right to maintain and strengthen their distinctive political, legal, economic, social, and cultural institutions. The UNDRIP is the key framework for addressing some of the global issues that undermine the rights of Indigenous peoples, such as climate change, threats to biological and cultural diversity, land grabbing, inequitable food production and distribution, and the curtailment of public services.

The UNDRIP highlights a number of communication issues such as access to information, media representation, intellectual property rights, ownership and control of the media, and cultural diversity. Without a rights-based approach to decision-making, media platforms, and culture, the rights of Indigenous people cannot be fully guaranteed. This belief has been echoed by numerous gatherings of Indigenous communicators, such as the International Encounter on Indigenous Peoples' Communication and Development, held in Bolivia in 2006, which reaffirmed the importance of communication as a fundamental element in the liberation, transformation, and development of society and the validation of the rights of Indigenous peoples.

Many of the 17 Sustainable Development Goals and targets are relevant to Indigenous peoples and have direct linkages to the human rights commitments in the UN Declaration on the Rights of Indigenous Peoples. There are six direct references to Indigenous peoples in the 2030 Agenda, including in Goal 2 related to agricultural output of Indigenous small-scale farmers, and Goal 4 on equal access to education for Indigenous children. Despite these positive developments, a number of Indigenous groups were disappointed with the lack of attention to issues such as the right to self-determination; the principle of free, prior, and informed consent; and collective rights (Indigenous People and the 2030 Agenda, 2016).

Communication can be a transformative factor for many Indigenous peoples because it can help strengthen their social fabric, improve governance processes, promote culture in all its diversity, and build bridges with other communities and social actors. These changes can help reinforce the vision enshrined in the UNDRIP and the goals promoted by Agenda 2030.

Key recommendations for development stakeholders are:

- Promote local processes of Indigenous community communication, and the development of networks of Indigenous communicators, through training, accompaniment, visibility, and access to resources.
- Provide legal and technical advice to Indigenous communities involved in communication processes, such as the establishment of community radio stations.
- Provide support to the development of national knowledge exchange networks between communicators (both from the community sector and from state and private sectors), Indigenous leaders, and researchers to achieve alliances.

CONCLUSION

Only concerted action by a coalition of those willing to devolve a measure of power to marginalized peoples and communities can resolve the conundrum of how to balance democratic cohesion with social justice. The infrastructures of communication can help maintain the status quo or they can help challenge it. Most often they do both. The spectrum runs from total control and censorship of mass and social media to the anarchy of speech and imagery that reinforce prejudice, racism, misogyny, and division. At its very worst, both lead to silencing and genocide. The model of the United Nations—in which countries agree principles of ethical conduct—can be applied to the technologies that inform and shape the digital era. We can agree (or we are beginning to agree) ethical principles for the use of nano-technologies, artificial intelligence, and cyberwarfare—although there will always be dissenters and malignant forces that try to seize them.

In the same way and with the same caveat, we can agree (or begin to agree) ethical principles and codes of conduct for digital communications and digital platforms. Applied fairly and equitably, responding to the urgent need for accessibility and affordability, and armed with functioning mechanisms at all levels for oversight and reform, a coalition of the United Nations, governments, civil society, and tech corporations could direct, monitor, and regulate the digital era in ways that benefit everyone and that greatly improve the chances of achieving the Sustainable Development Goals through their guarantee of genuine communication for all.

ANNEX: LIST OF ACTIVISTS WHO PARTICIPATED IN THE DRAFTING OF THESE RECOMMENDATIONS

1. Samuel Meshack, WACC Asia, India
2. Gitiara Nasreen, University of Dhaka, Bangladesh
3. Soonim Lee, Olive Tree Productions, South Korea
4. Niel Lopez, Resource Center for People's Advocacies in Southern Mindanao, Philippines
5. Jimmy Okello, Community Media Network Uganda, Uganda
6. Adeline Nsimire, Sauti ya Mwanamke Kijijini, Democratic Republic of Congo
7. Biak Hnin, Global Chin Christian Fellowship, Myanmar
8. Jose Enrique Africa, IBON Foundation, Philippines
9. Seck Medoune, Réseau Inter-Africain pour les Femmes, Médias, Genre et Développement, Sénégal
10. Suman Basnet, AMARC Asia Pacific, Nepal
11. Ashek Elahi, People's Research on Grassroots Ownership & Traditional Initiative, Bangladesh
12. Golam Mourtoza, Centre for Communication and Development, Bangladesh
13. Athanase Kabore, Farm Radio International, Burkina Faso

14. Ruth Omukhango, African Woman and Child Features Service, Kenya
15. Chirstopher Pasion, Pinoy Media Center, Philippines
16. Margaret Bukirwa, Uganda Media Women's Association, Uganda
17. Syed Tarikul Islam, Alliance for Cooperation and Legal Aid Bangladesh, Bangladesh
18. Sawssen Gharbi, Association Rayhana de femme de Jendouba, Tunisia
19. Vincent Rajkumar, Christian Institute for the Study of Religion and Society, India
20. Frank Jabson, Creative Centre for Communication and Development, Zimbabwe
21. Ramon Boultron, Asia Pacific Mission for Migrants, Hong Kong
22. Rey Asis, Asia Pacific Mission for Migrants, Hong Kong
23. Ramakrishnan Nagarajan, Ideosync Media Combine, India
24. Caesar Jonah David, National Council of Churches in India, India
25. Gerifel Cerillo, Karapatan Alliance Philippines, Philippines
26. Benjamin Alforque, Communication Foundation for Asia, Philippines
27. Kudzai Kwangwari, Zimbabwe Association of Community Radio Stations, Zimbabwe
28. Michael Beltran, Kalipunan Ng Damayang Mahihirap, Philippines
29. Ambrose Zwane, Swaziland Community Multimedia Network, Swaziland
30. Rhea Padilla, Altermidya—People's Alternative Media Network, Philippines
31. Sandra Chaher, Asociación Civil Comunicación para la Igualdad, Argentina
32. Nadia Ferrari, Equipo Latinoamericano de Justicia y Género, Argentina
33. Marcela Gabioud, World Association for Christian Communication—Latin America
34. Rokeya Kabir, Nari Progati Sangha, Bangladesh
35. Raquel Romero, Fundacion Colectivo Cabildeo, Bolivia
36. Abida Pehlic, Novi Put, Bosnia and Herzegovina
37. Vilma Peña, Observatorio Centroamericano de Género y Comunicación, Costa Rica
38. Carlos Terán Puente, Centro Ecuatoriano de Promoción y Acción de la Mujer, Ecuador

39. Sandra López Astudillo, Grupo de Apoyo al Movimiento de Mujeres del Azuay, Ecuador
40. Alisia Evans, FemLINK Pacific, Fiji
41. Sian Rolls, FemLINK Pacific, Fiji
42. [SEE 19 ABOVE]
43. Pat Phillips, WMW, Jamaica
44. Lucia Lagunes Huerta, Comunicación e Información de la Mujer (CIMAC), Mexico
45. Cirenia Celestino Ortega, Comunicación e Información de la Mujer (CIMAC), Mexico
46. Indu Tuladhar, Asmita Women's Publishing House, Media and Resource Organisation, Nepal
47. Olayide Akanni, Journalists against AIDS, Nigeria
48. Gbenga Osinaike, Journalists for Christ, Nigeria
49. Suheir Farraj, Women, Media and Development (TAM), Palestine
50. Alicia Noemí Stumpfs Vázquez, Kuña Roga, Paraguay
51. Amie Joof, Réseau Inter-Africain pour les Femmes, Médias, Genre et Développement (FAMEDEV), Senegal
52. Jelena Visnjic, BeFem—Feminist cultural Centre, Serbia
53. Dafne Sabanes Plou, Association for Progressive Communications (APC), South Africa
54. Margaret Sentamu, Uganda Media Women's Organization, Uganda
55. Pham Thi Minh Hang, Research centre for Gender, Family and Environment in Development (CGFED), Vietnam
56. Clare Paine, Christian Aid, United Kingdom
57. Jennifer Lee, Feminist Stories, USA
58. Sharon Bhagwan Rolls, femLINKPacific, Fiji
59. Shirley Struchen, World Association for Christian Communication—North America, USA
60. Glory Dharmaraj, Global Media Monitoring Project coordinator for North America region, USA
61. Karri Whipple, World Association for Christian Communication—North America, USA
62. Esther Franke, New School, Germany/USA
63. David Morales, WACC América Latina, Colombia
64. Raul Tacaj Xol Asociación Estoreña para el Desarrollo Integral (AEPDI), Guatemala
65. Samuel Macz Caal, Radio Nimlajacoc, Guatemala

66. Alma Montoya, Grupo Comunicarte, Colombia
67. Priscila Barredo, Observatorio Centroamericano de Género y Comunicación, Costa Rica
68. Liliana León, Asociación Voces Nuestras, Costa Rica
69. Elsa Chiquito, Radio Ixchel, Guatemala
70. Yesica Matias Manuel, Radio Xilotepek, Guatemala
71. Lorenzo Xajpot, Radio Sinakan, Guatemala
72. Moises Rioja, APG El Bananal, Argentina
73. Johannes Schwable, Comunicadores Populares por la Autonomía (COMPPA) México/Guatemala
74. Tania Ayma Calle, Centro de Educación y Comunicación para Comunidades y Pueblos Indígenas (CECOPI), Bolivia
75. Cesar Bernardez, Organización Fraternal Negra Hondureña (OFRANEH), Honduras
76. Maria Amorim e Avelar, Associação Beneficence Casa Caiada de Paraiba, Brazil
77. Bladimir Avila Urbano, Centro de Culturas Indígenas del Perú (CHIRAPAQ), Peru
78. Ary Regis, Sosyete Animasyon Kominikasyon Sosyal (SAKS), HaitI
79. Jose Luis Soto, Espacio de Comunicación Insular, Dominican Republic
80. Suleica Pineda, La Sandía Digital, México
81. Samanta Doudtchitzky, Asociación Crisol de Proyecto Sociales, Argentina
82. Victor Gómez, Colectivo Pro Derechos Humanos, Ecuador
83. Gissela Dávila, Asociación Latinoamericana de Educación Radiofónica (ALER), Ecuador
84. Graciela Navarro, Asociación Mundial de Radios Comunitarias (AMARC) Argentina, Argentina
85. Rosa Elena Vallejo, Centro Internacional de Estudios Superiores de Comunicación para América Latina (CIESPAL), Ecuador
86. Leonardo Félix, Agencia Latinoamericana y Caribeña de Comunicación (ALC), Argentina
87. Joara Marchezini, Artigo 19, Brazil
88. Dennis Christian Larsen, UNICEF
89. Avexnim Cojti, Cultural Survival, Guatemala/USA
90. Renato Joya, INTERCOM, Costa Rica

91. Luisa Ochoa, Profesora de la Escuela de Ciencias de la Comunicación Colectiva, Universidad de Costa Rica, Costa Rica
92. Marvin Amador, Profesor de la Escuela de Ciencias de la Comunicación Colectiva, Universidad de Costa Rica, Costa Rica

REFERENCES

Barja Daza, G., & Gigler, B.-S. (2007). The concept of information poverty and how to measure it in the Latin American context. In H. Galperin & J. Mariscal (Eds.), *Digital poverty: Latin American and Caribbean perspectives.* International Development Research Centre (IDRC). https://www.researchgate.net/publication/248381571_The_Concept_of_Information_Poverty_and_How_to_Measure_it_in_the_Latin_American_Context

Colle, R. D. (2008). The threads of development communication. In J. Servaes (Ed.), *Communication for development and social change.* Sage Publications.

Couldry, N., & Rodriguez, C. (2015). Chapter 13—Media and communications. *Rethinking society for the 21st century: Report of the International Panel on Social Progress.* https://www.ipsp.org/

CRIS Campaign. (2005). *Assessing communication rights: A handbook* (p. 22). Communication Rights in the Information Society Campaign. http://cdn.agilitycms.com/wacc-global/Images/Galleries/RESOURCES/COMMUNICATION-RIGHTS/Assessing-Communication-Rights.pdf

European Digital Rights (EDRi). (2014). Charter of Digital Rights. https://edri.org/wp-content/uploads/2014/06/EDRi_DigitalRightsCharter_web.pdf

Global Digital Report. (2018). https://wearesocial.com/us/blog/2018/01/global-digital-report-2018

Indigenous People and the 2030 Agenda—A Backgrounder. UN Permanent Forum on Indigenous Issues (2016). http://www.un.org/esa/socdev/unpfii/documents/2016/Docs-updates/backgrounderSDG.pdf

International Federation of Journalists. (2017). IFJ survey: One in two women journalists suffer gender-based violence at work. http://www.ifj.org/nc/en/news-single-view/backpid/1/article/ifj-survey-one-in-two-women-journalists-suffer-gender-based-violence-at-work/

Lakhani, N. (2016). 'It feels like a gift': Mobile phone co-op transforms rural Mexican community. *The Guardian.* https://www.theguardian.com/world/2016/aug/15/mexico-mobile-phone-network-indigenous-community

Macharia, S., et al. (2015). *Who makes the news? Global Media Monitoring Project 2015.* World Association for Christian Communication. http://whomakesthenews.org/gmmp/gmmp-reports/gmmp-2015-reports

Macharia, S., et al. (2020). *Who makes the news? Global Media Monitoring Project 2020*. World Association for Christian Communication. https://whomakes-thenews.org/gmmp-reports/gmmp-2020-reports/

Manyozo, L. (2011). Rethinking communication for development policy: Some considerations. In R. Mansell & M. Raboy (Eds.), *The handbook of global media and communication policy*. Blackwell Publishing.

Manyozo, L. (2012). *Media, communication and development: Three approaches*. Sage Publications.

Melkote, S. R. (2000). Reinventing development support communications to account for power and control in development. In K. G. Wilkins (Ed.), *Redeveloping communication for social change: Theory, practice, and power*. Rowman & Littlefield Publishers.

Melkote, S. R., & Steeves, L. (2001). *Communication for development in the third world*. Sage Publications.

Narayan, D., Chambers, R., Shah, M. K., & Petesch, P. (2000). *Voices of the poor: Crying out for change*. Oxford University Press. World Bank.

Ó Siochrú, S. (2017). *Spectrum innovation for small-scale community-owned mobile telephony: Strategic considerations*. World Association for Christian Communication (WACC) and World Association of Community Radio Broadcasters (AMARC).

Office of the High Commissioner for Human Rights. *Freedom of opinion and expression—Annual Reports*. http://www.ohchr.org/EN/Issues/Freedom Opinion/Pages/Annual.aspx

Reporters Without Borders. (2018). Brazil. Media Ownership Monitor. https://www.mom-rsf.org/en/countries/brazil/

Rey-Moreno, C. (2017). Understanding community networks in Africa. Internet Society. https://www.internetsociety.org/wp-content/uploads/2017/08/CommunityNetworkingAfrica_report_May2017_1.pdf

Segura, M. S., & Waisbord, S. (2016). *Media movements: Civil society and media policy reform in Latin America*. ZED Books.

Servaes, J. (1999). *Communication for development. One world, multiple cultures*. Hampton Press.

Servaes, J. (2006). Introduction. In J. Servaes (Ed.), *Communication for development and social change*. Sage Publications.

Sich, A., Bullock, J., & Roberts, S. (2018). What is the Cambridge Analytica scandal? *The Guardian*. https://www.theguardian.com/news/video/2018/mar/19/everything-you-need-to-know-about-the-cambridge-analytica-expose-video-explainer

UNESCO. (2008). *Media development indicators: A framework for assessing media development*. UNESCO.

UNESCO. (2017). *Developing Internet Universality Indicators*. Paris: UNESCO. https://en.unesco.org/internetuniversality/indicators

United Nations. (2015). Declaration. Transforming our world: The 2030 Agenda for Sustainable Development. https://sustainabledevelopment.un.org/post 2015/transformingourworld

United Nations Development Group. (2013). *A million voices: The world we want. A sustainable future with dignity for all.*

WACC Project Partners. (2018). *The New York Declaration: Gender and media post-2015.* World Association for Christian Communication (WACC). http://whomakesthenews.org/articles/from-bangkok-to-new-york-gender-media-post-2015

CHAPTER 3

Significance of Communication Studies to SDGs: (Re)setting Global Agendas

Chi Kit Chan and Paul S. N. Lee

Abstract This chapter explicates the significance of communication to the promotion and practices of Sustainable Development Goals (SDGs). It highlights how communication could contribute, and is indispensable, to the grand project of (re)setting global agendas for the sustainable goals.

Firstly, the dialogue of international and global communications has laid down highly relevant and important conceptual frameworks to apprehend the informational flow of contemporary world. Specifically, this strand of communication literature contemplates the role of states, inter-state relationship, non-state actors such as transborder conglomerates and social media giants, and the networks of news agencies and journalists in the shaping of world opinion. These studies inform us some crucial factors to attain SDGs as prominent global agendas.

Secondly, scholarly works on intercultural communication foster our sensitivity when adapting the visions of sustainable goals to various locales.

C. K. Chan (✉) • P. S. N. Lee
School of Communication, the Hang Seng University of Hong Kong,
Siu Lek Yuen, Hong Kong
e-mail: chikitchan@hsu.edu.hk

© The Author(s), under exclusive license to Springer Nature 61
Switzerland AG 2023
J. Servaes, M. J. Yusha'u (eds.), *SDG18 Communication for All,
Volume 1*, Sustainable Development Goals Series,
https://doi.org/10.1007/978-3-031-19142-8_3

Academic dialogues alike offer lessons on both the prospect and limits of multiculturalism and cultural hybridization when promoting social innovation and policy initiatives in various temporal and spatial contexts.

Lastly, in view of the contested discourses arising from varying and conflicting goals, motives, and vested interests in the execution of SDGs, the intellectual insights of the articulation between public opinion, policy agenda, mobilization of resources, social movement, and governance inform us both visionary and pragmatic strategies in such complicated circumstances. Here, the perspective of communication is an integral part of the efforts to help accomplish the SDGs alongside other disciplines.

In sum, communication is a much-needed jigsaw puzzle to complete the global momentum to (re)set SDGs as our universal goals. It plugs the strategic gap of shaping the world as well as local opinion, scrutinizes the cultural issues of introducing SDGs to different societies, and ushers in constructive and constitutive dialogues among various disciplines, contributing to social development for all.

Keywords SDGs • Communication • Global and international communication • Intercultural communication • Public opinion • Social movement • Governance

INTRODUCTION

There is a growing body of literature deliberating the implementation of Sustainable Development Goals (SDGs), the 17 goals outlined by the United Nations (UN) which list out the humanitarian visions and targets of global communities by 2030. Despite the common ground of making a better world, such visions and targets are frequently dragged into ambiguous policy and business agendas (Battaglia et al., 2020; Forestier & Kim, 2020; Marquis & Qian, 2014). Critics even dubbed the term "SDG-washing" (Heras-Saizarbitoria et al., 2021) to the cherry-picking of SDGs initiatives for organizational purposes and convenience, and their doubtful outcomes as well. Multiple, vague, and overlapping agendas in the name of SDGs are closely related to the debates concerning the indicators which could show the effectiveness of SDGs targets, especially when SDGs are understood differently in various nations (Gambetta et al., 2018). Fukuda-Parr and McNeil (2019) argue that the controversies surrounding the suitability of SDGs-indicators illustrate the politics of indexing, which is embedded in conflicting values, ideologies, and theories ascribed to what sustainability means. Pursuance of the global goals of sustainability has also been hindered by the question of motivation and mobilization. A prominent research direction on promoting SDGs is the enhancement of policy and corporate incentives, for instances, employing policy and fiscal encouragement for healthcare infrastructure (Siddiqui et al., 2020), using information and communication technologies (ICT) to alleviate carbon dioxide emission (Chien et al., 2021), reforming the reporting require-ment for Corporate Social Responsibility (CSR) in view of the significance of SDGs (García-Sanchez et al., 2020), and creating shared values which integrate SDGs in the organizational goals and business strategies of com-mercial enterprises (Olofsson & Mark-Herbert, 2020).

While SDGs present a set of visionary goals in view of the challenges to our globe in the twenty-first century, their roadmaps are fraught with communication headwind. These goals attempt to offer a more refining understanding and specific targets to a sustainable world, yet they are still inevitably subject to the uneasy process of agenda-setting: which should come first to our society among the 17 goals? How the targets enlisted by SDGs be compatible to the social expectation and public opinion of vari-ous communities? More ambitiously, how the politicians, activists, and experts from various disciplines could set the agendas of global public opinion for SDGs? These questions echo to the promotion of SDGs across regions and countries which are encountering different political and policy issues when embracing SDGs as their working targets. Equally important is the socio-cultural variation with which people must handle when setting indicators to measure the effectiveness of SDGs-related initiatives. Indicators and indexing tools which accessing and illustrating the accom-plishment and effort for SDGs often induce white-heat debates over con-tested discourses of sustainability, translation of social norms to quantified targets, interpretation of social reality, and even the objectivity and neu-trality of SDGs-indicators (Fukuda-Parr & McNeil, 2019, p. 7). Lastly, motivating popular support and implementation of SDGs targets also entails communication strategies such as effective usage of social media (Mulholland, 2019, pp. 11–12), organizational communication across various governmental and public units (Ocansey, 2018), and creative international campaigns based on scientific findings (Grorud-Colvert et al., 2010).

This chapter therefore will explicate the significance of communication studies to the promotion and implementation of SDGs. We will highlight how communication could contribute, and is indispensable, to the grand project of (re)setting global agendas for the sustainable goals. Firstly, the dialogue of international and global communications has laid down highly relevant and important conceptual frameworks to apprehend the informational flow in the contemporary world. Specifically, this strand of communication literature contemplates the role of states, inter-state relationship, non-state actors such as transborder conglomerates and social media giants, and the networks of news agencies and journalists in the shaping of world opinion. These studies show us some crucial factors to frame SDGs as prominent global agendas. Secondly, scholarly works on intercultural communication foster our sensitivity when adapting the visions of sustainable goals to various locales. Academic dialogues alike offer lessons on both the prospect and limits of multiculturalism and cultural hybridization when promoting social innovation and policy initiatives in various temporal and spatial contexts. Lastly, in view of the contested discourses arising from varying and conflicting goals, motives, and vested interests in the execution of SDGs, the intellectual insights of the articulation between public opinion, policy agenda, mobilization of resources, social movement, and governance inform us both visionary and pragmatic strategies in such complicated circumstances. Here, the perspective of communication studies is organically integrated with other disciplines, which include but not limit to sociology, political science, psychology, and urban studies. Communication is therefore a much-needed jigsaw puzzle to complete the global momentum to (re)set SDGs as our universal goals. It plugs up the strategic gap of shaping world opinion, scrutinizes the practical issues of introducing SDGs to different societies, and ushers in constructive and constitutive dialogue with other scholarly fields when human beings attempt to achieve a common ground of social development for all.

Setting Global Agenda for SDGs

Media researchers have been examining the significance of news representation to social agendas. The classical writing by Walter Lippmann (1922) depicted public opinion as "pictures in our heads" to the world beyond our immediate contacts, which is orchestrated and performed by journalists and their news sources from political and social elites. Decades of communication studies on media gatekeeping of social information (Berkowitz,

1990; Shoemaker, 1991; White, 1950) further explicate how news media perform the agenda-setting function (McCombs & Shaw, 1993) by assuming a powerhouse to set the priorities of what the people think about. While the rise of social media and online communication challenges the agenda-setting function of the printed press and broadcasters (Allan, 2006; Atton, 2002), media—both mainstream and alternative media—are still the key informational shortcut for the people to figure out salient and significant social agendas from an environment of "informational surplus" (Bennett & Iyengar, 2008). The significance of news representation and media agenda-setting should also be contemplated with the media political economy that shapes the formation of media agendas, the process which is conceptualized as agenda-building (Cobb et al., 1976; Cook, 1998). While the media have the power to set social agendas, their news agendas are also inevitably subject to the dynamics between political power, market economy, and the civil society. As in the late former British Prime Minister Margaret Thatcher's well-known words, the media hold the oxygen of publicity that political leaders need, but political leaders and dominant political institutions hold the "facts" and information that the news media need (Thatcher, 1985). Classic communication studies have been demonstrating how news agendas are framed by the consensus, conflicts, and negotiation among political leaders and social elites (Bennett, 1990; Hallin, 1986; Lee, 2002). Media scholars keep deliberating how the commercial logics such as advertising clientelism and market signals override journalistic professionalism in the setting of news agendas (Bagdikian, 2000; Curran, 2002; McManus, 1994). Despite the undeniable influence of political and market forces in the agenda-building process of news media, news nevertheless is widely positioned as a public good rather than purely a commercial commodity (Baker, 2002). Calls for public journalism which advocates a strong connection between media and communities (Glasser, 1999), initiatives of social movement activists to engage with news agendas by articulating their actions to journalistic values and practices (Ryan, 1991), and critics to media performance (Atton, 2002; Curran & Couldry, 2003) represent how civil society attempts to build up news agendas in media political economy.

Research logics of news agenda-setting, agenda-building, and media political economy are also manifested in studies of global communication and international communication, which have been investigating the formation of global agendas and the social momentum behind. Scholarly dialogue surrounding international communication—some place the significance of nation-state in the world order, such as the world system theory (Wallerstein, 2011), while some discuss the role of non-state actors and informational networks, such as in the network society theory (Castells, 2009)—has been explicating the global informational flow and its power implication. Classic literature of cultural imperialism highlights the political, business, social, and cultural edges of western states and media enterprises in the shaping of global information flow and media representation (Schiller, 1970, 1976). Academics have been deliberating to what extent global informational flow exhibits a balanced influence between the east, the west, and various regions (Sparks, 2007; Thussu, 2018a; Waisbord & Mellado, 2014). Sparks (2012) depicted the relative economic and corporate strength of the United States and western European countries in the media, publication, and entertainment industries, and thus argued that the informational flow at the global level is still largely not a balanced one, albeit the conceptual confusion demonstrated by the classic literature of cultural imperialism. However, Thussu (2018b) illuminated other alternative informational and media hubs which are indispensable to the "new" global communication order, namely the flourishing media and entertainment industries of mainland China and the rapid development of telecommunication and media industries in India.

Contested scholarly arguments over the national and regional influences on global informational flow underscore the significance of media political economy behind the global agendas. Setting global agendas for SDGs entails national and regional governing powers and their communication strategies, especially those of the strong states. Gilboa (2002) conceptualizes the state-media relationship against the backdrop of global communication and argued that global media images, especially the coverage of important or leaked diplomatic news, could affect both the domestic public opinion and states' policy decision to various extents. The communication networks between state leadership and media, and the political calculation of mobilizing media image for leveraging influence on the world public opinion have been deliberated by literature of public diplomacy and soft power (Hallin, 1986; Newsom, 1996; Nye Jr., 1990; Robinson, 2000; Servaes, 2012). Such effect of public diplomacy could be manifested in the media events—live broadcasting of highly important and historical occasions which involve global leaders or the substantial effort of state power (Dayan, 2008; Dayan & Katz, 1992). The deliberation and conclusion of the Paris Accord in 2015, which was the first international treaty setting global targets of carbon emission, reduction, and related regulations and visions, was a mega media event at a global level which attracted media and audience attention on climate change, and delineated specific global agendas and targets. A recent mega media event for climate change was the 26th United Nations Climate Change Conference of the Parties (COP26) in Glasgow, Britain, from 31st October to 12th November 2021. COP26 made climate change, carbon reduction, and sustainable development become global popular media topics, and served as a platform demonstrating international cooperation on global agendas amid white-heat conflicts among the great powers—Sino-American rifts over human rights issues and regional security, confrontation between Russia and European Union over the deployment of military defense systems in Eastern European countries, for example. Apart from mega media events at a global level, media campaigns for promoting SDGs at regional and national levels are also counted. A report written by the European Sustainable Development Network (ESDN) reiterated the significance of communication *of* and *about* sustainability (Mulholland, 2019, p. 5) when setting SDGs as the regional goals in European communities and part of the everyday concerns of people. The report further unleashed various communication campaigns for promoting SDGs in Europe—the social media campaign of "Commitment 2050" in Finland (Mulholland, 2019, pp. 11–12); the media and social campaign of "sustainability" orchestrated by German officials, business sectors, scientists, and leaders of civil society (Mulholland, 2019, pp. 13–14); and the television campaign conducted by the ministry of foreign affairs of Iceland for mobilizing and public awareness to and support for SDGs (Mulholland, 2019, p. 14).

Apart from the support of the state and media for promoting SDGs, the global network among social activists, non-governmental organizations (NGOs), and their emergence as a global public sphere is also highly significant to the communication and social mobilization for SDGs. As global informational flow has been dominated by the strong states and global news media, except for a few of resourceful NGOs, social activists and members of civil society could hardly become news figures in international news. Thrall et al. (2014) found that global news media have been focusing on a handful of globally known and well-established NGOs which enjoy sizable organizational capacity and robust international networks with states and media. However, the paradigm shift of media communication, thanks to the rise of the internet, social media networks, and their decentralizing influence on the gatekeeping function of mainstream media, is paving way for a growing public sphere at a global level (Castells,

2008). While reckoning the indispensable role of state power, market force, and global media in global communication, Castells argued that the Web 2.0 enables instant interactive bottom-up communication which could hardly be totally managed by the inter-states network (Castells, 2008, pp. 87–90). The "me-too" movement which went viral via social media platforms since 2017 was an illustrative example showing how gender equality and rights became a global agenda spiraling from the connective networks of Web 2.0. Promotion and implementation of SDGs could hardly miss this piece of the jigsaw puzzle. Meanwhile, social activists and their demands could also appear to be global agendas by derailing the global media events staged by the states and social elites: protests and disruptive activities against the media plots staged by the states in their media events could draw global attention on alternative discourses advocated by social activists (Dayan, 2008).

Studies of global communication shed light on the agenda-setting, agenda-building, and media political economy when deliberating the formation of global news agendas and informational flow. They are illustrative to promoting SDGs when the transnational and public bodies, business enterprises, members of civil society attempt to promote SDGs via setting global agendas. Prominent state powers in the globe—North America, Western Europe, Japan, Russia, China, and India—are unequivocally the heavyweights in the global informational flow. Yet, the global civil society and world opinion embedded in the networks of Web 2.0 are also significant to public diplomacy and soft power exercised by the states. Global communication thus is indispensable to stakeholders who engage in advocating and responding to the flourishing global concern of sustainability and SDGs (Yusha'u & Servaes, 2021).

Intercultural Communication: Shared Values for SDGs

While the accomplishment of SDGs counts on their salience in global agendas, how people from different parts of the world perceive them and more importantly, whether we can foster shared values and cultural identities for global citizenship, are crucial to turning those sustainable visions as operational targets in local communities. Here, communication studies—especially intercultural communication studies—could contribute to our apprehension to the formation of global citizenship across various societies. Global citizenship entails an empathy to public affairs which goes beyond one's immediate living communities and the sense of national affairs. Apart from global informational flow and its agendas, a cultural sense which surpasses ethnocentrism, embraces cultural diversity, and tolerates ethnical and racial differentiation is crucial to our understanding and affect to the fatal global issues which may not pose direct and immediate impact on the everyday life. After all, SDGs cover goals and targets whose social significance and cultural meanings vary across different parts of the world, despite they are the common fate to the globe. Fostering the intercultural communication between nations, societies, communities, classes, ethnics, and races is hence essential to the rise of global citizenship and the transborder empathy for pursuing SDGs.

Vision of global citizenship, which includes initiatives for SDGs, has been wrestling with mutual anxiety and distrust across nations and communities. Anxiety and uncertainty management (AUM) theory, which is a prominent topic in intercultural communication dialogue, has been tackling with misunderstanding and rivalry arising from coexistence of various ethnical and racial groups (Gudykunst, 1998; Logan et al., 2016; Nameni, 2020). In brief, AUM theorists highlight two paramount variables—anxiety to people who are not familiar with and uncertainty to engage them—which explicate people's unwillingness to and hostility toward intercultural communication (Gudykunst, 1995). Anxiety and uncertainty to intercultural communication cast shadow over the building of social trust in a multicultural context when people are blinded by ethnocentric bias based on race, ethnicity, nationality, and socio-cultural constructs alike, which could hardly be excluded in human societies (Nameni, 2020). Intercultural communication is especially salient when ethnocentrism is radicalized as fundamental ideologies which demonstrate exclusive tendency to cultural "others" (Wrench et al., 2006). Radicalized ethnocentrism is illustratively manifested in scholarly dialogues surrounding the neo-tribalization of nationalism when researchers explicate how ultra-nationalists and populist political discourses react to global issues, particularly migrants, refugees, and perceived threats from "outsiders" (Anbinder, 2006; Kastoryano, 2018; Lippard, 2011; Taggart, 2000). In view of the uncertain global risks, such as humanitarian crises resulting from regional instability, borderless and intangible networks of transborder terrorism, and the plight of transnational economic and financial turmoil which eventually paves the way for national fiscal debts and fragile public finance, public anxiety and uncertainties to future are captured by political discourses which mobilize people's frustration, anger, and fear for nationalism which envisions a defensive, exclusive, and intolerable homogeneity against conceived national enemies and cultural "others" (Chua, 2018; Triandafyllidou, 2021).

While acknowledging the issue of ethnocentrism and its radicalized consequences, studies of intercultural communication also pinpoint possibilities and approaches for cultural dialogue and mutual understanding. In his famous seminal work titled "Disjuncture and difference in the Global Cultural Economy", global anthropologist Arjun Appadurai conceptualized five types of global flow which are reshaping our social imaginary to human world: ethnoscapes (transborder and transcultural movement of people), mediascapes (transborder circulation of media content which is enabled by communication technologies), technoscapes (the global transmission of mechanical and informational technologies and innovation), finance-scapes (the global flow of capital and its relating informational indicators), and ideoscapes (circulation of mixed and even confrontational ideologies) (Appadurai, 1990). Appadurai's framework of global cultural economy captures the transborder momentum which propels a sense of global citizenship, as national and cultural borders could no longer effectively define people's perception to what the world is: we come into contact with people from other national and cultural territories (such as business elites, tourists, migrants, and even refugees), we could enjoy media content from other parts of the world, we commonly engage with various platforms of social media and search engines, our economies are vulnerable to major global stock markets and "hot money" from international investors, and we are exposed to various ideas, discourses, and ideologies which are different from those stemming from our own hometown via social media platforms and interpersonal communication with nonlocals. Despite varying impact of global cultural economy across locales, ethnocentrism is inevitably subject to cultural challenges and shocks against the backdrop of the aforesaid global movements.

Juxtaposition of radicalized ethnocentrisms and global cultural economy poses a pressing question on whether constructing shared values for SDGs is a viable vision. Here, studies of intercultural communication could shed light on several significant responses. Firstly, localization of global informational flow is the key to make global agendas echo to local concerns and context. For example, using the handover of Hong Kong from Britain to China as a case study of global media event, Lee et al. (2002) indicate how international news flow is (re)interpreted by the news frames stemming from various countries according to their own local agendas and national interests so that the people can understand the news values of the global information which is largely detached from their everyday life and local agendas. Likewise, scholarly dialogues surrounding SDGs have been deliberating how to actualize the visions of SDGs by operational policy and business indicators (Fukuda-Parr & McNeil, 2019; García-Sanchez et al., 2020). Gambetta et al. (2018) initiated an extensive scale of political comparative study to examine how the governments in Latin America localize SDGs via their policy goals and targets. Specifically, SDGs are enlisted as the policy targets of public expenditure on general public services (SDGs 16 and 17); defense (SDG 16); public order and safety (SDG 16); economic affairs (SDGs 7, 8, 9, and 12); environmental protection (SDGs 6, 12, 13, 14, and 15); housing and community ameni-ties (SDGs 6, 7, and 11); health (SDG 3); recreation, culture, and religion (SDG 4); education (SDG 4); and social protection (SDG 1, 2, 5, and 10) (Gambetta et al., 2018, p. 6). Although such framework of political com-parative study is not an exhaustive list for putting SDGs into local public expenditure and their respective policy areas, it highlights a regional attempt to "translate" the global vision of SDGs into specific and measur-able policy indicators. Similarly, the Global Reporting Initiative (GRI), Thomson Reuters database, and investment-indicators alike are essential policy and business incentives to encourage listed companies and transna-tional conglomerates to incorporate and localize SDGs as their vision and practices of corporate citizenship (García-Sanchez et al., 2020).

Secondly, studies of intercultural communication also underpin the sig-nificance of cultural identities and their formation under the global flow of information. Simply put, cross-cultural adaptation is a commonly seen for-mation process of cultural identities in view of the "melting pot" arising from hybridized flows and sources of cultural forces (Kim, 2007). Identity formation process in general is arising from socialization momentums from various collectivities, and multiple layers of cognitive and affective understanding of self in societies (Carbaugh, 2007; Kim, 2007). Such scholarly dialogues on identity formation and management could also be borrowed to apprehend the making of corporate identity which attempts to create shared values between SDGs and business goals (Olofsson & Mark-Herbert, 2020). While investment returns, business survival, and shareholders' benefit are indispensable goals to the commercial sector, a mature and inclusive investment and business community should be able to create shared values which make sustainability a common ground for investors, business management team, client network, and the publics

(Olofsson & Mark-Herbert, 2020, pp. 8–11). While we should not ideal-
ize the implementation of SDGs in the business world—especially the
problem of "SDG-washing" of which commercial corporates "cherry-
pick" SDGs and their selective targets for convenient responses to reporting requirements and investors' expectation (Heras-Saizarbitoria et al.,
2021)—literature of intercultural communication and identity formation
reminds us of the possibility of multiple identities and the potential of adding social goals into the corporate identity of the business sector.

Nevertheless, promoting SDGs entails construction of global citizenship which is built upon shared values for sustainability and the empathy
for the collective welfare of humankind, including the people who live
outside our cultural eyesight, and global issues which may not directly
matter to our immediate contacts and everyday life. While setting global
agendas for SDGs is essential, their localization to various places and win-
ning the hearts and mind of locals are equally important. In this regard,
scholarly deliberation of intercultural communication points us to both
opportunities and challenges. While ethnocentrism has been part of people's perception of the world outside, the global flows of population, capital, technologies, media images, and ideas are simultaneously making
inroads for a global vision which may transcend local perspectives and
national interests.

POLITICAL COMMUNICATION: REALPOLITIK FOR SDGS

Promoting SDGs, after all, is a realpolitik of political communication.
SDGs, however visionary and ideal, involve revising policy agendas and
priorities, reallocation of public resources, and mobilization for public
opinion. For example, Servaes (2009) has outlined the linkage between
communication, governance, and sustainable development by highlighting the significance of development communication in governance. Riding
on the conceptual dichotomy between the modernization paradigm
(which contends that international engagement is conducive and indispensable to social development) and dependency theory (which depicts
how the developed world exercises control and manipulation over the
developing world in modern era), Servaes formulates "the third way" of
development communication which examines the pre-conditions for the
media and communication to play a constructive role in sustainable development: an independent journalism working for public interest; effective
public institutions which facilitate public debate and participatory

decision-making by the public; a vibrant civil society which fosters public accountability, transparency, and clean governance; and economics and infrastructures which uphold the balance between government responsibility, public investment, and private-sector activities (Servaes, 2009, pp. 63–69). Thus, to achieve sustainable communication, a political campaign which mobilizes public opinion in support of SDGs and related policy reforms is needed.

While in general people seldom question the ethical justification and social needs for SDGs, recent studies of political communication bring out several observations about the contemporary communication environment to which organizations and people who advocate for SDGs should pay attention. Firstly, political communication nowadays is inevitably subject to informational disorder (Derakhshan & Wardle, 2017), or in a more well-known term, fake news, which started emerging in the scholarly dialogue when researchers discussed about parody, satire, and manipulation and fabrication of news materials since the early twenty-first century (Tandoc et al., 2018). Fake news even demonstrates a certain extent of agenda-setting power (Vargo et al., 2017). The "Pizzagate story"—which was found to be a hoax against Hillary Clinton during the 2016 American presidential election, was unfortunately perceived by a sizable number of Americans as probably true (Frankovic, 2016). Given its interchangeably and mixed usage with terms such as false news, inaccurate news, and propaganda, Derakhshan and Wardle reconceptualize the deliberation of fake news into misinformation, disinformation, and mal-information (Derakhshan & Wardle, 2017, p. 9). Simply put, misinformation refers to unintentional mistakes and factual errors, disinformation features with deliberately manipulated content with an intention to construct conspiracies or rumors, while mal-information is the deliberate disclosure of privacy and secrecy without the social value of public interest, such as revenge porn.

Albeit conceptually and empirically negotiable, the aforesaid framework is important to apprehend the current communication environment for policy advocacy, which includes promoting SDGs. In his seminal work on risk society and reflexive modernity, Ulrich Beck (1992, 2009) argues that given the pluralistic expert knowledge amid unfolding global risks, such as climate change, extreme weather, nuclear crises, and financial meltdown, professionals, pundits, and governments could hardly monopolize the definition of social facts, as prediction and conclusion by expert knowledge became unstable and refutable frequently. For instance, the well-known fact of global warming still receives scientific criticism and social skepticism which challenges its factual validity (Rensburg & Head, 2017). Divided and conflicting expert knowledge, coupled with the emergence of social distrust against news organizations and journalism (Tsfati et al., 2020, pp. 165–167), make fact-checking and the informational campaign against the malicious usage of news and social information an uphill battle, especially when the SDGs-related policy agendas are not in line with the vested interest of social stakeholders.

In addition to the informational disorder arising from rampant disinformation campaigns and fake news, promotion of global citizenship and SDGs must adapt the communication environment of digital and social media networks, which feature with fragmentated narrowcasting (Serazio, 2014). In brief, we are living in an age in which informational supply is much higher than demand, as digital communication, social media platforms, and users-generated content (UGC) enable people to conveniently create their own information (Bennett & Iyengar, 2008). Given such "informational surplus", people's reception and consumption of information becomes selective and niche-based with like-minded voices, as the term "echo chamber" in political communication has depicted (Barberá et al., 2015). Shedding light from the classic "two-step flow" theory, which highlights the significance of interpersonal networks and opinion leaders at local communities (Katz & Lazarsfeld, 1955), abundant informational supply in digital and social media platforms encourages people's reliance on their own "information shortcut" (Lupia & McCubbins, 2000)—the friends and reliable resource people whom they know—to pick up the convenient information from a sea of messages. Despite the emergence of global informational networks, thanks to digital and social media platforms, they simultaneously compete with online tribes of "echo-chambers" which are not conducive to the formation of public spheres for common social agendas (Serazio, 2014). Furthermore, narrowcasting in digital and social media environments could even be utilized by pro-government forces to construct their own defensive informational loops which aim to counter the social movements which fight for universal values (Lee, 2021).

A way to transcend the "echo-chambers" in digital and social media platforms to mobilize people's support for a common agenda is their affect-networks, which are the key momentum for mobilizing public opinion in a fragmented narrowcasting environment. Affect refers to the motivating force and energy of human beings resulting from a set of emotions triggered by cultural constructs such as identities, meanings, or experiences (Harding & Pribram, 2004, p. 873). Such power of emotions is vividly manifested in the formation of global networks of social movements when emotion is effectively utilized as a *quasi*-universal language to people coming from different parts of the world (Castells, 2015). Studies of large-scale social mobilization attempt to discern the mobilizing effects of different types of emotion. For example, perception of eminent and immediate social threat could rapidly mobilize people's swift action and radical responses which they do not think of (Cheng & Yuen, 2020); the feeling of guilt for not doing enough for the society could become the momentum for intergenerational understanding and supportive social movement networks (Tang & Cheng, 2021). While mobilizing people's emotion is theoretically viable in campaigning global crises of sustainability, such as the plight of climate change, such affect-networks could be a double-edged sword to fostering a sense of shared value for global citizenship. Recent studies of online political communication indicate that the issue of affective polarization in digital and social media platforms is jeopardizing people's willingness and capacity to receive alternative information, viewpoints, and listen to others who are not perceived as "us" (Liang & Zhang, 2021).

After all, campaigning sustainability and global citizenship is the political communication of public opinion. Literature of public opinion studies has been debating about people's rationality in political communication, such as electoral choice and political attitude. Classic writings by Lippmann (1922) and Converse (1964) cynically questioned people's wisdom and rationality in political choice and electoral affairs by enlisting voters' limited knowledge of and interests in public affairs, randomness of voting patterns, and ambiguous and self-contradictory tendencies in political attitudes and ideologies. Meanwhile, studies and research on public opinion and political communication have been arguing for a more pragmatic approach to understanding people's rationality and wisdom in public affairs. For instance, it is infeasible to ask people to acquire a great deal of political knowledge, yet they can still make an informed choice on critical moments such as a general election (Lupia & McCubbins, 2000; Popkin, 1991). Media sociologist Michael Schudson (1998) conceptualizes the idea of monitorial citizenship to apprehend public opinion: while people cannot afford paying full attention to public affairs all the time, they monitor the world via media coverage to see if something important happens, just like checking the surveillance camera from time to time to see if the children are approaching the swimming pool. John Zallar (2003) further develops the notion of monitorial citizenship by proposing the media function of "burglar alarm"—reminding the people of significant social issues when they are busy with everyday life. Studies of political communication and public opinion picture enable us to pull down the vision of global citizenship and SDGs to the earth of the everyday life of people. While some activists may be disappointed at people's lukewarm responses and inaction in view of climate change, humanitarian crises such as hunger, poverty, and shrinking biodiversity, communication research reminds us that to engage people in public affairs has been a difficult and strategic task. To persuade people walking away from their family life, work, and social circles for listening to a global vision entails a comprehensive understanding of the nature of public opinion: despite all the imperfections, people are willing to listen and act once they recognize that this is important news for them. Therefore, the next question is how to make global citizenship and SDGs a "new" and significant topic to the monitoring views of the media and people year after year, and decade after decade.

Conclusion

This chapter highlights the significance of communication studies for the promotion and implementation of a global vision of sustainability. In view of a growing body of literature about the policies, practices, and effectiveness of achieving SDGs, we propose that communication studies—especially global communication, intercultural communication, and political communication—are very relevant and crucial to initiate the scholarly and social dialogues for visions on global citizenship and sustainability. Global communication studies unravel the dynamics of setting agendas for global topics: action and politics initiated by the developed world and prominent state powers, the rise of a global civil society by the communication networks of activists around the world, and how the global media events such as the climate conference organized by the United Nations become an opportunity for activists to make an inroad for global media exposure. This research and experience informs us of the ways and strategies to set global agendas for SDGs. In addition, literature of intercultural communication reminds us that constructing shared values for global citizenship and sustainability is essential to putting the vision and targets of SDGs into workable and measurable local policy agendas and business goals.

Nevertheless, people from different societies perceive sustainability and SDGs from varying contexts and priorities. Localizing SDGs into political and socio-cultural practices at communities entails creating a common ground of global citizenship which enables our empathy to people and the plights which may not be visible in our immediate contacts. Scholarly dialogues surrounding political communication and public opinion depict the realpolitik of putting SDGs into action. While digital and social media platforms are connecting people from different parts of the world, we should be aware of its echo chambers with "affect polarization" which may not be conducive to promoting social tolerance and mutual understanding. Online mobilization via social media platforms usually features with people's emotion and corresponding affect-networks. Therefore, affect-networks can be counterproductive to our exposure to alternative views and acceptance of people who are not regarded as "us".

Campaigning for sustainability eventually matters to public opinion studies which investigate the rationality and wisdom of people who are usually busy with their own lives instead of paying attention to public affairs all the time. Public opinion studies offer us a pragmatic goal and approach to promote SDGs, particularly how to make SDGs a new and significant topic to people despite decades of deliberation. The basic momentum for executing SDGs is to keep people's attention and interest in related agendas and initiatives. On this ground, how to merge SDGs into various local affairs and agendas should be the prime question to get the ball rolling.

We want to emphasize that without a succinct cultural label which conveys the role of communication, there will be a missing jigsaw to the holistic picture of global citizenship and SDGs. Adding a clear SDG of "Communication for Sustainability" could tellingly explicate the essential role of effective communication among people and organizations in the promotion, education, and implementation of other SDGs. The first step to achieve social change is to inform, persuade, and enlighten people why change is needed. We believe that "Communication for Sustainability" is the gateway which makes an inroad to achieve other SDGs.

References

Allan, S. (2006). *Online news*. Open University Press.
Anbinder, T. (2006). Nativism and prejudice against immigrants. In R. Ueda (Ed.), *A companion to American immigration*. Blackwell.

Appadurai, A. (1990). Disjuncture and difference in the global cultural economy. *Theory Culture Society, 7,* 295–231.

Atton, C. (2002). News Cultures and New Social Movements: Radical journalism and the mainstream media. *Journalism Studies, 3*(4), 491–505.

Bagdikian, B. H. (2000). *The media monopoly.* Beacon Press.

Baker, C. E. (2002). *Media, markets, and democracy.* Cambridge University Press.

Barberá, P., Jost, J. T., Nagler, J., Tucker, J. A., & Bonneau, R. (2015). Tweeting from left to right: Is online political communication more than an echo chamber? *Psychological Science, 26*(10), 1531–1542.

Battaglia, M., Annesi, N., Calabrese, M., & Frey, M. (2020). Do agenda 2030 and sustainable development goals act at local and operational levels? Evidence from a case study in a large energy company in Italy. *Business Strategy & Development, 3*(4), 603–614.

Beck, U. (1992). *Risk society: Towards a new modernity.* Sage.

Beck, U. (2009). *World at risk.* Polity.

Bennett, W. L. (1990). Toward a theory of press-state relations in the United States. *Journal of Communication, 40*(2), 103–127.

Bennett, W. L., & Iyengar, S. (2008). A new era of minimal effects? The changing foundations of political communication. *Journal of Communication, 58,* 707–731.

Berkowitz, D. (1990). Refining the gatekeeping metaphor for local television news. *Journal of Broadcasting & Electronic Media, 34,* 55–68.

Carbaugh, D. (2007). Cultural discourse analysis: Communication practices and intercultural encounters. *Journal of Intercultural Communication Research, 36*(3), 167–182.

Castells, M. (2008). The new public sphere: Global civil society, communication networks, and global governance. In *The annuals of the American academy of political and social science,* vol. 616, *Public diplomacy in a changing world* (pp. 78–93). Sage Publications, Inc.

Castells, M. (2009). *Communication power.* Oxford University Press.

Castells, M. (2015). *Networks of outrage and hope: Social movements in the internet age.* John Wiley & Sons.

Cheng, E. W., & Yuen, S. (2020). Total mobilisation from below: Abeyance networks, threats and emotions in Hong Kong's freedom summer. *APSA Preprints.* https://doi.org/10.33774/apsa-2020-05j34

Chien, F., Anwar, A., Hsu, C., Sharif, A., Razzaq, A., & Sinha, A. (2021). The role of information and communication technology in encouraging environmental degradation: Proposing an SDG framework for the BRICS countries. *Technology in Society, 65.* https://doi.org/10.1016/j.techsoc.2021.101587

Chua, A. (2018). *Political tribes.* Bloomsbury.

Cobb, R., Ross, J. K., & Ross, M. H. (1976). Agenda-building as a comparative political process. *The American political science review, 70*(1), 126–138.

Converse, P. E. (1964). The nature of belief systems in mass public. In D. Apter (Ed.), *Ideology and discontent*. Free Press.

Cook, T. E. (1998). *Governing with the news: The news media as a political institution*. University of Chicago Press.

Curran, J. (2002). *Media and power*. Routledge.

Curran, J., & Couldry, N. (2003). The paradox of media power. In N. Couldry & J. Curran (Eds.), *Contesting media power: Alternative media in a networked world* (pp. 3–16). Rowman & Littlefield.

Dayan, D. (2008). Beyond media events: Disenchantment, derailment, disruption. In M. Price & D. Dayan (Eds.), *Owing the Olympic narratives of the new China* (pp. 391–402). The University of Michigan Press.

Dayan, D., & Katz, E. (1992). *Media events: The live broadcasting of history*. Harvard University Press.

Derakhshan, H., & Wardle, C. (2017). Information disorder: definitions. In *Proceedings of conference on understanding and addressing the disinformation ecosystem*, December 15–16, 2017, Annenberg School for Communication, USA.

Forestier, O., & Kim, R. E. (2020). Cherry-picking the sustainable development goals: Goal prioritization by national governments and implications for global governance. *Sustainable Development, 28*(5), 1269–1278.

Frankovic, K. (2016). Belief in conspiracies largely depends on political identity. *YouGov*. https://today.yougov.com/topics/politics/articles-reports/2016/12/27/belief-conspiracies-largely-depends-political-iden

Fukuda-Parr, S., & McNeil, D. (2019). Knowledge and politics in setting and measuring the SDGs: Introduction to special issue. *Global Policy, 10*(1), 5–15.

Gambetta, N., Fronti, I. C., Geldres-Weiss, V. V., Gómez-Villegas, M., & Jaramillo, M. (2018). *The Latin American governments' communication strategy in the voluntary national reviews: Is the speech aligned with the reality?* Working Paper of Universidad ORT Uruguay.

García-Sanchez, I., Aibar-Guzman, B., Aibar-Guzman, C., & Rodríguez-Ariza, L. (2020). "Sell" recommendations by analysts in response to business communication strategies concerning the Sustainable Development Goals and the SDG compass. *Journal of Cleaner Production, 255*. https://doi.org/10.1016/j.jclepro.2020.120194

Gilboa, E. (2002). Global communication and foreign policy. *Journal of Communication, 52*(4), 731–748.

Glasser, T. L. (1999). *The idea of public journalism*. The Guilford Press.

Grorud-Colvert, K., Lester, S. E., Airamé, S., Neeley, E., & Gaines, S. D. (2010). Communicating marine reserve science to diverse audiences. *Proceedings of the National Academy of Sciences of the United States of America, 107*(43), 18306–18311.

Gudykunst, W. B. (1995). Anxiety/uncertainty management (AUM) theory: Current status. In R. L. Wiseman (Ed.), *International and intercultural com-*

munication annual, vol. 19. Intercultural communication theory (pp. 8–58). Sage Publications, Inc.

Gudykunst, W. B. (1998). *Bridging differences: Effective intergroup communication* (3rd ed.). Sage.

Hallin, D. (1986). *The uncensored war: The media and Vietnam.* Oxford University Press.

Harding, J., & Pribram, E. D. (2004). Losing our cool? Following Williams and Grossberg on emotions. *Cultural Studies, 18*(6), 863–883.

Heras-Saizarbitoria, I., Urbieta, L., & Boiral, O. (2021). Organizations' engagement with sustainable development goals: From cherry-picking to SDG-washing? *Corporate Social Responsibility and Environment Management, 1–13.* https://doi.org/10.1002/csr.2202

Kastoryano, R. (2018). Multiculturalism and interculturalism: Redefining nationhood and solidarity. *Comparative Migration Studies, 6,* 17. https://doi.org/10.1186/s40878-018-0082-6

Katz, E., & Lazarsfeld, P. F. (1955). *Personal influence.* Free Press.

Kim, Y. Y. (2007). Ideology, identity, and intercultural communication: An analysis of differing academic conceptions of cultural identity. *Journal of Intercultural Communication Research, 36*(3), 237–253.

Lee, C. C. (2002). Established pluralism: US elite media discourse about China policy. *Journalism Studies, 3*(3), 343–357.

Lee, C. C., Chan, J. M., Pan, Z., & So, C. Y. K. (2002). *Global media spectacle: News war over Hong Kong.* State University of New York Press.

Lee, F. L. F. (2021). Countering the counterpublics: Progovernment online media and public opinion in Hong Kong. *International Journal of Communication, 15*(2021), 3397–3417.

Liang, H., & Zhang, X. (2021). Partisan bias of perceived incivility and its political consequences: Evidence from survey experiments in Hong Kong. *Journal of Communication, 71*(3), 357–379.

Lippard, C. D. (2011). Racist nativism in the 21st century. *Sociology Compass, 5*(7), 591–606.

Lippmann, W. (1922). *Public opinion.* Harcourt, Brace & Co.

Logan, S., Steel, Z., & Hunt, C. (2016). Intercultural willingness to communicate within health services: Investigating anxiety, uncertainty, ethnocentrism and help seeking behaviour. *International Journal of Intercultural Communication, 54,* 77–86.

Lupia, A., & McCubbins, M. D. (2000). The institutional foundation of political competence: How citizens learn what they need to know. In A. Lupia, M. D. McCubbins, & S. L. Popkin (Eds.), *Elements of reason: Cognition, choice and the bounds of rationality.* Cambridge University Press.

Marquis, C., & Qian, C. (2014). Corporate social responsibility reporting in China: Symbol or substance? *Organization Science, 25*(1), 127–148.

McCombs, M. E., & Shaw, D. L. (1993). The evolution of agenda-setting research: Twenty-five years in the marketplace of ideas. *Journal of Communication, 43*(2), 58–67.

McManus, J. H. (1994). *Market-driven journalism: Let the citizen beware?* Sage.

Mulholland, E. (2019). Communicating sustainable development and the SDGs in Europe: Good practice examples from policy, academic, NGOs, and media. *DSDN Quarterly Report, 51.*

Nameni, A. (2020). Research into ethnocentrism and intercultural willingness to communicate of Iraqi and Iranian medical students in Iran. *Journal of Intercultural Communication Research, 49*(1), 61–85.

Newsom, D. (1996). *The public dimension of foreign policy.* Indiana University Press.

Nye, J. S., Jr. (1990). *Bound to lead: The changing nature of American power.* BasicBooks.

Ocansey, R. C. (2018). *The role of communication in achieving sustainable development goal (SDG) 7 – The case of Ghana's energy sector.* MPhil thesis, University of Ghana, Accra.

Olofsson, L., & Mark-Herbert, C. (2020). Creating shared values by integrating UN Sustainable Development Goals in Corporate Communication – The case of Apparel Retail. *Sustainability, 12*(21), 8806. https://doi.org/10.3390/su12218806

Popkin, S. L. (1991). *The reasoning voter: Communication and persuasion in presidential campaigns.* University of Chicago Press.

Rensburg, W. V., & Head, B. W. (2017). Climate change skepticism: Reconsidering how to respond to core criticisms of climate science and policy. *Sage Open, 1,* 11. https://doi.org/10.1177/2158244017748983

Robinson, P. (2000). The policy-media interaction model: Measuring media power during humanitarian crisis. *Journal of Peace Research, 37,* 613–633.

Ryan, C. (1991). *Prime time activism: Media strategies for grassroots organizing.* South End Press.

Schiller, H. (1970). *Mass communications and American empire.* Augustus M Kelley.

Schiller, H. (1976). *Communication and cultural domination.* ME Sharpe.

Schudson, M. (1998). *The good citizen.* Free Press.

Serazio, M. (2014). The new media designs of political consultants: Campaign production in a fragmented era. *Journal of Communication, 64*(4), 743–763.

Servaes, J. (2009). Communication policies, good governance and development journalism. *Communicatio: South African Journal for Communication Theory and Research, 35*(1), 50–80.

Servaes, J. (2012). Soft power and public diplomacy: The new frontier for public relations and international communication between the US and China. *Public Relations Review, 38*(# 5), 643–651.

Shoemaker, P. J. (1991). *Gatekeeping.* Sage.

Siddiqui, S., Aftab, W., Siddiqui, F. J., Huicho, L., Mogilevskii, R., Friberg, P., Lindgren-Garcia, J., Causeic, S., Khamis, A., Shah, M. M., & Bhutta, Z. A. (2020). Global strategies and local implementation of health-related SDGs: Lessons from consultation in countries across five regions. *BMJ Global Health, 5*, e002859. https://doi.org/10.1136/bmjgh-2020-002859

Sparks, C. (2007). *Globalization, development and the mass media*. Sage.

Sparks, C. (2012). Media and cultural imperialism reconsidered. *Chinese Journal of Communication, 5*(2), 281–299.

Taggart, P. (2000). *Populism*. Open University Press.

Tandoc, E. C., Jr., Lim, Z. W., & Ling, R. (2018). Defining 'fake news': A typology of scholarly definitions. *Digital Journalism, 6*(2), 137–153.

Tang, G., & Cheng, E. W. (2021). Affective solidarity: How guilt enables cross-generational support for political radicalization in Hong Kong. *Japanese Journal of Political Science, 22*(4), 198–214. https://doi.org/10.1017/S1468109921000220

Thatcher, M. (1985). *Speech to American Bar Association* [Online]. Retrieved May 7, 2020, from http://www.margaretthatcher.org/document/106096

Thrall, A. T., Stecula, D., & Sweet, D. (2014). May we have your attention please? Human-rights NGOs and the problem of global communication. *The International Journal of Press / Politics, 19*(2), 135–159.

Thussu, D. (2018a). *International communication – Continuity and change* (3rd ed.). Bloomsbury Academic.

Thussu, D. (2018b). A new global communication order for a multipolar world. *Communication Research and Practice, 4*(1), 52–66.

Triandafyllidou, A. (2021). Nationalism in the 21st century: Neo-tribal or plural? *Nation and Nationalism, 26*, 792–806.

Tsfati, Y., Boomgaarden, H. G., Strömbäck, J., Vliegenthart, R., Damstra, A., & Lindgren, E. (2020). Causes and consequences of mainstream media dissemination of fake news: Literature review and synthesis. *Annals of the International Communication Association, 44*(2), 157–173.

Vargo, C. J., Guo, L., & Amazeen, M. A. (2017). The agenda-setting power of fake news: A big data analysis of the online media landscape from 2014–2016. *New Media & Society, 20*(5), 2028–2049.

Waisbord, S., & Mellado, C. (2014). De-westernizing communication studies: A reassessment. *Communication Theory, 24*(4), 361–372.

Wallerstein, I. (2011). *The modern world system I: Capitalist agriculture and the origins of the European world-economy in the sixteenth century*. University of California Press.

White, D. M. (1950). The "Gate Keeper": A case study in the selection of news. *Journalism Quarterly, 27*, 383–396.

Wrench, J. S., Corrigan, M. W., McCroskey, J. C., & Punyanunt-Carter, N. M. (2006). Religious fundamentalism and intercultural communication: The relationship among ethnocentrism, intercultural communication apprehension, religious fundamentalism, homonegativity, and tolerance for religious disagreements. *Journal of Intercultural Communication Research, 35*(1), 23–44.

Yusha'u, J., & Servaes, J. (Eds.). (2021). *The Palgrave handbook of international communication and sustainable development.* Palgrave Macmillan.

Zallar, J. (2003). A new standard of news quality: Burglar alarms for the monitorial citizens. *Political Communication, 20,* 109–130.

CHAPTER 4

Sustainable Development Goals and Communication as a Commons in the Context of Extractive Capitalism: Tensions and Possibilities

Víctor Manuel Marí Sáez

Abstract The need to include sustainable development goals in the debate on the Agenda 2030 poses two primary theoretical challenges: the analysis of the basic characteristics of the current socio-political context of extractive capitalism, and the ability to consider communication in an alternative post-capitalist horizon.

The first theoretical task of a contextual nature allows for identifying the basic characteristics of extractive capitalism (Gudynas, Disputes over capitalism and varieties of development. In Veltmeyer, H. & Záyago, E. (Eds.), *Buen Vivir and the challenges to capitalism in Latin America* (pp. 194–213). Routledge. https://doi.org/10.4324/9781003091516-13, 2020; Kidd, Extra-activism: Counter-mapping and data justice.

V. M. Marí Sáez (✉)
University of Cadiz, Cadiz, Spain
e-mail: victor.mari@uca.es

85
J. Servaes, M. J. Yusha'u (eds.), *SDG18 Communication for All, Volume 1*, Sustainable Development Goals Series, https://doi.org/10.1007/978-3-031-19142-8_4

Information Communication and Society, 22(7), 954–970. https://doi. org/10.1080/1369118x.2019.1581243, 2019) as an economic and political project diametrically opposed to that underlying the formulation of sustainable development goals. Both basic material goods (water, food, etc.) and social and communication rights are, in the framework of current capitalism, resources to be intensively exploited on the basis of a commodity logic.

On the contrary, a conception of (material and social) goods and communication as a commons implies a radically alternative worldview and political horizon. This approach includes a perspective of the economy, the environment and communication which encounters in the formulation of the commons a very useful theoretical template for constructing alternatives to extractive capitalism.

The subsequent development of the seminal works on the commons by authors like Hess & Ostrom (Understanding Knowledge as Commons: From Theory to Practice. MIT Press. https://doi.org/10.7551/mitpress/6980.001.0001, 2007) and Benkler (Commons and growth: The essential role of open commons in market economies. *University of Chicago Law Review, 80*(1), 499–555, 2013) in the field of communication can provide clues for research in this regard (Fuchs, The digital commons and the digital public sphere: How to advance digital democracy today. *Westminster Papers in Communication and Culture, 16*(1), 9–26. https:// doi.org/10.16997/wpcc.917, 2021). This alternative theoretical approach is not totally new, insofar as precedents worthy of being reproduced in the current context can be found in the history of communication for development (Servaes, *Approaches to development communication.* UNESCO, 2002). This is the case of the *dependentistas* who, back in the 1960s, had already discovered the delusion of considering underdevelopment as a stage of transition towards development, challenging the basis of the modernising development model inspired by functionalism. On the basis of these elements, it is possible to provide theoretical grounds for the proposed alternative.

Keywords Sustainable development goals • Commons • Sustainable communication • Postcapitalism • Digital communication

INTRODUCTION

The COVID-19 pandemic has highlighted even more the need to take into consideration the Sustainable Development Goals 18 (hereinafter SGD 18): "Communication for all", inasmuch as in this context the task of designing a coherent and comprehensive communication strategy in relation to the SGD 18 and the 2030 Agenda for Sustainable Development (hereinafter 2030 Agenda) has become increasingly more urgent (Oldekop et al., 2020). The pandemic has been accompanied by an infopandemic (Wang & Marí, 2021; Yusha'u & Servaes, 2021) which, more than ever before, makes it necessary to recall some of the lessons learned in the framework of the communication for development approach.[1]

It is therefore necessary to start from a communication framed in a specific context, which is none other than that of extractive (Gudynas, 2020; Kidd, 2019; Svampa, 2015, 2019) and digital capitalism (Fuchs & Mosco, 2015; Srnicek, 2017). The first concept (extractive capitalism) refers to one side of a new phase of global capitalist dynamics which depends predominantly on the exploitation and exportation of nature, while the second (digital capitalism) has to do with a dimension of the organisation of capitalism that is shaped by digital mediation. Somehow or other, digital capitalism is also a sort of extractivism. As much the material goods (water, food, etc.) as the social and communication rights are, within the framework of current capitalism, resources to be intensively exploited under a commodity logic.

Versus this economic and socio-political context, a number of practices governed by the logic of the commons have emerged and are already observable in reality. Each one of these contexts—the hegemonic of extractive and digital capitalism and the alternative of the commons—is accompanied by specific communication practices.

Taking these elements as a departure point, the main aim of this chapter is to put forward some theoretical keys for considering "communication for all" as a commons on a post-capitalist horizon, in order that their

---

[1] As Servaes and Lie (2015, p. 124) note, "The history of communication for sustainable development and social change or whatever other name is preferred—(e.g. development communication, devcom(m), com(m)dev, C4D, communication in/for (sustainable) development, communication for (sustainable) social change, communication and education for development and/or knowledge (management) for development)—is well documented (see, for instance, Gumucio-Dagron & Tufte, 2006; Manyozo, 2012; McAnany, 2012; Servaes, 1999; Servaes & Lie, 2013; Wilkins et al., 2014)."

alternative characteristics should be visible with respect to the type of communication preponderantly promoted in the framework of extractive and digital capitalism.

This alternative conception of communication and development is by no means new. For this reason, some of the critical visions of development and social change promoted—by the *dependentistas* (Katz, 2021; Servaes, 2002)—in the last third of the twentieth century, in addition to the subsequent communication alternatives developed during that period under the label of the "Latin American communication thought" (Beltrán, 1980; Marques de Melo, 1984)—need to be updated with a view to including the lessons learned from the theoretical work on the development and communication of these initiatives in communication as a commons.

To this end, the main characteristics of extractive and digital capitalism, in which the intention is to promote the SDG 18: "Communication for all" and the 2030 Agenda, are described in the first section. The following section revolves around those historical contributions of communication for sustainable development which can be reproduced at present, with a view to laying the foundations for an alternative digital communication understood under the logic of the commons. Lastly, the third section addresses some of the challenges that this alternative communication approach must meet on a post-capitalist horizon.

Contextualising: The SDG 18 and Communication for Sustainable Growth in the Age of Extractive and Digital Capitalism

Two Contradictory Inertias: The Good Intentions of the United Nations and the Predatory Logic of Capitalism

Regrettably, it has often been observed how international institutions like the United Nations (UN) are excessively naïve when releasing well-intentioned statements in relation to aspects like those being discussed here (i.e. the SDG 18). In many cases, these statements require a greater contextualisation when defining which material elements of the current socio-political context hinder such measures and which of them serve as catalysts for them.

In this connection, for Easterly (2015a, p. 323) the idealism and voluntarism of global institutions like the UN, when wondering what should be done to combat poverty in the world, yet again highlights, in this case as regards the SDG 18, "that action plans don't necessarily lead to action, that 'we' are not necessarily the right ones to act, and that there are alternative routes to progress". The general idea of a global alliance for development is seen as a further example of what this author calls "the tyranny of experts" (Easterly, 2015b), which needs to be reconsidered in the framework of a complex world (Ramalingam, 2013).

Furthermore, these statements and formulations on global alliances for development connect with the dominant trends of philanthrocapitalism (McGoey, 2012; Thorup, 2013) in which the so-called development industries (Mediavilla & García-Arias, 2019; Wilkins & Enghel, 2013) and the non-profit corporate complex (Gurcan, 2015; Rodríguez, 2007) establish the strategic lines along which the communication of solidarity and non-profit organisations flows.

Taking into account all these criticisms, however, it is true that, as noted by Servaes (2017, p. 7), the SDG 18 provides a look at development as an "engineering problem" to be solved from a top-down perspective. "Sixty years of countless reform schemes to aid agencies and dozens of different plans, and $2.3 trillion later, the aid industry is still failing to reach the beautiful goal [...]. The evidence points to an unpopular conclusion: Big Plans will always fail to reach the beautiful goal" (Easterly, 2006, p. 11, cited in Servaes, 2017, p. 7).

On the contrary, in the formulation of the SDG 18 some of the defects of the previous goals have been corrected, to the point that the current ones are aimed at overcoming the compartmentalisation of technical and policy work by promoting integrated approaches to the interconnected economic, social and environmental challenges confronting the world.

It is therefore important to perform a deeper analysis of the sociopolitical context in which the intention is to promote the SDG 18. And this is none other than that of the so-called extractive capitalism and neo-extractivism (Brand et al., 2016; Gudynas, 2020; Kidd, 2019; Svampa, 2015, 2019; Veltmeyer & Petras, 2014) and digital capitalism (Fuchs & Mosco, 2015; Schiller, 2000; Srnicek, 2017).

For Svampa (2019, p. 14), neo-extractivism is an exceedingly productive analytical category, originating from Latin America, which possesses a huge descriptive and explanatory potential, as well as a strong denunciative character and mobilising power. In turn, the concept has diverse nuances, since, according to Alberto Acosta (2011), extractivism is a mode of accumulation that first appeared some 500 years ago and which, since then, has been determined by the demands of the metropolitan centres of capitalism. For Gudynas, the term refers rather to a mode of appropriation, a type of extraction of vast amounts of natural resources for their exporting (Svampa, 2019, p. 15). In addition, Brand et al. (2016) believe that neo-extractivism is one side of a new phase of global capitalist dynamics which must be applied to all Latin American societies that, since the 1970s and especially since the year 2000, have depended predominantly on the exploitation and exportation of nature.

In a supplementary and convergent line with respect to the concept of extractive capitalism, there is the proposal put forward by David Harvey (2003, 2012) as regards expressing accumulation by dispossession. For this author, "the inability to accumulate through expanded reproduction on a sustained basis has been paralleled by a rise in attempts to accumulate by dispossession" (Harvey, 2003, p. 64). This term is useful for historically understanding the processes of accumulation within the capitalist system, in reference to both the transition from feudalism to capitalism and, nowadays, when perpetuating and legitimising neoliberal capitalism. It is especially interesting to become acquainted with the processes, mentioned by Harvey, by which this was achieved in the fledgling capitalism of the Middle Ages, namely primitive accumulation. These processes included, among others, the commodification and privatisation of land, the conversion of several types of ownership rights (communal, collective, state, etc.) into rights of exclusive private ownership, the suppression of access to the commons, the commodification of the labour force and the monetisation of exchanges and taxes, particularly on land (Harvey, 2003, p. 116).

Extractive capitalism is not totally different from the digital kind. To the contrary, the latter can be understood as a specific type of the former. For Fuchs (2021), digital capitalism is not a new phase of capitalist development, but rather a dimension of the organisation of capitalism that is shaped by digital mediation. In digital capitalism, "social processes such as the accumulation of power, capital accumulation, class struggles, political struggles, hegemony, ideology, commodification, or globalisation, are mediated by digital technologies, digital information, and digital communication" (Fuchs, 2021, p. 10). Daniel Schiller (2000) contends that digital capitalism has further empowered transnational corporations, while exacerbating existing social inequalities and offering supple tools to promote consumerism on a transnational scale.

In the initial stages of the citizenry's use of the Internet, it was expected that this new space would be more egalitarian and horizontal than the "space of places" (Castells, 1996). With time, however, the "spaces of flows", which is the Internet, in particular, and the digital world, in general, has been transformed into just another space of capital (Harvey, 2002), in which commodity logic governs increasing broader expanses.

Capitalism and the Struggle Against the Commons

Returning to the ideas of Harvey (2003) about accumulation by dispossession, it can be observed that in the transition from feudalism to capitalism, primitive accumulation[2] was achieved by the process of enclosure—namely, denying peasants and, in general, popular sectors of society access to common land—among other measures. By this process, the legal ownership and uses of hitherto common land was subsequently privatised. In his research on the formation of the working classes in England, Edward P. Thompson (1963) claims that the enclosure movement gathered pace throughout the fifteenth century, forming an integral part of the major transformation of European capitalism. This process started with the enclosure of common land and the change in its legal ownership.

These reflections on the enclosure movement have helped different authors to establish a series of continuities and discontinuities between the capitalist appropriation of the commons in the fifteenth century and current neo-extractive tendencies, through which, albeit in a different way but with a similar philosophy, the commons continues to be under attack. In this respect, for De Angelis (2011, 2012, 2017), while the purpose of the first enclosures was to establish private ownership as the basic pillar of capitalist society, the intention of the new enclosures is to multiply the spaces under private ownership or to recover those in which the system has had to give ground as a result of the class war (De Angelis, 2012, as cited in Galafassi & Composto, 2013, p. 78).

Under these processes and dynamics, it is possible to reinterpret, from a Marxist perspective, not only a contradiction between capital and labour but also, following O'Connor (2001), another one between capitalism and nature, which assailed the commons five centuries ago and which nowadays, in extractive capitalism, is besieging different types of existing commons.

---

[2] A term addressed in detail by Rosa Luxemburg (1871–1919), which Harvey includes in his work on the concept of "capitalism by dispossession".

De Angelis (2017) establishes a series of elements that are necessary for making commons systems available:

- Pooled material/immaterial resources or commonwealth;
- A community of commoners, that is, subjects willing to share, pool and claim commonwealth;
- Commoning, or doing in common, that is, specific multifaceted social labour (activity, praxis), through which commonwealth and the community of commoners are (re)produced together with the (re)production of stuff, social relations, affects, decisions and cultures (De Angelis, 2017, p. 119).

These three elements existed in the feudal system before the advent of the enclosure movement and the conformation of initial capitalism. By the same token, it is possible to identify these same elements in the contemporary practices of social movements and active citizens who defend and promote all types of commons. These include information and communication, which will be covered in greater detail in the following section. But it is important to stress the need to recover the lessons learned from the first enclosures and, in general, from the historiographical works of authors like Thompson to whom, as Thomas (2017) observes, reference is not usually made in the academic literature on communication for social change (CSC).

COMMUNICATION FOR SUSTAINABLE DEVELOPMENT IN A NEW CONTEXT

Certainly, the accelerated times in which we live, together with the postmodern tendency towards extolling the present and forgetting the past, hinder a historiographical approach that allows for learning interesting lessons for the present from research on the past. This occurs with those works of classic authors of the workers' movement, like Thompson, as well as in the field of communication for sustainable development itself. This is the reason why some of those lessons have been recovered in this section so as to help to identify problems and to shed light on possible alternatives.

Lessons Learned from the Stage of Dependency

In his classical periodisation of the stages and models of communication for development (ComDev), Jan Servaes (1999) refers to the stage of dependency (from the mid-1960s to the mid-1980s), which emerged in response to the modernising development designed from functionalist perspectives. Versus the modernising proposal emerging from northern powers such as the United States and Europe, there appeared a resistance movement that, initially, took shape in different Latin American countries, before spreading to other places and involving other social actors the world over. The movement would be led by the so-called *dependentistas* group, on which it is essential to dwell here in order to discuss some of its most important contributions.

After several decades of implementing functionalist and modernising development models, and following the confirmation of their failure to eradicate economic and social inequalities, it would be the countries of what was then known as the Third World, to wit, the periphery of the dominant world-system, that would identify the contradictions of a modernising process that generated a certain amount of development in the centres at the expense of exporting high levels of underdevelopment to the peripheries (Marí, 2011, p. 162).

Dependency theory reveals the falsehood of identifying underdevelopment as a stage (according to the theses of Rostow), challenging the basis of the modernising model. This new theoretical proposal, put forward by Fernando Henrique Cardoso and Enzo Faletto (1969), André Gunder Frank (1967), Paul Baran (1957), Ruy Mauro Marini (1974) and Theotonio dos Santos (1968), among others, would pave the way for the analytical structuralist model for the study of underdevelopment from the periphery.

Structuralist-based dependency theory has the following characteristic features:

- An analysis is performed in terms of totality. Underdevelopment is a global phenomenon in which the economy and the social and political spheres are interrelated.
- It is the interaction between central and peripheral countries, through economic and political relations, that is valued most. This implies addressing questions such as unequal exchanges, foreign debt, technological-financial dependency and so forth.

- Underdevelopment is defined in relation to the international economic system, in which the countries of the South have been given the role of providing the countries of the North with the raw materials that they need.
- The difference between development and underdevelopment is not one of level—greater or lesser income—but structural. A structure that was shaped in the colonial period and which is characterised by foreign dependency at a commercial, financial and technological level, among others.
- Colonialism is considered to be an important factor in the structuring of underdevelopment, and cultural imperialism, understood as the imposition of foreign cultural models far removed from the needs of the population (Mesa, 1990, p. 23).

It has been decades since the formulation of these theories and the particular contexts in which they were formulated have changed. Be that as it may, the dominant world-system continues to be capitalism and, therefore, a critique of this system as a whole is still necessary (Adorno, 2005 [1951]). The reflections of Katz (2018, 2021), who has revisited dependency theory 50 years after its formulation, point in this direction. He considers that dependency theory faces a new scenario in Latin America, in which a general reconsideration of Marxist dependency theory can be revived and expanded. The aforementioned neo-extractivism calls for a global response that could incorporate lessons gleaned from the experience of the *dependentistas*.

In the field of communication there are also many very important lessons that can be learned from the contributions of that period. There is a communication deriving from dependency, aimed at taking a step back from dependency in relation to the communication theories developed in the United States and the underlying geopolitical interests (Marí, 2021; Servaes, 2002). The critical movement connects, in turn, with the demands of the New World Information and Communication Order (NWICO) which, under the umbrella of the UNESCO, would give rise to one of the major milestones in the formulation and institutionalisation of an alternative approach to communication: the McBride Report (1980).

Versus Lasswell's model and Mass Communication Research, an alternative communication to the dominant system began to take shape, with different epicentres in Latin America. There was then a shift from communication theories at the service of the status-quo to theories aimed at the structural transformation of society and its necessary democratisation. Hierarchical communication models gave way to horizontal, participatory, popular and dialogic models (Navarro & Rodríguez, 2018). The project of cultural imperialism (Schiller, 1969) yielded to the formulation of national communication policies that allowed for repositioning communication in its points of intersection with local culture, citizenship and endogenous development (Bustamante & Corredor, 2016).

According to Gumucio (2011), dependency theories set the stage for many successful ComDev experiences in the world, in which the creation of community radio stations, participatory video and many other forms of educational and participatory communication were fostered. The communication aspect of dependency theory "has been described in many books and papers, including those published by Colin Fraser and Sonia Restrepo (1998), Andrew A. Moemeka (1994), Roberto C. Hornik (1988) and Jan Servaes (1989)" (Gumucio, 2011, p. 36).

But, despite these interpretations, an excessively fragmented communication research has prevailed, placing the accent on case studies and micro analyses, necessary but clearly insufficient for performing a critique on the systemic logics in which all these practices are immersed. The excessive fragmentation of both communication research and the communication practices of non-governmental organisations (NGOs) has reinforced the trend that some authors have dubbed as "NGO-isation" (Álvarez, 2009; Banks et al., 2015; Chouldry & Kapoor, 2012). It is a process characterised by the fragmentation of organised solidarity, which restricts its capacity for having a political impact for transforming society at an institutional and macrosocial level (Marí, 2022).

By and large, it is a systemic analysis of the field of communication that has been neglected (Marí & Martins, 2021, p. 314), considering the geopolitical dimension of research (Demeter, 2019) from a world-system perspective and from those of structurally determined core-periphery relations (Wallerstein, 1974, 1991). This theoretical approach allows for incorporating the idea of social totality in order to contextualise individual developments and, at the same time, to frame them in specific social and historical contexts. And, indeed, the confluences between postmodernity, which accepts an unequal and unjust present, and rampant neoliberalism tend to discredit the analysis of capitalism as a totality, in a context paradoxically characterised by the totalitarianism inherent to capitalism.

All in all, the contributions of the dependistas still need to be reinterpreted in the current context of extractive and digital capitalism, characterised by old and new features. The need to frame local experiences of domination and resistance in the broader context of systemic trends is still essential. From the point of view of communication, the insight that the researchers following this approach decades ago had to frame communication in the perspective of the struggles for democratising societies and for greater social justice, is still necessary and relevant.

Communication Understood as a Commons

As has been seen in the previous section, notwithstanding the fact that the term "commons" may seem, at first sight, a current formulation, it conceals a guiding thread that leads us to a moment when, in many places in Europe, there was a transition from feudalism to capitalism. Similarly, this connection is discovered in its application in the field of communication. In this sense, Birkinbine and Kidd (2020, p. 152) suggest rethinking the communication commons, after the proliferation of this term (commons) in past few years and especially as regards the use to which it has been put "in studies of the cultural and communication practices of social change movements that have actively worked against the privatization and 'enclosure' of public goods or other commons-based resources and of the exploitation of labor".

It is an operation not without its risks, since the commons are also being currently subsumed in the logic of capital (Birkinbine, 2020). For Birkinbine (2020), free and open source software (FLOSS) emerged as an alternative to proprietary software in the 1980s. However, both the products and production processes of FLOSS have become incorporated into capitalist production. Just as the commons have been used as a motivational frame for radical social movements, so too have they served the interests of free marketeers, corporate libertarians and states to expand their reach by dragging the shared resources of social life onto digital platforms so that they can be integrated into the global capitalist system. Once again, it can be seen how caution should be taken when placing the emphasis on the alternative nature of social and communication practices so as to identify the logics with which capital appropriated such initiatives, annulling or limiting their transformative potential.

Fuchs (2021) has formulated a series of principles revolving around the digital commons, which may be useful for reflecting on communication. To this end, the author establishes four types of commons according to the sphere of society in which they operate:

- Nature (natural commons), which implies common access to natural resources for everyone.
- Economy (economic commons), namely common ownership of the means of production.
- Politics (political commons), where basic political rights are guaranteed for all.
- Culture (cultural commons), where all humans are respected and able to understand each other and live together through common practices in everyday life so that friendships and a unity of diversity of lifestyles, identities and communities are possible.

On the basis of this scheme, Fuch proposes four types and dimensions of the digital commons, which are listed below (see Table 4.1).

Using this table as a reference, it is possible to observe that, in the strict sense of the word, the communication-related aspects would correspond to the fourth type of digital commons, that is, to those that have to do with the field of culture. But, using the theme of this chapter as a reference, it can be seen that, in the broadest sense of the word, the digital commons as to the spheres of "nature", "economy" and "politics" are

Table 4.1 Four types and dimensions of digital commons

Sphere of society	Type of the digital commons	Meaning of the digital commons
Nature	Natural digital commons: digital environmental sustainability	Common control of the mines where natural resources are extracted that form the physical foundations of digital technologies, sustainable environmental impacts of digital technologies that guarantee the common survival of nature, humans and society (e.g. green computing)
Economy	Economic digital commons: digital socialism	Common ownership of the digital means of production
Politics	Political digital common: participatory digital democracy	Collective governance of decisions about the use of digital resource
Culture	Cultural digital commons: digital friendships	Unity in diversity and common recognition and respect of everyone in digitally mediated communities so that friendships are enabled

Source: Fuchs (2021)

related to communication for sustainable development (Servaes, 2017; Servaes & Malikhao, 2007, 2014; Servaes & Lie, 2015). Furthermore, the third type of digital commons (politics) can be linked to the necessary communication, developmental and technological policies that ought to spawn an alternative conception of the SDG 18.

In this way, communication understood as a digital commons traverses the four spheres proposed by Fuchs, ultimately affecting, in an interrelated manner, issues that have to do with nature, economy, politics and culture.

Proposals for the SDG 18 Understood as a Commons

The previous section has been finished with a proposal for the digital commons and how, according to Fuchs (2021, p. 20), it could be the seed of a post-capitalist project. In recent years, the term "post-capitalism" has been employed in different ways (Cruddas & Pitts, 2020; Hudis, 2012; Mason, 2015; Srnicek & Williams, 2016) to refer to a series of processes that, in one way or another, lead to the end of the capitalist world. Either owing to the collapse of the capitalist system itself or due to political action aimed at eroding capitalism and gradually constructing alternatives, the term points to the shaping of a different society, governed by other principles and values in labour, production, consumption and communication.

This new context and this new horizon pose the huge challenge of recreating the principles of sustainable communication, even more so considering the lessons learned from the COVID-19 pandemic and the new problems that this situation poses for the promotion of the SDG 18.

As already noted, in his reflections on communication and sustainable development over the past years Servaes has already referred to the dynamic properties of this branch of communication. It is a mature field settled in sub-disciplines, which has found accommodation in different fields and areas of development and social change (Servaes & Lie, 2015, p. 141). In this same vein, although going into more detail, Servaes (2017, p. 2, original emphasis) suggests that

> *Communication for Sustainable Social Change* (CSSC) has started to address these specific concerns and issues of food security, rural development, and livelihood, natural resource management and environment, poverty reduction, equity and gender, and information and communication technologies (ICTs). However, perspectives on sustainability, participation, and culture in

communication changed over time in line with the evolution of development approaches and trends, and the need for effective applications of communication methods and tools to new issues and priorities.

For Servaes and Lie (2015), the future goals that should be met include
placing human and environmental sustainability at the centre of development and social change activities, bearing in mind that sustainable interventions are necessary to ensure a world worth living in for future
generations. This being the case, problems sometimes arise, as Karmasin
and Voci (2021) note in their empirical studies, when sustainability
becomes no more than an abstract guiding principle, hard to operation-
alise in its integration in European media and communication studies curricula. In this connection, these authors observe that the level of curricular
integration of sustainability aspects in the field of the media and communication is low (14%) and very low (6%).

Accordingly, on the basis of the theoretical discussion presented here it
is possible to formulate a number of lessons that can be useful for promoting the SDG 18: "Communication for all", understood under the logic of
the commons:

- In light of the proposals of extractive capitalism, there is a pressing
  need to consider the planet's different resources as common goods
  in the four dimensions developed above (nature, economy, politics
  and culture). If this urgent need was already a challenge when the
  SDG 18 were first formulated, it is now even more so in the current
  context of the pandemic and post-pandemic, which has highlighted
  the importance of considering medicines, information and communication as common goods that should be protected from commodity logic.
- Versus the predatory logic of the major corporations currently dominating digital capitalism, it is imperative to promote digital platforms, communication groups and scientific publications governed
  by the logic of the commons, maintaining their alternative character
  with respect to the mercantilist conception of these goods.
- It is essential to recover the triple dimension of the commons proposed by De Angelis (2017) in order to discover the importance of
  considering the three aspects involved together: material and immaterial resources, the community of commoners and commoning. In
  this connection there have been initiatives in the long tradition of

ComDev and CSC which can serve as inspiration, such as those revolving around community media implemented by social movements and active citizenship. Or, nowadays, in the context of extractive capitalism, those implemented by those who practice forms of what Kidd (2019) calls extra-activism.[3]

- It is now more pressing than ever to recover and recreate, in a new context, the holistic dimension of the analysis of reality and communication proposed by the dependentists, so as to overcome the excessive fragmentation of solidarity action (NGO-isation) and mainstream solidarity communication initiatives that tend to be designed from advertising and public relations perspectives, with little or no impact on the structural transformation of society.

In sum, there is still much work to be done to make the SDG 18 "Communication for all" a reality. And, in this process, the dynamic character of communication for sustainable development offers the keys for recreating, in the uncertain times of extractivism and the post-pandemic, theoretical and practical social models that allow for promoting a communication understood as a commons. Something that, on the other hand, has belonged to the meaning of the word "communication" (*communis*, in Latin) per se since time immemorial, although this original sense has been gradually deformed, blurred and even lost.

Acknowledgements This chapter has been written in the framework of the research project of the Agencia Estatal de Investigación (AEI), "Comunicación Solidaria Digital. Análisis de los imaginarios, los discursos y las prácticas comunicativas de las ONGD en el horizonte de la Agenda 2030" (PID2019-106632GB-I00/ AEI/10.13039/501100011033)I IP: Víctor Manuel Marí Sáez.

It is also the result of a research stay, funded by the Plan Propio de la Universidad de Cádiz (EST2021-051), which the author completed at the Centro de Ciencias Humanas y Sociales (CCHS) of the Consejo Superior de Investigaciones Científicas (CSIC), on the invitation of Prof Dr José Antonio Zamora Zaragoza. And it has

---

[3] In this connection, Kidd (2019, p. 956) suggests, "Inspired by their call, this article is part of a larger study of the use of contentious communications practices in the contest between capitalist extractivism and its contentious counterpart, extra-activism; in which I utilize the autonomist Marxist composition methodology elaborated by Nick Dyer-Witheford to query the forms of counter-power possible in a highly globalized capitalism (2008). I examine the communicative goals, vision, form, content, direction and circulation of specific struggles, situated within the larger cartography and changing composition of contentious subjects, technologies and media practices."

also been funded by the EU-Next Generation/Spanish Ministry of Universities (RD 289/2021 and UNI/551/2021)/Universidad de Cádiz (UCA/R155REC/2021).

References

Acosta, A. (2011). Buen Vivir: Today's tomorrow. *Development, 54*(4), 441–447. https://doi.org/10.1057/dev.2011.86

Adorno, T. (2005). *Minima Moralia: Reflections on a damaged life.* Verso. (Original from 1951).

Álvarez, S. (2009). Beyond NGOization? Reflections from Latin America. *Development, 52*(2), 175–184. https://doi.org/10.1057/dev.2009.23

Banks, N., Hume, D., & Edwards, M. (2015). NGOs, states, and donors revisited. Still too close for comfort? *World Develpment, 66,* 707–718. https://doi.org/10.1016/j.worlddev.2014.09.028

Baran, P. (1957). *La economía política del crecimiento.* Fondo de Cultura Económica.

Beltrán, L. R. (1980). A Farewell to Aristotle: Horizontal communication. *Communication, 5,* 5–41.

Benkler, Y. (2013). Commons and growth: The essential role of open commons in market economies. *University of Chicago Law Review, 80*(1), 499–555.

Birkinbine, B. (2020). *Incorporating the digital commons: Corporate involvement in free and open source software.* University of Westminster Press.

Birkinbine, B., & Kidd, D. (2020). Re-thinking the communication commons. *Popular Communication, 18*(3), 152–154. https://doi.org/10.1080/15405702.2020.1787094

Brand, U., Dietz, K., & Lang, M. (2016). Neo-extractivism in Latin America. One side of a new phase of global capitalist dynamics. *Ciencia Política, 11*(21), 125–159.

Bustamante, E., & Corredor, P. (2016). Las políticas de comunicación y la cultura en España. Balance de una articulación siempre precaria. In J. Rius & J. A. Rubio (Eds.), *Treinta años de políticas culturales en España. Participación cultural, gobernanza territorial e industrias culturales* (pp. 285–301). Universidad de Valencia.

Cardoso, F. H., & Faletto, E. (1969). *Dependencia y desarrollo en América Latina.* Siglo XXI.

Castells, M. (1996). *The information age: Economy, society and culture. Volume I. The rise of the network society.* Blackwell.

Choudry, A., & Kapoor, D. (2012). *NGOization: Complicity, contradictions and prospects.* Zed Books.

Cruddas, J., & Pitts, F. H. (2020). The politics of postcapitalism: Labour and our digital futures. *The Political Quarterly, 91*(2), 275–286. https://doi.org/1 0.1111/1467-923X.12853

De Angelis, M. (2011). Marx and primitive accumulation: The continuous character of capital's "enclosures". *The Commoner, 2*(1), 1–22. https:// thecommoner.org/wp-content/uploads/2019/10/Marx-and-primitive-accumulation-deAngelis.pdf

De Angelis, M. (2012). Marx y la acumulación primitiva. El carácter continuo de los "cercamientos capitalistas". *Theomai: Estudios sobre Sociedad, Naturaleza y Desarrollo, 26,* 39–59.

De Angelis, M. (2017). *Omnia Sunt Communia. On the Commons and the Transformation to Postcapitalism.* Zed Books.

Demeter, M. (2019). The World-Systemic Dynamics of Knowledge Production: The distribution of Transnational Academic Capital in the Social Sciences. *Journal of World-Systems Research, 25*(1), 112–144. https://doi.org/10.5195/ jwsr.2019.887

Dos Santos, T. (1968). *El nuevo carácter de la dependencia.* Centro de Estudios Socioeconómicos.

Dyer-Witheford, N. (2008). For a compositional analysis of the multitude. In W. Bonefeld (Ed.), *Subverting the present, imagining the future* (pp. 247–265). Autonomedia.

Easterly, W. (2006). *The White Man's burden. Why the West's efforts to aid the rest have done so much ill and so little good.* Penguin Books.

Easterly, W. (2015a). The trouble with the sustainable development goals. *Current History, 114*(775), 322–324.

Easterly, W. (2015b). *The tyranny of experts: Economists, dictators and the forgotten rights of the poor.* Basic Books.

Fraser, C., & Restrepo, S. (1998). *Communicating for development: Human change for survival.* TaurIs.

Fuchs, C. (2021). The digital commons and the digital public sphere: How to advance digital democracy today. *Westminster Papers in Communication and Culture, 16*(1), 9–26. https://doi.org/10.16997/wpcc.917

Fuchs, C., & Mosco, V. (2015). *Marx in the age of digital capitalism.* Brill.

Galafassi, G., & Composto, C. (2013). Acumulación por despojo y nuevos cerca-mientos: el caso de la minería a gran escala en la Patagonia argentina. *Cuadernos del Cendes, 83,* 75–103.

Gudynas, E. (2020). Disputes over capitalism and varieties of development. In H. Veltmeyer & E. Záyago (Eds.), *Buen Vivir and the challenges to capitalism in Latin America* (pp. 194–213). Routledge. https://doi.org/10.432 4/9781003091516-13

Gumucio, A. (2011). Comunicación para el cambio social: clave del desarrollo participativo. *Signo y Pensamiento, 30*, 26–39.

Gumucio-Dagron, A., & Tufte, T. (Eds.) (2006). *Communication for Social Change Anthology: Historical and contemporary readings.* CFSC Consortium.

Gunder Frank, A. (1967). *Capitalism and underdevelopment in Latin America: Historical studies of Chile and Brazil.* Monthly Review Press.

Gurcan, E. (2015). The nonprofit-corporate complex. An integral component and driving force of imperialism in the phase of monopoly-finance capitalism. *Monthly Review, 66*(11), 37–53.

Harvey, D. (2002). *Spaces of capital.* Routledge.

Harvey, D. (2003). *The new imperialism.* Oxford University Press.

Harvey, D. (2012). The "New" imperialism: Accumulation by dispossession. In B. Ollman & B. Anderson (Eds.), *Karl Marx* (pp. 213–237). Routledge.

Hess, C., & Ostrom, E. (2007). *Understanding knowledge as commons: From theory to practice.* MIT Press. https://doi.org/10.7551/mitpress/6980.001.0001

Hornik, R. (1988). *Development communication: Information, agriculture and nutrition in the third world.* Longman.

Hudis, P. (2012). Rosa Luxemburg's concept of a post-capitalist society. *Critique, 40*(3), 323–335. https://doi.org/10.1080/00111619.2012.697758

Karmasin, M., & Voci, D. (2021). The role of sustainability in media and communication studies' curricula throughout Europe. *International Journal of Sustainability in Higher Education, 22*(6), 42–68. https://doi.org/10.1108/IJSHE-10-2020-0380

Katz, C. (2018). *La teoría de la dependencia, cincuenta años después.* Batalla de Ideas.

Katz, C. (2021). The cycle of dependency 50 years later. Latin American Persp. (First Published Online, August 30). https://doi.org/10.1177/0094582X211018475

Kidd, D. (2019). Extra-activism: Counter-mapping and data justice. *Information Communication and Society, 22*(7), 954–970. https://doi.org/10.1080/1369118x.2019.1581243

Manyozo, L. (2012). *Media, communication and development: Three aproaches.* Sage.

Marí, V. M. (2011). *Comunicar para transformar, transformar para comunicar.* Editorial Popular.

Marí, V. M. (2021). Thinking communication for social change in Spanish here and now. *Arbor, 197*(801), a615. https://doi.org/10.3989/arbor.2021.801005

Marí, V. M. (2022). NGO-ization of the solidarity in the digital era. In Gonçalves, G. & Oliveira, E., (Eds.), *The Routledge Handbook of Nonprofit Communication.* Routledge. https://doi.org/10.4324/9781003170563

Marí, V. M., & Martins, C. (2021). Communication research, the geopolitics of knowledge and publishing in high-impact journals: The chronicle of a com-modification process foretold. *TripleC, 19*(2), 307–324. https://doi.org/10.31269/triplec.v19i2.1258

Marini, R. M. (1974). *Subdesarrollo y revolución*. Siglo XXI.

Marques de Melo, J. (1984). La investigación latinoamericana en comunicación. *Chasqui, 11*, 4–11.

Mason, P. (2015). *PostCapitalism: A guide to our future*. Penguin Books.

McAnany, E. G. (2012). *Saving the world: A brief history of communication for development and social change*. University of Illinois Press.

McBride, S. (1980). *Many voices, one world. Report by the international commission for the study of communication problems*. UNESCO.

McGoey, L. (2012). Philanthrocapitalism and its critics. *Poetics, 40*(2), 185–199.

Mediavilla, J., & García-Arias, J. (2019). Philathrocapitalism as a Neoliberal (Development Agenda) artefact: philanthropic discourse and hegemony in (financing for) international development. *Globalizations, 16*(6) https://doi.org/10.1080/14747731.2018.1560187

Mesa, M. (1990). *Tercer mundo y racismo en los libros de texto*. Cruz Roja Española.

Moemeka, A. (1994). *Communicating for development: A new pan-disciplinary perspective*. State University of New York Press.

Navarro, F., & Rodríguez, P. (2018). Conceptual approximations: Popular commu-nication, community communication and alternative communication. *Commons, 7*(2), 7–66. https://doi.org/10.25267/COMMONS.2018.v7.i2.02

O'Connor, J. (2001). La segunda contradicción del capitalismo. En J. O'Connor (Ed.), *Causas naturales. Ensayos de marxismo ecológico* (pp. 191–212). Siglo XXI.

Oldekop, J. A., Hotner, R., Hulme, D., et al. (2020). Covid-19 and the case for global development. *World Development, 134*, 1–4. https://doi.org/10.1016/j.worlddev.2020.105044

Ramalingam, B. (2013). *Aid on the edge of chaos: Rethinking international coopera-tion in a complex world*. Oxford University Press.

Rodríguez, D. (2007). The political logic of the non-profit industrial complex. In INCITE! (Ed.), *The revolution will not be funded: Beyond the non-profit indus-trial sector* (pp. 21–22). South End Press.

Schiller, D. (2000). *Digital capitalism: Networking the global market system*. MIT Press.

Schiller, H. (1969). *Mass communication and American Empire*. Kelley.

Servaes, J. (1989). *One world, multiple cultures: A new paradigm on communica-tion for development*. Acco.

Servaes, J. (1999). *Communication for development. One world, multiple cultures*. Hampton Press.

Servaes, J. (Ed.). (2002). *Approaches to development communication*. UNESCO.
Servaes, J. (Ed.). (2017). *Sustainable development goals in the Asian context*. Springer.
Servaes, J., & Lie, R. (2013). Sustainable social change and communication. *Communication Research Trends, 32*(4), 4–30.
Servaes, J., & Lie, R. (2015). New challenges for communication for sustainable development and social change: A review essay. *Journal of Multicultural Discourses, 10*(1), 124–148. https://doi.org/10.1080/1744714 3.2014.982655
Servaes, J., & Malikhao, P. (Eds.). (2007). *Communication and sustainable development. Selected papers from the 9th UN roundtable on communication for development*. FAO.
Servaes, J., & Malikhao, P. (2014). Communication for Development and Social Change: Three Development Paradigms, Two Communication Models, Many Applications and Approaches. In J. Hong (Ed.), *New Trends in Communication Studies Vol. 1* (pp. 20–45). Tsinghua University Press.
Srnicek, N. (2017). *Platform capitalism*. Polity Press.
Srnicek, N., & Williams, A. (2016). *Inventing the future. Postcapitalism and a world without work*. Verso Books.
Svampa, M. (2015). Commodities consensus: Neoextractivism and enclosure of the commnos in Latin America. *The South Atlantic Quarterly, 114*(1), 65–82. https://doi.org/10.1215/00382876-2831290
Svampa, M. (2019). *Las fronteras del neoextractivismo en América Latina: conflictos socioambientales, giro ecoterritorial y nuevas dependencias*. Calas.
Thomas, P. (2017). The contributions of Raymond Williams and E.P. Thompson to communication and social change theory and practice. *European Journal of Communication, 32*(5), 405–418. https://doi.org/10.1177/0267323117723968
Thompson, E. P. (1963). *The making of the English working class*. Victor Gollanez.
Thorup, M. (2013). Pro bono? On philanthrocapitalism as ideological answer to inequality. *Ephemera: Theory & Politics in Organization, 13*(3), 555–576.
Veltmeyer, H., & Petras, J. (Eds.). (2014). *The new extractivism: A post-neoliberal development model or imperialism of the twenty-first century?* Zed Books.
Wallerstein, I. (1974). *The Modern World-System: Capitalist Agriculture and the Origins of the European World-Economy in the Sixteenth Century*. Academic Press.
Wallerstein, I. (1991). *Geopolitics and Geoculture: Essays on the Changing World-System*. Cambridge University Press.
Wang, Y., & Marí, V. M. (2021). The Covid-19 pandemic in China and the entertainment education as communicative strategy against the misinformation. In J. Sierra Sánchez & A. Barrientos (Eds.), *Cosmovisión de la comunicación en redes sociales en la era postdigital* (pp. 675–698). McGraw-Hill.

Wilkins, K., & Enghel, F. (2013). The privatization of development through global communication industries: Living Proof? Media. *Media, Culture & Society, 35*(2), 165–181. https://doi.org/10.1177/0163443712468606

Wilkins, K. et al. (2014). *The handbook of development communicatin and social change*. John Wiley & Sons.

Yusha'u, M. J., & Servaes, J. (2021). Communication for sustainable development in the age of COVID-19. In M. J. Yusha'u & J. Servaes (Eds.), *The Palgrave handbook of international communication and sustainable development* (pp. 3–30). Palgrave Macmillan.

CHAPTER 5

Six Information and Communication Dynamics That Call for the Adoption of an 18th Sustainable Development Goal

Andrea Ricci

Abstract Coordinated policies ought to be launched to counter the detrimental effects on the development of the six forces that shape contemporary information and communication ecosystems. The first force is the logarithmic growth of information, particularly, but not only in the social media landscape. The second force is produced by the phenomena of the reflectivity of information and the impacts of reverb tails. The third force comes from the presumed recipients of information which have increasingly inconstant and insufficient attention. The fourth force is played by competition which disaggregates communities, including those of media and intelligence practitioners. The fifth force is brought by propaganda

The opinions expressed within this chapter are solely the author's and do not reflect the opinions and beliefs of the European External Action Service (EEAS).

A. Ricci (✉)
European External Action Service, Brussels, Belgium

© The Author(s), under exclusive license to Springer Nature
Switzerland AG 2023
J. Servaes, M. J. Yusha'u (eds.), *SDG18 Communication for All,*
Volume 1, Sustainable Development Goals Series,
https://doi.org/10.1007/978-3-031-19142-8_5

which dominates in a time erroneously considered as peaceful. The sixth force is introduced by oblivion and its growing black hole, the edges of which seem to start just after real time experiences.

The six forces strike at the very core the metabolism of development; fostering the growth of cultures which hamper progress; limiting the understanding of 'what works' to an elite of monads with little capacity or willingness to coalesce; even endangering—with intelligence failures or ineffective risk analysis—the survival of individuals, companies, and State organisations. The sequence of strategic intelligence failures since 9/11, the incapacity to stop climate change, the unfolding of the COVID pandemic, the challenges brought by globalisation and social media to companies' growth and individuals can all be analysed under the lens of epistemic and cultural disservices induced by the influence of the six forces. The forces have in the past already challenged society. Today the energy behind the forces is dangerous: in stark contrast with the amount of information and communication at our disposal, basic certainties seem unknowable, weak, and questionable. Acts of governance are necessary to inverse the polarity at each of these six levels, truly supporting all other sustainable development goals (SDGs).

Keywords Information overload • Information directionality • Attention • Competition • Propaganda • Oblivion

INTRODUCTION

In 1827 Johann Wolfgang von Goethe wrote to his grand nephew Alfred Nicolovius a prophetic letter. He described his post-Napoleonic era as accelerating forward with dangerous speed. He employed the term *velociferisch*, a crasis between the words fast and Luciferus. The industrial revolution is for him an age of excess: nothing has the time to mature, «one moment is consumed by the next, and the day spent in the day; so that a man is always living from hand to mouth» (Bailey Sounders, 1908, p. 68).

Osten (2013) underlines that Goethe had realised the compulsory unleashing of the booming public sphere of his time: «Daily criticisms in fifty different places,…a sort of half culture of the masses; for the more talented, they constituted a noxious mist, a descending poison » (Goethe,

2019). Goethe, an observer of the globalisation of culture in his time (Pizer, 2000), once exclaimed «Have we not already newspapers for every hour of the day!». He was probably not exaggerating, if we consider that in Great Britain alone, in the single month of January 1827, 845 issues of 105 newspapers were in circulation.

Few years before, in 1824, the word 'star' was first used in England to describe the capacity for a single actress to sell out the entire capacity of a theatre (Van Krieken, 2019a): numerous women, from Sarah Bernhardt, to George Sand, Rosa Bonheur, and Lola Montez, were to achieve public celebrity status through their eccentric and intellectual qualities. Their contemporary heiresses are today Lady Gaga, Chiara Ferragni, Amelie Nothomb, J. K. Rowling, or Anna Gavalda.

In 1857 the Sepoy Mutiny, a violent uprising against British rule in India, also known as the 'Indian rebellion', triggered an active propaganda campaign in England both in printed form and through political cartoons (Summers, 2015). Today, some 45 million pages of recent google news carry the term propaganda, and A. I. (Artificial Intelligence) enabled deep fakes are producing a step-change in psy-ops and information warfare.

Much like today, the first half of the nineteenth century was marked by the effects of an expansive wave of globalisation. The colonial state was to bring to society a much greater set of products, due to its impact on manufacturing and trade, and many options and novelties in terms of infrastructure, science, and education. It was an age of acceleration. It wasn't uncommon back then to feel overwhelmed by overflows. Littau (2006) underlines in this respect the 'countless warnings' in the nineteenth century about «too much print, too much writing, too much reading».

Within the limits of comparative history, it is possible to reflect on the commonalities between historical phases characterised by a rampant growth of information and communication flows and its by-products: from celebrity production, to propaganda, from the excitement deriving from new intelligence on business opportunities, to the disorienting or even threatening sense of information overload.

The simultaneous presence of cofactors like globalisation waves, technical breakthrough in the production or the distribution of information and knowledge, economic growth and market liquidity, entrepreneurship and maecenatism, can be identified in several historical periods.

Way before the nineteenth century, these phenomena were already gathered, albeit in different proportions: between 1250 and 1350, before the European hegemony (Abu-Lughod, 1989); in 1536 when in Venice the official news (*fogli avvisi*) on the crisis with the Turkish empire were on sale for a *gaxeta* (the name of the two *soldi* coin); or later, in the seventeenth and eighteenth century, when the Portuguese, Spanish, Dutch, and British empires created the conditions for heightened levels of material and immaterial exchanges (Hopkins, 2011).

THE SIX FORCES

Today, the information and communication ecosystems that surround us are dominated by the same forces which were active during Goethe's time. The big difference lies in their intensity. In this chapter, I argue that these forces are so great today that they have the potential, if unchecked, to negatively affect cognitive mechanisms in key public policies. They create a context in which the nature of policy change and its implementation become increasingly problematic, dysfunctional, and unsustainable. A context in which social evolution can slow down drastically. A context in which countries can be brought against a form of 'civilisational ceiling' (Bronner, 2021) or even accelerate instability and economic decline. It seems therefore paradoxical, against the large array of analyses reviewed here, all focusing on the negative externalities generated in the cognitive sphere by the internet and social media in particular, that one of the greatest policy exercises for global progress, the sustainable development goals (SDGs), omits to integrate an information and communication dimension.

The forces which materialise today in our information and communication ecosystems affect, at its core, the metabolism of development, hampering progress through its epistemic pathways. From a policy making perspective, six of these forces have a very peculiar relevance for the nature of their individual by products, but also, and above all, by their capacity to stack up, multiplying their impact on communities.

Grounded in practice and in literature, this work aims at addressing the concerns of SDGs policy makers and policy analysts. My hope is to contribute to the debate on the enlargement of the blueprint for peace and development which the SDGs represent. To achieve this, in the first section of the chapter, I will first review what we know already of these energy factors and then describe the reasons why each of the forces can condition policy makers.

In the following section, I will focus on intelligence at large (secret, open, business, strategic intelligence) as a *progress catalyser* and explain how the new context set by the six forces blocks the cognitive pathways that lead to meaningful decisions and sustainable change.

In the third section, I will explain why *SDG goals are wicked problems* and show how the forces concur to produce 'cognitive (perfect) storms', such as Sri Lanka's very problematic plunge into organic farming in 2021.

Finally, I will examine a set of structures or typologies of projects which might provide controls over the negative influence of the six forces.

My argument is that an urgent call for action is needed to unite developed and developing countries in a new dimension of partnership. We need a new development goal: to restore the full evolutionary potential of mission-critical expert knowledge; protecting it from the impact of the six forces. But let us first discover, or re-discover, the six forces.

INFORMATION OVERLOAD

The first force is generated by the growth of information in all its forms: data, texts, videos or pictures. Some 3.2 billion images and 720,000 hours of video are circulated every day on social media (Angus et al., 2020). According to former Google's CEO, Eric Schmidt, the latest estimate of size of the internet is 5 million terabytes (but only 0.004% has been indexed by Google). One last figure: the global internet traffic in 2021 was equivalent to 135 times the volume of the entire global internet in 2005 (CISCO, 2016).

Everyone has an awareness of this facet of reality. The Google Ngram Viewer, which measures how a word or phrase has occurred in a corpus of books over the years, shows that the concept of *information explosion*, had a sudden a spike towards the end of the 1960s. From that moment onwards, the correlated notion of *information overload* has never ceased to grow in popularity.

There have been a variety of theoretical reference points for the writers working with the concept of the geometric growth of information, including Bell (1976) and Touraine (1971) 'Post Industrial Society', Habermas' (1991) 'structural transformation of the public sphere', Castells' (2010) 'Network Society' trilogy, Norris' (2001) digital divide', Lyon's (2013), and Webster's (2014) 'Information Society'. The common and central argument in these works is that the growth of information is positively correlated with disintermediation and the reshuffling of key social hierarchies, speed, virtualisation (the decline of physical boundaries and distances), innovation-driven economic growth, the rise of investments in new forms of internet-centric businesses, a growing competition between traditional media and social media, and the strategic role played by searching and filtering tools.

In contrast with positive narratives on the information society, Morehead (2000) and Servaes (2003) highlighted that this explosion was and still is leaving behind large cohorts of *information have-nots*. In a similar critical vein, George Akerlof, Michael Spence, and Joseph Stiglitz (Stiglitz, 2000; Barkley Rosser, 2003), by examining the actions of uninformed agents in a market characterised by asymmetric information, paved the way to the understanding that information is highly expensive and does not grow in equal proportions for each subject.

Information asymmetry actually creates an environment where *strong signals* kill *weak signals*. Signal strength orients value allocation and attention in favour of a relatively small number of strong information entities. Weak signals, notwithstanding the intentions of the publishers or the predictive relevance of the information they carry, behave like *functional secrets*. This peculiar category of secrets is growing in size every day. In this context, selective attention can become quite prejudicial, particularly for policy based organisations.

Claude Silberzahn, a former DGSE (Directorate General for External Security) Chief, famously said (Silberzahn, 1995): 'what is secret is deducted from what is open: all that is open and all that is being opened'. Silberzahn invited us to critically question the boundaries of an effective *horizon scan*: in a world characterised by information asymmetry, the value chain of secrecy must start from open sources, which constantly reveal new, important findings on the issues that surround us.

Few years before Silberzahn, Richard Saul Wurman (1989) with *Information Anxiety* had already warned us of the widening gap between what 'we understand and what we think we should understand', considering the ever growing set of new information been produced on any given subject. Wurman (1989, p. 39) identified three key *catalysers* able to reduce information anxiety: adequate transmission (voluntary information sharing), adequate memorisation, and adequate understanding. We shall see later on how the growth of some of the six forces has greatly reduced the sequence of reactions induced by Wurman's *enzyms*, reducing the overall access to critical intelligence (on virtually any subject, of personal and collective interest).

One of the key consequences of the first force for policy makers is that functional secrets are silently becoming much more significant in quality and quantity than traditional, normative secrets. From risk analysis, to strategic forecasting and planning, from intelligence collection, to policy options development, functional secrets, lost in a sea of open sources, can be game-changers for States or organisations which have the right tools and a modern intelligence strategy.

Old strategies assume limitless analytical assets and are quite dysfunctional when coping with information asymmetry. New strategies assume less peer based cooperation, and leverage on technologies which extract value from open sources.

With the six forces, policy makers focusing on security issues or economic sovereignty must view open sources as precursors of secrecy, and must adopt an ultra wide angle lens when monitoring insecurity and opportunities. No matter where violence occurs, the seeds of that violence might inseminate diasporic communities in any sub-urban area. No matter where science reveals a new process which alters the strategic relevance of a commodity, that transformation may change the future of a local territory, which is currently struggling for socio-economic survival.

Defective Information Directionality

The second force is produced by the peculiar way information now travels on media. Increasingly, signals loose their directionality: their initial aim is dissociated from their final target. This specific phenomenon appears to augment with the geometric growth of the sources and the ever greater mobility of the audience. Projecting with greater power a signal in a specific direction with increased performance and reduced interference from unwanted sources is, for many (both individuals and organisations), an increasingly difficult and unreliable process; a major source of frustration, costs, and uncertainty.

A first crucial element that policy makers must factor in, with a *second force-regulated ecosystem*, is the cost of precision targeting. Communication directionality has been profoundly altered by the impact of programmatic/algorithmic advertising on Google, social media, but also, and increasingly so, on digital audio, display, and connected television. Against the background of a *programmatic* directionality of communications, several collinear changes are materialising, including: the inevitable decline of linear TV and printed press (The Trade Desk, 2020; Digital News Report 2021, p. 14), a broad re-regulation of the gatekeeping function (Westley & MacLean, 1957), and the re-definition of key theoretical concepts which have structured communication theories until the early 1990s and the birth of the World Wide Web.

The notion of feedback has, for example, evolved into the notion of *audience activation* and *engagement* both implying real time bidding (for attention) from the advertisers' side. Primary or reference groups (Riley & Riley, 1951, 1959) have lost social structure importance in favour of transversal *buzz* or *viral eruptions* (Meerman Scott, 2011, p. 95; Beauvisage et al., 2011). The difference between public and private signals in interpersonal communication (Barnlund, 2008, 2013) has morphed into the expression 'you are what you publish'. Message contextualisation now occurs with tags and keywords and, as Instagram hashtags eloquently prove, it's very often artificial.

The 2021 Reuters Institute Digital News Report shows that information *reflectivity* (sharing news via social media, messaging or email) is a reality for 37% of the news consumers surveyed in 44 countries around the world. Information sharing increases the length of reverb tails (the decay of information once the direct signal has stopped), and this occurs both:

- superficially (59% of people sharing information have only read the title of the article—Gabielkov et al., 2016);
- through plagiarism (Cage et al., 2018);
- through tactical 'newsjaking' (injecting one's ideas into a breaking news story to attract traffic—Meerman Scott, 2011);
- or through organic 'echo chambers' (crowded by users in homophilic clusters, dominating online interactions on Facebook and Twitter—Cinelli et al., 2021).

For policy makers, information reverberation has ambiguous connotations: on one side it's functional to the cognitive strategies of propagandists (repetition augments the life span and retention of information in short term memory), it can confere a sense of naturalness and acceptability to State policies. On the flip side, it can also have adverse effects: when, for example, the chaotic interaction between the State's and its antagonists' respective reverberations generates noise detrimental to the intelligibility of all signals.

Policy makers should retain that—under the impact of the second force—*policy relevant signals* which are not sustained by advertising investments are too weak to be heard organically. Without adequate funds, there is no enzymatic reaction and the cognitive pathway is locked.

Audience activation is uncertain by default because *visibility algorithms*—our modern gatekeepers—are both constantly updated and their rationale is kept deliberately secret. A conspicuous level of advertising investment can trigger the gate opening. An even greater level of advertising investments can reveal, through inverse engineering, the precise contours of a visibility algorithm, before it's changed again. Public communicators are therefore either forced to try to collect the free crumbs of algorithmic intelligence fallen off the tables of actors which operate way above them in the (publicity) food chain, or contribute to the spending in digital advertising (estimated at 455.3$ bill. worldwide in 2021; Statista Research Department, 2021), accepting the fees of independent media buying platforms which promise the 'precision to reach the right audience anywhere'.

Scarce Attention

The third force is produced by the increasingly volatile and insufficient audience attention. Klapp (1986) was one of the first voices to link the information society's information overload, to entropy, loss of quality of life, but also redundancy, noise, and boredom.

In the mid-1990s, Google's NGRAM showed the start of a massive spike of collective interest for the question of the *attention economy*, described by numerous scholars as:

- by-product of the web's hyperlinked architecture (Turow & Tsui, 2008);
- as the new currency of business (Davenport & Beck, 2002);
- as the real source of value in advertising (cost per *valuable* impression or qCPM—Nelson-Field, 2020);
- as the true by-product of capitalist narratives on efficiency and techno-determinism (Odell, 2019);
- as a new economic system based on the commodification of personal data and attention (for the benefit of an oligopoly of *surveillance capitalists*—Zuboff, 2019);
- or, finally, as the true driver of the ever growing interest to become a celebrity, a *brand* or a *mental capitalist* (the latter, in the academic sphere—Franck, 2019; van Krieken, 2019b).

Gerald Bronner (2021) provides a mature reflection on how our capital of almost five hours per day of *mental freedom* is used today. He points out that in France, and arguably in many developed countries, people have today five times more attention capital than in the 1900s and eight times more compared to the 1800s (Mermet, 2013). Yet, recent statistics from eMarketer (Zalani, 2021) indicate that the average US adult spends 3 hours and 54 minutes on their mobile devices, whereas Statista reveals that more than 40% of the US adults spend between 5 and 7 hours on their smartphones. The key point made by Bronner is that a *revelation* on the true nature of people' cognitive preferences is emerging from clinical psychology and analyses of online behaviours (Liu et al., 1998; Rozin & Royzman, 2001; Nielsen & Sarason, 1981; Haselton & Nettle, 2006; Siegrist & Cvetkovich, 2001; Bronner, 2021, pp. 127–149; Krasnova et al., 2013; RSPH, 2017; Deaner et al., 2005; Stephens-Davidowitz, 2017): in a deregulated cognitive market, relations between content demand and offer are fluid, and this freedom abandons crowds to the effect of *addictive loops* which are deeply enrooted in evolutionary human neurophysiology. Bronner in particular warns against the overstimulation of the dopaminergic pathways by *likes* and notifications (Haynes, 2018), but also against the brain's obsessive-compulsive hypersensitivity to negative messages, conflictuality, risks, fear, sex, information incompleteness (produced e.g. by *clickbait* links), narcissism (insta-egocentric information, selfies), social benchmarking/validation, fake news, and the large nomenklatura of micro celebrities.

What policy makers should retain of the third force are three keywords: loss of productivity, radical intolerance, and *new poors*. These are all bad metabolites which are generated by a cognitive pathway deregulated by attention modifications.

The third force puts productivity at risk at any level of social development: in a pre-social media era, studies already indicated that 28% of an average working day was hijacked in the US by interruptions and other attention related issues (increased errors and anxiety) with an estimated cost of 588$ billion yearly (Spira & Feintuch, 2005; Spira, 2005; Bailey & Konstan, 2006).

Secondly, social media induced anxiety fosters radicalisation. Social media interest for risks, religiously motivated violence, or mortality tends to increase prejudice, intolerance to deviance, and people's interest for authoritarian ideas (Greenberg et al., 1990). As Bronner observes (2021, pp. 123–180):

It's understandable that people that feel insecure because they think they live in a poisoned world, or in decadence, or simply because they believe they are losing their autonomy and their sovereignty, claim back full control of their environment.

We contemplate the emergence [therefore] of these societies where frustration cyclically turns into a form political anger which seeks culprits: the State, the elites, oligarchs, the system....

This background gives opportunities to new populists to produce a kind of *cognitive demagogy* (Bronner, 2021, p. 300) where politicians fake a proximity with the base, and deal with the pathologies of the system either pretending that more *transparency* is thaumaturgic, or, alternatively, advocating *participatory* democracy solutions, where the delegitimisation of experts goes hand in hand with the overvaluation of popular common sense.

Thirdly, policy makers should consider that the digital divide is not separating today the information haves from the have nots, but it's actually creating cohorts of *cognitive poors*, with the most disadvantaged communities spending the biggest part of their mental freedom on smartphones screens (Bronner, 2021 p. 350).

COMPETITION

The fourth force is played by the extraordinary web-centric competition and its off-line impact on cognitive circuits.

We know from microeconomics that competition is affected by product features, number of sellers, barriers to entry, information availability, and location. All these factors exist online and have quasi perfect conditions for synergy. Information products are easy to manufacture, there's a plethora of players due to the democratisation of both access and software production tools, and finally, the web offers a solution to the constraints of time and space. Two hundred years after Goethe's remarks, Bronner argues (2021, p. 13):

anyone can pour his/her own world representation in this ocean [of ideas]..., [this is] not the first time in history that belief and methodic thought are in competition—but it's the first time ....that someone with a social account contradicts an Emeritus Medicine professor on vaccines, while having a far greater set of followers than the professor himself.

A key point for policy makers is that online, and, increasingly, off-line too, information quality deteriorates under the effect of competition. The availability of a key cognitive enzyme—time—is inadequate. There is no time to verify, and there is too much collective pressure to bury the previous information with a new one, meant to captivate the limited attention available. Popular information is very often of bad quality (Weng et al., 2012; Qiu et al., 2017) and in stark contrast with utopian visions of cyberspace based on Thomas Jefferson's ideas ('truth can stand by itself', Jefferson, 1785, p. 170).

A second important reminder for policy makers, active in capacity-building, is that competition disaggregates communities. When this occurs within the media ecosystem, the result is a growing risk aversion from the publishers' side, and a uniformisation towards consensual content, in line with the expectations of the majority. When competition occurs within the intelligence community, the result is a far greater risk of strategic surprise and intelligence failures. When think tanks in countries in transition are in an adversarial posture, strong departmental affiliations with specific ministries become even stronger, drastically weakening interaction with research counterparts and producing a broad governance problem.

Policy makers should retain that, 20 years after the call for action advocated by the 9/11 Commission Report (2004), the culture of the *need to know* is still much, much stronger than the culture of the *need to share*. In a hyper competitive environment, the poor fluidity of high value information is the great antagonist to progress and the kind of partnerships advocated by the SDGs.

PROPAGANDA

The fifth force is brought by propaganda, which truly dominates the public sphere in many societies.

In *The Early Political Web (1995–2005)* (Ricci, 2013) I scrutinised the largest dataset of political parties available at the time of writing (n = 2073) and concluded that the early adopters of the political web already showed little interest to practice true, inclusive, deliberative, participatory democracy.

From 2001 onwards, numerous scholars (Bunt, 2003, 2018; Vacca, 2021; Conway & MacDonald, 2021) have pointed out how the web has been a crucial factor to foster digital jihad, as a form of militant propaganda. The internet has provided violent political groups with training tools, logistical solutions (including Daesh travel guides to enter Syria from Turkey), and adequate encryption to operate undetected by national security organisations.

Tristan Harris, former design ethicist at Google, in his hearings in front of the US legislators (CNBC Television, 2019; Center for Humane Technology, 2020) stressed that the bulk of communication online is based on a business model which exploits an *invisible asymmetric power relation* between social media (which are still treated as fiduciaries) and web users. His thesis is that multi-million dollar revenues of online corporations are based on algorithmically promoted polarisation and persuasion techniques that range from the *pull-to-refresh news, infinite scrolling feeds,* and *AI enabled loyalty prediction.*

Several genuses of epistemic disservices (classic forms of propaganda, disinformation, or complex *influence operations*—IO) affected the 2016 elections in the US, in the Philippines, but also the 2014 and 2019 polls in Indonesia (Oxford Analytical Aug. 13, 2021). Facebook (Facebook, 2021) acknowledges that since 2017 the platform was used by 150 CIB (Coordinated Inauthentic Behavior) networks, mainly originating from Russia, Iran, Myanmar, US and Ukraine. These CIBs have been, inter alia, responsible for encouraging violence against the Muslim Rohingya in Myanmar, aiding a bloodshed which pushed nearly one million refugees across the border into Bangladesh (APHR, 2020).

The existing Western policy response against online propaganda is producing little impact. Third party fact checking services produce far less information than CIB networks. US parliamentary scrutiny on Facebook has not drastically altered the company's practices (Facebook's generously funded Oversight Board is probably the only remarkable change so far).

« Facebook does not have the systems to manage the scale of the enterprise they now have», underlines David Kirkpatrick, author of *The Facebook Effect*, in a BBC Tech Tent (2021) interview, « ...Of the 3 million employee/hours to tackle disinformation in 2020 only 13% goes outside the US, for a service which is 90% outside the United States». Worse: «Facebook knows, in acute detail, that its platforms are riddled with flaws that cause harm, often in ways only the company fully understands». That is the key take-away of Wall Street Journal *Facebook files*, produced on the basis of the documents leaked by Frances Haugen.

Fundamentally, the problem remains twofold: on one side, the goals embedded in the business model of social media remain the same, and on the other, many societies seem incapable of fighting fake news. In an attempt to counter disinformation and COVID vaccine resistance, Thailand, Malaysia, Singapore, and Vietnam have tried to impose fines and other corrective measures to fake news, but observers have argued that the pandemic has only worsened the discretionary aspects of these legislations (Oxford Analytical Aug. 13, 2021). Similar controversial results on the criminalisation of social media posts, critical of the government, have occurred in Tanzania in 2020, and in Uganda in 2019.

Large countries tend to be even more heavy handed. The preferred authoritarian solution to the restoration of political control, notably in electoral periods, is a shutdown of the internet. In the developing world, 29 countries have operated shut downs in 2020: India alone, the world's largest democracy, has generated 109 documented shutdowns in 2020, and 21 between January and May 2021 (Oxford Analytica June 29, 2021).

Policy makers should note that the fifth force does not only materialise with trolls factory located in Russia or China. A 2019 report by the Oxford's University Computational Propaganda Research Project (Bradshaw & Howard, 2019) has provided evidence of disinformation campaigns in 70 countries with India, Iran, Pakistan, Saudi Arabia, and Venezuela as growing state actors. According to the Pew Research Centre, the impact of misinformation is a key concern for 11 emerging economies (Silver, 2019).

Many know that the data points generated through the use of Facebook have been used by Cambridge Analytica to influence the course of 200 elections in 68 countries. In contrast, few know that recent research indicates that psychological profiling can be predicted without interacting with the application programming interface of social media platforms (only mouse movements and clicks patterns suffice—Khan et al., 2008, 2015—or, alternatively, other patterns collected with smartphones—Stachl et al., 2020).

Since the creation of the Propaganda Commission in Rome in 1622, it has never been so easy to create cognitive devices that can hit many thousands of people simultaneously. The analysis of a dataset of rumor cascades on Twitter from 2006 to 2017, spread by ~3 million people, shows that the top 1% of false news diffused to between 1000 and 100,000 people, whereas *Jeffersonian truth* rarely diffused to more than 1000 people (Vosoughi et al., 2018). Lies have a far greater kinetic efficiency online than truth because they correspond to the general cognitive preferences of the public (Acerbi, 2019). Lies can leverage on the compound product of cultural stereotypes, tens of cognitive biases, the surprise effect and the full gamut of our psychological weaknesses, from anxiety to narcissism (Bronner, 2003).

Policy makers should retain these essential points on the strength of propaganda today. Social media are providing incentives to media, politicians, and political activists to post divisive content which circulates faster and more widely, particularly on Facebook which is dominating news sourcing. The by-product of widespread propaganda (misinformation or fake news) requires a constant and very significant drain of resources—from both individuals and organisations—to qualify and eventually invalidate not only reported news, but also, increasingly, argumented analysis. The Brandolini law (also known as the *bullshit asymmetry principle*—Brandolini, 2013) eloquently states that it takes far more time to disproof a propaganda device than to manufacture it. The cost of truth—in an info-obese world—has never been so high.

The practical issue is that too often and in too many fields, the information and communication ecosystem is the stage of hostilities between two parties which reciprocally accuse one another to push an *un-evidenced policy* in the public sphere or to use their *un-evidenced ideology* to influence a given community.

A common reply given to mainstream media when they interview anti-vax communities is: 'I do my own research, and I have come to the conclusion that they are hiding the truth'. A persistent, growing perception of being manipulated, or of being victims of a logical fallacy or cognitive illusion, affects the public of many debates. A massively deregulated cognitive market, or the market of ideas, argues Bronner, massively raises public uncertainties.

OBLIVION

The sixth force—the collective failure to remember—is correlated to the first, but operates on its own, in the background of the cognitive scene. Hermann Ebbinghaus' forgetting curve (only one hour after learning, retention of a subject lowers to 44%) has quite a different significance today if one considers, in parallel, Buckminster Fuller and Kuromiya's

(1978) *knowledge doubling curve* (knowledge doubles every 25 years since the end of World War II).

There is no doubt that, whether we speak of knowledge or unstructured data, whether we agree or not to Buckminster Fuller's definition of knowledge, whether we prefer instead to focus on the speed with which knowledge becomes obsolete (Fritz Machlup's *knowledge half-life*) or whether we argue that the rate of *half-life* varies very much with topic area (Arbesman, 2014), information growth is seemingly unstoppable and geometric. The point here is that this growth generates an enormous pressure to discharge short term memory both at personal (by decay, interference, or repression) and at an organisational (organisational memory loss) level.

The sixth force has three interesting dimensions:

First, a neurophysiological one. The *velociferish* focus on short term and discontinuity does not help the audience sort real from fake. It's the contemporary curse of mankind, as Jacques Ellul (1965) wrote in *Propagandes*:

> Precisely because he is in the bath of current news, this type of man is characterised by a psychological fragility which puts him at the disposal of the propagandist. Never there is confrontation between event and truth. There is no relationship between the event and the person. Current news never [directly] concern anybody.

Secondly, the sixth force is reinforced institutionally and structurally. Loss of organisational memory is on the rise because very few organisations have inscribed this process among the important internal corporate functions or have dedicated assets invested in memory preservation (Langenmayr, 2016).

Thirdly, the sixth force is sociologically reinforced. The decline of historical knowledge in the US is already tangible and measurable (BA History represents less than 2% of all undergraduate degrees—Brookings, 2016; Schmidt, 2018), it's financially motivated (Malcolm, 2013), and frankly dangerous for citizens. As the *New Yorker* noted in 2019, halfway through the Trump Presidency: «A nation whose citizens have no knowledge of history is asking to be led by quacks, charlatans, and jingos» (Alterman, 2019).

The sixth force threatens policy makers at various levels. A focus on 'short term supports and resistances', often the result of individual and organisational choices (Laverty, 1996; Marginson & McAulay, 2008) induces governments to abandon prior governments' (development) plans without considering the wider national implications. The dangerous, but evolutionary, preference for intuition (Daniel Kahneman's *System 1*) sets the boundaries of oblivion's black hole almost on the edges of live experiences.

A COALITION TO ANTAGONISE DEVELOPMENT COMMUNICATION

To resume: the context in which policy makers, today, have to create sustainable change is characterised by six stacked and mutually reinforcing dynamics. Functional secrets are growing; State communication on policies is too weak to be heard organically; lack of attention creates cognitive poors; competition tends to deteriorate information quality and weakens all the key actors of cognitive cycles (media, intelligence agencies, and think tanks); social media are providing everyone incentives to post divisive content; and the geometric growth of information generates an enormous pressure to discharge short term memory both at personal and organisational levels.

Policy change or policy reform are tough businesses, in these circumstances.

I argue that the interplay between the six forces or the sequential stacking of their impact is already very clearly showing its capacity to endanger the road to social progress for both developed and developing countries. The forces coalesce to antagonise the very process of *development communication* which Servaes and Malikhao (2005) define as:

> The sharing of knowledge aimed at reaching a consensus for action that takes into account the interests, needs and capacities of all concerned.

Communication media—to paraphrase Fair (1989)—become here the *magic demultipliers*, decelerating and reducing the benefit of development.

Traditional theoretical paradigms in development communication studies (modernisation, dependency, multiplicity, participation, all comprehensively reviewed in Servaes & Lie, 2013) applied in a scenario dominated by the six forces, lead to new, disarming research questions:

- Through the *modernisation theory* lens we can easily quantify the raise in access to mobile internet solutions everywhere around the world, but we can hardly quantify the losses in terms of *cultural capital* both in the north and in the south.
- Through the *dependency theory* lens we can still see the systemic interdependencies, but we can hardly distinguish the victimiser from the the victim,
- Through the *cultural multiplicity* theory we can still perceive the contours of homogenous communities, but these can be much less explained in terms of of geography (centre vs. Periphery, global vs. National vs. Local). Instead, Bourdieu's multifactorial cultural consumption patterns appear to be much more relevant today. Yet, these complex patterns are hard to exploit as, today, preferences change at warp speed.
- Through the *participatory* lens, we understand that the point of departure, the community, should remain the locus of 'information sharing, knowledge, trust, commitment, and a right attitude in development projects' (FAO, 2007, p. 4). Yet, we see in the largest democracies of both north and south, (geographical) communities that regress to a tribal state, challenged by (online/non-geographical) hierarchies. People refuse to live next to neighbours who don't share their politics; negotiation and compromise are perceived as betrayal, and advocacy communication is not effective because there is not enough attention capital. The Freirian argument (participatory communication works because is based on the *theology of the respect of others* and because collective solutions have their own cogency— Servaes & Malikhao, 2005) is not negated by elites, but by masses that lack self-management.

This is an environment which encourages individuals and organisations to take absurd decisions (Morel, 2002), constantly making 'radical and persisting errors'. It's also a context which generates unforgivable lost opportunities, retrogression, and dissolution.

THE STACKED IMPACT OF THE FORCES ON INTELLIGENCE AND ON GROWTH

Let me now briefly focus on the details of the *stacking* of the six forces. This is important because, as in systems theory or Gestalt, the *whole is something besides the parts.*

The disturbing charm of the interaction between the six forces lies in its simplicity. It could be qualified as a series of harmful reactions occurring in a deregulated metabolism.

Information overload augments oblivion and paves the way for propaganda. It becomes complex for individuals and organisations to collect vital *functional secrets* on policy issues because too many pre-requisites are necessary to really exploit *open* sources. Competition at personal, organisational, local, national, and international level antagonises the culture of the need to share. Survival intelligence, even when fully based on open sources, is expensive and jealously guarded. The cognitive market, instead, is inundated with either strong signals, with limited actionability, or with epistemic disservices. When governmental organisations try to lead in an increasingly competitive geopolitical environment using the tool of visibility, their signal (if not boosted financially and algorithmically) is inaudible to mission-critical targets. An audience exists, but it does not *convert*. Conversion (which in our case could be simply, policy adoption) does not happen. There is not enough attention, there is a problem with communication directionality and the signal is often perceived as *un-evidenced*, as questionable, as a politically motivated *influence operation*.

The forces influence at many levels the cognitive pathways that shape key executive functions of the State. Interesting evidence of their impact can be found by focussing on the intelligence gathering function. By framing the notion of intelligence at large (secret, open, business, strategic) it is actually possible to understand how the six forces can put to a severe test both:

- the strenuous pursuit of sovereign interest, which represents the realist primary strategy to survive in a competitive environment (Antunes & Camisão, 2018) and
- the Western model of development, which emphasises economic growth through industrialisation and technological change (Servaes, 2013).

SOVEREIGN INTEREST AND INTELLIGENCE FAILURES

Big data, artificial intelligence, grid computing, or ultrafast supercomputers are all considered to be key for State survival in a competitive environment. Yet all these assets, most of which in the hands of a very small global elite, have failed to provide decisive support when sovereign interests were massively at stake.

In the realm of both domestic and external security in the past 20 years, the greatest intelligence superpowers (US, UK, France, Germany, India, Pakistan, Israël, Russia, Iran) have accumulated a considerable amount of *intelligence failures*. Some of the most notable ones, from the oldest, to the newest, include: the 9/11 attacks, the Moscow theatre siege, the Indian parliament attack, the case of Irak's WMDs, the siege of Lal Masjid (the *Red Mosque* in Pakistan), the second Lebanon war, the Arab spring, the death of Kim Jong Il, several terror attacks in major capitals (London, Madrid, Mumbai, Paris, Brussels, Berlin, Vienna, Christchurch), the killings of General Qassem Soleimani, of Iraqi militia leader Abu Mahdi al-Muhandis, and Brigadeer-General Mohsen Fakhrizadeh, the Nagorno-Karabakh conflict, the Covid-19 pandemic, the Capitol attack in Washington and finally Kabul's rapid collapse. This very last failure, and some others in this list, have occurred in a country which can count on an intelligence community composed by 17 State agencies, 1271 governmental organisations, 1931 private companies, and 845,000 professionals (Swab, 2019).

Providing an explanation for this sequence of strategic surprises is of course a complex task. All these failures raise fundamental questions about which kind of intelligence—in a world dominated by the first and fifth force (a plethora of viewpoints and propaganda)—can influence—even beyond the realm of hard security—CEOs, journalists, scientists, or presidents. Betts (1978) usefully reminds that strategic surprises are inevitable and that:

> In the best known cases of intelligence failures, the most crucial mistakes have seldom been made by the collectors of raw information, occasionally by professionals who produce finished analyses, but most often by the decision makers who consume the product of intelligent services.

I argue that in addition to the responsibility of the ultimate decision makers, the combined impact of the six forces has added new and important challenges to the IC (Intelligence Community).

For developed countries for example, big data, and the first force, offer the potential for un-precedented data visualisation and predictive capabilities based on computational lexicography applied to both conflict prevention and the broad applications of *culturomics* (sociological research based on high volume text analysis—Leetaru, 2011). On the other side, while these technologies demonstrate very well in contrived environments, in order to perform in real production settings they require massive (and often unforeseeable) financial investments for customisation and, crucially, highly trained resident staff. The question of training goes actually way beyond data mining, and it boils down to the capacity of imagining hypotheses, identify anomalies and asking the right questions. Mastering historical references (sixth force), possessing a wealth of information on actors (local personalities) rather than working almost exclusively on factor analysis, being skilled in sourcing, being capable of cancelling noise (second force) or understanding the role of echo chambers, and reverb tails sequences; all this matters in intelligence analysis performance.

Most AI powered datamining platforms require the bespoke development of several data import solutions. Very often these platforms cannot process effectively existing content without further software development and adequate ontologies. Few typical customisations for intelligence analysis work include the creation of a precise vocabulary to define security incidents, scripts to filter duplicata, subtle coding providing correct qualification of nodes' relationships, or comprehensive tables of equivalence, notably when working with locations and people's names in non European languages.

Despite the marketing pitch ('Non technical employees can build and edit the automated processes required to extract the data that they need') most solutions cannot be run by resident staff. This deepens the dependence of security agencies from outsourcing companies as eloquently shown by the documents leaked in 2013 by Edward Snowden, by the 2015 Hacking Team emails, or by the 2017 Vault 7 Wikileaks files.

Big data is therefore not necessarily a guarantee for more intelligence, also because these big data tools have to focus on precise targets to be productive. As targeting is influenced by political masters and bilateral cooperation between agencies, weak signals emerging from low intensity conflicts are *children of a lesser God*, and disappear under the pressure of strong signals. The risk of being confronted with a sudden and dangerous emergency developing from a blind spot has become a constant feature of the global IC. Total horizon scanning is a theoretical construct in a big data/big propaganda environment. As the capacity of some IC communities to collect data augments, the extreme argument made by Sageman (2014) becomes more and more cogent:

> We have a system of terrorism research in which intelligence analysts know everything but understand nothing, while academics understand everything but know nothing

Productive interactions between analytical communities are largely insufficient: between open and closed communities, but also within the same community.

The fourth force (competition) plays a critical role here perpetuating the pillarisation (too much specialisation at agency level), confessionalisation (military vs. civilian), and ideologisation (open vs. secret sources) of the intelligence eco-system. The IC's inability to function as a single team is problematic everywhere. In the States, it has been the subject of more than 40 major studies since the creation of the CIA in 1947 (Zegart, 2009).

Emerging and developing countries have far greater issues in taming the impact of six forces on the IC, particularly the first one. When they are not factionalised, politicised, and compromised by political leaders in pursuit of political vendettas, their natural reflex is to perpetuate past processes and narrow their production focus to absolutely essential domestic targets. Scarcity of all other means inflates the role of the often abundant humint (human intelligence), whose production largely constitutes the bulk of intelligence trade with allies.

The investment in technological platforms targets mobile communications (22 emerging markets and developing countries have used FinFisher surveillance software, 19 have used Circles, and Pegasus has been used by 45 countries according to recent reports); and very little money goes to pay-per-view analysis from quality open sources. Knowledge asymmetry (deriving from the over dependence on surveillance data) and cognitive poverty, are aggravated by the isolation of the IC community, which in developing countries rarely establishes communication exchanges with academia.

The result is that, in a global information system dominated by propaganda and influence operations, policy makers in developing countries have incentives to rely on information and narratives which are popular within their factions or within relevant regional organisations. These narratives represent an information homogenisation around themes that have immediate, intuitive appeal (imperialism, colonialism, white supremacy, capitalism, olygarchism, etc.), and represent a decision making support with a very low entry costs, but also without guarantees on quality and absence of manipulative purposes.

If fear and negative news are particularly functional types of information to travel across modern media systems, their impact is greater in developing countries: their leadership has a lesser capacity to invest in compensatory (analytical) processes and a much greater incentive to cede to short term influences (powerful families, armed forces, political parties, ultra high net worth individuals, neighbouring countries with common cultural traits) or develop a neo-populist or authoritarian response to uncertainty, as we can see in Brazil, Philippines, Tanzania, Turkmenistan, Belarus, or Venezuela.

WESTERN MODEL OF DEVELOPMENT AND GROWTH

If intelligence failures show that the six forces should be a source of concern for realists, the shortcomings generated by the forces when policy reform is attempted in EMDCs (and elsewhere) should keep the neoliberals up at night as well. The forces have the potential to seriously erode growth from a micro and a macro perspective: the case of Sri Lanka's jump to organic farming, which will close this section, is an excellent illustration of the stacked impact of the forces.

In a *microeconomic* framework, sub-optimal information for decision making (e.g. in financial management, in performance monitoring, in regulatory compliance), is magnified by info-overload, by propaganda and the high costs of valuable, mission-critical information. Technology to manage exploding corporate data (when and where this is the case), puts companies in front of difficulties comparable to those that intelligence organisations face, when dealing with big data.

Customers service, talent recruitment, and strategic planning are departments which greatly depend on the decoding of functional secrets. Social science research techniques can provide help, but there's is often no resident expertise in this field in SMEs and SMIs, so the solution requires costly externalisations. When investment capital is unavailable, *jumps* in performance become unlikely. This explains the limited adoption of social media by developing countries SMEs (South Africa, Ghana, Pakistan, Bangladesh) which simply do not have the funds to afford the costs of precision targeting in marketing communication (Makhitha, 2016; Amoah, 2020; Amoah & Jibril, 2020; Rahman et al., 2020; Islam & Ozuem, 2019). De facto, for many small companies everywhere in the world, social media cannot represent technological assets for growth, because making money with social media costs too much money.

In a *macro-economic* perspective, for emerging markets or developing countries, social progress and growth are challenged by the six forces when administrations interact with aid donors. More specifically, EMDCs struggle with strategic planning, with governmental coordination, and with overflowing priorities.

Emerging and developing countries administrations painfully cope with donors' project requirements when they are asked to contribute to multi annual indicative plans for loans, grants, or other typologies of external assistance. *Results based management* (R.B.M.) requires S.M.A.R.T. objectives, R.A.C.E.R. indicators and the capacity to clearly distinguish between *outputs*, *outcomes*, and *impact* of planned activities. Forced to operate in a scarcity environment (Mullainathan & Shafir, 2013), EMDCs administrations often fail to have the right expertise to cope with the combination of information overload produced by multi annual plans and the formal requirements of R.M.B. The results is that they either fail to produce valuable long term planning for their own national or public interest or they increase their dependence on donors, loosing the full ownership of the initiatives.

Insufficient administrative coordination affects various typologies of donor supported policy implementation. It's the result of structural capacity issues, but also of competition. Poor coordination endangers *decentralisation processes* (e.g. in Angola, Uganda, Malawi, Ghana, Tanzania, Rwanda—Crawford, 2008); the *diversification of the economy* (which is an issue for almost all, but few African countries such as Egypt, South Africa, Togo, and the countries of the East African Federation); *interventions on root causes of conflict* (e.g. in Congo Brazzaville or Cameroon); or the implementation of *security sector reforms* (e.g. in Burkina Faso and, again, in Cameroon), when public finances are not managed with the needed efficiency or transparency.

These difficult policy contexts become easily a terrain for propaganda, either through the influence of external actors, or by the government itself, trying to divert public attention from the economic situation by fabricating scapegoats, such as minorities, or *the West*.

A third type of struggle emerges paradoxically when the combined intervention of multiple donors generates *overflowing priorities*. High level political agendas end up reading like A to Z lists of *wicked problems*: from Human Rights, to SMEs Growth, from Decentralisation, to Regional Development, from Climate Change, to Fight against Drugs, from Market Access issues, to 'Foreign Investment with a priority to circular economy'.

WICKED PROBLEMS AS THE SIX FORCES 'PERFECT STORMS'

It's increasingly clear that wicked problems are 'perfect storms' characterised by the most powerful concurrence of the six forces. These special policy issues are so tough to solve because they are so deeply conditioned by the forces. Their multifaceted nature is genetically programmed to generate information overload; the nexus of interdependent, nested, and conflicting priorities is just perfect to exacerbate propaganda and competition; their complexity and duration in time promotes forgetting and increases the gap with cognitive poors; the multiplicity of the actors involved in their solution increases information directionality and attention problems.

The trouble is that many *development goals* are actually *wicked problems*.

Climate change is an excellent example of policy interdependence and is a major source of tensions between actors with diverging interests. Think of the issue of methane mitigation and the interests of livestock producers; the raise of domestic production of palm oil and environmental fallout in biodiverse areas; the triangle (in China, e.g.) between post-Covid stimulus, a likely increase of carbon emissions and national concerns about energy security.

The road towards *digitalisation* is equally a good example of a wicked problem. In Africa, key government activities, including elections, customs, visas, and taxes are being digitised in 18 sub-Saharian countries, including Kenya, Rwanda, and South Africa. While all this contributes to democracy, to solving public finance issues and reducing corruption, cybersecurity, and data protection have not improved with equal speed, as incidents during elections or attacks against banks have showed eloquently. Cybersecurity and data protection were, in this case, the nested *weak signals* that this policy implementation neglected.

On a daily basis, well structured and sophisticated analytical communities in developed countries struggle with complex, seemingly insurmountable social problems, with ill defined issues, disputable (in a pluralistic society) viewpoints, and parts of the puzzle which seem to be the expression of another problem. Developed economies choose to approach wicked problems through *intellectual competition*: think tanks challenge one another in the *market of ideas* until, at the end of the process, government rationally arbitrates for the best policy solution. In principle, the one that has survived to the peer review. Unfortunately, under the effect of the forces (propaganda, overload, and forgetting), experts are today rapidly challenged in the public space, recommendations are either discredited or rapidly forgotten, and key functional secrets in an adversarial ecosystem remain un-discovered or cannot be put to fruition effectively.

When facing wicked problems or overflowing priorities, leaders in developing and emerging countries have incentives to produce social mobilisation on the basis of artificial problem simplifications. The narrative is in line with the standards of Davos, but their policy is poorly researched. If they choose to act differently, they are forced to struggle with political factions and with the consequences of scarcity in relevant administrative and political communities.

Developing countries technocrats, notwithstanding the support they receive from donors or the civil society fail to have the resources (including by-partisan expertise) to decompose a wicked problem in all its components and to find the parameters to solve the complex equation. They fail to master the necessary tools and techniques to collect the relevant *functional secrets* from the available info glut. They clearly perceive a widening gap between what they understand and what they should understand: that is, the *principal component* needed to introduce change in policy issues such as migration, youth employment, or the lowering of the national dependency from the revenue generated by commodities.

An illustration of a *big* principal component analysis failure is Sri Lanka's recent bid to become the world's first fully organic farming country. In an attempt to make strides on SDG3 (Good Health and Well Being) and SDG13 (Climate Change), while at the same time increasing agricultural revenues (thanks to organic premium prices), effectively copying with the impact of COVID on public finances and repaying money borrowed in the past, the government stopped the import of chemical fertilisers and pesticides on May 6, 2021. The decision had a massive intuitive appeal: simple savings seemed to be able to generate lots of positive externalities.

Sadly, the abrupt and unaccompanied country-wide transition to organic farming, was followed by a food crisis (crop production reduced by 25% to 35%, price of some vegetables multiplied by 5, rice price up by 30%), a fertilisers black market and a sudden policy reversal, characterised by multiple corrective interventions on media ('the crisis has nothing to do with organic'), and the purchase of 30,000 tons of potassium chloride ('sold' to the public as an 'organic fertiliser'—De Costa, 2021; Al Jazeera, 2021).

Intense pro and anti government propaganda preceded and followed the decision. The move had been prepared in a ten points strategic policy document entitled 'Vistas of Prosperity and Splendour' (Ministry of Finance, Sri Lanka 2021). It had been announced by the President in the margins of the UN Food Systems Summit in September 2021, and again in the COP26 (Glasgow) the following November. The decision was itself the government's response to the accusation of having caused, with its subsidised and State controlled fertilisers policy, an 'agricultural kidney disease' epidemic among the country's farmers (Nulkar, 2021; Marambe, 2021). Clearly the goal could not 'be easily achieved' as Basil Rajapaksa, Chairman of the Presidential Task Force on Economic Revival, reportedly said publicly (ColomboPage, 2021).

A whole series of functional secrets—information no one was really protecting—did not come to the attention of decision makers or was not acted upon. Among them, some crucial intelligence that could have played the role of *principal factor* for the government's decision process.

For example:

- International organic certification is not automatic.
- Scientific literature indicates that organic farming is 15% to 20% less productive that intensive farming.
- Most importantly: a national survey organised by Verité Research (Ranwala, 2021) in July 2021 indicated that 91% of Sri Lanka's farmers used fertilisers, 76% of them relied *heavily* on chemical fertiliser, but only 20% declared have adequate knowledge in using alternatives; 63% of the farmers hadn't received any guidance on organic cultivation and 59% didn't have access to people with such knowledge (Ranwala, 2021).

This failure is leaving the country in the middle of a mudslinging, propaganda storm where it's not possible to know any more what causes kidney failures among farmers, what is the real role of criminals that profit from fertilisers' regulation, if organic fertiliser and compost can alone suffice in providing the required nutrition to plants, or what is a realistic timeframe for a transition to organic for Sri Lanka. This failure is also discrediting in Asia (and beyond) organic agriculture with headlines such as 'How the organic agriculture ideology destroyed the Sri Lankan economy' (Adriano, 2021).

So, what can be done to prevent these political catastrophes?

APPROACHES TO TACKLE THE SIX FORCES

The six forces produce a massive *hand break effect* on the information and communication ecosystem: they tend to weaken and compress any piece of crucial intelligence, including key findings that can really help progress and sustainable development.

Several operational approaches can produce broad cognitive benefits to the actions and partnerships needed to achieve the existing 17 SDGs. Each one of these methods requires to divert part of the existing development funds to new objectives. Here are some of the options:

- A 'whole society approach': this would allow tackling the six forces by producing training for governmental officials, civil servants, journalists, and by starting bespoke education in schools, professional education centres and universities. Being applied in other contexts such as conflict prevention or public health, this approach entails the combination of an horizontal dimension of policy coordination (between different instruments, policy domains, and processes going on the ground at community level); and a vertical dimension based on inclusivity (reaching communities at every level, from elite to grassroots).
- Incorporating intelligence functions into the Presidency or the PM office: this structural intervention can speed up reforms, but poses long term dangers of more abuses.
- The creation of dedicated structures for economic intelligence: modelled after the French SISSE (Service de l'information stratégique et de la sécurité économiques) these would allow the focused fusion of only 'growth-relevant' functional secrets.
- Funding policy oriented scenario analysis bodies: along the lines of UNDP's PAPEP (Projecto Politico y Escenarios Perspectivos) which

has done an excellent job in Latin America through the interaction between high level policy makers and practitioners of strategic foresight. *Futuribles*, in Paris, represents another model of excellence, bridging public and private sector through foresight training and consulting.

- Funding social enterprise projects like *Thinking the Unthinkable*, which aims at facilitating radical change through bespoke advisory work, customised horizon scans, and analytical research on *unthinkables (black swans)*.
- Extending the support for the political, legal, and financial independence of the existing think tanks in emerging markets and developing countries, with a new focus on cooperative initiatives. The specific objective here would be to merge the existing model of the *virtual think tank* with the model of *intelligence fusion centres*, active in the field of counter terrorism.
- Creating development oriented *rapid expeditionary teams*: these could be activated in conflict prone countries with a mix of open source intelligence collection, reports by faith based groups, academic studies, baseline surveys prepared by economist, satellite imagery, and consultancy with private firms. The USAID Global Development Lab has commissioned a study to look into the feasibility of these *rapid expeditionary development* (RED) teams modelled after special forces.
- Supporting a big change in the quality of the formats and design of governmental information, would also be an effective option too, as Wurman showed creating the TED Talks after his success with *Information Anxiety*.

Servaes (2013, 2017) usefully reminds the ever growing list of wicked problems or *global risks* identified on a yearly basis by the World Economic Forum's *Global Risks Report*. Experts consulted in Davos underline that:

> Decision makers need to improve understanding of incentives that will improve collaboration in response to global risks... Communication and information sharing on risks must be improved by introducing greater transparency about uncertainty and conveying it to the public in a meaningful way

Servaes insists that one of the imperatives for a sustainable future is to consider communication and culture as an end in itself, 'crucial to effectively tackle the major problems of today', a key to antagonise propaganda.

Many voices call for a cultural revolution, based on the idea that income, productivity, and gross national product are essential aspects of human development, but they are 'not the sum total of human existence' (Servaes, 2017, p. 2). Such a revolution would be a key to antagonise competition.

The Buddhist monk and philosopher, Phra Dhammapidhok, stresses that sustainability is about ecology, economy, and *evolvability*, or the potential of human beings to develop themselves into less selfish persons, in harmony with their environment. Others, like Gallup, Richard Layard (Emeritus at LSE), the Sustainable Development Solutions Network (SDSN) or the Earth Institute at Columbia University, consider that the cultural revolution should be based on the eighteenth century enlighten-ment goal for society: happiness of the people.

Through different approaches (western, eastern, fusion), we under-stand that the common concern is to get the right goals into our troubled societies. It's a communication challenge. Against this background, it's key, notes Servaes, to include in the frame of sustainable development, *Communication for Sustainable Social Change*, as an essential field of study and intervention.

I argue that another common need and an important control responsi-bility to be assigned to leaders, is the uninterrupted production of *survival intelligence*; the kind of intelligence which is cogent enough to elicit the collaboration, the trust, and the collective solutions expected by so many. My restorative formula for deregulated cognitive metabolisms would therefore be based on focused, targeted, *Information and Communication for Sustainable Social Change*.

CONCLUSIONS

The SGDs have been criticised from several angles. They have been pre-sented as a 'bureaucratic process out of control' (Economist, 2015); they have also been attacked:

- for their utopian vision (Kenny, 2015),
- for their incapacity to take into consideration the inequalities in the international system (as David Taylor suggests 'ensuring the

sustainability of one place, one location, one country, might undermine the sustainability of other places'—Trinity College, 2021),

- for their failure to address root causes (economic models, power relations, social structures) of gender issues of feminist concern (Consortium on Gender, Security and Human Rights, 2017),
- for their reliance on old models of industrial growth incompatible with the commitment to hold global warming below the 2° Celsius threshold (Hickel, 2015, 2020),
- for their mis-measurement of poverty (Hickel, 2015),
- for their failure 'to reflect on the root causes of the huge and persistent poverty-related human rights deficit' (Pogge & Sengupta, 2016),
- for their failure to produce quantified targets and indicators than can be effectively monitored (Langford, 2016).

Since September 2015, date of the adoptions of the goals, 35% of the countries listed in the UNDP Human Developed Index have regressed and lost positions in the ranking. Some 58% of the countries with medium human development and 59% of the countries with low development index have equally lost positions in the same period.

Against these criticisms and data, I argue with Langford that, 'ultimately the most important question for the SDGs is one of effectiveness'. The burning issue is not whether the underlying theory holds promise, but rather, as Sachs (2015) stresses, the point is if this vector of information is actually proving essential for social mobilisation for the goals, if it creates peer pressure and if it has the capacity to spur epistemic communities. The answer in this respect should be positive as SDGs represent for the donor community the tool which performs *matrix transfer molding* for development policies worldwide. SDGs perform, a sort of *editorialisation du Monde* to use a category dear to Bronner: they provide, as Wurman suggested, a useful format to convey signal with efficacy.

Nietzsche, in a chapter on Poets in *Thus spoke Zarathustra*, wrote: 'we know little, we study even less and therefore we are obliged to lie'. It's an illustration of the 'civilisational ceiling' created by the six forces and breaking that ceiling requires all hands on deck. This implies the capacity to create truces in competition allowing meaningful progress, through shared survival intelligence. It also implies the capacity to develop a strategic vision to guide our attention. If we use the lens provided by Innis in his *Empire and Communications* (1950), we can understand that the six forces left unchecked, may affect durably power balances, leaving virtual and geopolitical space to those entities that master the weaponisation of these forces. Maybe, like Goethe recommended, we need to slow down and find a more virtuous balance between rhythms of progress and retrogression, of evolution and dissolution. Maybe an 18th goal could be added, paraphrasing Churchill, to the list of the existing 17 SDGs: to produce expert knowledge and rigorously guide government in helping the plain man, who knows where it hurts.

REFERENCES

9/11 Commission Report: Reorganization, Transformation, and Information Sharing. (2004). Retrieved August 9, 2021, from https://www.govinfo.gov/content/pkg/GAOREPORTS-GAO-04-1033T/html/GAOREPORTS-GAO-04-1033T.htm

Abu-Lughod, J. L. (1989). *Before European hegemony: The world system AD 1250–1350.* Oxford University Press.

Acerbi, A. (2019). Cognitive attraction and online misinformation. *Palgrave Communications, 5*(1), 1–7. https://doi.org/10.1057/s41599-019-0224-y

Adriano, F. (2021, September 30). How the organic agriculture ideology destroyed the Sri Lankan economy. *The Manila Times.* https://www.manilatimes.net/2021/09/30/business/agribusiness/how-the-organic-agriculture-ideology-destroyed-the-sri-lankan-economy/1816512

Al Jazeera, (ENG). (2021, October 20). Sri Lanka reverses organic farming drive as tea suffers [News]. https://www.aljazeera.com/news/2021/10/20/sri-lanka-organic-farming-tea-export-suffers

Alterman, E. (2019, February 4). The decline of historical thinking. *The New Yorker.* https://www.newyorker.com/news/news-desk/the-decline-of-historical-thinking

Amoah, J. (2020, July 2). *Social media and its impact on the financial performance on SMEs in developing countries: A literature review.* https://doi.org/10.34190/ESM.20.097

Amoah, J., & Jibril, A. B. (2020). Inhibitors of social media as an innovative tool for advertising and marketing communication: Evidence from SMEs in a developing country. *Innovative Marketing, 16,* 164–179. https://doi.org/10.21511/im.16(4).2020.15

Angus, D., Dootson, P., & Thomson, T. J. (2020). *3.2 billion images and 720,000 hours of video are shared online daily. Can you sort real from fake?* The Conversation. Retrieved August 7, 2021, from http://theconversation.com/3-2-billion-images-and-720-000-hours-of-video-are-shared-online-daily-can-you-sort-real-from-fake-148630

Antunes, S., & Camisão. (2018, February 27). Introducing realism in International Relations theory. *E-International Relations.* https://www.e-ir. info/2018/02/27/introducing-realism-in-international-relations-theory/

Arbesman, S. (2014). *The half-life of facts: Why everything we know has an expiration date.* Penguin Books Australia.

ASEAN Parliamentarians for Human Rights. (2020). ASEAN's Rakhine crisis. Assessing the regional response to atrocities in Myanmar's Rakhine State. APHR Bangkok. www.aseanmp.org

Bailey, B. P., & Konstan, J. A. (2006). On the need for attention-aware systems: Measuring effects of interruption on task performance, error rate, and affective state. *Computers in Human Behavior, 22*(4), 685–708. https://doi. org/10.1016/j.chb.2005.12.009

Bailey Sounders, T. (1908). *The maxims and reflections of Goethe; trans. By Thomas Bailey Saunders.* Macmillan and Co., Limited; University of Pennsylvania. https://www.sas.upenn.edu/~cavitch/pdf-library/Goethe_Maxims_ Reflections%20copy.pdf

Barkley Rosser, J., Jr. (2003). A Nobel Prize for asymmetric information: The economic contributions of George Akerlof, Michael Spence and Joseph Stiglitz. *Review of Political Economy, 15*(1), 3–21. https://doi.org/10.1080/ 09538250308445

Barnlund, D. C. (2008). A transactional model of communication. In *Communication theory* (2nd ed.). Routledge.

Barnlund, D. C. (2013). A transactional model of communication. In *Language behavior* (pp. 43–61). De Gruyter Mouton. https://www.degruyter.com/ document/doi/10.1515/9783110878752.43/html

Beauvisage, T., Beuscart, J.-S., Couronné, T., & Mellet, K. (2011). Le succès sur Internet repose-t-il sur la contagion? Une analyse des recherches sur la viralité. *Tracés,* 151–166. https://doi.org/10.4000/traces.5194

Bell, D. (1976). *The coming of post-industrial society: A venture in social forecasting* (Reissue ed.). Basic Books.

Betts, R. (1978). Analysis, war, and decision: Why intelligence failures are inevitable. *WorldPolitics, 31*(1), 61–89.

Bradshaw, S., & Howard, P. N. (2019). *The global disinformation order 2019 global inventory of organised social media manipulation.* Càmputational Propaganda Research Project—Oxford University. https://demtech.oii.ox. ac.uk/wp-content/uploads/sites/93/2019/09/CyberTroop-Report19.pdf

Brandolini, A. (2013). Twitter. https://twitter.com/ziobrando/status/ 289635060758507521

Bronner, G. (2003). *L'empire des croyances.* Presses Universitaires de France. https://doi.org/10.3917/puf.bronn.2003.01

Bronner, G. (2021). *Apocalypse cognitive.* Presses Universitaires de France.

Brookings, J. (2016, March 1). *New data show large drop in history bachelor's degrees | Perspectives on history | AHA.* https://www.historians.org/publications-and-directories/perspectives-on-history/march-2016/new-data-show-large-drop-in-history-bachelors-degrees

Buckminster Fuller, R., & Kuromiya, K. (1978). *Critical path* (2nd ed.). St. Martin's Griffin.

Bunt, G. R. (2003). *Islam in the digital age: E-Jihad, online fatwas and cyber Islamic environments.* Pluto Press.

Bunt, G. R. (2018). *Hashtag Islam: How cyber-Islamic environments are transforming religious authority (Islamic civilization and Muslim networks).* University of North Carolina Press.

Cage, J., Herve, N., & Viaud, M.-L. (2018). The production of information in an online world: Is copy right? *Sciences Po LIEPP Working Paper N°72.* https://spire.sciencespo.fr/hdl:/2441/1ikqf7qv0m8h7q6lmc4ng73ueq/resources/wp72-cage-herve-viaud.pdf

Castells, M. (2010). *The information age trilogy* (Rev. ed.). Wiley–Blackwell.

Center for Humane Technology. (2020, January 24). *Tristan Harris Congress testimony: Technological deception in the social media age.* https://www.youtube.com/watch?v=LUNErhONqCY

Cinelli, M., Morales, G. D. F., Galeazzi, A., Quattrociocchi, W., & Starnini, M. (2021). The echo chamber effect on social media. *Proceedings of the National Academy of Sciences, 118*(9). https://doi.org/10.1073/pnas.2023301118

CNBC Television. (2019, June 25). *Congress holds hearing on use of persuasive technology on the internet—06/25/2019.* https://www.youtube.com/watch?v=yjKV_j_mFIQ

ColomboPage, N. (2021, April 29). Sri Lanka: President vows to make Sri Lanka the first country in the world to be free of chemical fertilizers. ColomboPage: Sri Lanka Internet Newspaper. http://www.colombopage.com/archive_21A/Apr29_1619712437CH.php

Consortium on Gender, Security and Human Rights. (2017). Feminist_Critiques_of_the_SDGs_-_Analysis_and_Bibliography_-_CGSHR.pdf. (n.d.). Retrieved September 2, 2021, from https://genderandsecurity.org/sites/default/files/Feminist_Critiques_of_the_SDGs_-_Analysis_and_Bibliography_-_CGSHR.pdf

Conway, M., & MacDonald, S. (2021). *Islamic state's online activity and responses.* Routledge.

Crawford, G. (2008). Poverty and the politics of (de)centralisation in Ghana. In G. Crawford & C. Hartmann (Eds.), *Decentralisation in Africa* (pp. 107–144). Amsterdam University Press. https://www.jstor.org/stable/j.ctt46msxc.6

Davenport, T. H., & Beck, J. C. (2002). *The attention economy: Understanding the new currency of business* (Rev. ed.). Harvard Business Review Press.

De Costa, W. A. J. M. (2021). 100% organic agriculture: A costly experiment leading to national disaster—II. Retrieved January 17, 2022, from http://island. lk/100-organic-agriculturea-costly-experiment-leading-to-national-disaster-ii/

Deaner, R., Khera, A., & Platt, M. (2005). Monkeys pay per view: Adaptive valuation of social images by rhesus macaques. *Current Biology: CB, 15*, 543–548. https://doi.org/10.1016/j.cub.2005.01.044

Digital News Report 2021. (2021). Reuters Institute for the Study of Journalism. Retrieved October 23, 2021, from https://reutersinstitute.politics.ox.ac.uk/ digital-news-report/2021

Ellul, J. (1965). *Propagandes*. Armand Colin.

Facebook. (2021). *IO-Threat-Report-May-20-2021.pdf*. Retrieved September 17, 2021, from https://about.fb.com/wp-content/uploads/2021/05/IO-Threat-Report-May-20-2021.pdf

Fair, J. E. (1989). 29 years of theory and research on media and development: The dominant paradigm impact. *Gazette (Leiden, Netherlands), 44*(2), 129–150. https://doi.org/10.1177/001654928904400204

Food and Agriculture Organization of the United Nations (Ed.). (2007). *Communication and sustainable development: Selected papers from the 9th UN roundtable on communication for development.* Research and Extension Division, Natural Resources Management and Environment Dept., Food and Agriculture Organization of the United Nations.

Franck, G. (2019). The economy of attention. *Journal of Sociology, 55*(1), 8–19. https://doi.org/10.1177/1440783318811778

Gabielkov, M., Ramachandran, A., Chaintreau, A., & Legout, A. (2016). Social clicks: What and who gets read on Twitter? *ACM SIGMETRICS Performance Evaluation Review, 44*, 179–192. https://doi.org/10.1145/2964791.2901462

Global_2021_Forecast_Highlights. (2016). CISCO: VNI complete forecast highlights. https://www.cisco.com/c/dam/m/en_us/solutions/service-provider/vni-forecast-highlights/pdf/Global_2021_Forecast_Highlights.pdf

Goethe, J. W. von. (2019). *The Collected Works of Johann Wolfgang von Goethe: Novels, plays, essays & autobiography (200+ titles in one edition): Wilhelm Meister's travels, faust part one and two, Italian Journey...* e-artnow.

Greenberg, J., Pyszczynski, T., Solomon, S., Rosenblatt, A., Veeder, M., Kirkland, S., & Lyon, D. (1990). Evidence for terror management theory II: The effects of mortality salience on reactions to those who threaten or bolster the cultural worldview. *Journal of Personality and Social Psychology, 58*(2), 308–318. https://doi.org/10.1037/0022-3514.58.2.308

Habermas, J. (1991). *The structural transformation of the public sphere: An inquiry into a category of bourgeois society* (6th Printing ed.). The MIT Press.

Haselton, M. G., & Nettle, D. (2006). The paranoid optimist: An integrative evolutionary model of cognitive biases. *Personality and Social Psychology Review, 10*(1), 47–66. https://doi.org/10.1207/s15327957pspr1001_3

Haynes, T. (2018, May 1). Dopamine, smartphones & you: A battle for your time. *Science in the News.* https://sitn.hms.harvard.edu/flash/2018/dopamine-smartphones-battle-time/

Hickel, J. (2015, September 23). Five reasons to think twice about the UN's Sustainable Development Goals |. *Africa at LSE.* https://blogs.lse.ac.uk/afri-caatlse/2015/09/23/five-reasons-to-think-twice-about-the-uns-sustainable-development-goals/

Hickel, J. (2020). The world's Sustainable Development Goals aren't sustainable. *Foreign Policy.* Retrieved September 2, 2021, from https://foreignpolicy.com/2020/09/30/the-worlds-sustainable-development-goals-arent-sustainable/

Hopkins, A. G. (2011). *Globalisation in world history.* Random House.

Innis, H. A. (1950). *Empire and communications* (1st ed.). Clarendon Press.

Islam, M., & Ozuem, W. (2019, June 10). *The impact of social media on social entrepreneurship in a developing country.* https://www.researchgate.net/profile/Md-Islam-347/publication/333677213_The_impact_of_social_media_on_social_entrepreneurship_in_a_developing_country/links/5cfeaa34a6fdccd13091bf31/The-impact-of-social-media-on-social-entrepreneurship-in-a-developing-country.pdf

Jefferson, T. (1785). *Thomas Jefferson, 1743–1826. Notes on the State of Virginia.* Retrieved August 4, 2021, from https://docsouth.unc.edu/southlit/jefferson/jefferson.html

Kenny, C. (2015, May 27). *MDGs to SDGs: Have we lost the plot?* Center For Global Development. https://www.cgdev.org/publication/mdgs-sdgs-have-we-lost-plot

Khan, I., Brinkman, W.-P., Fine, N., & Hierons, R. (2008). Measuring personality from keyboard and mouse use. *369*, 38. https://doi.org/10.1145/1473018.1473066

Khan, I. A., Khalid, O., Jadoon, W., Shan, R. Us., & Nasir, A. N. (2015). *Predicting programmers' personality via interaction behaviour with keyboard and mouse* [Preprint]. PeerJ PrePrints. https://doi.org/10.7287/peerj.preprints.1183v1

Klapp, O. (1986) *Overload and boredom: Essays on the quality of life in the information society (Contributions in Sociology)* Hardcover. Praeger.

Krasnova, H., Wenninger, H., Widjaja, T., & Buxmann, P. (2013, February 18). *Envy on Facebook: A hidden threat to users' life satisfaction?* International Conference on Wirtschaftsinformatik (WI) / Business Information Systems.

Langenmayr, F. (2016). The concept of the organizational memory funtion. In F. Langenmayr (Ed.), *Organisational memory as a function: The construction of past, present and future in organisations* (pp. 67–87). Springer Fachmedien. https://doi.org/10.1007/978-3-658-12868-5_3

Langford, M. (2016). Lost in transformation? The politics of the Sustainable Development Goals. *Ethics & International Affairs, 30*(2), 167–176. https://doi.org/10.1017/S0892679416000058

Laverty, K. J. (1996). Economic "Short-Termism": The debate, the unresolved issues, and the implications for management practice and research. *The Academy of Management Review, 21*(3), 825–860. https://doi.org/10.2307/259003

Leetaru, K. (2011). Culturomics 2.0: Forecasting large-scale human behavior using global news media tone in time and space. *First Monday*. https://doi.org/10.5210/fm.v16i9.3663

Littau, K. (2006). *Theories of reading: Books, bodies, and bibliomania*. Polity.

Liu, S., Huang, J.-C., & Brown, G. L. (1998). Information and risk perception: A dynamic adjustment process. *Risk Analysis, 18*(6), 689–699. https://doi.org/10.1111/j.1539-6924.1998.tb01113.x

Lyon, D. (2013). *The information society: Issues and illusions*. John Wiley & Sons.

Makhitha, K. (2016). Risks of using social media as a marketing tool for small producers in a developing country. *Risk Governance and Control: Financial Markets & Institutions, 6*. https://doi.org/10.22495/rcgv6i4c3art1

Malcolm, H. (2013). USA TODAY. Retrieved August 8, 2021, from https://www.usatoday.com/story/money/personalfinance/2013/08/14/finances-affect-college-major/2649665/

Marambe, B. (2021). A tragedy of relying on misinformation. Retrieved February 13, 2022, from http://island.lk/a-tragedy-of-relying-on-misinformation/

Marginson, D., & McAulay, L. (2008). Exploring the debate on short-termism: A theoretical and empirical analysis. *Strategic Management Journal, 29*(3), 273–292.

Meerman Scott, D. (2011). *Newsjacking: How to inject your ideas into a breaking news story and generate tons of media coverage* (1st ed.). Wiley.

Mermet, G. (2013). *Francoscopie 2013 edition*. Larousse.

Ministry of Finance, S. L. (2021). Ministry of Finance—Sri lanka. Ministry of Finance, Sri Lanka. Retrieved January 17, 2022, from https://www.treasury.gov.lk/national-policy#policy_7

Morehead, J. (2000). Information haves and have nots. *The Reference Librarian, 34*, 131–143. https://doi.org/10.1300/J120v34n71_10

Morel, C. (2002). *Les décisions absurdes*. Bibliothèque des Sciences humaines—GALLIMARD.

Mullainathan, S., & Shafir, E. (2013). *Scarcity: Why having too little means so much*. Penguin UK.

Nelson-Field, K. (2020). *The attention economy and how media works: Simple truths for marketers* (1st ed., 2020 ed.). Springer.

Nielsen, S. L., & Sarason, I. G. (1981). Emotion, personality, and selective attention. *Journal of Personality and Social Psychology, 41*(5), 945–960. https://doi.org/10.1037/0022-3514.41.5.945

Norris, P. (2001). *Digital divide: Civic engagement, information poverty, and the Internet worldwide* (1st ed., 1st Printing). Cambridge University Press.

Nulkar, G. (2021, September 22). Sri Lanka's organic farming crisis: Learning from failures. https://www.downtoearth.org.in/blog/agriculture/sri-lanka-s-organic-farming-crisis-learning-from-failures-79138

Odell, J. (2019). *How to do nothing: Resisting the attention economy* (1st ed.). Melville House Pub.

Osten, M. (2013). *"Alles veloziferisch" oder Goethes Entdeckung der Langsamkeit.* Wallstein Verlag.

Pizer, J. (2000). Goethe's "World Literature" paradigm and contemporary cultural globalization. *Comparative Literature, 52*(3), 213–227. https://doi.org/10.2307/1771407

Pogge, T., & Sengupta, M. (2016). Assessing the sustainable development goals from a human rights perspective. *Journal of International and Comparative Social Policy, 32*(2), 83–97. https://doi.org/10.1080/21699763.2016.1198268

Qiu, X., Oliveira, D., Shirazi, A., Flammini, A., & Menczer, F. (2017). Limited individual attention and online virality of low-quality information. *Nature Human Behaviour, 1*, 0132. https://doi.org/10.1038/s41562-017-0132

Rahman, R., Mohsin, S., El-Gohary, H., Abbas, M., Khalil, H., Altheeb, S., & Sultan, F. (2020). Social media adoption and financial sustainability: Learned lessons from developing countries. *Sustainability, 12*, 27–52. https://doi.org/10.3390/su122410616

Ranwala, C. (2021, August 27). Farmers' pulse—Independent survey. Verité Research. Retrieved January 16, 2022, from https://www.veriteresearch.org/farmerspulse/

Ricci, A. (2013). *The Early Political Web, 1995–2005: A ten-year observational research seeking evidence of eDemocracy in the information architecture of political parties web sites worldwide.* http://hdl.handle.net/2013/

Riley, M. W., & Riley, J. W., Jr. (1951). A sociological approach to communications research. *Public Opinion Quarterly, 15*(3), 445–460. https://doi.org/10.1086/266329

Riley, M. W., & Riley Jr, J. W. (1959). Mass communication and the social system. *Sociology Today.*

Rozin, P., & Royzman, E. B. (2001). Negativity bias, negativity dominance, and contagion. *Personality and Social Psychology Review, 5*(4), 296–320. https://doi.org/10.1207/S15327957PSPR0504_2

RSPH (Royal Society for Public Health). (2017). *Instagram ranked worst for young people's mental health.* Retrieved August 3, 2021, from https://www.rsph.org.uk/about-us/news/instagram-ranked-worst-for-young-people-s-mental-health.html

Sachs, J. D. (2015, March 30). *Why the Sustainable Development Goals matter | by Jeffrey D. Sachs*. Project Syndicate. https://www.project-syndicate.org/commentary/sustainable-development-goals-shift-by-jeffrey-d-sachs-2015-03

Sageman, M. (2014). The stagnation in terrorism research. *Terrorism and Political Violence, 26*(4), 565–580. https://doi.org/10.1080/09546553.2014.895649

Schmidt, B. M. (2018, November 26). *The history BA since the great recession | Perspectives on History | AHA*. https://www.historians.org/publications-and-directories/perspectives-on-history/december-2018/the-history-ba-since-the-great-recession-the-2018-aha-majors-report

Servaes, J. (2003). *The European information society—A reality check*. Intellect Books.

Servaes, J. (2013). Introduction: Imperatives for a sustainable future. In J. Servaes (Ed.), *Sustainable development and green communication: African and Asian perspectives* (pp. 1–39). Palgrave Macmillan UK. https://doi.org/10.1057/9781137329417_1

Servaes, J. (2017). *Introduction: From MDGs to SDGs* (pp. 1–21). https://doi.org/10.1007/978-981-10-2815-1_1

Servaes, J., & Lie, R. (2013). Sustainable social change and communication. *Communication Research Trends, 32*, 4–30.

Servaes, J., & Malikhao, P. (2005). Participatory communication: The new paradigm? In *Media and glocal change: Rethinking communication for development* (p. 14). CLACSO, Consejo Latinoamericano de Ciencias Sociales.

Siegrist, M., & Cvetkovich, G. (2001). Better negative than positive? Evidence of a bias for negative information about possible health dangers. *Risk Analysis, 21*(1), 199–206. https://doi.org/10.1111/0272-4332.211102

Silberzahn, C. (1995). *Au cœur du secret: 1500 jours aux commandes de la DGSE, 1989–1993*. Fayard.

Silver, L. (2019). Misinformation and fears about its impact are pervasive in 11 emerging economies. *Pew Research Center*. Retrieved October 24, 2021, from https://www.pewresearch.org/fact-tank/2019/05/13/misinformation-and-fears-about-its-impact-are-pervasive-in-11-emerging-economies/

Spira, J. B. (2005). The high cost of interruptions. *KM World, 14*(8), 1–32. https://www.interruptions.net/literature.htm#:~:text=8)%2C%20 1%2B32%20%5B-,PDF%20167KB,-%5D

Spira, J. B., & Feintuch, J. B. (2005). *The cost of not paying attention: How interruptions impact knowledge worker productivity: Executive Summary*, Basex. https://www.interruptions.net/literature.htm#:~:text=Executive%20 Summary%2C%20Basex%20%5B-,PDF,-%5D

Stachl, C., Au, Q., Schoedel, R., Gosling, S. D., Harari, G. M., Buschek, D., Völkel, S. T., Schuwerk, T., Oldemeier, M., Ullmann, T., Hussmann, H., Bischl, B., & Bühner, M. (2020). Predicting personality from patterns of behavior collected with smartphones. *Proceedings of the National Academy of Sciences, 117*(30), 17680–17687. https://doi.org/10.1073/pnas.1920484117

Statista Research Department. (2021). *Digital advertising spending worldwide from 2019 to 2024.* Statista. Retrieved August 2, 2021, from https://www.statista.com/statistics/237974/online-advertising-spending-worldwide/

Stephens-Davidowitz, S. (2017). *Everybody lies: Big data, new data, and what the Internet can tell us about who we really are* (Illustrated ed.). Dey Street Books.

Stiglitz, J. E. (2000). The contributions of the economics of information to twentieth century economics*. *The Quarterly Journal of Economics, 115*(4), 1441–1478. https://doi.org/10.1162/003355300555015

Summers, C. C. (2015). The Indian Rebellion of 1857. *Tenor of Our Times, 4*(6), 9. https://scholarworks.harding.edu/cgi/viewcontent.cgi?article=1052&context=tenor

Swab, A. J. (2019). *Black budgets: The US government's secret military and intelligence expenditures.* Harvard Law School Briefing Papers on Federal Budget Policy, Briefing Paper No. 72. https://scholar.harvard.edu/files/briefingpapers/files/72_-_swab_-_black_budgets.pdf

Tech Tent—A turning point for Facebook?—BBC Sounds. (Released On: 24 September 2021). Retrieved October 24, 2021, from https://www.bbc.co.uk/sounds/play/w3ct1nhh

The Trade Desk. (2020, May 11). *In Human Terms, Episode 14: The Decline of Linear TV.* Retrieved August 2, 2021, from https://www.youtube.com/watch?v=tBlueHLmWPQ&list=PLZ8wbDOdQUSuVb5P-XEHAYufxDl5QKsbF&index=4&t=37s

Touraine, A. (1971). *The post-industrial society,: Tomorrow's social history: classes, conflicts and culture in the programmed society* ([1st American ed.] ed.). Random House.

Trinity College Dublin. (2021). *Are the Sustainable Development Goals the best approach to sustainability?* FutureLearn. Retrieved September 2, 2021, from https://www.futurelearn.com/info/blog

Turow, J., & Tsui, L. (2008). The hyperlinked society: Questioning connections in the digital age. *New Media World.* https://doi.org/10.3998/nmw.5680986.0001.001

Unsustainable goals. (2015, March 26). *The Economist.* https://www.economist.com/international/2015/03/26/unsustainable-goals

Vacca, J. (2021). *Online terrorist propaganda, recruitment, and radicalization: Vacca* (1st ed.). CRC Press.

van Krieken, R. (2019a). *Celebrity society: The struggle for attention.* Routledge and CRC Press. https://www.routledge.com/Celebrity-Society-The-Struggle-for-Attention/Krieken/p/book/9781138295063 van Krieken, R. (2019b). Georg Franck's 'The Economy of Attention': Mental capitalism and the struggle for attention. *Journal of Sociology, 55*(1), 3–7. https://doi.org/10.1177/1440783318812111

Vosoughi, S., Roy, D., & Aral, S. (2018). The spread of true and false news online. *Science, 359*(6380), 1146–1151. https://doi.org/10.1126/science.aap9559

Webster, F. (2014). *Theories of the information society.* Routledge.

Weng, L., Flammini, A., Vespignani, A., & Menczer, F. (2012). Competition among memes in a world with limited attention. *Scientific Reports, 2*, 335. https://doi.org/10.1038/srep00335

Westley, B. H., & MacLean, M. S. (1957). A conceptual model for communications research. *Journalism Quarterly, 34*(1), 31–38. https://doi.org/10.1177/107769905703400103

Wurman, R. S. (1989). *Information anxiety* (1st ed.). Doubleday.

Zalani, R. (2021). *Screen time statistics 2021: Your smartphone is hurting you.* (2020, May 6). ECM. https://elitecontentmarketer.com/screen-time-statistics/

Zegart, A. B. (2009). *Spying blind.* Princeton Press.

Zuboff, S. (2019). *The age of surveillance capitalism: The fight for the future at the new frontier of power.* Profile Books Ltd.

The Role of Strategic Communication in Gender Equality Activism and Collective Action: Illustrating the Need for SDG18

Naíde Müller

Abstract Civil society organizations are recognized as contributing to the efficiency and stability of democratic governments. Strategic communication is also a determining factor for social mobilization in the achievement of legitimacy and participatory and democratic adhesion. What unites activists is the common goal of achieving social and political change for the societies of the future. However, several areas of strategic communication, namely public relations, have long failed to recognize activism-related activities as an integral part of discipline and practice. The ability of public

This research was supported by the Portuguese national funding agency for science, research and technology, Foundation for Science and Technology (FCT), Ph.D. Grant Nr. SFRH/BD/144467/2019.

N. Müller (✉)
Faculty of Human Sciences, Catholic University of Portugal (UCP), Lisbon, Portugal
e-mail: ncaldeira@ucp.pt

relations to influence human behavior through communication is recognized. That is why this area has a role to play in the communication strategies of activists defending human rights and sustainable development. In the context of the UN Sustainable Development Goals, this role would be better understood and debated if SDG18 (Communication for All) were included in the 2030 Agenda itself.

In this chapter I resort to a case study built on an ethnographic approach (between January and June 2021) to UMAR, a feminist NGO based in Portugal, and the consultation of 12 communication experts to illustrate the areas where public relations and activism intersect and to show how these intersections could be better understood and debated if SDG18 were included in the 2030 Agenda.

Keywords Strategic communication • Public relations • Activism • Collective action

INTRODUCTION

The existence of social capital (which values the collective over individualism) is fundamental for the development of modern societies (Bourdieu, 1986; Coleman, 1988; Putnam, 1993). The social capital of the third sector is associated with "values of civic spirit, ethical consensus, associativism whose social interaction results in a climate of trust and the ability to work together towards a common goal" (Sá & Pequito, 2015, p. 14).

Contemporary social movements have spread by contagion in a world virtually connected and characterized by the fast and viral dissemination of images and ideas. According to USC Annenberg's 2020 Global Communication Report, a new generation of activists, motivated by the lack of trust in political institutions, will become increasingly influential in the coming years.

Because strategic communication is the intentional use of communication by organizations to promote their mission, the contribution of this field of research and practice to the mobilization and participation of citizens is essential (Frandsen & Johansen, 2017; Hallahan et al., 2007; Holtzhausen & Zerfass, 2014). However, several areas of strategic communication, namely public relations—an area of increasing global economic relevance (Guttmann, 2020)—have long not recognized activism-related activities as an integral part of discipline and practice (Dozier & Lauzen, 2000; Dutta, 2009). This article begins with a literature review on the need to reframe public relations perspectives on activism and activists.

The study approaches the relevance of SDG18 (Communication for all) in achieving the 2030 Agenda for Development (Lee & Vargas, 2020; Yusha'u & Servaes, 2021). In addition to other reasons related to access to fair media representation, communication platforms, media literacy education, participation in decision-making processes, and free and independent media systems, including SDG18 in the 2030 Agenda, would also provide greater attention and reflection by activist organizations and civil society interest groups on the importance of adequate communication strategies to achieve their goals.

The ability of public relations to influence human behavior through communication is recognized (Servaes, 2012; Verčič, 2008), which is why strategic communication and public relations have a role to play in the communication strategies of activists defending human rights and sustainable development. This role would be better understood and debated if SDG18 (Communication for all) were included in the 2030 Agenda itself.

Methodologically I resorted to a case study based on an ethnographic approach that lasted six months (between January and June 2021) to UMAR, a Portuguese feminist nongovernmental organization (NGO) founded in 1976. I also interviewed 12 communication and public relations experts on their perspective of how the same communication strategies that have successfully established mass consumption as a way of life can be used by contemporary activists to increase shared global views such as the 2030 Agenda. This research illustrates the areas where public relations and activism intersect by showing how these intersections could be better understood and debated if SDG18 (Communication for all) were included in the 2030 Agenda.

Reframing Public Relations Perspectives on Activism and Activists

It is recognized that civil society organizations contribute to the efficiency and stability of democratic governments and to the development of modern societies (Bourdieu, 1986; Coleman, 1988; Putnam, 1993). Strategic communication is also a determining factor for social mobilization in the achievement of legitimacy and participatory and democratic adhesion (Negri & Hardt, 2005; Norris, 2002; Toro & Werneck, 2004; Kunsch et al., 2007). Various forms of activism throughout history have contributed to the appearance of "hybrid multifunctional voluntary organizations" (Hasenfeld & Gidron, 2005) that have fought for social change. Depending on their legal nature and the causes they advocate, interest groups within the third sector and the organizations they establish to achieve their objectives can vary substantially, showing areas where third-sector organizations mix with social movements (Ferreira, 2004; Hasenfeld & Gidron, 2005; Martins, 2003). Furthermore, evidence indicates that activist networks are becoming transnationally involved due to an increasing coordination of communication and action based on the proliferation of the Internet and digital cultures (Harrebye, 2016; Rheingold, 2002).

Contemporary social movements have spread by contagion in a world virtually connected and characterized by the fast and viral dissemination of images and ideas. This multifaceted dissent is not only caused due to poverty, the economic crisis, corruption, and a lack of democracy. At its origin lies the "humiliation caused by the cynicism and arrogance of people in power" (political, financial, or cultural) that unite "those who transformed fear into indignation, and indignation into hope for a better humanity" (Castells, 2013, pp. 10–11). The new powers of the media, the culture of networks, and fluidity and horizontality are increasingly influencing the constitution and functioning of social movements (Castells, 2007).

According to USC Annenberg's 2020 Global Communication Report, a new generation of activists, motivated by the lack of trust in political institutions, will become increasingly influential in the coming years. The study also mentions that these new activists use modern public relations tools to raise awareness of a broad spectrum of social and environmental issues. They tend to be younger, nonwhite, urban, female, well-educated, and tech-savvy. They also are more likely to organize voters online than protest in public. Notably, they are open to cooperation with brands, and their values often align with good and responsible business values.

But the field of public relations is still seen as the defender of corporate and capitalist interests, and consequently resistant to outside voices such as activists, NGOs, union members, protesters, and whistle-blowers (Adi, 2020). This context demonstrates the need for new ways to look ahead to activism and public relations.

As Ciszek and Logan (2018) observed, much of the existing literature within public relations and dialogic communication comes from a collaborative approach, and this can be problematic because it reduces attention from the critical role that contestation and tension can have, neglecting other methods of activist social change that perform a confrontational communication (Ganesh & Zoller, 2012, p. 73). Agonism recognizes the "value of permanent contest, dissensus, and performance in vibrant public spaces which expose and test the legitimacy of those who hold power and privilege" (Davidson, 2016, p. 145). Agonistic theory, explained in detail in the work of Chantal Mouffe (1998), is defined by Ganesh and Zoller (2012, p. 77) as "pluralist views of democratic processes that treat social conflict as central."

A postmodern approach to public relations "allows one to consider PR [public relations] as a narrative, a way of talking about the world, the people in that world, and PR's relationship with those people" (Radford, 2012, p. 50) and this is in line with the assumptions of critical theory. A critical knowledge of the signs and symbols of culture allows one to understand the dominant ideologies and power dynamics and eventually permits a comprehension of different publics instead of dominating them or calculating their behavior (Mickey, 1995). Postmodernism in public relations reflects on how to address emancipation at the intersection of research, praxis, society, and organizations (Edwards, 2006; Holtzhausen, 2000; L'Etang, 2009). Public relations can produce and maintain powerful dominant discourses, but they can also subvert and resist these discourses (Holtzhausen, 2000, 2012; Holtzhausen & Voto, 2002).

Because strategic communication is fundamental to promote social change, its applicability in an organizational context is relevant for activist movements. It facilitates the organization of collective action, the call for civic participation, and the relations with other social actors. Ciszek (2017) research showed that activists are producers of strategic communication for social change and that activism and public relations are not incompatible; they both occupy fluid social spaces influenced by cultural and economic forces.

From this perspective, the same communication strategies that successfully established mass consumption as a way of life can be used to voice sustainable pro-democratic movements (Acaroglu, 2014) and enhance shared global visions (Tafra-Vlahović, 2012) (such as human rights and the 2030 Agenda) for sustainable development.

As cited in the USC Annenberg's 2020 Global Communication Report, Fred Cook, director, USC Center for Public Relations, says that "having historically been viewed as adversaries, modern activists have more in common with their corporate counterparts than many professionals realize. Both groups are addressing critical societal issues through purposeful communications and civic engagement. New Activism requires a new perspective from PR."

SDG18—Communication for All: Enhancing Civil Society Advocacy

Communication is a complex process that has "always been about power and exclusion and that transformative potential has constantly faced obstacles" (Lee & Vargas, 2020, p. 6). "Communication enables meanings to be exchanged, makes people who and what they are and motivates them to act" (Lee & Vargas, 2020, p. 18); it is the "lifeblood of society" (Lee & Vargas, 2020, p. 24), which is why communication is so important for social change and in achieving the UN's Sustainable Development Goals. The political control of communication turns out to be an exercise in power. In this way, "political and social change—and with them sustainable development—depend on unfettered access to communications" (Lee & Vargas, 2020, p. 44).

Communication and information poverty constitute a critical multidimension of poverty, with millions of people on every continent lacking access to fair media representation, communication platforms, media literacy education and knowledge, participation in decision-making processes, and free and independent media systems. And these issues are crucial to the United Nations' 2030 Agenda for Sustainable Development and its 17 Sustainable Development Goals (SDGs). All human rights depend on the recognition, implementation, and protection of communication rights (Lee, 2004). The correlation between access to information and communication and the structural causes of poverty has been widely recognized (McNamara, 2000, 2003). In addition to being a source of knowledge, information is also a source of improvement of economic, social, political, and cultural freedoms (Gigler, 2001). Likewise, strategic communication has positive effects on poverty reduction providing opportunities to reconfigure the relationships among government, donors, and civil society (Mozammel, 2011). But, as Gigler & Bailur (2014) point out, this debate needs to move beyond issues related to simple access to information and communication and start focusing more on assessing the effects of the prevalent use, generation, and sharing of information by citizens.

According to the UN SDG Progress Report 2020, the COVID-19 pandemic affected the SDGs' social indicators by reversing several positive trends and increasing several inequalities within and between countries. The pandemic reinforced the need for a global collaborative response from governments, the private sector, civil society, and the general public to achieve the goals. "Communication saves lives" is how the international professional and academic associations of public relations and communicators recently addressed the need for ethical and effective communications to handle the COVID-19 pandemic (EUPRERA, 2021).

In this context, SDG18 (Communication for all) is inevitable in achieving the 2030 Agenda for Development (Lee & Vargas, 2020; Yusha'u & Servaes, 2021). Including SDG18 in the 2030 Agenda would also provide greater attention and reflection by activist organizations and civil society interest groups on the importance of adequate communication strategies to achieve their goals.

What separates activism from other types of collective action is the solidarity that unites activists—the main authors of social movements—around the common goal of achieving social and political change for the societies of the future (Jordan, 2002). Regardless of how these activists are organized, from a historical point of view, activism played an important role in ending slavery, challenging dictatorships, protecting workers from exploitation, protecting the environment, promoting women's equality, opposing racism, and many other important issues (Martin, 2007). Such associations are representative of a vibrant civil society that is essential "in the struggle for more open, inclusive, and democratic media ecosystems" (Lee & Vargas, 2020, p. 85), and strategic communication approaches can help activists to develop and implement clear, common agendas and objectives. Activists also need access to the tools to produce and disseminate knowledge and to interact with several publics and stakeholders. As power and influence relations are the DNA of public relations (Berger & Reber, 2013), this area of study and practice can contribute and be a tool for activists to be publicly recognized as "truly legitimate" (Lee & Vargas, 2020, p. 85).

Activism and social movements can be considered as a form of public relations work concerned with advocacy,[1] promotion, events, lobbying,[2] and public affairs, communicating with a wide range of audiences, clearly oriented toward social change and the achievement of idealized goals. In this way, public relations can be understood as an intervention aimed at collective action (L'Etang, 2016).

But most protests remain "an unconscious collective response, an act of collective anger, rather than a strategy rationally designed to transform political reality, (...) which tend to dissipate as soon as the moment of anger passes" (White, 2016, pp. 63–64). As White (2016) argues, the "future of activism is a struggle to capture the imagination of humanity" (p. 173).

The notion of "soft power" originally appears in the realm of international relations and means the ability to get what you want through attraction rather than coercion or payments (Nye, 2004), and this also requires imagination. In this context, public relations emerges as an example of applied communication sciences such as corporate communication, organizational communication, and strategic communication, among other designations that, despite their differentiating specificities, share a common idea: that the combination of science knowledge and the development of experience through training can generate better results in inducing influence, attraction, or commitment, that is, that communication management exceeds spontaneous communication (Verčič, 2008). As influence, attraction, and commitment are intrinsic constitutive functions of public relations, they represent a way of exercising "soft power" (Servaes, 2012; Verčič, 2008).

The power of influence, attraction, or commitment of public relations is achieved through communicative and symbolic discursive logics. Power is thus disposed in the public arena through structures of meaning. This meaning that results from discursive capacity influences (a) mentality (how the construction of language and vocabulary shape what we think and how we think, which in turn shapes the way we speak and act on a

---

[1] "Advocacy, in essence, implies gaining political commitment and policy support through organised social action with the involvement of committed individuals, support from influential forces and the involvement of concerned sectors of society" (Servaes & Malikhao, 2012, p. 241).

[2] "Lobby definitions tend to converge on its main objective, which is to influence legislative decisions through lawful means, and it is an important resource for citizens to achieve social change" (Alemanno, 2017).

subject), (b) the self/I (identity and identification), and (c) society (which consists of culturally represented relationships, based on narratives) (Heath et al., 2009, p. 206).

"Language in action, that is communication, is an individual human need—as basic as food, clothing and shelter" (Lee & Vargas, 2020, p. 30). And the ability of public relations to influence human behavior through communication is recognized (Servaes, 2012; Verčič, 2008), which is why strategic communication and public relations have a role to play in the communication strategies of activists defending human rights and sustainable development. This role would be better understood and debated if SDG18 (Communication for all) was included in the 2030 Agenda itself.

METHODOLOGY: PUBLIC RELATIONS ETHNOGRAPHIC APPROACH

The sociocultural theoretical traditions in public relations have presented ethnography as a methodology with innovative potential for the advancement of research (Everett & Johnston, 2012; L'Etang et al., 2012; Xifra, 2012). It is also recognized that the need to place research in public relations more broadly as "cultural and ideological practice involved in complex intercultural processes and away from technocratic concerns" "can help in developing an understanding of public relations work in international society and its relations with the world of life and the public sphere" (L'Etang, 2006, p. 393). Though it is not yet a widely used methodology, when investigators intend to make descriptive inferences that characterize the interactions between an organization's culture and its social environment, ethnography has been recognized as a methodological imperative in public relations (Everett & Johnston, 2012). In public relations research, ethnography will examine how a group understands, experiences, and adapts to its environment (Sutton & Anderson, 2004; Winthrop, 1991).

RESEARCH DESIGN

The purpose of this investigation is to articulate the empirical data with the existing theories about the phenomena under observation. Following the methodological imperative in public relations ethnographic research proposed by Everett and Johnston (2012), the study's analytical design was based on two data collection stages. In the first moment, I resorted to an ethnographic immersion in the organizational dynamics of UMAR using participant observation, interviews, informal conversations with the different members of the team, social media monitoring, and analysis of documents, compiled in a field diary (a document in which all the information and interactions are noted daily).

In a second stage, I consulted experts from 12 communication and public relations agencies associated with APECOM—Portuguese Association of Council Companies in Communication and Public Relations—to understand their position on the topic under study. I focused on the interviewees' designated "expert position" (Demo, 1995) and asked all 12 experts the same question:

> In your perspective, how can the same communication strategies that have successfully established mass consumption as a way of life be used by contemporary activists to increase shared global views such as the 2030 Agenda?

Through these two moments of data collection and analysis, I intended to answer the following research question: What is the real or potential role of strategic communication in gender equality activism and collective action, and how does SDG18 relate to this topic?

Case Study: *Ethnographic Immersion UMAR and Expert Consultation*

UMAR is a nonprofit NGO based in Portugal and founded in 1976 after the Carnation Revolution of 1974, also known as the 25th of April, that made Portugal transition from an authoritarian regime to become a democracy. UMAR is today an association dedicated to awakening feminist consciousness in Portuguese society. For 45 years, UMAR has managed to unite several generations of women and to open spaces for intervention by younger women with a feminist agenda of new and "old" causes, such as the right to contraception and abortion, the fight against domestic violence, parity in political decision-making bodies, or international involvement in initiatives such as the World March of Women (UMAR, 2021).

UMAR works within the scope of human rights and the UN 2030 Agenda, namely the fifth objective: Achieve gender equality and empower all women and girls. UMAR's activity highlights the areas where third-sector organizations mix with social movements (Ferreira, 2004). UMAR's fieldwork includes involving itself with women in their major concerns and social struggles, but also as a way to build feminist daily lives and cultures, valuing the diversity of women's ways of understanding life and the world. In this way, the construction of the feminist agency is articulated with cultural activity, organizing events of a public nature including pressure, denunciation, proposals, contests, protests, and tributes, as well as parties, gatherings, concerts, poetry sessions, and so on (UMAR, 2021).

Data Sampling and Sources

Within ethnography, the amount of time the researcher should spend in the field has not been established, but some authors have defined a period from three months to two years depending on the research design (Everett & Johnston, 2012; Fetterman, 1998; Hammersley & Atkinson, 2007). This study's data were collected over six months—January to June 2021— by the author as part of her doctoral research. The methods used for data collection were adapted to the organization's reality and the interviewees, considering the confinement and restrictions imposed by the COVID-19 pandemic during part of the observation period. Between January and April 2021, UMAR's teams and the interviewees worked from home, communicating through videoconferences on platforms like Zoom. UMAR does not have a formal communication team. Communication is handled more or less spontaneously by people from different nuclei. There is one person who has no training in communication who assumed this responsibility with regard to managing online social media (Facebook and Instagram) and media relations.

In this sense, the field diary was fed through meetings and conversations, and the monitoring of UMAR actions via Facebook and Instagram and through attending their online events, like live talks and conferences on different topics. I also analyzed UMAR's 2021 activity plan and other documents. From April onward, it was possible to follow UMAR's work in the field, in demonstrations and other in-person events. As in the study of Everett and Johnston (2012), a qualitative method for data collection was used, based on "participant observation (experiencing), interviewing (enquiring) and studying materials prepared by others (examining)" (Wolcott, 2009, p. 10), paying attention to the details in the expressions of culture, framed in their context (Ybema et al., 2009).

Ethical considerations, mainly related to managing the observer–participant relationship, need to be addressed during all the ethnographic research stages (Fetterman, 1998). I addressed this issue by making the researcher's role explicit through all the interactions and asking for permission to record the conversations and quote the people involved. The researcher's role and the investigation's objectives were explained in the document of informed, clarified, and free consent to participate in the study signed by Manuela Tavares and Sara Anselmo, members of the association's Board of Directors.

A list of all interviewees at both stages of the investigation is provided in Table 6.1.

Table 6.1   List of interviewees, institutions, and expertise

List of interviewees	
INSTITUTIONS	EXPERTISE
UMAR	Co-founder and Board of Directors (Lisbon Center)
UMAR	Board of Directors (Lisbon Center)
UMAR	Board of Directors (Lisbon Center)
UMAR	Association Member (Lisbon Center)
UMAR	Association Member (Lisbon Center)
UMAR	Association Member (Lisbon Center)
UMAR	Board of Directors (Braga Center)
UMAR	Board of Directors (Coimbra Center)
UMAR	Association Member (Coimbra Center)
APECOM-associated agencies	
Atrevia	President Portugal
M Public Relations	Executive director
Midlandcom	Director
Wisdom Consulting	CEO
Guess What PR	Partner
Multicom	General director
Global Press Communication & PR Consulting	Account Director
Quintela & Reis Consultores	Managing partner
Companhia das Soluções	Communication Director
Central de Informação	General director
Llorente & Cuenca	Partner and General Director
JLM & Associados	Administrator

DATA ANALYSIS AND REDUCTION

Through ethnographic immersion and interviews, a very high quantity of data was obtained, and that required a careful selection process of meaning units. Converting data through description, analysis, and interpretation is not a linear process in ethnographic approaches (Wolcott, 2009). In the first stage of description, fieldwork observation data were documented in the field diary, and all recorded interviews were transcribed as they were undertaken (Baszanger & Dodier, 2004).

To select the information relevant to this study from the ethnographic approach to UMAR, two main selection criteria/categories were used (obtained from the literature review): (a) type of activism, according to the typology of activism proposed by Harrebye (2016, p. 3), and (b) main communication and organizational challenges (Ruão & Kunsch, 2014).

To analyze the responses of the communication experts, I resorted to NVivo software.[3] The analysis started by reading, identifying, and classifying codes suggested by the data rather than collected from the literature (Lansisalmi et al., 2004). Coding was operationalized as nodes (meaning structures) and managed by computer-assisted qualitative data analysis.

FINDINGS: ETHNOGRAPHIC IMMERSION UMAR

Type of Activism

According to the typology of activism proposed by Harrebye (2016, p. 83), UMAR fits into various types depending on the issues being handled. But the kind of activism that prevails is "confrontational" with a "fundamental logic" based on "denunciation," which, not directly appealing to civil disobedience, aims at "open/transparent" and fair procedures, resorting to "challenging slogans" like "Against patriarchal justice and sexist violence! They messed with one, they messed with all of us!" This style is "provocative" and rebellious (with a propensity for "tension in the relationship with institutional agents"). For example, on the topic of sexual harassment that was much debated in Portugal in April and May 2021 because of the denunciation of public figures, similar to the #MeToo movement in the US in 2017, UMAR used a narrative of

---

[3] QSR International. (2021). NVivo Qualitative Data Analysis Software. https://www.qsrinternational.com/nvivo-qualitative-data-analysis-software/home.

"confrontational" criticism and of disobedience to social customs, claim-
ing "open/transparent procedures" and using a challenging slogan—"If
you can look, see. If you can see it, act!"—in a tone that represented a
"provocative" call to action.

Main Communication and Organizational Challenges

Through the participant observation and online conversations and interviews with activists from UMAR, the main communication and organizational challenges identified were:

1. Precarious professional situation of those engaged in this type of
   activism. The working conditions of those working in NGOs in
   Portugal are known: "Insufficient collaborators in many NGOs;
   Difficulty in finding qualified workers, especially in the areas of management and marketing (...); Risk of burnout due to the accumulation of functions, exhaustion or psychological demand for the work
   performed at all levels of the hierarchy; low salaries paid to employees (...); Low financial capacity of the organization to integrate
   human resources working exclusively in areas such as external communication or fundraising" (Franco, 2014, p. 207). One of the
   UMAR interviewees mentioned, "I am going to be 58 years old,
   and I have never known any work experience other than precarious-
   ness." Another added: "[A] paternalistic approach and a romanti-
   cized welfare culture that does not allow people to talk openly about
   money in this area." One of the members of the UMAR board
   explained, "I am a project technician in an NGO, but people think
   this is a playful job, not credible."
2. Dependence on public funding. UMAR also provides public services such as shelters for women who are victims of violence, as well
   as training in victim support techniques, in line with its perspective
   that these are services that replace the function of the state. Despite
   a common assumption that UMAR members practice a left-wing
   feminism (politically), they claim that ideologically they see no
   impediment to establishing partnerships with private entities for
   fundraising and/or communication support activities. But as with
   many NGOs, a lack of resources can itself prevent sustainable ongoing funding, because fundraising efforts require staffing for this purpose, which UMAR lacks. Even in these circumstances, UMAR

claims that it maintains a critical public voice based not only on contesting but also on suggesting concrete solutions to problems.

However, when UMAR members go to Parliament to present proposals or participate in political committee hearings, they feel a lack of support in training and preparing arguments.

3. Lack of representation in the mainstream media, especially on television. "Gender issues in media content remain pertinent" and "the power to change lies with governments, the media, and ordinary audiences" (Lee & Vargas, 2020, p. 7). However, UMAR's experience with the media confirms other authors' perspectives about the need to discuss an inclusive media agenda because there is a "representation crisis" between journalists and social movements in Portugal (Alves, 2013, p. 135). In a collective context of voters' disinterest in the political system, the media in Portugal continue to not encourage journalists' receptiveness to the messages of the new social movements, nor do they welcome their messages in the news agenda without prejudice or stigmas (which does not mean without scrutiny and rigor) (Alexandre, 2019, p. 339). In an interview, an activist and member of the UMAR board said, "We only manage to appear in the media when there is violence"; another said, "[J]ournalists want nothing to do with us, they always listen to the same most powerful or influential institutional figures." This confirms that "the conventional criteria for news are obsessed with the news value of "prominence": the VIPs with political and economic power, and the "stars" of entertainment and of sports" (Lee & Vargas, 2020, p. 34). If, on the one hand, activists do not resort to communication tools that allow them to position themselves as credible media sources, on the other hand, the predominant media public image associated with new social movements is one of incitement to conflict or associated with irrelevance. This leaves contemporary activists with a dilemma: Is it still necessary to resort to violence, drama, and victimization to get media representation?

Expert Consultation

Regarding the consultation of communication experts from APECOM-associated agencies, as seen in Fig. 6.1, the categories for this type of consultation are the following (by order of highest frequency with which they were mentioned):

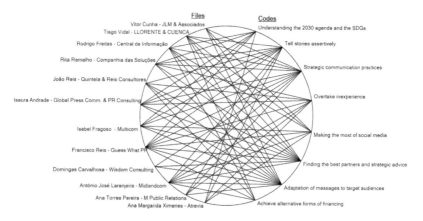

Fig. 6.1 Visual representation of the connections between respondents and response categories (NVivo software)

Strategic Communication Practices. The 12 experts interviewed mentioned that companies and organizations in general are reviewing their relationships with interest groups in terms of good practices as well as social and environmental responsibility. Communication practices reveal a much more realistic management concern with these issues. The culture of the financial firm—pure and hard, and seeking only profit—is falling behind, and this could be an opportunity for a new type of partnership between companies, NGOs, and other interest groups. One of the respondents mentioned: "Communication strategies are a tool, and as such can be used to achieve any goal."

Adaptation of Messages to Target Audiences. Almost all respondents (11) agreed on the need for case-by-case analyses. One of the interviewees emphasized that "when it comes to massification, the objective of organizations of this type, or of a large majority, is for their message to reach as large an audience as possible, but it is necessary to start somewhere, and eventually this analysis will be very important." This means that turning these actions into advertising actions may not be the best solution for the things one wants to defend, which, in this case, are intangible in the sense of being moral and social values and of fighting for the good of other people in society and not for the sale of a particular product or service. Because people are all different, specific communication tools and communication strategies must be increasingly oriented toward the right audience in order to increase these shared global views, as happened in the past with certain products that came to be associated with a certain status or lifestyle. Another respondent stated that "people have to be impacted by major global causes through fractioned or segmented narratives connected to their daily reality. People, publics, are not homogeneous, they play several different social roles. And it is necessary to adapt the narratives to the different social roles or concerns that each person may have."

Finding the Best Partners and Strategic Advice. Ten of the experts consulted agreed that strategic communication areas such as public relations can be crucial for activism around the 2030 Agenda, in helping to find the partners that can give strategic advice and support in the implementation of communicative actions. One of the interviewees stated, "[F]or me communication and relationships are an instrument for democracy, and I am proud to be part of this change." Communication agencies and other similar entities already have best practices and techniques on their side, so the causes of clients that often are commercial entities could be replaced by other types of causes. Other interviewee even alluded to this, saying, "So, I would say that it is almost on the side of the players, of the activists, looking for people like us, rather than anything else, because there is the will and the tools to start on this path." Other referred that "it's necessary to find true ambassadors and if we work professionally and strategically with these ambassadors, we can be able to have great results, that a brand would have to invest financially to achieve because the ambassador would not be available to do it in a graceful way."

Tell Stories Assertively. Nine interviews agreed that there is a need in activist communication for a more rational and assertive way to tell stories based on facts. To achieve credibility and legitimacy to operate in the public space, there is a need, as one of the interviews noted, for "well-grounded information that tells a credible story about the subject we are trying to frame." In the words of another respondent, "Let's say that a good part of the people who are involved in activism, whatever it may be, is more for emotional reasons than for political or social reasons. There is no planning, there is no determination of goals and a set of procedures to achieve these goals, because the interest is emotional." Assertiveness in framing the stories was identified as an important factor for activist communication strategies. Other interviewee commented: "Massive sending of superficial information no longer works." Another added: "Everything that involves people, ideas, convictions and causes has an emotional dimension that I don't know how to quantify, but it is huge and communication strategies in this area have to take this into account."

Overtake Inexperience. Seven respondents mentioned, directly or indirectly, the issue of inexperience. It is natural that this type of activism that brings together people from the most diverse areas to collaborate for joint causes does not use (due to a lack of knowledge or lack of access) communication strategies that have long been efficiently used by other private or public entities. One of the interviewees said, "In this context, where inexperience is also paramount, reliable strategic communication will prepare these activists to achieve their goals." Another respondent said, "To have space in the media we have to be on the media agenda of the day. It's not about being on the long-term media agenda. TV news schedules are made and managed during the day. It takes a great capacity to adjust to the day's agenda, to create news angles that have to do with that moment, with that context."

Making the Most of Social Media. Six respondents reported that strategic digital communication is essential to work on causes related to the 2030 Agenda. One of the interviews said that "more than 30 years ago, certain social topics, environmental issues, or animal rights, were not a public issue, and the fact that they are now was enhanced by social media and also by an awareness of these values." Another interviewee referred that "the digital environment has profoundly transformed public relations, creating greater opportunities for engagement with specialized audiences, but also bringing greater challenges in the management of these relations and information flows." Another interviewee offered a reminder that "mainstream media nowadays, fortunately, are one channel among many. Communication with segmented communities, namely digital, is increasingly a reality." One respondent added, "The purpose of this activist communication is always the same is to draw attention, is to sell a message. If you make a well-made viral video that is posted on the networks and after a few hours was seen by millions of people, that's an impact."

Achieve Alternative Forms of Financing. It was also mentioned, by five experts, that strategic communication can help activist groups to rethink ways to finance their activities. One of the interviews noted that "As far as Portugal is concerned, it is also a question of scale. There is not enough critical mass in many movements to achieve alternative forms of financing, for example." According to another, "The big challenge regarding this possibility [using strategic communication tools to increase shared global views such as the 2030 Agenda] has to do with the search for financing. PR campaigns are thought to cost less than other types of campaigns such as advertising, but this is not true. Depending on the project, larger teams are needed to work with different channels and different audiences and doing this in an integrated manner is quite costly. I would say that, for this to happen, a professional approach to strategic communication planning for these movements is needed, which can involve partnerships with communication agencies." Other respondent said, "[W]hen I talk about resources, in terms of causes and global agendas, I believe that more than financial resources, we are talking about having time and motivated people."

Understanding the 2030 Agenda and the SDGs. Confirming something that had already been mentioned by UMAR activists, five respondents agreed that the 2030 Agenda and the SDGs have all the potential to act as aligners to a global communication strategy. However, it is still necessary to achieve greater collective and individual engagement with this agenda. One of the respondents said, "I don't think this potential is generating the desired effects from a communication and engagement standpoint. I actually think most people have no idea what it is. It's a global message that is being used by companies, but I don't think there is a deep understanding of what this global strategy is. And here I think that everyone fails a little bit, the media, the government, the companies, the citizen himself." One of the interviews said, "There is a need to almost, I would say, uncomplicate this agenda and transport this agenda to real and tangible situations."

Discussion and Conclusion

Although is not yet widely recognized and documented in the public relations literature, there are several forms of organizational communication (beyond the commercial and corporate ones) that are "bold, inventive and effective" (Demetrious, 2013, p. 2). Invoking the strength of global collective action and connection, UMAR activists fighting for gender equality managed to mobilize, during the observation period, several collectives, and associations of intersectional feminism, and mobilized its followers in Portugal to carry out online and offline symbolic protests and community solidarity actions during the COVID-19 pandemic, in line with global claims in the scope of human rights and the 2030 Agenda.

Through an ethnographic immersion in UMAR and consultation with specialists in communication, it was possible to confirm that there is an emancipatory, subversive, and transformative potential of public relations for social change. This potential can be observed through different perspectives: (a) production of social meanings and their interference in power relations; (b) development of advocacy and activism campaigns for social and political change; (c) negotiation of cultural identities and practices; and (d) reputation management and political and media communication (Daymon & Demetrious, 2013).

With regard to the research question, the SDGs are all interrelated, and the glue between them are communicative processes. As Lee and Vargas (2020, p. 42) pointed out, "it is difficult to imagine that universal access to sexual and reproductive healthcare services (SDG 3, Target 3.7) can be achieved unless women and girls can obtain accurate knowledge about reproductive health and are able to participate in decision-making processes about healthcare priorities." Strategic communication in general and public relations particularly have the capacity to impact the quality of media representations about gender, which negatively affect the achievement of more ambitious changes in this area. By enabling effective organization and mobilization of increasingly influential activists, strategic communication can also positively impact the ability of these precursors of social change on gender equality to pressure political and economic powers. Strategic communication, in its various areas, is essential to deal with the tensions of misinformation and disinformation exacerbated by the COVID-19 pandemic and by the increase in extreme populisms that are not supportive of gender equality and related agendas. To this extent, SDG 18—Communication for All—will reinforce the realization of SDG5 on gender equality.

In the logic of activist participation—"critical," "assertive," or "indignant" citizens, who pose new challenges to the political status quo (Sá & Pequito, 2015)—the third sector is essential for the quality of democracy and for social innovation. Concerning gender equality activism, based on confrontational and rebellious communication like the one practiced by UMAR, it is possible to say that its members are producers of strategic communication who use, though in an amateur way, various public relations tools.

Strengthening the role of strategic communication in gender equality activism and collective action will require strong efforts. These efforts are influenced not only by activists but also by structural problems of the third sector in Portugal, like the precarious professional situation of those engaged in this type of activism, dependence on public funding, and the lack of representation in the mainstream media, especially on television.

The biggest challenges identified by and with activists during participant observation were corroborated by the communication experts consulted, confirming the existence of a "representation crisis" between journalists and social movements in Portugal (Alves, 2013, p. 135).

These experts also indicated the main areas where strategic communication could support activists working under the 2030 Agenda: (a) taking advantage of the changes that are happening in corporate cultures and that are generating new communication practices in terms of social and environmental responsibility; (b) adapting messages to target audiences; (c) finding the best partners and strategic advice; (d) telling stories assertively; (e) overtaking inexperience; (f) making the most of social media; (g) achieving alternative forms of financing; and (g) understanding the 2030 Agenda and the SDGs.

On the one hand, activists say that ideologically they see no impediment to establishing partnerships with private entities for fundraising and/ or communication support, confirming the findings of USC Annenberg's 2020 Global Communication Report. On the other hand, the communication and public relations experts mentioned that one of the possible paths to enhancing the communication strategies of these groups is a closer relationship between these organizations and private companies that are really concerned with these topics of social change. Given this scenario, there may be paths and bridges to be explored in an innovative logic of win–win partnerships between activists and private companies. A study from Parcha and Kingsley Westerman (2020) revealed that a "corporate statement on a controversial social issue is effective in changing an individual's attitude toward the issue depending on how much the issue is relevant to the individual's goals and/or if the corporate statement is supported by other corporations" (p. 350).

Activist organizations need to understand that the culture of dependence on public funding that has been taken for granted for many years needs to be transformed; otherwise, the organizations run the risk of being unable to seize opportunities, becoming arms of the civil society co-opted by political parties that capitalize on their dissatisfaction. "Public funding will be increasingly scarce and social capital will gain more and more importance in order to guarantee the economic, financial and strategic sustainability of organizations of this nature" (Azevedo et al., 2010, p. 17). The way to prepare for the current changes is to be "increasingly demanding on themselves by becoming professional" (Azevedo et al., 2010, p. 27). The increasingly evident competition in the market of ideas and struggles for change and social causes reinforces the growing trend toward the adoption of business practices by third-sector organizations, and communication is a preponderant factor in this process (Balonas, 2012).

It was also possible to observe that the 2030 Agenda is not a framework that is used by these activists, neither in direct communication with their audiences nor with the media audience. These activists consider it "too vague and far removed from their real daily challenges," and to this extent "greater integration of communication and information issues into the SDGs and their targets would have strengthened the vision of Agenda 2030" (Lee & Vargas, 2020, p. 43). This leads us to the relation of SDG18 (Communication for all) with the role of strategic communication in gender equality activism.

The inclusion of SDG18 on the 2030 Agenda could enhance civil society advocacy, allowing it to broaden and explore the debate on the contributions of the various dimensions of communication for these struggles. After all, "no matter the issue—poverty, conflict resolution, self-determination, migration, health, land, housing, the climate crisis—little can be done without effective communication" (Lee & Vargas, 2020, p. 2). Strategic communication practices can help to achieve greater collective and individual engagement with the 2030 Agenda.

This case study illustrates the areas where public relations and activism intersect by showing how these intersections could be understood and debated more deeply if SDG18 (Communication for all) were included in the 2030 Agenda.

References

Acaroglu, L. (2014). *Make a change—A handbook for creative rebels and change agents*. Disrupt Design.

Adi, A. (2020). *Protest public relations—Communicating dissent and activism*. Routledge.

Alemanno, A. (2017). *Lobbying for change: Find your voice to create a better society*. Icon Books.

Alexandre, R. (2019). O papel do jornalismo na mobilização cívica. In A. Corrêa D'almeida, *Reforma do Sistema Parlamentar em Portugal—Análises e instrumentos para um diálogo urgente*. Principia.

Alves, T. C. (2013). Média, movimentos sociais e democracia participativa: As mensagens políticas nos cartazes da manifestação de 15 de setembro de 2012. *Estudos em Comunicação, 14*, 123–136.

Azevedo, C., Franco, R., et al. (Eds.). (2010). *Gestão de Organizações Sem Fins Lucrativos—o desafio da inovação social.* Imoedições.

Balonas, S. (2012). O fator comunicação na profissionalização do terceiro setor. In *V Jornadas de Publicidade* "Publicidade, públicos e redes de influência na actualidade digital". Universidade Católica Portuguesa. http://hdl.handle.net/1822/27641

Baszanger, I., & Dodier, N. (2004). Ethnography: Relating the part to the whole. In D. Silverman (Ed.), *Qualitative research: Theory, method and practice* (2nd ed.). Sage Publications.

Berger, B. K., & Reber, B. H. (2013). Power and influence in public relations. In K. Sriramesh, A. Zerfass, & J.-N. Kim, *Public relations and communication management, current trends and emerging topics.* Routledge.

Bourdieu, P. (1986). The forms of capital. In J. Richardson, *Handbook of theory and research for the sociology of education* (pp. 241–258). Greenwood.

Castells, M. (2007). *A era da informação: economia, sociedade e cultura: o poder da identidade.* Fundação Calouste Gulbenkian.

Castells, M. (2013). *Redes de indignação e esperança: movimentos sociais na era da internet.* Zahar.

Ciszek, E., & Logan, N. (2018). Challenging the dialogic promise: How Ben & Jerry's support for Black Lives Matter fosters dissensus on social media. *Journal of Public Relations Research, 30*(3), 115–127. https://doi.org/10.1080/1062726X.2018.1498342

Ciszek, E. L. (2017). Activist strategic communication for social change: A transnational case study of lesbian, gay, bisexual, and transgender activism. *Journal of Communication, 67*(5), 702–718. https://doi.org/10.1111/jcom.12319

Coleman, J. S. (1988). Social capital in the creation of human capital. *The American Journal of Sociology, 94*, S95–S120.

Davidson, S. (2016). Public relations theory: An agonistic critique of the turns to dialogue and symmetry. *Public Relations Inquiry, 5*(2), 145–167. https://doi.org/10.1177/2046147X16649007

Daymon, C., & Demetrious, K. (2013). *Gender and public relations: Critical perspectives on voice, image and identity.* Routledge.

Demetrious, K. (2013). *Public relations, activism, and social change: Speaking up.* Routledge.

Demo, P. (1995). *Metodologia científica em ciências sociais.* Atlas.

Dozier, D., & Lauzen, M. (2000). Liberating the intellectual domain from the practice: Public relations, activism, and the role of the scholar. *Journal of Public Relations Research, 12*(1), 3–22.

Dutta, M. J. (2009). On Spivak. In O. Ihlen, B. van Ruler, & M. Fredriksson (Eds.), *Public relations and social theory: Key figures and concepts* (pp. 278–299). Routledge.

Edwards, L. (2006). Rethinking power in public relations. *Public Relations Review,* *32*(3), 229–231. https://doi.org/10.1016/j.pubrev.2006.05.013

EUPRERA. (2021, April 15). Statement on communication of Covid-19 pandemic. https://euprera.org/covid-comm-statement

Everett, J. L., & Johnston, K. A. (2012). Toward an ethnographic imperative in public relations research. *Public Relations Review,* *38*(4), 522–528. https://doi.org/10.1016/j.pubrev.2012.05.006

Ferreira, S. (2004). O papel de movimento social das organizações do terceiro sector em Portugal. Atas dos ateliers do V° Congresso Português de Sociologia, Sociedades Contemporâneas: Reflexividade e Acão Atelier: Classes, Movimentos e Lutas Sociais. https://estudogeral.sib.uc.pt/handle/10316/44071

Fetterman, D. M. (1998). *Ethnography: Step by step* (2nd ed.). Sage.

Franco, R. C. (Coord.). (2014). Diagnóstico das ONG em Portugal, Fundação Calouste Gulbenkian and EEA Grants.

Frandsen, F., & Johansen, W. (2017). Strategic communication. In C. R. Scott & L. K. Lewis (Eds.), *The international encyclopedia of organizational communication* (pp. 2250–2258). Wiley-Blackwell.

Ganesh, S., & Zoller, H. M. (2012). Dialogue, activism, and democratic social change. *Communication Theory,* *22*(1), 66–91. https://doi.org/10.1111/j.1468-2885.2011.01396.x

Gigler, B. S. (2001, July/August). Empowerment through the Internet: Opportunities and challenges for Indigenous peoples. In: Technology for Social Action. TechKnowLogia.

Gigler, B.-S., & Bailur, S. (2014). Closing the feedback loop: Can technology bridge the accountability gap? Directions in development—Public sector governance. Washington, DC: World Bank. © World Bank. https://openknowledge.worldbank.org/handle/10986/18408 License: CC BY 3.0 IGO.

Guttmann, A. (2020). *PR industry market size worldwide 2018–2022.* Statista.com. https://www.statista.com/statistics/645836/public-relations-pr-revenue

Hallahan, K., Holtzhausen, D., van Ruler, B., Verčič, D., & Sriramesh, K. (2007). Defining strategic communication. *International Journal of Strategic Communication,* *1*(1), 3–35. https://doi.org/10.1080/15531180701285244

Hammersley, M., & Atkinson, P. (2007). *Ethnography: Principles in practice* (3rd ed.). Routledge.

Harrebye, S. F. (2016). *Social change and creative activism in the 21st century: The mirror effect.* Palgrave Macmillan.

Hasenfeld, Y., & Gidron, B. (2005). Understanding multi-purpose hybrid voluntary organizations: The contributions of theories on civil society, social movements and nonprofit organizations. *Journal of Civil Society,* *1*(2), 97–112. https://doi.org/10.1080/17448680500337350

Heath, R. L., Motion, J., & Leitch, S. (2009). Power and public relations: Paradoxes and programmatic thoughts. In K. Yamamura (Ed.), *12th Annual*

International Public Relations Research—Conference Research that Matters to the Practice. University of Miami.

Holtzhausen, D. R. (2000). Postmodern values in public relations. *Journal of Public Relations Research, 12*(1), 93–114. https://doi.org/10.1207/S1532754XJPRR1201_6

Holtzhausen, D. R. (2012). *Public relations as activism: Postmodern approaches to theory & practice*. Routledge.

Holtzhausen, D. R., & Voto, R. (2002). Resistance from the margins: The postmodern public relations practitioner as organizational activist. *Journal of Public Relations Research, 14*(1), 57–84.

Holtzhausen, D. R., & Zerfass, A. (2014). *The Routledge handbook of strategic communication*. Routledge.

Jordan, T. (2002). *Activism! Direct action, hacktivism and the future of society*. Reaktion Books.

Kunsch, M., Krohling, M., & Kunsch, W. L. (2007). Relações Públicas Comunitárias: A comunicação numa perspetiva dialógica e transformadora. Summus Editorial.

L'Etang, J. (2006). Public relations and propaganda: Conceptual issues, methodological problems, and public relations discourse. In J. L'Etang & M. Pieczka (Eds.), *Public relations: Critical debates and contemporary practice* (pp. 23–40). Lawrence Erlbaum.

L'Etang, J. (2009). Radical PR—Catalyst for change or an aporia? *Ethical Space: The International Journal of Communication Ethics, 6*(2), 13–18.

L'Etang, J. (2016). History as a source of critique. In J. L'Etang, D. McKie, N. Snow, & J. Xifra (Eds.), *The Routledge handbook of critical public relations*. Routledge.

L'Etang, J., Hodges, E. M., & Pieczka, M. (2012). Cultures and places: Ethnography in public relations spaces—Editorial. *Public Relations Review, 38*(4), 519–521. https://doi.org/10.1016/j.pubrev.2012.05.013

Lansisalmi, H., Peiro, J., & Kivimake, M. (2004). Grounded theory in organizational research. In C. Cassell & G. Symon (Eds.), *Essential guide to qualitative methods in organizational research*. Sage.

Lee, P. (Ed.). (2004). *Many voices, one vision. The right to communicate in practice*. Southbound.

Lee, P., & Vargas, L. (2020). *Expanding shrinking communication spaces*. Centre for Communication Rights. Southbound.

Martin, B. (2007). Activism, social and political. In G. L. Anderson & K. G. Herr (Eds.), *Encyclopedia of activism and social justice* (pp. 19–27). Sage.

Martins, S. da Cruz. (2003). Novos associativismos e tematizações na sociedade portuguesa. *Sociologia, Problemas e Práticas, 43*, 103–132. http://www.scielo.mec.pt/scielo.php?script=sci_arttext&pid=S0873-65292003000300009&lng=en&tlng=

McNamara, K.S. (2000, March/April). Why wired? The importance of access to information and communication technologies. *International Journal of Technologies for the Advance of Knowledge and Learning.*

McNamara, K. S. (2003). Information and communication technologies, poverty and development: Learning from experience. A Background paper for the InfoDev Annual Symposium. Washington, DC: The World Bank.

Mickey, T. J. (1995). *Sociodrama: An interpretive theory for the practice of public relations.* University Press of America.

Mouffe, C. (1998). "The radical centre: A politics without adversary". *Soundings*, 9, 11–23, https://banmarchive.org.uk/soundings/soundings-issue9-summer-1998/the-radical-centre/

Mozammel, M. (2011). Poverty reduction with strategic communication: Moving from awareness raising to sustained citizen participation. Communication for Governance and Accountability Program (CommGAP). World Bank, Washington, DC. © World Bank. https://openknowledge.worldbank.org/handle/10986/27362 License: CC BY 3.0 IGO.

Negri, A., & Hardt, M. (2005). *Multidão—Guerra e democracia na Era do Império.* Campo das Letras.

Norris, P. (2002). *Democratic phoenix: Reinventing political activism.* Cambridge University Press.

Nye, J. S. (2004). *Soft power: The means to success in international relations.* Public Affairs Press.

Parcha, J. M., & Kingsley Westerman, C. Y. (2020). How corporate social advocacy affects attitude change toward controversial social issues. *Management Communication Quarterly, 34*(3), 350–383. https://doi.org/10.1177/0893318920912196

Putnam, R. D. (1993). What makes democracy work? *National Civic Review, 82*, 101–107. https://doi.org/10.1002/ncr.4100820204

Radford, G. P. (2012). Public relations in a postmodern world. *Public Relations Inquiry, 1*(1), 49–67. https://doi.org/10.1177/2046147X11422143

Rheingold, H. (2002). *Smart mobs: The next social revolution.* Perseus.

Ruão, T., & Kunsch, M. (2014). A Comunicação Organizacional e Estratégica: Nota Introdutória. *Comunicação e Sociedade, 26*, 7–13.

Sá, J. de, & Pequito, C. (2015). *Capital Social, Economia Social e Qualidade de Democracia em Portugal.* Campos de Comunicação.

Servaes, J. (2012). Soft power and public diplomacy: The new frontier for public relations and international communication between the US and China. *Public Relations Review, 38*(5), 643–651.

Servaes, J., & Malikhao, P. (2012). Advocacy communication for peacebuilding. *Development in Practice, 22*(2), 229–243. https://doi.org/10.1080/09614524.2012.640980

Sutton, M. Q., & Anderson, E. (2004). *Introduction to cultural ecology*. Altamira Press.

Tafra-Vlahović, M. (2012). The role of public relations in the growth of sustainable consumerism. *International Journal of Management Cases, 14*. https://doi.org/10.5848/APBJ.2012.00024

Toro, J. B. A., & Werneck, N. M. D. (2004). *Mobilização social: um modo de construir a democracia e a participação*. Autêntica.

UMAR. (2021). UMAR: Uma Associação com 30 anos de História. http://www.umarfeminismos.org/index.php/quemsomos

Verčič, D. (2008). Public relations and power: How hard is soft power? In A. Zerfass, B. van Ruler, & K. Sriramesh (Eds.), *Public relations research*. VS Verlag für Sozialwissenschaften.

White, M. (2016). *The end of protest: A new playbook for revolution*. Knopf.

Winthrop, R. H. (1991). *Dictionary of concepts in cultural anthropology*. Greenwood Press.

Wolcott, H. F. (2009). *Writing up qualitative research* (3rd ed.). Sage.

Xifra, J. (2012). Public relations anthropologies: French theory, anthropology of morality and ethnographic practices. *Public Relations Review, 38*(4). https://doi.org/10.1016/j.pubrev.2012.05.003

Ybema, S., Yanow, D., Wels, H., & Kamsteeg, F. (Eds.). (2009). *Organizational ethnography*. Sage.

Yusha'u, M. J., & Servaes, J. (2021). *The Palgrave handbook of international communication and sustainable development*. Palgrave Macmillan.

OTHER SOURCES

UN SDG Progress Report 2020, July 2020. https://unstats.un.org/sdgs/report/2020/The-Sustainable-Development-Goals-Report-2020.pdf

USC Annenberg's 2020 Global Communication Report. https://annenberg.usc.edu/news/research-and-impact/study-predicts-growth-and-democratization-activism

Media Literacy and Conflict: Understanding Mediated Communication for the Achievement of Peace and Development

Valentina Baú

Abstract In advocating for the establishment of *SDG18—Communication for All*, this chapter discusses the importance of media literacy among groups who have experienced conflict, with particular focus on the youth. Drawing on the 'essential competencies of digital and media literacy' articulated by Hobbs, a framework is built to discuss the role that communication for development (C4D) projects implemented in conflict-affected realities can play when media literacy is placed at the centre.

V. Baú (✉)
Western Sydney University, Institute for Culture and Society (ICS),
Sydney, NSW, Australia
e-mail: v.bau@westernsydney.edu.au

© The Author(s), under exclusive license to Springer Nature Switzerland AG 2023
J. Servaes, M. J. Yusha'u (eds.), *SDG18 Communication for All,*
Volume 1, Sustainable Development Goals Series,
https://doi.org/10.1007/978-3-031-19142-8_7

By existing on the margins of formal education media literacy can be incorporated into initiatives that lie outside traditional curriculum design and can be shaped into C4D interventions that aim for critical consciousness, agency and empowerment. While discussing how these interventions can be built to have a positive impact on young people living in conflict-affected realities, this chapter reveals how targeting media literacy through a communication-specific goal is essential for development.

Keywords Media literacy • Mediated communication • Peace and development • Young people

INTRODUCTION

In advocating for the establishment of *SDG18—Communication for All,* this chapter discusses the importance of media literacy among groups who have experienced conflict, with particular focus on the youth. Drawing on the 'essential competencies of digital and media literacy' articulated by Hobbs (2010), a framework is built to discuss the role that communication for development (C4D) projects implemented in conflict-affected realities can play when media literacy is placed at the centre.

There is a growing recognition today that communication-based development interventions that are inclusive, participatory and locally driven can contribute meaningfully to processes of social change. *SDG16—Peace, Justice and Strong Institution* aims at promoting peaceful and inclusive societies, access to justice and accountable institutions. In the achievement of this goal and its targets, in particular, access to communication and information is critical. Not only can media and communication facilitate participation, peaceful conflict resolution and trust in institutions, but they can also strengthen civil society and secure good governance by informing citizens and enabling them to drive the public agenda. Yet, in the current presentation of both this and other SDGs, the role of communication remains largely veiled.

This chapter argues the importance of media literacy as a critical component of development, in order to ensure that individuals are able to understand information and engage in meaningful communication exchange though the media. A lack of literacy among young people living in realities of conflict can be regarded as an obstacle for the establishment of a sustainable peace; hence, the formulation of a communication-focused goal that addresses not only information poverty but also misinformation through media is key. Moreover, providing young people with the skills to produce content and to take action in society as a result of their experience on the media are also critical outcomes of media literacy that must not be left untapped. It is also argued that C4D projects, thanks to their change-driven strategic design to the use of the media, represent useful avenues for the development of these critical skills in the youth.

The chapter begins with an overview, informed by the literature, of the role that communication can play in the achievement of the SDGs through the provision of media literacy. The role of the media in conflict is subsequently debated, highlighting both the useful and the dangerous function that these platforms perform in shaping the dynamics of the conflict. After that, a framework is presented for the development of C4D projects aimed at providing young people living in conflict with media literacy skills that are contextually relevant. Built around Hobbs' (2010) five essential competencies of media literacy, the framework presented generates ideas on three critical stages that C4D projects should incorporate in order to deliver effective skills to the youth. These are

1. understanding harmful media messages;
2. developing peace-oriented participatory content;
3. upholding and promoting peace.

Lastly, a discussion is offered on the importance of SDG18 for the promotion of media literacy and its essential skills and on how these, ultimately, contribute to the current development agenda.

Media Literacy and the Role of Communication in the SDGs

With the saturation of media and the increasing level of media consumption in societies around the world, specific skills are needed to deal effectively with the information received. The media can exert a strong influence on people's attitudes, beliefs and perceptions; therefore, the issue at stake is how people respond to media exposure, and whether or not they have the ability to 'comprehend, interpret, critically analyse and compose text' (Koltay, 2011, p. 212). The European Commission (2007) has highlighted different levels of media literacy, the most critical of which include (1) being comfortable with all forms of media, from print to digital, and using them actively to access information but also for entertainment, intercultural dialogue and learning; (2) being able to assess critically both quality and accuracy of media content; and (3) using media to disseminate content in a way that is informed and creative.

While a number of different literacies have been explored in the academic scholarship, the term media literacy encompasses all types of mediated texts, including print, audiovisual, electronic and telephony, which form an integrated media environment (Koltay, 2011). Aufderheide (1992) defines a media literate person as someone who 'can decode, evaluate, analyse and produce both print and electronic media. The fundamental objective of media literacy is a critical autonomy relationship to all media' (p. 1). Koltay (2011) also adds that among the various components of media literacy, analytic competencies have been especially emphasised; this is because critical evaluation is an important requirement for both examining and constructing media messages.

The significance of media literacy is not simply dictated by the growing media consumption. It is also justified by the significant role that information plays in the contexts of development, democracy, participation and active citizenship. This is particularly true for young people, who are the recipients of a great quantity of media messages (Koltay, 2011). Research has shown that, through media literacy, young people learn how to ask relevant questions, search for appropriate information, gauge the quality of it and engage in discussions with others: this strengthens their participation in civic and political life (Martens & Hobbs, 2015). Participating actively in society through both political and civic engagement not only strengthens democratic practices; it also allows citizens to contribute in shaping the path to development. With the strong focus on inclusion and representation that exists in the 2030 development agenda presented through the SDGs, practices and avenues that enable citizens to participate should also be regarded as an essential component that needs to be clearly articulated in a goal.

As Hobbs (2010) explains, media literacy has also undergone its own evolution from being a term indicating mainly the ability to read, write and listen to media, to a concept that refers to the 'ability to share meaning through symbol systems in order to fully participate in society' (p. 16).

With the emergence of new channels, the idea of text has also expanded to include 'any form of expression or communication in fixed and tangible form that uses symbol systems, including language, still and moving images, graphic design, sound, music and interactivity' (pp. 16–17).

Ranieri (2019) argues that the process of becoming media literate involves three stages. Firstly, the media are accessed not only in a material but also in a cognitive way; this refers to the ability, besides reading and writing, to research and consult media purposefully. Secondly, there is a strong critical understanding of the media landscape; this is demonstrated in the evaluation of media content and in considering opportunities and limitations. Lastly, available skills include the creation and production of messages, with an awareness of the audience's characteristics and an ability to tailor the message based on these. It is interesting to note that whilst critical understanding and evaluation of the media were initially the main goals of media literacy programmes, the current digital context has called for the recognition of the importance of content creation skills as part of the learning (Ranieri, 2019).

Mihailidis (2019) contends that media literacy must be developed with 'civic intentionality'. This means that interventions in this field should stay true to their claims of contributing to people's empowerment by enabling individuals to participate and better engage in civic life. This author offers five constructs to make media literacy more 'intentional' in its civic-driven endeavour:

- Caring: media literacy encourages people to consider how media can support interventions that bring us together.
- Critical consciousness: media literacy encourages to go beyond the media text and look at its connection with oppression, power, transgression and boundaries.
- Imagination: particularly appropriate for young people, media literacy here builds a creative space that allows one to 'explore alternative realities through cultural icons that can connect, subvert, and inspire' (p. 114).
- Persistence: media literacy facilitates connection between knowledge and action, and helps in developing commitment to a cause with the deployment of relevant media tactics that support this.
- Emancipation: through media literacy, people question the role of powerful media institutions and structures, can negotiate boundaries and avoid restrictive technologies.

These ideas make clear the importance that the media and communication have for connecting, informing, reflecting, creating and more. In spite of this tangible need for both skills and channels that drive these processes, SDG18 remains missing from the global goals. Some of the leaders who took part in drafting the 2030 agenda for development acknowledged that communication would inevitably play a key role in achieving the SDGs (Yusha'u, 2021). The sections that follow make a case for the value of media literacy in building effective, peace-oriented mediated communication at times of conflict. This not only contributes directly to development goal 16 but also brings benefit to the agenda more broadly.

MEDIA IN CONFLICT: OPPORTUNITY OR THREAT?

A report by Oxfam (2008, cited in Baksh et al., 2009, p. 5) identifies as the objectives of peacebuilding those of 'develop(ing) trust, safety, and social cohesion within and between communities; strengthen(ing) social and cultural capacities to resolve disputes and conflict; and promot(ing) inter-ethnic and inter-group interaction and dialogue'. It also highlights that people themselves are the best foundations on which peace is built; therefore, engaging with different actors at the local level, from families to community leaders, is essential to ensure that a shared understanding of peace is created and that this is promoted meaningfully. At the same time, the United Nations encourage 'the involvement of media, especially the mass media, in promoting a culture of peace and non-violence, with particular regard to children and young people' (United Nations, 2018, p. 5).

In contexts of conflict, the media are purposefully used to promote and rebuild peace using three main approaches in media programmes:

- Informational media: These programmes adopt news media to deliver reliable, accurate and unbiased information, which is critical both during and immediately after conflict in order to prevent dangerous rumours from spreading.
- Entertainment media: Programmes using these productions embed peace-related messages into well-liked formats such as radio or TV drama, reality shows, music and so forth. This approach is also known as edutainment.
- Participatory media: These see the involvement of community members in the production of the media intervention. Their participation

typically involves script-writing, storytelling, interviewing and editing, with the aim of communicating messages that are important to the community in the process of re-establishing peace (Paluk, 2012).

For over twenty years now, media interventions adopting different approaches and methodologies have been designed and implemented to reframe conflicts around the world, develop trust and harmony between communities, re-establish balance in unequal power relationships, and combat hate speech and propaganda from violent actors (Legatis, 2015). There have been many instances in which the media, including social media, have been effective at promoting peace and reconciliation, such as in the post-conflict truth-telling process in Liberia (Best et al., 2011) and during the post-Apartheid testimony hearings (Krabill, 2001). As Paluk (2012) explains:

> Media programmes aimed at rebuilding communities target multiple outcomes. Some programmes attempt to increase social tolerance and cooperation generally, or toward certain stigmatised or previously victimised groups such as ethnic minorities or women who have experienced sexual violence. Programmes also attempt to promote politically knowledgeable and active citizens who know their rights and who participate in democratic processes like voting. Finally, media are used to promote economic and physical health in the aftermath of conflict with programmes that promote financial literacy and vaccinations. (p. 285)

Yet, while the media can be useful instruments for rebuilding social relations and assisting communities in re-opening a path to peace, both economically and politically, it is also recognised how these same instruments can be used to fuel conflict, particularly through stereotyping and by stirring up hatred. The negative portrayals of minorities in the media during conflicts such as the war in former Yugoslavia, the genocide in Rwanda, and even the Kenya Post-Election Violence through SMS and blogging are examples of how powerful these channels can be in inciting hate (Paluk, 2012). Even people who have been displaced by violence find themselves having to face additional types of conflicts, such as racism and xenophobic attacks, which are expressed through the media (Moyo, 2021). Hence, we can resolve that the media are not merely reporting conflict, but they are also actively driving some of its dynamics (Allen & Seaton, 1999).

With the power of the media now being widely recognised, it has been acknowledged at the same time that media manipulation by the hands of those who control them or own them is a recurring practice, based on the economic or political environment in which these platforms are operated (Moyo, 2021). In particular, Cottle (2006) has argued that, through their role in assigning meaning to our social world, news media can also serve as instruments to promote ideology. At the same time, other studies have shown how ideology can also be disguised into entertainment media programmes (Moyo, 2021).

Authors such as Kempf (2005, cited in Legatis, 2015, p. 4) have indicated that conflicts are often based on societal constructions, and that one of the ways to untangle these frameworks is by deconstructing them and transforming them into new discourses that focus on peace. From this perspective, it is useful to bear in mind that, in the communication landscapes of conflict-affected countries, a multitude of discourses compete with one another and try to prevail. Different social actors, both state and non-state, have constructed these discourses and are attempting to drive them in the direction they feel is appropriate. Such actors may include politicians, religious institutions, non-governmental organisations (NGOs), the corporate sector, paramilitaries and private security companies, other armed forces, the police and even the media. All of them adopt a range of techniques and make use of specific opportunities to gain approval for their own benefit; at the same time, they use strategies to suppress or delegitimise opposing discourses. Ultimately, through a number of different methods, these actors work to control where and how communication is flowing, and prevent reliable information that could harm their interests from circulating (Legatis, 2015).

In a discussion on the media in Africa, Moyo (2021) highlights a tendency in the media to 'simplify complex realities through ethnicisation or tribalisation of issues—pitting one group against another and not looking for any grey areas in between. This ethnical/tribal shorthand creates an easy "them" and "us" dichotomy for reporting, which inadvertently solidifies previously held stereotypes' (p. 94). This author emphasises how a lack of media literacy and an increase in fake news make media platforms even more predisposed to manipulation. Within this context, Okigbo (2015) underlines how conflict prevention, especially in relation to inter-ethnic conflict, is built on effective communication and the development of a shared understanding. When conflict occurs, it is evidence that communication has failed.

During conflict, false information is often disseminated also with the intent of misleading the in-country adversarial group—such as local rebels or overseas actors—including foreign governments, exiled militia or even diaspora. However, these messages also end up having an impact on innocent civilians (Fiedler & Kovats, 2017). Within this context, instead of encouraging division, the media can choose to adopt strategies that aim for resolving conflict, promoting dialogue and cross-conflict understanding and supporting reconciliation efforts. This can be achieved not only through news media (though these are often the primary focus) but also by utilising other genres and formats such as entertainment programmes, folk theatre, billboards, music and storytelling (Loewenberg, 2009). Thus, an awareness that different channels exist and of how they can be understood and operated is crucial to be able to make effective use of these in a targeted effort to rebuild peace.

Media Literacy Through C4D for Young People in Conflict

As Lee and Vargas (2020) have highlighted, a lack of media literacy is one of the key manifestations of communication and information poverty. During and after conflict, this type of poverty threatens both the achievement and the preservation of peace. With the current convergence of traditional and digital media, media literacy has gained even more importance, particularly in the lives of young people experiencing violent conflict, who are exposed to a diverse range of information channels. Lee and Vargas (2020) state that 'low levels of media literacy among youth affected by conflict prevent them from critically engaging with media content that normalises or glamourises conflict' (p. 96). Hence, a key question that needs to drive the design of media literacy interventions is how these should respond to the surfacing of polarisation, bias and mistrust that both mainstream and grassroots media seem to have brought about (Mihailidis, 2018); this is particularly relevant in context of conflict.

Hobbs (2010) has developed a framework for media literacy that sees the promotion of this practice as a set of five competencies that work together in a spiral. This progression (shown in Table 7.1) moves towards people's empowerment and active participation in learning through both their consumption and creation of media content.

Table 7.1   Essential Competencies of Media Literacy, from Hobbs, 2010, p. 19

Essential Competencies of Digital and Media Literacy

1. **ACCESS** Finding and using media and technology tools skillfully and sharing appropriate and relevant information with others
2. **ANALYZE & EVALUATE** Comprehending messages and using critical thinking to analyse message quality, veracity, credibility and point of view, while considering potential effects or consequences of messages
3. **CREATE** Composing or generating content using creativity and confidence in self-expression, with awareness of purpose, audience and composition techniques
4. **REFLECT** Applying social responsibility and ethical principles to one's own identity and lived experience, communication behavior and conduct
5. **ACT** Working individually and collaboratively to share knowledge and solve problems in the family, the workplace and the community, and participating as a member of a community at local, regional, national and international levels

Wilkins and Mody (2001) have recognised Communication for Development (C4D) as the intentional and strategic use of media and communication technologies in order to achieve positive change in society. Okigbo (2015) expands that by explaining that C4D is a practice in which communication principles, products, methods and processes are systematically and purposefully adopted in order to reach a desirable change. Wilkins (1996) emphasises that the intention of influencing an audience towards a particular change needs to be explicit when working with this framework. In line with that, there are different types of interventions that can be designed to develop media literacy of young people living in conflict-affected or conflict-prone areas. These interventions can be useful not only to de-escalate conflict but also to prevent its occurrence in the first place.

The discussion presented below wants to demonstrate how C4D projects targeting young people can be designed to contribute to the development of a media literacy that raises critical consciousness, a sense of agency and empowerment in contexts of conflict, based on the 'essential competencies of media literacy' set out by Hobbs (2010). Figure 7.1 shows the framework around which this discussion has been built.

Also Hobbs (2010) states that community education for media literacy can be more effectively built through strategic work of NGOs. This framework suggests how C4D projects aimed at developing media literacy can be designed by these organisations. The discussion below unpacks each

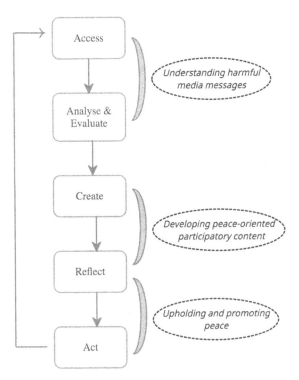

Fig. 7.1 Design framework of C4D interventions aimed at developing media literacy during conflict (drawing on Hobbs' 2010 Media Literacy Essential Competencies)

step of the framework with a specific focus on interventions targeting young people who have experienced conflict.

Understanding Harmful Media Messages

Those who are literate in their media consumption understand that the media industry has a role in shaping knowledge we hold of both ourselves and the world we live in. Hence, this type of literacy allows individuals to prevent internalisation of media representations that may disseminate a negative image of particular groups or that propagate harmful worldviews. Individuals who are media literate also understand the role they play and the responsibilities they have in this landscape. As a result, media literacy empowers people as they become more fluent with communication channels (including technology) and are better placed to locate, evaluate and use information (French, 2015).

It is essential to be able to understand the complex nature of misinformation in order to recognise the difference between misinformation and accurate information. Misinformation is propagated through a large number of channels, which may include social media, messaging apps, but also speeches given in Parliament or other high-level events; traditional community networks can also be a source (Cunliffe-Jones et al., 2021). Projects that provide young people with opportunities to analyse multimedia messages critically play a very important role. In particular, when young people are given the tools to solve problems through the use of advocacy and social communication, they can begin to regard themselves as active participants in what is happening in their communities (Hobbs, 2010). This is very important in contexts of violent conflict, where the youth are too often passive recipients of messages that incite to violence and hatred.

Currently, young people around the world are expected to develop literacy skills in a number of areas that range from written literacy to digital literacy, health literacy, news literacy and others. Arguing for the need for a 'misinformation literacy', Cunliffe-Jones et al. (2021) emphasise the importance of gaining knowledge on the different forms that both misinformation and accurate information can take, the processes in place to produce these, how they are distributed and who they are consumed by, including who may believe that misinformation is true and share it. In particular, these authors put forward four domains in which skills must be developed: (1) knowledge of the *context* in which either false or accurate information is produced; (2) knowledge of the sources of *creation* of that information, including motivations they may have; (3) knowledge of the *content*, that is, whether information presented is fact or opinion, and how deception can occur; and (4) knowledge of the process of *circulation* of information.

The dissemination of news on channels such as social media during conflict can make a significant difference on the outcome of certain events. While armed actors attempt to control the content and reach of the information that is being circulated, local communities are also reliant on accessing information in order to stay safe. This is why it is vital that not only is information accessible, but also that people can interpret it and decode it critically to understand the situation around them (Fiedler &

Kovats, 2017). In a discussion on the importance of media literacy during the conflict in South Sudan, Fiedler and Kovats (2017) contend that improved literacy 'in recognising virulent, biased and dehumanising language that can incite violence, could equip people with vital tools, [...] helping them to filter, understand, and critically interpret content spread online and therefore facilitate the responsible use of the Internet and social media' (p. 372). These authors go on to say that strengthening literacy skills in digital media by assessing the facts and distilling them from the circulation of rumours 'can help make up for the deficits in the access to and interaction with traditional media' (ibid.). This is particular important for the realities of young people, who are active users of social media and even more so when other channels become disrupted by the violence.

Patrão et al. (2021) have shown that participatory ways to develop people's media literacy using creative methods are effective, particularly when these are designed to promote civic responsibility and agency amongst learners. Thanks to its flexible approaches, Communication for Development lends itself effectively to the conception of interventions that can deliver crucial media literacy skills. Moreover, media literacy can also be applied to different types of content, from informational to entertaining (Hobbs, 2010).

Developing Peace-Oriented Participatory Content

In contexts that allow for the employment of media technologies, the use of video and other digital media can be crucial for young people to engage in a process of storytelling where their interests and problems can be shared (Hobbs, 2010). The process of participatory content creation is unique not only for its approach in building information, but also for developing media literacy through direct engagement (Munro & Pringle, 2009).

Activities that promote dialogue, reflection, collaboration, creativity, independent thinking and social responsibility should be carried out when working on developing and sharing messages (Hobbs, 2010). C4D projects can be designed around these practices in order to provide young people with a space to not only create but also reflect on the content they are producing and its potential impact.

The introduction of the Internet and the growth in popularity of social media have made possible for anyone who has access to these platforms to bring people together under the flag of a common cause, and to circulate misinformation and rumours that could assign the blame to a particular group or individual with the potential to escalate violence and conflict. In countries where the information needs of the population cannot be met effectively by traditional media due to interference and control from the government, it is particularly important to ensure that information circulated through mobile communication and social media is accurate (Fiedler & Kovats, 2017). This is why engaging young people in C4D initiatives that tap into their creativity to produce their own online content is a great avenue to develop an understanding of the importance of these forms of mediated processes, while using communication to promote peace at the same time.

The process of working together using a medium also creates a meaningful interaction among those involved. Individuals can be taught how to produce content that relates to their own realities, making the learning process more relevant and more sustainable. This is particularly useful in conflict-affected realities. As exemplified by Munro and Pringle (2009), 'holding structured, focused discussion through community radio on key areas of conflict, with experts, opinion pieces, perhaps drama and music as well as opportunities for listeners to participate can be particularly effective if learners are given the opportunity to design and develop some or all of the components of the programme' (p. 19). This makes clear the crucial role that C4D can play when initiatives are designed to deliver media literacy skills through the involvement of the youth in participatory media and communication projects. These can be purposefully built to address the roots of the conflict and make visible the different experiences of those affected by it.

Upholding and Promoting Peace

Thanks, in particular, to the introduction of technology, there has been a substantive increase in both quantity and quality of information that reaches communities. Yet, this greater access to information is not in itself sufficient if people do not have the skills to act upon it (NDI, 2014). The United Nations define a culture of peace as a set of 'values, attitudes and behaviours that reflect and inspire social interaction and sharing based on the principles of freedom, justice and democracy, all human rights, tolerance and solidarity, that reject violence and endeavour to prevent conflicts by tackling their root causes to solve problems through dialogue and negotiation [...]' (United Nations, 1997, p. 1). From this definition, it becomes clear how media literacy can facilitate both the development and the promotion of these skills and value set.

In particular, Mihailidis (2018) emphasises that media literacy 'should prioritise a civic intentionality where interventions are designed to bring people together in support of solving social problems, reinventing spaces for meaningful engagement [and] creating positive dialogue in communities' (p. 159). This author asserts that building these capacities 'depends not only on how we are able to deconstruct and critically engage with media texts, but also we understand their impact on our ability to co-exist in communities, and leverage media to better support a common good' (p. 159).

Hence, a focus on capacity building at the local level is essential to enable an environment where people can discuss and resolve conflict. This approach to creating peace also reinforces social cohesion (Baksh et al., 2009). More specifically, media literacy strategies that aim at behaviour change and drive communication content towards a positive messaging that promotes dialogue rather than responding to abuse must be introduced. Learning such skills involves a shift from a passive user of communication technologies, to one that is aware, for example, of the function of social media and utilises available channels 'as active vehicles of communication and empowerment' (Fiedler & Kovats, 2017, p. 375).

Another important aspect that C4D projects have the potential to address effectively in this area is the issue of identity. By being more aware of who they are, young people can become better skilled at recognising when an attempt to manipulate their emotions with the aim of steering them towards hatred is taking place. In doing so, they can also find their voice to further their rights and make clearer choices on who they want to become (Gagliardone et al., 2015). Thus, gaining skills in understanding and using the media offers the opportunity to learn when and how one can position themselves, particularly in relation to their social and political environment, and reflect on where they belong. Through C4D, this process can take place using participatory approaches and connecting young people with their purpose through the use of communication.

WHAT SDG18 MEANS FOR MEDIA LITERACY

Even though media literacy plays a significant role in anything related to media and everyday life, it is very rare to see it indicated as a specific objective in media and communication interventions. It has also been seldom evaluated as part of broader programmes. Yet, as we have seen, this practice has changed dramatically from being primarily focused on enabling people to evaluate bias and accuracy of information, to including the provision of skills for creating and distributing content. In other words, citizens are not only just consumers but also producers of media. They not only need to be able to analyse information provided by the media critically, but also to express themselves creatively through the media (Burgess, 2013).

In order to participate in contemporary society effectively, people need to have access to information that allows them to take critical decisions for their lives and those of their communities. This also enables them to be engaged in public life. It is therefore crucial to strengthen people's capacity to both consume and produce information in public conversations on important matters (Hobbs, 2010).

When the information and communication needs of specific groups in society are regularly disregarded, especially in the context of development, a number of complications that may include language barriers, different access to media and even prejudice, amongst others, begin to shape relationships within a society (Lee & Vargas, 2020). It also means that selected accounts will remain absent from both the social and political voice of that society. This, in turn, creates a form of social exclusion that can exacerbate conflict.

When communication and information, however, are recognised as rights, then a lack of access to these or the inability to make the most of what they have to offer can be acknowledged as a form of poverty. Media literacy, along with the availability of platforms that make genuine and culturally relevant participation possible, is essential to prevent or transform hardship. In this context, C4D is accepted to be a key tool to bring about processes of social change through its various approaches to the use of media (Lee & Vargas, 2020).

Media literacy that is intentionally built with the aim of instilling civic responsibility and developing a sense of community is one that focuses on 'creative problem solving, the use of physical and online spaces for meaningful engagement, and media processes and practices that support positive community dialogue and collaboration' (Mihailidis, 2019, p. 108). These elements also explain why information and communication must be considered when setting the development agenda: ensuring that people access information that concerns them and their society, and hold the key to understand it, facilitates the achievements of other important objectives related to development and ensures sustainability (Lee & Vargas, 2020). With SDGs 9 and 17 addressing the need for access to the Internet and mobile telephony for everyone, and SDG16 recognising the necessity for accountability, transparency in institutions, and a decision making process that is inclusive and participatory in order to achieve peace, it is clear that media and communication are playing a key role in the 2030 development agenda. This is why a communication-focused SDG is now needed more than ever. In its targets, this goal provides an opportunity to make media literacy a central element in the pursuit of sustainable development. Even when looking at SDG5, the importance of information and communication technology in advancing women empowerment becomes clear. As French (2015) states, 'promoting media literacy will [...] be essential to achieve the development goal of gender equality in and through the media' (p. 34). In line with these ideas, increasing access to the Internet or other digital platforms and creating meaningful spaces for people to voice their views and opinions in society, will not contribute to development unless individuals have the ability to use these tools effectively.

As Wilkins (1996) states, communication can lead to change by creating a connection that brings together both individuals and groups. Yet, while social transformation can be instigated by the use of mediated campaigns, the power to change remains with the people. This is why media literacy is the key for individuals and communities to both consume and produce media with the aim of creating meaningful exchange, harmony and debating solutions to their problems. Therefore, this chapter suggests that Target 1 of SDG18, as proposed by Lee and Vargas (2020), is amended as follows:

Target 1.1 *By 2030, ensure the existence of spaces and resources __and the__* *__acquisition of skills__ for men and women, in particular the poor and vulnerable, to engage in transparent, informed and democratic public dialogue and debate.*

Conclusions

This chapter has brought to light the crucial role that media literacy plays in the 2030 development agenda, both as part of a communication-oriented goal such as SDG18 and as a central component of C4D projects targeting young people in conflict. A lack of media literacy among the youth makes them more vulnerable to violent propaganda. The acquisition of skills that allow this group to understand media messages effectively and to use media channels purposefully, with a focus on peace, can bring an important contribution to development.

After clarifying the link between media literacy and communication, and the function the latter has in the achievement of the SDGs, a framework for the design of C4D interventions aimed at developing media literacy during conflict has been presented. Turning to the 'essential competencies of digital and media literacy' formulated by Hobbs (2010), the framework identifies three conceptual components that can be applied to the design of C4D projects that aim to develop media literacy.

In particular, learning to understand harmful media messages, developing peace-oriented participatory content, and taking action to uphold and promote peace have been recognised to be key stages in the development of a media literacy that wants to raise critical consciousness and a sense of agency. Harnessing the design of C4D projects through this structure can empower young people living in realities of conflict to shape and direct the representation of the events they are living, to feel connected with their identity, and to actively support peace as individuals.

While arguing for the importance of establishing a communication-focused goal as part of the development agenda, this chapter has also maintained that media literacy is a vital component in the achievement of this goal. *SDG18—Communication for All* is a crucial reminder, both for world leaders and for citizens, that what lies at the core of all processes, including development ones, is the ability to communicate ideas, to remain open to reactions, to establish and facilitate dialogue, and to share knowledge that can benefit society broadly. The media are channels that can drive these processes: therefore, literacy in this area needs to be regarded as an essential instrument that can assist useful interaction between all parties, which will ultimately bring progress in development.

References

Allen, T., & Seaton, J. (1999). *The media of conflict. War reporting and representations of ethnic violence.* Zed Books.

Aufderheide, P. (1992). *Media Literacy: A report of the national leadership conference on media literacy.* Aspen Institute. Retrieved October 15, 2021, from https://files.eric.ed.gov/fulltext/ED365294.pdf

Baksh, R., Munro, T., & Robb, C. (2009). Introduction: Setting the context. In R. Baksh & T. Munro (Eds.), *Learning to live together: Using distance education for community peacebuilding* (pp. 1–11). Commonwealth of Learning.

Best, M., Long, W. J., Etherton, J., & Smith, T. (2011). Rich digital media as a tool in post-conflict truth and reconciliation. *Media, War & Conflict, 4*(3), 231–249.

Burgess, J. (2013). *Media Literacy 2.0: A sampling of programmes around the world*. CIMA. Retrieved October 18, 2021, from https://www.cima.ned.org/resource/media-literacy-2-0-a-sampling-of-programs-around-the-world/

Cottle, S. (2006). *Mediatised Conflict: Developments in media and conflict studies*. Open University Press.

Cunliffe-Jones, P., Gaye, S., Gichunge, W., Onumah, C., Pretorius, C., & Schiffrin, A. (2021). The state of media literacy in Sub-Saharan Africa 2020 and a theory of misinformation literacy. Part one. In P. Cunliffe-Jones, A. Diagne, A. Finlay, S. Gaye, W. Gichunge, C. Onumah, C. Pretorius, & A. Schiffrin (Eds.), *Misinformation policy in Sub-Saharan Africa: From laws and regulations to media literacy* (pp. 9–98). University of Westminster Press.

European Commission. (2007). *A European approach to media literacy in the digital environment*. Commission of the European Communities. Retrieved October 15, 2021, from https://www.cedefop.europa.eu/en/news-and-press/news/european-approach-media-literacy-digital-environment

Fiedler, A., & Kovats, S. (2017). Digital media literacy in conflicts. The increasing role of social media in South Sudan. In B. S. De Abreu, P. Mihailidis, A. Y. L. Lee, J. Melki, & J. McDougall (Eds.), *International handbook of media literacy education* (pp. 368–379). Routledge.

French, L. (2015). Media literacies for empowering females and reducing gender inequalities. In G. Lister (Ed.), *Media support in sustainable development and culture of peace* (pp. 34–38). UNESCO.

Gagliardone, I., Gal, D., Alves, T., & Martinez, G. (2015). *Countering online hate speech*. UNESCO.

Hobbs, R. (2010). *Digital and media literacy: A plan of action*. The Aspen Institute. Retrieved October 18, 2021, from https://www.aspeninstitute.org/wp-content/uploads/2010/11/Digital_and_Media_Literacy.pdf

Koltay, T. (2011). The media and the literacies: Media literacy, information literacy, digital literacy. *Media, Culture & Society, 33*(2), 211–221.

Krabill, R. (2001). Symbiosis: Mass media and the Truth and Reconciliation Commission of South Africa. *Media, Culture & Society, 23*(5), 567–585.

Lee, P., & Vargas, L. (2020). *Expanding shrinking communication spaces*. Southbound.

Legatis, R. (2015). *Media-related peacebuilding in processes of conflict transformation*. Berghof Handbook for Conflict Transformation. Berghof Foundation.

Loewenberg, S. (2009). Open communication. In J. de Rivera (Ed.), *Handbook on building cultures of peace* (pp. 176–189). Springer.

Martens, H., & Hobbs, R. (2015). How media literacy supports civic engagement in a digital age. *Atlantic Journal of Communication, 23*, 120–137.

Mihailidis, P. (2018). Civic media literacies: Re-imagining engagement for civic intentionality. *Learning, Media and Technology, 43*(2), 152–164.

Mihailidis, P. (2019). *Civic Media Literacies: Re-imagining human connection in an age of digital abundance.* Routledge.

Moyo, D. (2021). A critical reflection on the role of the media in conflict in Africa. In J. Maweu & A. Mare (Eds.), *Media, conflict and peacebuilding in Africa. Conceptual and empirical consideration* (pp. 87–100). Routledge.

Munro, T., & Pringle, I. (2009). Using open and distance learning for community development. In R. Baksh & T. Munro (Eds.), *Learning to Live Together: Using distance education for community peacebuilding* (pp. 13–22). Commonwealth of Learning.

NDI. (2014). *Citizen participation and technology. An NDI study.* National Democratic Institute. Retrieved October 21, 2021, from https://www.ndi.org/sites/default/files/Citizen-Participation-and-Technology-an-NDI-Study.pdf

Okigbo, C. C. (2015). Recursive inter-ethnic violence and the failure of development communication in Africa. In S. Gibson & A. L. Lando (Eds.), *Impact of communication and the media on ethnic conflict* (pp. 77–88). IGI Global.

Paluk, E. L. (2012). Media as an instrument for reconstructing communities following conflict. In K. J. Jonas & T. A. Morton (Eds.), *Restoring civil society: The psychology of intervention and engagement following crisis* (pp. 284–298). John Wiley & Sons.

Patrão, C., Soeiro, D., & Parreiral, S. (2021). Media, literacy and education: Partners for sustainable development. In M. J. Yusha'u & J. Servaes (Eds.), *The Palgrave handbook of international communication and sustainable development* (pp. 215–233). Palgrave.

Ranieri, M. (2019). Literacy, technology, and media. In Hobbs, R. & Mihailidis, P. (Eds.), *The international encyclopedia of media literacy* (pp. n/a). John Wiley & Sons.

United Nations. (1997). *UN resolutions 52/13: Culture of peace.* UN General Assembly. Retrieved October 21, 2021, from http://www.un-documents.net/a52r13.htm

United Nations. (2018). *UN resolution 73/126. Follow-up to the declaration and programme of action on a culture of peace.* UN General Assembly. Retrieved October 21, 2021, from https://www.un.org/pga/73/wp-content/uploads/sites/53/2019/08/Resolution-A_RES_73_126_2018-The-Culture-of-Peace.pdf

Wilkins, K. G. (1996). Development communication. *Peace Review, 8*(1), 97–103.

Wilkins, K. G., & Mody, B. (2001). Reshaping development communication: Developing communication and communicating development. *Communication Theory, 11*(4), 385–396.

Yusha'u, M. J. (2021). SDG18 – The missing ventilator: An introduction to the 2030 Agenda for development. In M. J. Yusha'u & J. Servaes (Eds.), *The Palgrave handbook of international communication and sustainable development* (pp. 53–75). Palgrave.

CHAPTER 8

Creating Safe Communication Spaces Amidst the Disinformation Quandary

Yvonne T. Chua and Rachel E. Khan

Abstract The COVID-19 pandemic has highlighted global reliance on communication not only for health information, but also for socioeconomic survival. But it has also brought to the fore malicious actors who spread disinformation or the so-called fake news alongside (and at times, surpassing) truthful information, thereby causing public confusion and risky behavior. Disinformation undermines one of the underlying goals of communication for all: the formation of an informed and critical citizenry so essential to democracy and development. Its agents exploit a gamut of communication media—offline and online, as well as state media, legacy media, social media, messaging apps that can be villains or victims, or both, depending on the role they play. The content they create and the tools and tactics they deploy range from the tried and tested to highly innovative ones that demand a multipronged and multisectoral anti-disinformation approach. Using the COVID-19 pandemic as a take-off

Y. T. Chua • R. E. Khan (✉)
University of the Philippines, College of Mass Communication (UP-CMC) in Diliman, Quezon City, Philippines
e-mail: ytchua@up.edu.ph; rekhan2@up.edu.ph

© The Author(s), under exclusive license to Springer Nature Switzerland AG 2023
J. Servaes, M. J. Yusha'u (eds.), *SDG18 Communication for All*, *Volume 1*, Sustainable Development Goals Series, https://doi.org/10.1007/978-3-031-19142-8_8

point, this chapter discusses the ecology of false information and a scoping review of its effects of sustainable development goals (SDGs). The chapter also discusses the processes by which disinformation is spread from the obscurity of the internet to the sphere of public and private communication platforms. As important, it will explore multistakeholder efforts in countering fake news, and simple, appropriate tools and responses that citizens can use to safeguard spaces for communication.

Keywords Disinformation • Fake news • Sustainable development • Communication • Public sphere • Infodemic

INTRODUCTION

As social beings, communication is the hinge of human interaction and collaboration. And yet, it is usually relegated as an appendage in development plans and strategies.

The drafting of the 2030 Sustainable Development Goals (SDGs) in 2015 was no exception. As pointed out by Lee and Vargas (2020), "Conspicuous by its absence was a dedicated Goal addressing the essential role played by communication." They noted that communication is mentioned as related targets under Goal 5 on "Gender Equality" and Goal 16 on "Peace, Justice and Strong Institutions" but was not deemed important enough to be raised as a goal itself.

We concur with Lee and Vargas (2020) that an 18th SDG should be dedicated to *Communication for All* to ensure "unfettered access to the information and knowledge essential to democracy, empowerment, responsible citizenship, and mutual accountability" (p. 13).

This is especially needed today as free, transparent, accessible communication and information are being challenged on many fronts. In this chapter, we focus on the threat posed by disinformation, which has disrupted several economic, social, and cultural rights, including people's right to a standard of living adequate for the health and well-being of themselves and of their family. Specifically, the chapter addresses disinformation as a disruptive communication phenomenon retarding the ability of nation-states to meet the 2030 SDG agenda.

The rapid spread of disinformation or "fake news" alongside (and at times, surpassing) truthful information undermines one of the underlying goals of communication for all: the formation of an informed and critical citizenry so essential to democracy and development. We argue that effective communication is a crosscutting goal for sustainable development and that an SDG 18 dedicated to *Communication for All* can bring attention and resources needed to combat the subtle but increasing threat of disinformation while building safe spaces for truthful information and honest interactions.

COMMUNICATION AS A HUMAN RIGHT

Communication as a human right is enshrined under Article 19 of the Universal Declaration of Human Rights (UDHR), which clearly states:

> Everyone has the right to freedom of opinion and expression; this right includes freedom to hold opinions without interference and to seek, receive and impart information and ideas through any media and regardless of frontiers. (United Nations, 1948)

While the UDHR is not binding, the multilateral covenant known as the United Nations International Covenant on Civil and Political Rights (ICCPR) is. Article 19 of the UN ICCPR echoes the UDHR in protecting freedom of information and of expression.

But long before these global declarations, many nations have already recognized communication as a right in their Constitutions or State laws. A prime example is the 1789 French Declaration of the Rights of Man, which guaranteed the "free communication of ideas and opinions." Similarly, the First Amendment of the United States Constitution, as penned by James Madison in 1791, reads:

> Congress shall make no law respecting an establishment of religion or prohibiting the free exercise thereof; or abridging the freedom of speech, or of the press; or the right of the people peaceably to assemble, and to petition the Government for a redress of grievances.

In the last century, democratic nations have strengthened this right to freedom of the press and of expression with the so-called Sunshine laws that seek to make government actions and transactions more transparent.

According to the freedominfo.org, a network of press freedom advocates, 119 nations have some sort of Freedom of Information Act in place.[1]

Development advocates recognize that for sustainable goals to be achieved, people should be able to assert their rights and let governments know their needs even as free and open communication is essential. In recent years, it can be noted that the landscape of development cooperation has significantly changed from being only at the level of government to being more inclusive and involving citizen stakeholders (OECD/Dev, 2014).

For these types of collaboration to be effective, the citizen stakeholders should have the ability to access timely, truthful, and reliable information. A report from the OECD/Dev (2014) noted, "Communication is central to accountability and with many actors (donors, partner governments, NGOs, private sector, etc.) all playing a part in the development effort it is difficult to imagine telling a complete story without partnerships" (p. 8).

While access to information can be facilitated by establishing laws, dealing with disinformation is more complex. The catch-22 for disinformation is that enacting laws that penalizes so-called fake news may result in working against legitimate media and information sources.

A study commissioned by the European Parliament showed that access to information could become a collateral victim of laws governing disinformation. While acknowledging that disinformation threatens human rights on various levels, the study also noted, "the inverse challenge is that counter-disinformation policies can also restrict freedoms and rights" (Colomina et al., 2021, p. 18). In fact, a recent report by the Poynter Institute showed that, in many cases, laws or regulations that enable the prosecution of persons for producing or distributing false information are being used to silence legitimate media from reporting the truth or preventing the State leaders' political opposition from voicing their opinions (Funke & Flamini, 2021).

As we discuss in the latter part of the chapter, disinformation threatens human rights on various levels, starting with undermining the ability of people to make informed decisions. Marginalized populations bear the brunt of the backlash of false narratives that are associated with a rise in digital violence, intimidation, and harassment. Ethnic groups, migrants, and women, in particular, have been targeted by state-sponsored or -tolerated

---

[1] List of countries with FOI regimes as of September 2017, freedominfo.org.

disinformation and trolling, drowning out the critical voices of dissent or of vulnerable sectors (USAID, 2021; Colomina et al., 2021).

This impacts the United Nations' SDGs as well, which are also under significant threat from disinformation.

Understanding Disinformation

The propagation of fabricated or misleading information for various motivations has been a feature of human communication since ancient times. Around 44 BC, Octavian was said to have etched short and sharp "Twitter-worthy slogans" onto coins to smear Mark Antony's reputation (Posetti & Matthews, 2018, p. 2). In a speech, Pope Francis traced the first instance of disinformation, the "first fake news," to the strategy employed by the serpent or "snake tactic" to deceive Adam and Eve into partaking of the fruit of forbidden tree of the knowledge of good and evil (Vatican, 2018).

For the most part, technology has been blamed for the dramatic amplification of false information: the Gutenberg printing press, radio, telephone, television, the internet, and now social media and private or encrypted messaging apps. As *The Guardian* observed, "The use of propaganda is ancient, but never before has there been the technology to so effectively disseminate it" (Nougayrede, 2018).

As of October 2021, about 62 percent of the world's total population or 4.9 billion people use the internet close to seven hours a day, more than twice the amount of time they spend watching television.[2] The increased usage is attributed to pandemic restrictions on mobility. Social media, in particular, dominate the world's online activities: More than 95 percent of working-age internet users rely on social networks and messaging services (Kemp, 2021).

Technology has afforded nearly everyone the chance to self-publish, leading to an explosion of information online. This in turn has chipped away at the role of the news media as the primary provider of information and poses risks to authentic journalism that supplies reliable and verified information. Eight in 10 adults consume news online, significantly more than the 64 percent who say they watch news on television. Overall, 56 percent access news content through social media, of which 44 percent turn to Facebook (Newman et al., 2021).

---

[2] https://datareportal.com/reports/digital-2021-july-global-statshot.

The proliferation of false or misleading information online is not lost on internet users. Still in the grip of the COVID-19 pandemic, self-reported exposure to misinformation about the coronavirus and other health issues, politics, celebrities, climate change, immigration, and products and services averages 73 percent in 46 media markets. Some countries such as Nigeria, Kenya, the Philippines, and Peru record a high 89 percent to 90 percent. Globally, trust in news content on social media is a mere 24 percent amid concerns over misinformation (Newman et al., 2021).

Online information has unleashed a plethora of terms and concepts associated with false and fraudulent information—some new, some old: problematic information, fake news, hoax, rumors, misinformation, disinformation, satire, parody, propaganda, computational propaganda, advertising, post-truth, and alternative facts.

Communication scholars and institutions, such as the United Nations Educational, Scientific and Cultural Organization (UNESCO), largely adopt Wardle and Derakhshan's (2017) framework, which defines disinformation as "information that is false and deliberately created to harm a person, social group, organization, or country" (p. 20). The intent to harm differentiates disinformation from misinformation, which has no intention to harm, and from malinformation, whose purpose is also to harm but purveys genuine information. Misinformation, disinformation, and malinformation comprise what has been dubbed as the "information disorder" (Wardle & Derakhshan, 2017, p. 6; Wardle, 2020) as illustrated in Fig. 8.1.

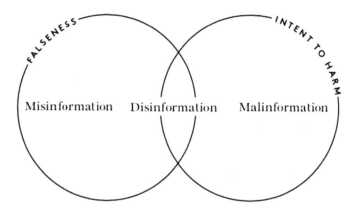

Fig. 8.1 Information disorder model, Wardle (2020)

The European Commission's high-level group (HLEG) on fake news and online disinformation has appended another motivation to disinformation: profit. Disinformation, it said, "includes all forms of false, inaccurate, or misleading information designed, presented, and promoted to intentionally cause public harm or for profit" (European Commission, 2018a, p. 5).

In favoring the term disinformation, communication experts view the more popular phrase "fake news" as problematic and "woefully inadequate" (Wardle & Derakhshan, 2017, p. 5). It not only encompasses too many types of information, including honest mistakes in news reporting, but populist leaders have also deployed the term against news organizations whose coverage they find unfavorable.

A systematic literature review on disinformation suggested a "normalized" all-inclusive typology of disinformation spanning three dimensions: facticity, the degree to which information relies on facts; verifiability, the origins and genuineness of the information; and motivation, the driving force behind an act (Kapantai et al., 2020). In all, it listed 11 types of disinformation: fabricated, click bait, imposter, misleading connection, conspiracy theories, fake reviews, hoaxes, trolling, biased or one-sided, pseudoscience, and rumors (p. 14).

CONCEPTUAL FRAMEWORK

Different lenses have been used to examine disinformation in a bid to come up with multidimensional solutions to the problem.

Wardle and Derakhshan (2017) break down the concept of disinformation and other types of information disorder into three main elements or "AMI": *agent* (the creator, producer, and distributor of the information and their motivation); *message* (the type, format, and characteristics of the information); and interpreter (the receiver's interpretation and action taken, if any, on the message).

On the other hand, the UNESCO Working Group on Freedom of Expression and Addressing Disinformation expands the AMI framework to make a distinction between those fabricating disinformation and those distributing content. It classifies the former as *instigators* (direct or indirect) and the latter as *agents* ("influencers," individuals, officials, groups, companies, institutions). They form part of its five-hybrid framework called IAMIT that depicts the "life cycle" of disinformation: *instigators, agents, messages, intermediaries* (the rough equivalent of channels), and *targets/interpreters* (Bontcheva & Posetti, 2020).

Another conceptual framework, dubbed "ABC," highlights the three key vectors characteristic of viral disinformation. Manipulative *actors* knowingly engage in viral deception campaigns that are covert to hide the actor's identity and intent. Deceptive *behavior* pertains to the techniques actors use to amplify their content, from automated tools to manual trickery. "Coordinated inauthentic behavior," the use of fake accounts or a network of accounts to mislead people or the platform, is one example. Harmful *content* is the outcome seen on social media posts and for sure, the most visible vector (Francois, 2019).

Alaphilippe (2021) suggested adding a "D" to Francois' key vectors, as he noted that *distribution* played a key part in disinformation, which spreads largely due to today's digital platforms. Disinformation actors have benefitted from loopholes and weaknesses of digital platforms and applications such as Facebook, TikTok, and YouTube despite efforts to filter out disinformation sources by detecting network algorithms.

Despite the differences in parlance, Harold Lasswell's classic 5Ws communication process (1948) remains highly applicable. His *Who says What in Which channel to Whom and with What effect* is a systems theory model that can be adopted to analyze the communication of disinformation while incorporating factors such as manipulative actors and the audience's cognitive biases into the model to help explain online deception (see Fig. 8.2).

Applying Lasswell's model to disinformation, we see that *sources* can be manipulative even as they capitalize on well-known or credible sources through mimicry and by quoting supposed but nonexistent experts. *Messages* on social media are accompanied by popularity ratings (likes, shares, or comments) that serve as a set of heuristics or mental shortcuts that can affect how people evaluate the messages. Social media and private messaging apps now serve as primary *channels*, transmitting the messages to various *audiences* who usually engage in selective exposition, especially those that match their beliefs and disposition to avoid inconsistency. Thus, the overall *effect* of disinformation is its ability to fool ordinary folks into

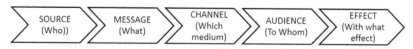

Fig. 8.2 Lasswell's process of communication model (1948)

sharing (albeit unwittingly) the source's false information to friends and family, while at the same time lending their own credibility to the false information.

Various studies and media reports have identified five key actors behind the spread of disinformation: states, politicians and governments, the media, social movements, and ordinary people. States resort to disinformation in the form of propaganda or information warfare to meddle in other states' affairs. Politicians and governments use disinformation to retain power. The media, often in collusion with political or business elites, distort the facts in creating public opinion. Social movements such as anti-women and anti-migrant groups employ disinformation tactics to discredit and discriminate against vulnerable groups. Ordinary people, meanwhile, often unintentionally spread false or misleading narratives because of their low media literacy (López-García et al., 2021; Alaphilippe, 2021).

Without doubt, disinformation has far-reaching consequences. It has played a significant role in undermining democracy and good governance, free and fair elections, access to information, rule of law, protection of human rights, independent media, and civil society action (USAID, 2021). Disinformation costs the global economy US$78 billion every year (Prevency, 2020).

Meanwhile, the surfeit of information–both true and false–has generated the so-called infodemic. The term, a portmanteau of "information" and "epidemic," was originally coined by journalist and political analyst David Rothkopf in a 2003 *Washington Post* column. "A few facts, mixed with fear, speculation, and rumor, amplified and relayed swiftly worldwide by modern information technologies, have affected national and international economies, politics, and even security in ways that are utterly disproportionate with the root realities," wrote Rothkopf (2003).

The term has been adopted by the World Health Organization to describe the rapid and far-reaching spread of mis and disinformation during health crises, from SARS to AIDS to COVID-19.

DISINFORMATION THREATENS SDGs

As noted earlier, disinformation impacts the United Nations' Sustainable Development Goals. A study for the Broadband Commission for Sustainable Development (Bontcheva & Posetti, 2020) identifies several of these SDGs as:

- SDG 3 on healthy lives and promotion of well-being for all ages
- SDG 4 on inclusive and equitable quality education
- SDG 5 on gender equality
- SDG 16 on peaceful and inclusive societies, including SDG 16.10 on public access to information and fundamental freedom

However, we note that the impact of disinformation has not been limited to the above-mentioned goals. In fact, disinformation affects others, such as SDG 10 on reduced inequality, especially for migrants, and SDG 13 on climate action. We shall discuss briefly the impact of disinformation on these sustainable development goals.

SDG3 Good Health and Well-being

The UN considers SDG 3 as a crosscutting goal even as it acknowledges that sustainable development can only be achieved when the people are healthy and unencumbered by debilitating diseases. Under this goal, the UN envisions the end of epidemics such as AIDS, tuberculosis, malaria, and other communicable diseases by 2030 as well as the attainment of universal health coverage and access to safe and effective medicines and vaccines for all.

However, the diseases listed in the SDG have taken a backseat to COVID-19 when the pandemic was declared in March 2020. The WHO reports that the global death toll of COVID-19 has reached 4.9 million with some 244 million confirmed cases as of October 2021.[3] It also records a total of 6.2 billion COVID-19 vaccines having been administered worldwide.

Undoubtedly, the COVID-19 pandemic has negated any gains made for this goal. In fact, the WHO reported in April 2021 that the COVID-19 pandemic has disrupted essential health services in non-COVID-19 illnesses. Henrietta Fore, UNICEF executive director, observed, "The COVID-19 pandemic continues to pose serious challenges to global health beyond the impact of the disease itself" (World Health Organization, 2021).

While the pandemic has demonstrated the importance of universal health coverage, it also highlights another aspect: the need for timely and reliable information. The 2021 UN Sustainable Goals Report noted, "The

---

[3] https://covid19.who.int/.

pandemic has taught us that the weaknesses in data and information systems present an added and enormous challenge to decision makers" (Zhenmin, 2021) The report also noted that the pandemic showed a need to invest in information systems (p. 2). Many nations also needed to boost their health communication capacities. Even in developed nations like the United Kingdom, official health information received less public attention than rumors and trivial news about the coronavirus (Khan, 2020).

Ironically, the lack of useful data is also accompanied by a surfeit of information—some true and many false. In a gathering of foreign policy and security experts in March 2020, WHO Director-General Tedros Adhanom Ghebreyesus observed, "We're not just fighting an epidemic; we're fighting an infodemic" (UN Department of Global Communications, 2020).

Symptomatic of the infodemic is the belief in disinformation about the COVID-19 and, conversely, the mistrust of scientific information (Roozenbeek et al., 2020; Agley & Xiao, 2021).

Global research studies showed that misinformation about COVID-19 had spread at a rapid rate, especially through social media like Facebook and Twitter with common rumors and conspiracy theories across nations and languages (Islam et al., 2020; Roozenbeek et al., 2020; Mian & Khan, 2020; Agley & Xiao, 2021). Researchers also noted that rumors circulating were primarily related to supposed cures of the disease from eating garlic in the United States to drinking cow urine in India. Misinformation also led to violence against health workers, including being evicted from their apartments to various acts exhibiting Asian hate (Islam et al., 2020).

Mian and Khan (2020) noted that medical disinformation is not new even as the same can be said of the HIV pandemic and epidemics such as the Ebola virus and the SARS-Asian Flu. Agley and Xiao (2021) said disinformation about the Ebola outbreak in Congo in 2019 could be linked to violence, including targeted attacks on healthcare providers.

Roozenbeek et al. (2020) observed that the unfortunate consequence of the infodemic on the coronavirus is the "increased susceptibility to misinformation," which in turn leads to their noncompliance or outright unwillingness to conform to health-safety protocols or to avail of the COVID-19 vaccine.

SDG 4 *Quality Education*

A 2020 global survey[4] conducted by the Strategic Transformation Support Unit of UNESCO revealed that education was regarded as the top solution for addressing global challenges, whether it is climate change, lack of water, or loss of biodiversity.

Within the SDG framework, education is seen as "central to the realization of the 2030 Agenda for Sustainable Development" (UNESCO, 2017). The UN goal aims to ensure inclusive and equitable quality education and promote lifelong learning opportunities for all.

However, disinformation counteracts this goal. In 2019, a document of the UNESCO Broadband Commission for Sustainable Development noted, "Disinformation works against the purpose of education and learning. On the other hand, digital knowledge and skills, as well as media and information literacy, are essential in order to provide Broadband users with understanding of ethics, human rights, and how to defend against the automation, fabrication, and dissemination of disinformation" (UNESCO, 2019, p. 2).

In studying university faculty responses to disinformation, a study found that professors generally recognized the dangers posed by disinformation but still lacked consensus in how to tackle it in the classroom (Weiss et al., 2020). The study also found that the proliferation of information on the internet resulted in a decrease in critical thinking. The researchers observed that the technologies that allow targeted content of social media feeds have obscured sources of reliable and factual information and make internet users ability to process information "less efficient and make their decision-making less accurate" (Weiss et al., 2020, p. 3).

The study's findings are echoed by Guy Berger, UNESCO director for Freedom of Expression and Media Development, who said, "When there is rising hatred, xenophobia, and gender discrimination, as well as anti-science, all being promoted through disinformation, we see an urgency in integrating MIL [media and information literacy] in Global Citizens Education."[5]

---

[4] https://en.unesco.org/news/world-2030-public-survey-climate-change-and-biodiversity-loss-biggest-concern-far.

[5] https://en.unesco.org/news/unesco-shares-its-work-media-and-information-literacy-hlpf-side-events.

SDG 5 Gender Equality

The UN envisions gender equality and the empowerment of women and girls by 2030 through SDG 5. It seeks to end all forms of discrimination and violence against women and girls in both the public and private spheres and increase women's participants in political, economic, and public life, including opportunities for leadership through their representation in national parliaments, local governments, and managerial positions. Enabling technology, in particular, information and communications technology (ICT) is viewed as a means to empower women.

The Broadband Commission's study in 2020, however, observed that online disinformation is often used to target groups such as women and gender identity-based communities which may lead to violence, hatred, and discrimination. The algorithms used by social media and search engines to prioritize content, including disinformation, have been shown to lead to bias and work against inclusivity (Bontcheva & Posetti, 2020).

Research provides evidence of gendered disinformation, even during the pandemic, that ultimately leads to violence against women and girls (VAWG), and violence against women in politics (VAW-P). The international Consortium for Elections and Political Process Strengthening or CEPPS (2021) defines gendered disinformation as "false, misleading, or harmful content that exploits gender inequalities or invokes gender stereotypes and norms, including to target specific individuals or groups." It pays attention to the gendered impact or risk of disinformation on women, girls, men, boys, and people with diverse sexual orientations and gender identities.

A five-country study of online violence against women in Asia (UN Women, 2020) listed the dissemination of false information among the nine factors that could contribute to the risk of ICT VAWG of online violence.

During the COVID-19 pandemic, misogynistic narratives have been adapted to fit the disinformation landscape and negatively impacted on women's rights. For example, women have been framed as spreaders of COVID-19 or transmitters of disinformation. Gendered disinformation and anti-vaccine claims have been merged to push false narratives (e.g., cells from aborted fetuses were used in vaccines). Female politicians are depicted as incapable of prioritizing relevant policies and thus unfit for decision-making. All these are designed to "produce either a negative representation of women as enemies and opponents in public debate or a pitiful depiction of women as victims, often in order to push a social or political agenda" (Sessa, 2020).

The National Democratic Institute, which is part of the CEPPS, has focused on "state-aligned" gendered disinformation or "disinformation created and shared not only by those who may have been directly coordinated by the government, but also by informal networks of actors who use gendered disinformation to try to shield the state from critique or democratic threat, in particular by women in public life" (Judson et al., 2020, p. 7).

Weaponizing emotion and preexisting misogynistic tropes, state-aligned gendered disinformation is governed by six "rules": (1) to convince others that women are devious an unfit for politics, (2) denounce women as too stupid for public life, (3) make them afraid to talk back, (4) praise women for being sexy but condemn them for being sexual, (5) show that the strong men will save them, and (6) demonize the values women hold. Gendered disinformation is ultimately a form of online VAW-P, which covers "all forms of aggression, coercion, and intimidation of politically active women simply because they are women" (National Democratic Institute, 2019, p. 12).

The escalation of online falsehoods against women in politics prompted more than 100 current and former legislators in the U.S. and around the world to write Facebook in 2020 demanding a stop to the spread of gendered disinformation and misogynistic attacks against women leaders (States News Service, 2020). The signatories, who include U.S. Speaker Nancy Pelosi, herself a victim of viral cheap fakes, cited a study that nearly 42 percent of women parliamentarians have seen extremely humiliating or sexually charged images of themselves spread through social media. They also cited another study that found that women elected officials in the U.S. were attacked more often than their male counterparts by fake news accounts, and that these attacks were more likely to be focused on personal traits or character.

SDG 10 Reduce Inequalities

The UN believes the road to equality within and among countries is through social, economic, and political inclusion of all regardless of age, sex, disability religion, economic status or race, ethnicity, or origin. It also seeks to protect migration and mobility of people and urges countries to implement well-managed migration policies. That has hardly been the case for migrants and refugees in the U.S., Europe, Asia, and elsewhere in the world, no thanks to disinformation. Disinformation actors further fan the animosity toward migrants by injecting messages with religious overtones.

In Europe, migration has been a key subject of disinformation campaigns since the "refugee crisis" in 2015 when the influx of refugees and migrants, most of them fleeing war and persecution in countries such as Syria, Afghanistan, Iraq, and Eritrea, reached staggering new levels (Spindler, 2015).

In four European Union member states, disinformation narratives between May 2019 and July 2020 linked migration to existing insecurities, depicting it as a threat to three partly overlapping areas: *health*, *wealth*, and *identity*. Migrants were depicted as violent criminals, potential terrorists, or a COVID-19 infection risk. They were supposedly social benefits cheats who posed unfair competition for jobs or drained community resources. They were made to appear as a hostile invasion force that threatened European or Christian traditions or were poised to replace white Europeans (Butcher & Neidhardt, 2020).

Disinformation agents preyed on the Global Compact for Safe, Orderly and Regular Migration (GCM), an intergovernmental agreement prepared under the auspices of the UN that highlights the need for more international cooperation to manage migration effectively, insinuating it would lead to an end of the European people. In the end, nine EU member states refused to endorse the agreement.

Based on the *EUvsDisinfo* database, most of the disinformation narratives from 2018–2021 about migrants and minority groups in the EU concern migrants or Muslims. The stories perpetuated longstanding narratives such as migrants/Muslims are a threat to European cultural identity, a criminal threat, and an economic threat (Szakács & Bognár, 2021). The campaigns are said to have had "chilling effect" on nongovernmental organizations who, when vilified, avoid being associated with the issue. As well, politicians have weaponized disinformation to clamp down on dissent.

An analysis of anti-refugee disinformation and hate messages in Greek, German, and English in 2020 detected a transnational network of actors, including far-right extremists and elements of the political right, who often share common audiences and use similar tactics. The networks did not act in isolation; there had been instances of cross-border mobilization (Institute for Strategic Dialogue, 2021).

The ethnic cleansing of the Rohingya Muslims in Myanmar in 2017 is emblematic of the lethal consequences of a cocktail of disinformation and hate speech spread via Facebook against a community of migrants singled out for their ethnicity and religion by a predominantly Buddhist state. More than 24,000 Rohingyans died at the hand of state forces, triggering their exodus from Myanmar and creating a colossal refugee crisis in Asia (Habib et al., 2018).

Facebook belatedly banned Myanmar's commander-in-chief and military officials from its platform for violating community standards of hate speech laced with false narratives such as Islam being a global threat to Buddhism or the rape of a Buddhist woman by a Muslim man (Mozur, 2018). State-run media, however, continued to frame the Rohingya as a homogenous group capable of violence and a threat to national peace and stability and dismissed as "fake news" international documentation of the mass atrocities in Rakhine where the Rohingya population mostly lives (Kironska & Peng, 2021).

SDG13 Climate Action

The UN sees the climate crisis continuing unabated unless urgent steps are taken to combat climate change. Under this goal, the UN hopes to place climate change in the policy agenda of governments and implement the UN framework convention on climate change. At the same time, its primary target is to strengthen the resilience and adaptive capacities of nations in the face of climate disasters.

This tall order has a direct adversary in climate change denialists and disinformation campaigners.

Public hearings in 2019 by the U.S. House of Representatives Committee on Oversight and Reform revealed that the fossil fuel industry contributed to disinformation on climate change long before the existence of social media (Keane, 2020). As early as 1981, fossil fuel companies like Shell, Chevron, and Exxon were aware of their industry's impact on emissions of carbon dioxide and other greenhouse gasses through the findings of their own scientists. However, instead of facing the problem, they funded campaigns that sought instead to discredit climate change scientists (Keane, 2020; Gramling, 2021).

Dossiers of letters, memos, and internal documents of several fuel companies compiled by the Union of Concerned Scientists showed that there was a deliberate campaign of disinformation in the 1990s, which aimed to "deliberately sow confusion and block policies designed to reduce the heat-trapping emissions that cause global warming" (Mulvey & Sulman, 2015, p. 2). Among the revelations of the said documents is an investment in scientific research by a Smithsonian-affiliated scientist of an estimated US$1.2 million aimed at debunking climate change (Mulvey & Sulman, 2015).

Another study by Stephan Lewandowsky of the University of Bristol (2020) noted that prior to the 1990s there was little difference in the level of concern over climate change among Republicans and Democrats in the United States. By the year 2000, however, there was a marked polarization between the two parties, and in 2016, only 40 percent of Republicans believed that climate change was worrisome vis-à-vis 84 percent of Democrats (p. 3).

Lewandowsky (2020) noted that "countless surveys have shown a strong association between right-wing or libertarian worldviews and the rejection of climate science," which he attributed to the misinformation campaign in the 1990s (p. 3). An inventory of strategies adopted in the climate disinformation by various academic studies can be summed up as follows (Lewandowsky, 2020; Porter et al., 2019; Mulvay & Sulman, 2015; Freudenburg & Muselli, 2013):

- Question (or sow doubt) regarding the scientific consensus on climate change;
- Highlight scientific uncertainty and demand certainty as a condition for climate action;
- Discredit individual scientists to undermine their studies;
- Discredit institutions (including academic journals); and
- Project pseudoscientific alternatives through social media.

SDG 16.10 Ensure Public Access to Information

At a time that reliable information and fact-based reports are needed the most, many governments used the "disinfodemic" (Bontcheva & Posetti, 2020), or the overabundance of pandemic-related misinformation, as a pretext to restrict the flow of information and press freedom. This goes against the very heart of SDG 16.10, which seeks to ensure public access to information, safeguard fundamental freedoms, and protect journalists and media workers from killings and attacks under SDG 16 on peace, justice, and strong institutions.

As of February 2021, 127 countries have adopted laws on access to information, but the UN noted that implementation of the laws could be improved. In addition, the pandemic has slowed the pace of progress in this area. No countries or territories passed such laws in 2020, and a number of countries and territories temporarily suspended existing legal guarantees (United Nations Economic and Social Council, 2021).

Public access to state-held information could have helped stem the tide of disinformation unleashed by the pandemic, which has targeted various sectors of society, including journalists. But the ranks of state leaders dubbed as "predators of press freedom" have further swollen (Reporters Without Borders, 2021a). In their arsenal are tools and techniques to demonize independent and critical media that often include a state-linked networked disinformation offline and online. An oft-repeated false rhetoric is that the media are purveyors of fake news or are part of destabilization attempts (Turcilo & Obrenovic, 2020).

The year 2020 closed with at least 577 press freedom violations worldwide linked to COVID-19 (International Press Institute, n.d.). At least 91 countries were found to have imposed restrictions on the news media as a response to the pandemic (Repucci & Slipowitz, 2020). Press freedom violations encompassed arrests, detentions, civil lawsuits, and criminal investigations against journalists and media organizations; restrictions on access to information; physical or verbal attacks, including online intimidation or smear; and censorship.

Eighteen countries passed "fake news" laws targeting the disinfodemic but autocrats have conveniently parlayed into censorship tools them. By May of 2021, the count of countries where journalism had been blocked or constrained, for reasons related to the pandemic or not, had climbed to 132, characterized by a "dramatic deterioration in people's access to information and an increase in obstacles to news coverage" (Reporters Without Borders, 2021b).

These have further disrupted the traditional media landscape, which has already lost much ground to social media and messaging apps as information providers and to orchestrated and organic disinformation campaigns targeting journalists. It has translated to a loss of trust in journalism as a credible and independent source of information. The level of public mistrust of journalists is disturbing: Six in ten people in 28 countries said journalists deliberately try to mislead the public by reporting information they know to be false (Edelman, 2021).

In particular, women journalists have been targeted by orchestrated and organic disinformation campaigns against the media. Nearly three-fourths of women journalists surveyed by UNESCO and the International Center for Journalists said they had experienced online violence. Two in five said the online attacks appeared linked to orchestrated disinformation campaigns. Reporting on disinformation is also an emerging trigger for online attacks. Political actors are the second most frequently noted sources of attacks and abuse after anonymous or unknown attackers (Posetti et al., 2020).

Orchestrated attacks on journalists can chill critical journalism. For example, the women journalists in UNESCO's study said they responded to online violence by self-censoring on social media, withdrawing from all online interaction, or avoiding audience engagement.

Declines in press freedom, in turn, have negative consequences on the economy. A recent longitudinal study of 97 countries found that a decline in press freedom resulted in a one to two percent drop in real gross domestic product. Subsequent recoveries in press freedom cannot easily reverse the negative economic effects of deteriorating press freedom (Nguyen et al., 2021).

CREATING SAFE SPACES: THE ROLE OF AN SDG

One of the biggest challenges in harnessing communication toward sustainable development is the need to uphold press freedom and free speech while combatting disinformation. With *Communication for All* as the 18th Sustainable Development Goal, governments can be urged to view disinformation as a whole-of-society problem instead of a compartmentalized issue. As such, a whole-of-society response would improve the integrity of the information environment (United States Department of Homeland Security, 2019) and safeguard democracy as well as contribute to the fulfillment of the development goals.

Wardle and Derakhshan (2017) espouse a multistakeholder, multifaceted framework directed at national governments, technology companies or platforms, education ministries, media organizations, civil society, and funding bodies.

This holistic approach is cognizant of the fact that disinformation is a complex problem that would require a collaborative response. In fact, the Broadband Commission (Bontcheva & Posetti, 2020) noted that this requires an expanded list of stakeholders: intergovernmental and other international organizations; individual states; legislators and policy makers; political parties and other political actors; electoral regulatory bodies and national authorities; law enforcement and the judiciary; internet communications companies; journalists and fact-checkers; civil society organizations; advertising brokers; and universities and applied and empirical researchers.

Combining Lasswell's model with the previously discussed disinformation frameworks, especially that of Francois (2019) and Alaphilippe (2021), we propose the following conceptual framework to support a multistakeholder, multifaceted response to disinformation that addresses the various stages of false information (see Fig. 8.3).

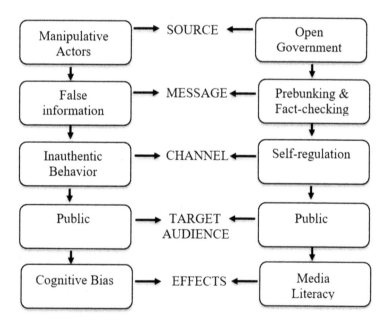

Fig. 8.3   Proposed model of combatting disinformation

As noted earlier, disinformation is a complex problem and has no easy solutions. By identifying the disinformation dilemma within the communication process, solutions can be pursued, and the problem tackled on the different levels of engagement or as a whole-of-society approach.

Addressing the Source

As noted earlier, manipulative actors engage deliberately in viral deception campaigns (Francois, 2019). These campaigns are usually covert designed to make their identity difficult to trace.

Instead of laws against disinformation that may abridge fundamental freedoms, including freedom of expression, states are being called on to respond to disinformation by adhering to *open government* principles, specifically, to protect access to information and support free and independent media (Matasick et al., 2020; Freedom House, 2021; UNESCO, 2021).

The OECD noted that a proactive public communication strategy might be a better method of combatting disinformation. This strategy should (1) provide citizens with truthful and accurate information; (2) prebunk or debunk false or misleading information; (3) educate citizens about consuming and sharing content responsibly; (4) support a better understanding of public attitudes; and (5) engage citizens in a collective response to the infodemic (OECD, 2020b, p. 5).

OECD sees *participatory communication* embedded in public communication, the two-way dialogue with citizens certainly benefiting governments because it would help them gain better insights into citizens' needs and respond to these more directly. Participatory communication—the "two-way sharing of information among communication equals" (Servaes, 2008, p. 23)—has long been emphasized as being integral to communication for development and social change, including as a possible solution to worldwide poverty (Servaes & Malikhao, 2016).

An example of not just a two-way but also a ground-up communication strategy was employed by the Bangladesh government and humanitarian organizations to stem the spread of misinformation among vulnerable Rohingya refugees during the pandemic. A contextualized risk communication and community engagement (RCCE) response was instrumental in identifying how and where the refugees obtained false or misleading information about COVID-19 and how these formed their perceptions. This, in turn, enabled the government and organizations to target these sources of misinformation (Mahmud, 2020).

Empowering small-scale deliberative forums or participative deliberation such as this to find out how communities generate, consume, and engage with information is deemed a rights-led and empowering approach to counter-disinformation (Colomina et al., 2021).

Balancing the Message

Fact-checking or debunking falsehoods has emerged as one of the most publicly visible and fastest interventions against disinformation.

According to Dobbs (2012), the modern-day *fact-checking movement* can be traced to the pre-internet presidency of Ronald Reagan when some newspapers began assigning specific reporters to check the narratives of politicians and started handing out "Pinocchio verdicts" on some of their claims (p. 3). Efforts at fact-checking grew with the inception of the internet and the rise of blogs. By 2004, the *Washington Post* took the lead in establishing a fact-checking team, distinct from their beat reporters, and gave them a separate section in the newspaper in 2007.[6]

Recognizing the rising number of community fact-checkers, the Florida-based Poynter Institute launched the International Fact-checking Network (IFCN) in 2015 to promote excellence and collaboration in the global fight against disinformation. The organization has become a sort of accreditation body that verifies the legitimacy of the fact-checking organizations around the globe even as it provides support and continuing education for fact-checkers (Poynter, n.d.).

The need for these types of collaboration has been extremely evident with the COVID-19. Launched weeks before the SARS-COV-2 was declared a pandemic, the database of the CoronaVirusFacts Alliance led by the IFCN has since aggregated more than 10,000 fact checks on the coronavirus published in 40 languages from fact-checkers in more than 70 countries (Poynter, n.d.). Meanwhile, WHO (n.d.) has urged the public to, among other things, turn to fact-checkers to help flatten the infodemic curve. UNESCO, UNDP, and the OECD are among international institutions that have thrown their support for independent fact-checking organizations (Bontcheva & Posetti, 2020; OECD, 2020a; UNDP, 2020).

---

[6] https://www.washingtonpost.com/politics/2019/01/07/about-fact-checker/.

The positive reviews fact-checking has received can also be attributed in part to the growing body of research documenting its effectiveness. A recent study that ran simultaneous experiments in four diverse countries showed fact checks reduced belief in misinformation by at least 0.59 points on a five-point scale, with most of their effects still detectable more than two weeks later (Porter & Wood, 2021). The findings imply that fact-checking can help mitigate the threat of mis and disinformation.

But disinformation studies also point to what they consider as a more effective accuracy-promoting intervention: *prebunking* (Jolley & Douglas, 2017; Cook et al., 2017; Bryanov & Vziatysheva, 2021; Lewandowsky et al., 2021; Van der Linden et al., 2021).

Anchored on the inoculation theory, prebunking entails preemptively exposing people to a weakened strain of misinformation that is gaining traction and warning them of misleading or manipulative argumentation strategies. This is intended to build people's "cognitive antibodies" and, consequently, their resilience to subsequent manipulation attempts.

Inoculation techniques could range from exposing news consumers to conspiracy theories (Bryanov & Vziatysheva, 2021) to educational games, such as putting them in the shoes of fake news producers to think proactively about how people might be misled to achieve a goal (Roozenbeek & Van der Linden, 2018). A recent study has found evidence of inoculation retention lasting for weeks and further suggests boosters just like a real vaccine for long-term immunization against misinformation (Roozenbeek et al., 2020).

Clearing Up the Channels of Distribution

Since 2018, Facebook, Twitter, and other social media platforms have initiated *self-regulation* measures to address disinformation.

In 2020, Twitter suspended some 23,750 accounts that were posting pro-Beijing narratives and another 150,000 accounts that were amplifying these messages. It also froze about 1000 accounts linked to Russian political propaganda and a network of 7340 fake accounts linked to the ruling party in Turkey. Similarly, Facebook had deleted some 300 pages and accounts in both 2019 and 2020 linked to Philippine and China-based networks from its platform and from Instagram that exhibited coordinated inauthentic behavior (Gleicher, 2019; Davidson & Fonbuena, 2020).

At the instigation of the European Commission, online companies such as Facebook, Twitter, Microsoft, Google, and TikTok are signatories of a

Code of Practice to address online disinformation.[7] Consequently, platforms have also been taking actions to increase the visibility of authoritative sources, especially regarding the COVID-19 pandemic. These companies have also developed tools that facilitate access to reliable information.

Communication and technology scholars believe that artificial intelligence can provide tech-based solutions such as algorithm filters, browsers, apps, and plug-ins that can help combat disinformation. Anderson and Rainie (2017) observed that the right technology can "help label, filter or ban misinformation and thus upgrade the public's ability to judge the quality and veracity of content" (p. 6).

But legislators and others are suggesting more *regulatory remedies*, such as a software liability law, greater transparency laws, and the unbundling of social networks like Facebook to prevent network domination (Anderson & Rainie, 2017). "We cannot leave it to American companies to determine which information EU citizens can or cannot see. They cannot determine our view on the world, that window should be as big as possible," said Magdalena Adamowicz, a member of the European Parliament (Nicolas, 2020).

Similarly, California Senator Bill Hertzberg is pushing for the regulation of automated bots on the Internet (Diresta, 2019). Automated bots are AI internet software that can access online platforms without human intervention. These have been used to mislead users by artificially inflating follower counts, likes, and retweets and they have been used to manipulate online polls.

Decreasing the Impact of Disinformation

The variety of techniques used to manipulate the reach, virality, and impact of disinformation campaigns can range from automated tools to paid engagement or troll farms. Regardless of method, this seeks to undermine democratic space through inauthentic behavior by manipulative actors (Francois, 2019).

While steps are being made by social media companies to curtail the distribution of false information, greater effort can be made to inoculate the public against infodemics.

---

[7] https://digital-strategy.ec.europa.eu/en/policies/code-practice-disinformation.

For starters, multilateral organizations can support existing fact-checking collaborative efforts, such as the Belgium-based, EU-wide *Eufactcheck.eu*, the Mexican *Verificado*, the Indonesian *Masyarakat Anti Fitnah Indonesia* (Mafindo), and the Philippine *Tsek.ph*. These organizations are already on the ground fighting disinformation despite limited resources.

Greater emphasis can also be given to *Media and Information Literacy* (MIL), which can play a key role in empowering people to find, critically evaluate, use, and contribute to credible information so they could make informed judgments and decisions, and critically engage in sustainable development. In fact, in marking World Press Freedom Day in May 2021, UNESCO acknowledged that developing media and information literacy "offers a long-term and systemic policy response to disinformation and hate speech" (2021, p. 11). A media and information literate citizenry, it further said, "becomes a necessary node in the business model for viable and transparent media and digital communication companies, thus contributing to the sustainable development goals" (p. 12).

MIL was first proposed by the Grunwald Declaration on Media Education and adopted by 19 nations during UNESCO's 1982 International Symposium on Media Education. A report prepared for the U.K.'s Office of Communications said three specific types of media literacy skills—critical thinking, evaluation strategies, and knowledge of the operation of news and media industries—have been found to positively influence the ability to critically engage with misinformation (Edwards et al., 2021). Moreover, individuals with higher digital literacy, numerical literacy, health literacy, and cognitive skills also appear better at assessing health-related statements, according to a study (Vidgen et al., 2021).

Meanwhile, American scholars Michelle Amazeen and Erik Bucy (2019) noted that news literacy has been associated with a decreased likelihood of people falling for disinformation. In particular, people with greater levels of procedural news knowledge are more likely to accurately recognize digital disinformation, including native advertising and fabricated headlines, they said.

Social listening is another strategy in countering deceptive behavior. Instead of monitoring suspected manipulative actors, social listening is the effort to gain insights into the sentiments and dominant narratives about specific issues circulating online in order to be able to correct false information with counternarratives if needed (CEPPS, 2021).

In the context of disinformation, a counternarrative refers to "a communication strategy that tries to directly oppose a particular false claim or narrative by uncovering lies and untruths and by discrediting disinformation actors" (Butcher & Neidhardt, 2020, p. 4).

Counternarratives are better than state interference, including legislation that may restrict free speech. Udupa et al. (2020) noted that counternarratives resulted in positive outcomes, for example, support for certain groups such as victims of violence, increased public awareness around racism and other issues, free legal advice to victims, and greater enforcement of laws criminalizing racism. At the same time, however, they cautioned that counternarratives could unwittingly make disinformation and hateful speech newsworthy.

Closely related to counter narratives are *alternative narratives*, which promote a story of subject different from what disinformation actors push. Butcher and Neidhardt (2020) said:

> Alternative narratives focus on what society stands for, rather than against. Unlike counternarratives, alternative narratives do not seek to respond directly to or rebuke an existing false narrative, but rather try to reframe the debate and shift the attention away from the threats and fears propagated by disinformation actors. (p. 4)

Alternative narratives especially target those in the "movable middle" or those most open to changing their views (Butcher & Neidhardt, 2020, p. 5). In fact, these groups may also be more liable to being influenced by disinformation.

CONCLUSION

Disinformation, as discussed above, should be seen as a violation of the right to information since it robs people of an atmosphere of transparency and access to quality information needed to make informed choices. Moreover, disinformation can exacerbate poverty, "adding ignorance to the already heavy burden the poor have to bear in terms of physical deprivation" (Lister, 2016).

By 2030, the danger of disinformation can be reduced significantly only if a collaborative response across and within governments, the private sector, civil society, and the media is pursued. This strongly suggests the need for adopting *Communication for All* as a sustainable development goal not only to facilitate collaboration but also to ensure that a more participatory approach is implemented.

The European Commission's action plan against disinformation shows the way forward. The Action Plan promoted a coordinated and joint response across nations in addressing disinformation campaigns. Among the many actions taken, the members had set-up a Rapid Alert System, which provided real-time alerts on disinformation campaigns and helped EU members to share data and assessment and coordinate their responses (European Commission, 2018b), at the same time, enabling time and resource efficiency.

Collaboration would also promote effective and participatory public communication. The escalation of disinformation during the pandemic further highlighted the need for public communication which, according to the OECD (2020b), entails "providing information for the public interest that is factual, transparent, and separate from political communication" (p. 5) to be effective in supporting policy and combatting disinformation and gaining public trust.

As noted earlier, one of the biggest challenges in harnessing communication toward sustainable development is the need to uphold press freedom and free speech while combatting disinformation. With *Communication for All* as the 18th Sustainable Development Goal, governments will be encouraged to combat disinformation through media literacy education, greater support for media institutions, and other innovations instead of resorting to restrictive legislation.

References

Agley, J., & Xiao, Y. (2021). Misinformation about COVID-19: Evidence for differential latent profiles and a strong association with trust in science. *BMC Public Health, 21.* https://doi.org/10.1186/s12889-020-10103-x

Alaphilippe, A. (2021). Adding a D to the ABC disinformation framework. *TechStream.* The Brookings Institute. Retrieved October 2, 2021, from https://www.brookings.edu/techstream/adding-a-d-to-the-abc-disinformation-framework/

Amazeen, M. A., & Bucy, E. P. (2019). Conferring resistance to digital disinformation: The inoculating influence of procedural news knowledge. *Journal of Broadcasting & Electronic Media, 63*(3), 415–432. https://doi.org/10.1080/08838151.2019.1653101

Anderson, J., & Rainie, L. (2017). *The future of truth and misinformation online.* Pew Research Center. Retrieved October 7, 2021, from https://www.pewresearch.org/internet/2017/10/19/the-future-of-truth-and-misinformation-online/

Bontcheva, K., & Posetti, J. (Eds.). (2020). *Balancing act: Countering digital disinformation while respecting freedom of expression.* Broadband Commission for Sustainable Development and UNESCO. Retrieved September 7, 2021, from https://www.broadbandcommission.org/Documents/working-groups/FoE_Disinfo_Report

Bryanov, K., & Vziatysheva, V. (2021). Determinants of individuals' belief in fake news: A scoping review determinants of belief in fake news. *PLOS One.* https://doi.org/10.1371/journal.pone.0253717

Butcher, P., & Neidhardt, A. H. (2020). *Fear and lying in the EU: Fighting disinformation on migration with alternative narratives.* Foundation for European Progressive Studies. Retrieved September 27, 2021, from https://www.epc.eu/content/PDF/2020/Disinformation_on_Migration.pdf

Colomina, C., Margalef, H. S., & Youngs, R. (2021, April). *The impact of disinformation on democratic processes and human rights in the world.* European Parliament Policy Department. Retrieved September 7, 2021, from https://www.europarl.europa.eu/RegData/etudes/STUD/2021/653635/EXPO_STU(2021)653635_EN.pdf

Consortium for Elections and Political Process Strengthening (CEPPS). (2021). *Countering disinformation.* Retrieved October 9, 2021, from https://counteringdisinformation.org/topics/embs/0-overview-emb-approaches

Cook, J., Lewandowsky, S., & Ecker, U. (2017). Neutralizing misinformation through inoculation: Exposing misleading argumentation techniques reduces their influence. *Plos One.* https://doi.org/10.1371/journal.pone.0175799

Davidson, H., & Fonbuena C. (2020, September). Facebook removes fake accounts with links to China and the Philippines. *The Guardian.* Retrieved October 24, 2021, from https://www.theguardian.com/technology/2020/sep/23/facebook-removes-fake-accounts-with-links-to-china-and-philippines

Diresta, R. (2019, July 24). A new law makes bots identify themselves—That's the problem. *Wired.* Retrieved October 24, 2021, from https://www.wired.com/story/law-makes-bots-identify-themselves/

Dobbs, M. (2012). *The rise of political fact-checking: How Reagan inspired a journalistic movement.* New America Foundation. Retrieved October 9, 2021, from https://www.issuelab.org/resources/15318/15318.pdf

Edelman. (2021). *Edelman Trust Barometer 2021.* Retrieved September 27, 2021, from https://www.edelman.com/sites/g/files/aatuss191/files/2021-03/2021%20Edelman%20Trust%20Barometer.pdf

Edwards, L. Stoilova, M., Anstead, N., Fry, A., El-Halaby, G., & Smith, M. (2021). Rapid evidence assessment on online misinformation and media literacy: Final report for Ofcom. Retrieved September 22, 2021, from https://www.ofcom.org.uk/__data/assets/pdf_file/0011/220403/rea-online-misinformation.pdf

European Commission. (2018a). *A multi-dimensional approach to disinformation: Report of the independent high-level group (HLEG) on fake news and online disinformation*. Retrieved September 7, 2021, from https://op.europa.eu/en/publication-detail/-/publication/6ef4df8b-4cea-11e8-be1d-01aa75e

European Commission. (2018b, December). *Joint communication on the Action Plan against disinformation*. Retrieved October 7, 2021, from https://ec.europa.eu/info/publications/action-plan-disinformation-commission-contribution-european-council-13-14-december-2018_en

Francois, C. (2019). *Actors, behaviors, content: A disinformation ABC*. U.S. Congressional Committee on Science, Space and Technology. Retrieved September 7, 2021, from https://science.house.gov/imo/media/doc/Francois%20Addendum%20to%20Testimony%20-%20ABC_Framework_2019_Sept_2019.pdf

Freedom House. (2021). *Freedom in the World 2021. Democracy under siege*. https://freedomhouse.org/report/freedom-world/2021/democracy-under-siege

Freudenburg, W., & Muselli, V. (2013). Reexamining climate change debates: Scientific disagreement or scientific certainty argumentation methods (SCAMs)? *American Behavioral Scientist, 57*. https://doi.org/10.1177/0002764212458274

Funke, D., & Flamini, D. (2021). *A guide to anti-misinformation actions around the world*. Poynter Institute. Retrieved September 7, 2021, from https://www.poynter.org/ifcn/anti-misinformation-actions/

Gleicher, N. (2019). *Removing coordinated inauthentic behavior from the Philippines*. Meta. Retrieved September 7, 2021, from https://about.fb.com/news/2019/03/cib-from-thephilippines/

Gramling, C. (2021, May 18). Climate change disinformation is evolving. So are efforts to fight back. *Science News*. Retrieved October 1, 2021, from https://www.sciencenews.org/article/climate-change-disinformation-denial-misinformation

Habib, M., Jubb, C., Ahmad, S., & Pallard, H. (2018). *Forced migration of Rohingya: The untold experience*. Ontario International Development Agency. Retrieved September 7, 2021, from https://doi.org/10.2139/ssrn.3242696

Institute for Strategic Dialogue. (2021). *The networks and narratives of anti-refugee disinformation in Europe*. Retrieved September 7, 2021, from https://www.isdglobal.org/wp-content/uploads/2021/07/The-networks-and-narratives-of-anti-migrant-discourse-in-Europe.pdf

International Press Institute. (n.d.). *IPI COVID-19 press freedom tracker*. Retrieved July 7, 2021, from https://ipi.media/covid19

Islam, M. S., Sarkar, T., Khan, S., Mostofa Kamal, A., & Hassan, S. (2020). COVID-19–related infodemic and its impact on public health: A global social media analysis. *The American Journal of Tropical Medicine and Hygiene, 103*(4),

1621–1629. https://www.ajtmh.org/view/journals/tpmd/103/4/article-p1621.xml

Jolley, D., & Douglas, K. (2017). Prevention is better than cure: Addressing anti-vaccine conspiracy theories. *Journal of Applied Social Psychology*, *47*(8), 459–469. https://doi.org/10.1111/jasp.12453

Judson, E., Atay, A., Krasodomski-Jones, A., Lasko-Skinner, R., & Smith, J. (2020). *Engendering hate: The contours of state-aligned gendered disinformation online*. National Democratic Institute. Retrieved September 27, 2021, from https://www.ndi.org/sites/default/files/Engendering-Hate.pdf

Kapantai, E., Berberidis, C., Christopoulou, A., & Peristeraset, V. (2020). A systematic literature review on disinformation: Toward a unified taxonomical framework. *New Media & Society*, 1–26. https://doi.org/10.1177/146144482095929

Keane, P. (2020, September 20). How the oil industry made us doubt climate change. *BBC*. Retrieved October 1, 2021, from https://www.bbc.com/news/stories-53640382

Kemp, S. (2021, July 21). *Digital 2021 July Global statshot report*. DataReportal. Retrieved September 27, 2021, from https://datareportal.com/reports/digital-2021-july-global-statshot

Khan, R. E. (2020, July 31). Viral news on the coronavirus: Does it contribute to health communication? *TRIPODOS*, *47*(1), 49–66. https://doi.org/10.51698/tripodos.2020.47p49-66

Kironska, K., & Peng, N. (2021). How state-run media shape perceptions: An analysis of the projection of the Rohingya in the state-run Global New Light of Myanmar. *South East Asia Research*, *29*(1), 16–31.

Lasswell, H. (1948). The structure and function of communication in society. In L. Bryson (Ed.), *The communication of ideas* (p. 117). Institute for Religious and Social Studies.

Lee, P., & Vargas, L. (2020). *Expanding shrinking communication spaces*. The Centre for Communication Rights and Southbound Penang.

Lewandowsky, S. (2020). Climate change disinformation and how to combat it. *Annual Review of Public Health*, *42*, 1–21. https://doi.org/10.1146/annurev-publhealth-090419-102409

Lewandowsky, S., Cook, J., Schmid, P., et al. (2021). *The COVID-19 vaccine communication handbook. A practical guide for improving vaccine communication and fighting misinformation*. https://sks.to/c19vax

Lister, G. (2016, May 3). Free speech and access to information: Key to citizen empowerment and sustainable development. *UNESCO Insights*. UNESCO. Retrieved October 11, 2021, from https://en.unesco.org/world-press-freedom-day-2016/insights

López-García, X., Costa-Sánchez, C., & Vizoso, Á. (2021). Journalistic fact-checking of information in pandemic: Stakeholders, hoaxes, and strategies to fight disinformation during the COVID-19 crisis in Spain. *International Journal of Environmental Research and Public Health, 18*(3), 1227. https://doi.org/10.3390/ijerph18031227

Mahmud, E. (2020). Risk communication: Community engagement to counter misinformation in Rohingya refugee camps. OECD. Retrieved September 22, 2021, from https://www.oecd-ilibrary.org/sites/e8f2389a-en/index.html?itemId=/content/component/e8f2389a-en

Matasick, C., Alfonsi, C., & Bellantoni, A. (2020). Governance responses to disinformation: How open government principles can inform policy options. OECD. Retrieved September 22, 2021, from https://www.oecd.org/gov/open-government/working-paper-governance-responses-to-disinformation.htm

Message of his holiness Pope Francis for World Communications Day. (2018, January 24). *Vatican News*. Retrieved September 27, 2021, from https://www.vatican.va/content/francesco/en/messages/communications/documents/papa-francesco_20180124_messaggio-com

Mian, A., & Khan, S. (2020). Coronavirus: The spread of misinformation. *BMC Medicine, 18*(89). https://doi.org/10.1186/s12916-020-01556-3

Mozur, P. (2018, October 15). A genocide incited on Facebook, with posts from Myanmar's military. *The New York Times*. Retrieved September 7, 2021, from https://www.nytimes.com/2018/10/15/technology/myanmar-facebook-genocide.html

Mulvay, K., & Sulman, S. (2015). *The climate deception dossiers*. Union of Concerned Scientists. Retrieved October 1, 2021, from https://www.ucsusa.org/resources/climate-deception-dossiers

National Democratic Institute. (2019). *Tweets that chill. Analyzing online violence against women in politics*. Retrieved September 27, 2021, from https://www.ndi.org/sites/default/files/NDI%20Tweets%20That%20Chill%20Report.pdf

Newman, N., Fletcher, R., Schulz, A., Robertson, C., & Andi, S. (2021). *Digital news report 2021*. Reuters Institute. Retrieved July 31, 2021, from https://reutersinstitute.politics.ox.ac.uk/s

Nguyen, J., Valadkhani, A., Nguyen, A., & Wake, A. (2021). Press freedom and the global economy: The cost of slipping backwards. *Journalism Studies, 22*(4), 399–417. https://doi.org/10.1080/1461670X.2021.1873822

Nicolas, E. (2020, June 16). Self-regulation not working' on fake news, EU warned. *EUObserver*. Retrieved October 24, 2021, from https://euobserver.com/coronavirus/148648

Nougayrede, N. (2018, January 31). In this age of propaganda, we must defend ourselves. Here's how. *The Guardian*. Retrieved September 27, 2021, from https://www.theguardian.com/commentisfree/2018/jan/31/propaganda-defend-russia-technology

OECD. (2020a). *Combatting COVID-19 disinformation on online platforms.* Retrieved September 22, 2021, from https://www.oecd.org/coronavirus/ policy-responses/combatting-covid-19-disinformation-on-online-platforms-d854ec48/

OECD. (2020b). *Transparency, communication and trust: The role of public communication in responding to the wave of disinformation about the new coronavirus.* Retrieved September 22, 2021, from https://www.oecd.org/coronavirus/ policy-responses/transparency-communication-and-trust-the-role-of-public-communication-in-responding-to-the-wave-of-disinformation-about-the-new-coronavirus-bef7ad6e/

OECD/Dev. (2014). Good practices in development communication. Retrieved August 5, 2021, from https://www.oecd.org/dev/DevCom%20 Publication%20Good%20Practices%20in%20Development%20 Communication.pdf

Porter, E., & Wood, T. (2021, September). The global effectiveness of fact-checking: Evidence from simultaneous experiments in Argentina, Nigeria, South Africa, and the United Kingdom. *PNAS, 118*(37), e2104235118. https://doi. org/10.1073/pnas.21042351

Porter, E., Wood, T., & Bahador, B. (2019, July–September). Can presidential misinformation on climate change be corrected? Evidence from Internet and phone experiments. *Research and Politics,* 1–10. https://doi. org/10.1177/2053168019864784

Posetti, J., Aboulez, N., Bontcheva, K., Harrison, J., & Waisbord, S. (2020). *Online violence against women journalists: A global snapshot of incidence and impacts.* UNESCO. Retrieved September 27, 2021, from https://www.icfj. org/sites/default/files/2020-12/UNESCO%20Online%20Violence%20 Against%20Women%20Journalists%20-%20A%20Global%20Snapshot%20 Dec9pm.pdf

Posetti, J., & Matthews, A. (2018). *A short guide to the history of 'fake news' and disinformation.* International Center for Journalists. Retrieved September 27, 2021, from https://www.icfj.org/news/short-guide-history-fake-news-and-disinformation-new-icfj-learning-module

Poynter. (n.d.). The CoronaVirusFacts/DatosCoronaVirus Alliance database. Retrieved September 22, 2021, from https://www.poynter.org/ifcn-covid-19-misinformation/page/1031/

Prevency. (2020, June). *What is disinformation?* Retrieved September 27, 2021, from https://prevency.com/en/what-is-disinformation/

Reporters Without Borders. (2021a). *2021 "Press freedom predators" gallery—Old tyrants, two women and a European.* Retrieved September 27, 2021, from https://rsf.org/en/news/rsfs-2021-press-freedom-predators-gallery-old-tyrants-two-women-and-european

Reporters Without Borders. (2021b). *2021 World Press Freedom Index: Journalism, the vaccine against disinformation, blocked in more than 130 countries*. Retrieved September 27, 2021, from https://rsf.org/en/2021-world-press-freedom-index-journalism-vaccine-against-disinformation-blocked-more-130-countries

Repucci, S., & Slipowitz, A. (2020). *Democracy under lockdown: The impact of COVID-19 and the struggle for global freedom*. Freedom House. Retrieved September 27, 2021, from https://freedomhouse.org/report/special-report/2020/democracy-under-lockdown

Roozenbeek, J., Freeman, A., Schneider, C., Dryhurst, S., & Kerr, J. (2020). Susceptibility to misinformation about COVID-19 around the world. *Royal Society Open Science, 7*. https://doi.org/10.1098/rsos.201199

Roozenbeek, J., & Van der Linden, S. (2018). The fake news game: Actively inoculating against the risk of misinformation. *Journal of Risk Research, 22*(5), 570–580. https://doi.org/10.1080/13669877.2018.1443491

Rothkopf, D. J. (2003, May 11). When the buzz bites back. *Washington Post*. Retrieved October 1, 2021, from https://www.washingtonpost.com/archive/opinions/2003/05/11/when-the-buzz-bites-back/bc8cd84f-cab6-4648-bf58-0277261af6cd/

Servaes, J. (2008). *Communication for development and social change*. SAGE. https://doi.org/10.1177/097317411000500110

Servaes, J., & Malikhao, P. (2016). Communication is essential for global impact. *Procedia Engineering, 159*, 316–321.

Sessa, M. G. (2020). *Misogyny and misinformation: An analysis of gendered disinformation tactics during the COVID-19 pandemic*. EU Disinfo Lab. Retrieved September 7, 2021, from https://www.disinfo.eu/publications/misogyny-and-misinformation:-an-analysis-of-gendered-disinformation-tactics-during-the-covid-19-pandemic/

Spindler, W. (2015, December 8). *2015: The year of Europe's refugee crisis*. UN Refugee Agency. Retrieved September 27, 2021, from https://www.unhcr.org/news/stories/2015/12/56ec1ebde/2015-year-europes-refugee-crisis.html

States News Service. (2020). *Democratic Women's Caucus, Speaker Pelosi send letter to Facebook demanding it stop the spread of gendered disinformation and misogynistic attacks against women leaders*. Retrieved September 27, 2021, from https://speier.house

Szakács, J., & Bognár, E. (2021). *The impact of disinformation campaigns about migrants and minority groups in the EU*. European Parliament. Retrieved September 27, 2021, from https://www.europarl.europa.eu/RegData/etudes/IDAN/2021/653641/EXPO_IDA(2021)653641_EN.pdf

Turcilo, L., & Obrenovic, M. (2020). *Misinformation, disinformation, malinformation: Causes, trends, and their influence on democracy*. Hoenrich Boll

Foundation. Retrieved September 27, 2021, from https://www.boell.de/sites/default/files/2020-08/200825_E-Paper3_ENG.pdf

Udupa, S., Gagliardone, I., Deem, A., & Csuka, L. (2020). *Hate speech, information disorder, and conflict.* Social Science Research Council. Retrieved September 22, 2021, from https://s3.amazonaws.com/ssrc-cdn1/crmuploads/new_publication_3/the-field-of-disinformation-democratic-processes-and-conflict-prevention-a-scan-of-the-literature.pdf

UN Department of Global Communications. (2020, March 31). UN tackles 'infodemic' of misinformation and cybercrime in COVID-19 crisis. Retrieved August 7, 2021, from https://www.un.org/en/un-coronavirus-communications-team/un-tackling-%E2%80%98infodemic%E2%80%99-misinformation-and-cybercrime-covid-19

UN Women. (2020). *Online violence against women in Asia: A multicountry study.* Retrieved September 27, 2021, from https://asiapacific.unwomen.org/-/media/field%20office%20eseasia/docs/publications/2020/12/ap-ict-vawg-report-7dec20.pdf?la=en&vs=4251

UNESCO. (2017). *Unpacking Sustainable Development Goal 4.* Retrieved October 1, 2021, from sdg4education2030.org: https://sdg4education2030.org/the-goal

UNESCO. (2019, August 5). Call for proposals for a research report on freedom of expression and addressing disinformation on the internet. Retrieved October 1, 2021, from https://en.unesco.org/sites/default/files/unesco_wg_freedom_of_expression_and_disinformation_call_for_proposals.pdf

UNESCO. (2021). World Press Freedom Day 2021: Information as a public good. Retrieved September 22, 2021, from https://en.unesco.org/sites/default/files/wpfd_2021_concept_note_en.pdf

United Nations. (1948). *Article 19 Universal Declaration of Human Rights.*

United Nations Development Programme. (2020). *Responding to COVID-19 information pollution.* Retrieved September 22, 2021, from https://www.undp.org/publications/responding-covid-19-information-pollution

United Nations Economic and Social Council. (2021). *Progress towards the Sustainable Development Goals.* Retrieved September 27, 2021, from https://undocs.org/en/E/2021/58

United States Department of Homeland Security. (2019). *Combatting targeted disinformation campaigns: A whole-of-society issue.* Retrieved October 9, 2021, from https://www.dhs.gov/sites/default/files/publications/ia/ia_combatting-targeted-disinformation-campaigns.pdf

USAID. (2021). *Disinformation primer.* Retrieved September 27, 2021, from https://pdf.usaid.gov/pdf_docs/PA00XFKF.pdf

Van der Linden, S., Dixon, G., Clarke, C., & Cook, J. (2021). Inoculating against COVID-19 vaccine misinformation. *EClinicalMedicine, 33*, 100772. https://doi.org/10.1016/j.eclinm.2021.100772

Vidgen, B., Taylor, H., Pantazi, M., Anastasiou, Z., Inkster, B., & Margetts, H. (2021). *Understanding vulnerability to online misinformation*. The Alan Turing Institute. Retrieved September 27, 2021, from https://www.turing.ac.uk/sites/default/files/2021-02/misinformation_report_final1_0.pdf

Wardle, C. (2020, September). *Understanding the disinformation disorder*. Retrieved December 15, 2021, from https://firstdraftnews.org/long-form-article/understanding-information-disorder/

Wardle, C., & Derakhshan, H. (2017). *Information disorder: Toward an interdisciplinary framework for research and policymaking*. Council of Europe. https://rm.coe.int/information-disorder-toward-an-interdisciplinary-framework-for-researc/168076277c

Weiss, A., Alwan, A., & Garcia, E. (2020). Surveying fake news: Assessing university faculty's fragmented definition of fake news and its impact on teaching critical thinking. *International Journal for Educational Integrity, 16*(1). https://doi.org/10.1007/s40979-019-0049-x

World Health Organization. (2021, April 23). *COVID-19 continues to disrupt essential health services in 90% of countries*. Retrieved September 30, 2021, from https://www.who.int/news/item/23-04-2021-covid-19-continues-to-disrupt-essential-health-services-in-90-of-countries

World Health Organization. (n.d.). *Let's flatten the information curve*. Retrieved September 22, 2021, from https://www.who.int/news-room/spotlight/let-s-flatten-the-infodemic-curve

Zhenmin, L. (2021). *View from the pandemic: Stark realities, critical choices*. United Nations Economic and Social Affairs.

Communicating the SDGs: Formulating Performance Metrics for Higher Education Institutions

Jude William Genilo and Kamolrat Intaratat

Abstract The Times Higher Education (THE) Impact Rankings is a measure that shows how global higher education institutions (HEIs) work toward the fulfillment of the United Nations' Sustainable Development Goals (SDGs). To formulate its measurement, THE (in collaboration with Vertigo Ventures) sought guidance from the Theory of Change (ToC), which has four components: (1) teaching (disseminating knowledge and producing people to address world problems); (2)

J. W. Genilo (✉)
Department of Media Studies and Journalism, University of Liberal Arts
Bangladesh (ULAB), Dhaka, Bangladesh
e-mail: jude.genilo@ulab.edu.bd

K. Intaratat
School of Communication Arts, Sukhothai Thammathirat Open University
(STOU), Nonthaburi, Thailand
e-mail: kamolrat.int@stou.ac.th

© The Author(s), under exclusive license to Springer Nature
Switzerland AG 2023
J. Servaes, M. J. Yusha'u (eds.), *SDG18 Communication for All,*
Volume 1, Sustainable Development Goals Series,
https://doi.org/10.1007/978-3-031-19142-8_9

research (creating knowledge to address world problems); (3) steward-ship (managing resources and caring for stakeholders); and (4) outreach (directly acting in society). THE developed performance metrics under each of the four ToC components for every SDG. After obtaining data for the different performance metrics, THE produces: (1) an overall ranking of universities based on the top three SDGs for each individual university plus SDG 17; and (2) individual rankings of universities based on perfor-mance in each SDG.

The Impact Rankings gained traction among higher educational insti-tutions worldwide. In the 2019 edition, 450 universities from 76 coun-tries participated. In the 2020 edition, this increased to 735 universities from 89 countries. In 2021, around 1117 universities from 98 countries joined. Unfortunately, the Impact Rankings did not include a goal on the role of communication in achieving the SDGs. With this omission, THE has excluded the important work universities have undertaken in commu-nication for development, particularly toward the achievement of the SDGs.

In light of this, this paper investigated the initiatives and undertakings of the top ranked universities in the Impact Rankings 2021 toward Communicating the SDGs. The top ranked universities included: (1) University of Manchester; (2) University of Sydney; (3) RMIT University; (4) La Trobe University; and (5) Queen's University. The findings indi-cated that these universities allocated a lot of time, energy and resources in communicating the SDGs—through their teaching (degree programs); research (books, book chapters and research papers); stewardship (web-sites, student-run media and campus-based platforms); and community outreach (social media accounts, news articles, blogs, podcasts, video recordings and opinion pieces). Based on their endeavors, the paper rec-ommended performance metrics and indicators for possible inclusion in future THE Impact Rankings.

Keywords Sustainability education • Times higher education impact ranking • Sustainable development goals • Higher education institutions • Communicating the SDGs • University Ranking

INTRODUCTION

In September 2015, after intense negotiations, 193 United Nations (UN) Member States agreed to adopt 17 Sustainable Development Goals (SDGs) and its 169 targets as part of the document: "Transforming Our World: The 2030 Agenda for Sustainable Development." The document serves as a guide for all countries to solve the world's most pressing problems by 2030—ending poverty and hunger, addressing climate change, protecting the planet, living healthy fulfilling lives, creating just and inclusive communities, achieving gender equity, realizing quality education, among others. To be able to achieve these complex socio-economic and environmental objectives, societal transformation is a must; all sectors need to collaborate, interconnect and act responsibly. There is a need to "contribute to strong institutions and partnerships" (De la Poza et al., 2021).

One sector crucial in implementing the SDGs is the universities. Higher Education Institutions (HEIs) engage in teaching and learning, campus operations and community leadership. Bhowmick et al. (2018) mentioned that the "unique functions and expertise of universities are critical for overcoming the wide range of interconnected social, economic and environmental challenges which is covered by the SDG agenda." They even went so far as to say, "the SDGs will not be achieved without this sector."

To illustrate, target 12.8 under SDG 12 (Responsible Consumption and Production) reads, "people everywhere have the relevant information and awareness for sustainable development and lifestyles in harmony with nature" (SDSN, 2015). For this target to be attained, HEIs need to develop in students the knowledge, skills, attitudes, and values to become responsible global citizens, professionals and consumers. Educating for sustainable development, thus, "empowers and equips the current and future generations to meet their needs using a balanced and integrated approach to the economic, social and environmental dimensions of sustainable development" (Leicht et al., 2018).

In terms of research contribution, De La Poza et al. (2021) rationalized that measuring SDGs require "in-depth thought about fundamental issues on the power of data to shape knowledge control to not be bound by politics," which only universities can provide. They asserted that universities could provide answers to questions relating to SDG achievements such as "What is measured," "Who finances and does the measuring," and "How are data collected, interpreted and disbursed." Moreover, universities have the capacity to generate and disseminate interdisciplinary and transdisciplinary knowledge—engaging academic disciplines with societal needs.

With regards to forming partnerships for the SDGs, HEIs have a long tradition of advocating for liberal ideals and communicating social and behavioral changes in their spheres of influence. They have been seen as neutral and trusted stakeholders—making it easier for them to engage in partnership and disseminate information about the goals. The Sustainable Development Solutions Network (2020) enumerated the attributes that enable universities help society address the SDGs as follows: reach, responsibility, access to learners, learning and teaching expertise, broad expertise, and special societal role. With these attributes, El-Jardali et al. (2018) added that HEIs can pursue partnerships for the SDGs such as in strengthening science-policy interface, providing neutral platforms for cross-sectoral dialogue, supporting integrated and coherent policies and actions for SDGs, getting involved in the political process, strengthening transdisciplinary learning and educational interactions, and demonstrating commitment to effective engagement and impact.

Dobson and Edersheim (2021) mentioned that global universities can even make greater and wider impacts by making higher education accessible (SDG 4) to more students, particularly those from underserved areas such as women and girls (SDG 5). Moreover, they have an important role in increasing economic growth (SDG 8) for a peaceful and just society (SDG 16). Unlike single institutions, they can expand international reach—inviting new members and incorporating institutions—through their network.

In a 2018 survey, covering 180 Participatory Research in Asia (PRIA) university partners, Tandon and Chakrabarti (2018) found out that around 75 percent of respondents felt that partnerships are important to influence powerful stakeholders while nearly 70 percent believed that partnerships are forged to solve particular problems. "Partnership is formed around a particular issue or a set of issues," they explained. The survey also revealed that more than 90 percent of respondents partnered with non-government organizations (NGOs), 80 percent with community-based organizations, 73.7 percent with the government, nearly 70 percent with international agencies, 68.4 percent with academia, 68 percent with the private sector, and 42 percent with the media.

Guiding Universities and Measuring Progress Toward the SDGS

To help universities contribute in the fulfillment of the SDGs, several initiatives have been undertaken—forming university partnerships, formulating guidebooks and manuals, devising assessment tools and creating impact rankings on sustainability for HEIs. In 2012, 300 universities partnered with the UN to form the Higher Education Sustainability Initiative (HESI). HESI members commit to teach sustainable development across all disciplines, encourage research and dissemination of sustainable development knowledge and green campus, and support local sustainability efforts, and engage/share information with international networks. In other words, HESI is a unique interface between teaching and learning, research and policy making.

Another pioneering HEI partnership is the International Sustainable Campus Network (ISCN), non-profit association with over 80 colleges and universities representing over 30 countries. ISCN members have been working together to holistically integrate sustainability into campus operations, research and teaching. In its 2020–2023 strategic plan, it aims to elevate its presence with key peer networks, agencies, and funders as well as enhance member value through robust exchange and engagement platforms. Since 2013, it has published the best campus sustainability practices in its annual report and since 2008, it has given the International Sustainable Campus Excellence Awards to recognize sustainable campus projects that demonstrate leadership, creativity, effectiveness, and outstanding performance in the areas of whole systems approach, partnerships for progress and cultural change for sustainability.

To guide universities in undertaking sustainability, some organizations have developed manuals, guidebooks, and assessment tools. The European University Association (EUA), for one, in December 2018, produced a manual to explain how universities can facilitate social, environmental, and economic development. It divided the SDGs into three broad areas—well-being, environment, and economy—emphasizing that HEIs play a central role in each of them. Well-being includes SDGs 1, 2, 3, 4, 5, 6, 10 and 11; environment covers SDGs 7, 13, 14 and 15; and economy involves SDGs 8, 9 and 12. The remaining SDGs—16 and 17—are for the development of universities as strong institutions.

In September 2020, Sustainable Development Solutions Network (SDSN) formulated a guide for "Accelerating Education for the SDGs in Universities." The guide provides a five-step process for implementing

Education for the SDG (ESDGs): (1) mapping activities; (2) building capacity and ownership; (3) identifying priorities, opportunities and gaps; (4) integrating, implementing and embedding the SDGs; and (5) monitoring, evaluating and communicating. The document also enumerated the common approaches in implementing ESDGs as follows: awareness-raising, interdisciplinary introductory units, discipline-specific units, integration into the existing discipline curriculum, SDG-focused project-based units, SDG-focused co-curricular activities, SDG-focused leadership programs, student-led activities, Massive Open Online Courses (MOOCs) and other online content and sustainable development degrees.

In October 2020, SDSN with the Gothenburg Centre for Sustainable Development and the University of Gothenburg developed the SDG Impact Assessment Tool. The said tool is a free, online resource for research and educational institutions, companies, entrepreneurs, civic organizations and public agencies to make self-assessments of their SDG impacts. Using the tool, HEIs can identify relevant sustainability perspectives in a simple and structured approach; assessing an object's impact on each of the 17 SDGs as either direct positive, indirect positive, no impact, indirect negative, direct negative or more knowledge needed. In this manner, HEIs can reflect and learn collaboratively about the SDGs and the links between them using the following steps: (1) gather forces; (2) define, refine, draw the line; (3) sort the SDGs; (4) assess impact; and (5) choose strategy forward.

To further encourage university participation, the University of Indonesia (UI) launched in 2010 the GreenMetric World University Ranking. In April 2009, UI hosted the International Conference on World University Rankings. During the conference, a number of experts observed that ranking systems did not give credit to HEIs who were making efforts to reduce their carbon footprint and combat global climate change. Given this, UI established the said ranking system to measure university performance on 39 indicators under six criteria: (1) Setting and Infrastructure; (2) Energy and Climate Change; (3) Waste; (4) Water; (5) Transportation; and (6) Education. In 2020, 912 universities from 84 countries participated in the rankings—up from 95 universities in 35 countries in 2010.

According to Usher and Savino (2006), universities rankings are gaining popularity "due to the public demand for transparency and information that institutions and governments have not been able to meet on their own." Individuals and families find comparative information useful to determine potential salary premium. Employers, on the other hand, need the rankings to adjust their expectations of various university graduates. Governments take their cue from rankings to determine university quality, international standards, and economic credibility. In this sense, universities need to participate in rankings because they need to. Hence, to show their commitment to the SDGs, universities may find it wise to join the GreenMetric World University Ranking and THE Impact Ranking.

Developing the THE Impact Rankings

The Times Higher Education (THE), formerly known as The Times Higher Education supplement (THES), started as a United Kingdom-based magazine reporting on higher education news and issues. THE became known for the annual Times Higher Education (THE)—Quacquarelli Symonds (QS) World University Rankings, which was first published in 2004. Five years later, THE broke with QS and partnered with Thomson Reuters instead. It developed a new methodology and published every year the following rankings: World Reputation Rankings, World University Rankings, and Young University Rankings. In 2013, THE signed a new deal with Elsevier—continuing the said rankings and publishing new ones such as Asia University Rankings (2013), Emerging Economies University Rankings (2014), Latin America University Rankings (2016), Japan University Rankings (2017) and WSJ/THE College Rankings (2017).

In June 2018, the THE held the THE Young Universities Summit in Florida to discuss and consult with interested parties the ways to measure the impact of a university. Later called THE Impact Rankings, the measure shows how global HEIs work toward the fulfillment of the SDGs. To formulate its measurement, THE (in collaboration with Vertigo Ventures) developed a Theory of Change (ToC), which illustrated the ways a university contributes to society. These included: (1) teaching (disseminating knowledge and producing people to address world problems); (2) research (creating knowledge to address world problems); (3) stewardship (managing internal resources and caring for stakeholders); and (4) community outreach (directly acting in society). De la Poza et al. (2021) explained the theoretical basis for the ToC; putting together the proposed model of Dziminska et al. (2020) and the internal community stewardship acknowledged by Bhowmick et al. (2018). The former explained about how universities might engage in promoting the SDGs in the three HEI core areas of teaching, research and serving society. The latter elaborated that universities needed to create a sense of identity among their stakeholders, which include students, faculty, and staff.

TOC is basically an illustration of how a desired change is expected to happen. It focuses on mapping out what an initiative does and how these lead to desired goals. In the study's context, the change agents are HEIs and the desired changes are the SDGs. HEIs contribute to change through teaching, research, stewardship, and community outreach.

Based on the ToC, THE developed performance metrics under each of the four aspects for every SDG. For example, as stated in the Methodology 2022, to measure the teaching aspect of SDG 2 (Zero Hunger), universities need to provide data regarding the number of graduates from agriculture and aquaculture courses, including sustainability aspects. To measure the research aspect of SDG 3 (Good Health and Well-being), Elsevier collects data (from the Scopus dataset) on a university's paper views, clinical citations and publications. It does this by tracking keywords relating to the said SDG. Since 2018, it has created search queries to aid institutions track and demonstrate progress toward the SDGs.

To assess the stewardship aspect of SDG 11 (Sustainable Cities and Communities), universities must discuss its sustainable practices such as commuting, remote working, affordable housing for employees, affordable housing for students, pedestrian priority on campus, local authority collaboration on planning and development, planning and development on new build standards and building on brownfield sites. To monitor the outreach aspect of SDG 4 (Quality Education), universities are required to supply information regarding public resources for lifelong learning, public events for lifelong learning, vocational training events, educational outreach activities beyond campus and lifelong learning access policy.

After obtaining data for the different performance metrics, THE produces: (1) an overall ranking of universities based on the top three SDGs for each individual university plus SDG 17; and (2) individual rankings of universities based on performance in each SDG. The Impact Rankings gained traction among higher educational institutions worldwide. In the 2019 edition, 450 universities from 76 countries participated. Also, THE collected data on 11 of the 17 SDGs during that period. In the 2020 edition, THE expanded data gathering to all 17 SDGs. Around 735 universities from 89 countries participated. In 2021, around 1117 universities from 98 countries joined.

Unfortunately, akin to the UN, THE Impact Ranking did not include a goal on the role of communication in achieving the SDGs. With this omission, THE might have unintentionally excluded the important work universities have undertaken in communication for development, particularly toward the achievement of the SDGs. The next section discussed the repercussions of such an oversight given that it is extremely difficult to achieve the SDGs without articulating the role of communication.

Communicating the SDGs

The 2030 Agenda for Sustainable Development incorporated specific communication-related targets, particularly on awareness-raising, education, and access to information. Under SDG 4 (Quality Education), target 4.7 sees all learners acquiring the knowledge and skills needed to promote sustainable development and global citizenship. Under SDG 12 (Responsible Consumption and Production) and SDG 13 (Climate Action), targets 12.8 and 13.3 call for public awareness and education to promote sustainable consumption and production as well as climate change. Under SDG 16 (Peace, Justice and Strong Institutions), targets 16.6 and 16.10 mandate nations to establish accountable and transparent institutions and ensure public access to information.

With such specific targets, during a European Sustainable Development Network (ESDN) workshop, Mulholland (2018) declared that a direct mandate has been given to SDG communicators. He proceeded to discuss the magnitude and reach required to attain the SDGs. In terms of magnitude, he mentioned that all countries have accepted the SDG targets—states are not alone in working toward the goals but are responsible entities to realize the goals. In terms of reach, he explained that the "line of communication must be taken further, so that those levels closest to civil society, the local and municipal levels, as well as other stakeholder groups are also informed on priorities, as they will be the agents of 'on the ground change' regarding meeting the targets of the SDGs." The OECD Development Communication Network (2016) added that SDG communicators have a formal mandate and specific targets to raise awareness, build knowledge, and inspire people for sustainable development. Moreover, they need to tell people how development happens and understand the perceptions of new audiences.

To help SDG communicators, the OECD Development Communication Network (2016) recommended the crafting of new narratives for sustainable development; understanding SDG audiences; forging new partnerships; maximizing digital technologies and innovations; and mobilizing resources for public engagement. In line with this, the Hub likewise devised ten peer learning areas relating to vision and strategy, people and partnerships and tools, resources and innovation.

Communication scholars and groups like Lee and Vargas (2020), WACC (2019) and Yusha'u (2021) felt that the existing targets relating to communication were insufficient to attain the SDGs. Yusha'u observed that there were only a few passing communication-related targets in the SDGs. In the same light, the WACC recommended specific communication-related targets for SDG 5 (Gender Equality), SDG 9 (Industry, Innovation and Infrastructure), SDG 16 (Peace, Justice and Strong Institutions) and SDG 17 (Partnership for the Goals). According to WACC (2019), gender inequality is a key dimension of communication and information poverty. SDG 5 is affected by how women and girls are represented in media, have access to media platforms, and gain information/knowledge. The issue of access to Information and Communication Technologies (ICTs), including the internet, should be highlighted in SDG 9. National governments should provide universal access to basic telecommunication services to all its citizens, even those living in remote places. As SDG 17 focuses on finance, technology, capacity, trade, effectiveness and monitoring Agenda 2030 implementation, WACC (2019) asserted that more structural issues are afoot with digital communication, including open and democratic access, in terms of developing new infrastructure and governance models. Regarding SDG 16, open and democratic access to ICTs underpins social inclusion, peaceful conflict resolution, rule of law, trust in institutions and enabling participation.

Lee and Vargas (2020) argued that genuine sustainable development and equitable access to ICTs requires an additional SDG—SDG 18: Communication for All. This additional SDG expands and strengthens public civic spaces through equitable and affordable access to ICTs and platforms, media pluralism and media diversity. It provides a framework to enable, empower, and transform to guarantee media access, safety, diversity, and public participation. The call for this additional SDG has been supported by Yusha'u (2021), who highlighted the role of communication during the COVID-19 pandemic, stating that the SDGs were on life support and the omitted SDG on communication served as the ventilator. The writings of Lee and Vargas, Yusha'u and Servaes underscored Traber's likening of communication to the human body's nervous system. He wrote, "if the nervous system or the immune system breaks down, the wellbeing of the entire body is in jeopardy. Similarly, no modern democracy can exist, let alone flourish, without a certain level of information and participation" (Traber, 2019).

In many ways, the above-mentioned communication scholars asserted the central role communication plays in attaining the SDGs. For them, there is no way to attain the SDGs other than through communication. In this manner, an additional SDG on communication is warranted; it is not enough to simply integrate communication-related SDG targets into the existing document. At the level of HEIs, a case in point are Spanish universities who were mindful of the link between communication and the SDGs. De Filippo et al. (2020) analyzed how 50 private and public Spanish universities communicated their commitment to sustainability. The study looked at sustainability content in the website, sustainability governance structures, scientific papers, and social media. The findings indicated that there is intensified interest in sustainability among Spanish universities in recent years, especially in associating sustainability to designate governing bodies. Universities could not fulfill their role in pursuing the SDGs without the full use of communication.

A Closer Look at the Top Ranked Universities

The paper aimed to recommend an additional performance metric for communicating the SDGs (possibly, SDG 18), which may be considered for inclusion in future THE Impact Ranking exercises. To undertake this, the paper needed to explore the SDG-related communication activities of HEIs with respect to the ranking system's ToC. Table 9.1 presents the indicators explored in the paper under each ToC aspect.

Data gathering on the said indicators took place from September to October 2021. Data were gathered from the university's website, strategic plan, and social media accounts, particularly Facebook, Twitter, YouTube, Instagram, and LinkedIn. Regarding the selection of universities for inclusion in the study, the main criterion was that the university was among the top five ranked in the THE Impact Ranking for 2021. Table 9.2 describes the said universities in terms of their foundation year, location, and vision.

The top university ranked for 2021 was the University of Manchester (UOM). The university traced its history to 1824 as the Manchester's Mechanics Institution. In 2004, the Victoria University of Manchester and the University of Manchester Institute of Science and Technology (UMIST) merged to form UOM. The next three top ranked universities

Table 9.1 Study framework showing ToC aspects and their indicators

No.	ToC aspect	Indicators
1	Teaching	• Undergraduate and graduate programs that produce professionals trained in communicating the SDGs such communication studies, film studies and media studies.
2	Research	• Keywords, tags and subjects of books, book chapters and research papers relating to communication, media, sustainability and SDGs.
3	Stewardship	• Content on sustainability as well as SDG-related policies, programs and activities featured in the university website. • Content on sustainability as well as SDG-related policies, programs and activities featured in campus-based media. • Content on sustainable as well SDF-related initiatives in other internal communication channels.
4	Community Outreach	• Activities and reach of university social media accounts. • SDG-related news featured in the university website. • SDG-related advocacies featured in university blogs, podcasts, video recordings and opinion pieces.

are all located in Australia. The University of Sydney (USYD), ranked 2, is a public research university with eight academic faculties and schools.

The Royal Melbourne Institute of Technology (RMIT), ranked 3, began as a night school offering classes in art, science, and technology. Now, it has 4 academic colleges and 15 academic schools. La Trobe University (LTU), ranked 4, has its main campus located in Melbourne suburb of Bundoora. It is a public research university and is part of the Innovative Research Universities. Queen's University (QU), ranked 5, is a public research university in Canada organized into eight faculties and schools.

Communicating the SDGs: Teaching and Research

In the THE Impact Ranking 2021 methodology, the aspect of teaching was measured by the number and proportion of graduates belonging to fields of study that relates to a particular SDG. For example, graduates from agriculture and aquaculture addressed SDG 2 (Zero Hunger), health professions for SDG 3 (Good Health and Well-being), from any program providing primary school teaching qualifications for SDG 4 (Quality Education), and from law and enforcement courses for SDG 16 (Peace,

Table 9.2 Top ranked universities included in the study

Rank	University	Foundation year	Location	Vision
1	University of Manchester (UOM)	1824	Manchester, United Kingdom	We will be recognized globally for the excellence of our people, research, learning and innovation, and for the benefits we bring to society and the environment.
2	University of Sydney (USYD)	1850	Sydney, Australia	Since our inception, we have believed in education for all and leadership that improves lives in all the communities that we serve.
3	Royal Melbourne Institute of Technology (RMIT)	1887	Melbourne, Australia	A global university of technology, design, and enterprise.
4	La Trobe University (LTU)	1964	Melbourne, Australia	A university known for making a positive difference in the lives of our students, partners, and communities. We will become an even more valued and relevant university because of the way we respond to their needs in this time of great local and national crisis.
5	Queen's University (QU)	1841	Kingston, Ontario, Canada	Queen's longstanding reputation for offering its students an exceptional educational and extra-curricular learning experience. Today, we are as well known in our excellence in research and graduate and professional programs as for the quality of our student learning experience.

Source: University Websites and Strategic Plans

Justice and Strong Institutions). It can also be evaluated by the number and proportion of students belonging to particular socio-economic groups such as students with disability for SDG 10 (Reduced Inequalities) and females graduating from STEM courses for SDG 5 (Gender Equality). It may also be assessed by looking at education programs addressing specific SDGs such on climate for SDG 13 (Climate Action).

For communicating the SDGs, the paper focused on undergraduate (as shown in Table 9.3) and graduate (as shown in Table 9.4) programs that produce professionals trained in communication. It was undertaken by analyzing the university website, particularly under courses, faculties, and departments sections.

Table 9.3 Communication-related undergraduate programs in the top five ranked universities

Rank	University	Communicated-related programs
1	UOM	BA Film Studies and Film Studies in combination with other courses.
2	USYD	BA (Media and Communications); Bachelor of Advanced Studies (Media and Communications).
3	RMIT	Bachelor of Communication (Professional Communication); Bachelor of Communication (Advertising); Bachelor of Communication (Public Relations); Bachelor of Media and Communication (Honours); Bachelor of Communication (Journalism); Bachelor of Communication (Media); Bachelor of Design (Communication Design); Bachelor of Arts (Photography).
4	LTU	Bachelor of Media and Communication; BA in Screen, Media and Performance.
5	QU	Bachelor's in Film and Media; Bachelor's in Media and Performance Production.

Table 9.4 Communication-related graduate programs in the top five ranked universities

Rank	University	Communicated-related programs
1	UOM	MA Film Studies; MA Intercultural Communication; MA Digital Technologies, Communication and Education; MSc Science and Health Communication; PhD Anthropology, Media and Performance; PhD Social Anthropology with Visual Media
2	USYD	Master of Moving Image; Master of Health Communication; Master of Digital Communication and Culture; Master of Media Practice; Master of Strategic Public Relations;
3	RMIT	Master of Advertising; Master of Design (Media and Communication); Master in Writing and Publishing; Master of Communication; PhD (Media and Communication)
4	LTU	Master of Strategic Communication;
5	QU	MA and PhD in Screen Cultures and Curatorial Studies

The results indicated that the top ranked universities conducted a myriad of courses relating to communication. Some courses were more generalist such as Communication Studies and Media Studies. Other courses were particularly suited for certain professions such as Journalism, Advertising, Public Relations, Strategic Communication, Writing, and Publishing. There were courses that were media production-intensive such as Film, Photography, Digital Technologies, and Communication Design. There was one course on Health Communication, which indicated the need to produce communication professional in various development aspects. The findings illustrated the amount of resources allocated to and variety of approaches in teaching communication undertaken by the said universities.

For the aspect of research, THE Impact Rankings relied on Elsevier for data collection. As mentioned earlier, Elsevier provided information based on the Scopus dataset on research undertaken by university faculties for each SDG. The dataset is based on a query of keywords associated with each SDG. For example, searches with keywords such "poverty," "paucity," "destitution" and "shortage" would be categorized under SDG 1 (No Poverty). Published works with keywords such as "hunger," "malnutrition," "starvation" and "famine" would make them fall under SDG 2 (Zero Hunger). From the information given by Elsevier, the THE Impact Rankings would measure the number of publications, citation indexes and research collaborations of the university for each SDG.

Since keywords formed the basis of classifying studies, the paper explored the same for books, book chapters and research papers relating to communicating the SDGs. Concretely, it utilized the information provided on the RMIT website—given that it listed studies undertaken by its faculty. To search for publications particular to communicating the SDGs, the following terms were explored in the university website browser: "communication," "media," "development communication," "sustainability" and "SDGs." The search showed 25 results of such publications undertaken by RMIT faculty from 2011 to 2021. After obtaining the list, each publication was probed on the Internet. The keywords, tags and/or subjects for each publication were then collected and analyzed to constitute an initial dataset for publications relating to communicating the SDGs. The list, which included publication date, author/s and keywords, was presented in Appendix.

Fig. 9.1   Tag Cloud Visualizing Keywords of RMIT searches on communicating the SDGs

To visualize the resulting keywords, a tag cloud was created using https://tagcrowd.com/. There was a total of 256 words entered into the tag cloud. Figure 9.1 demonstrated that the most common keywords were as follows: "media," "journalism," "communication," "studies," "digital," "news," "policy," "political" and "mobile." Other prominent keywords were "education," "development," "environment," "learning," "literacy," "technology," "information," "identity," "platform," among others. Using the keywords, studies on communicating the SDGs can be identified. Having identified studies on communicating the SDGs, it is now possible for Elsevier through its Scopus dataset to provide information on the number of publications, citations, and research collaborations of a university on this.

Communicating the SDGs: Stewardship

In the THE Impact Ranking, the aspect of stewardship was measured based on the management of internal resources and the care for stakeholders for each of the SDGs. For example, employment policies on unions, modern slavery, discrimination, equivalent rights outsourcing and pay scale equity were highlighted for SDG 8 (Decent Work and Economic Growth). Sustainable practices on remote working, sustainable commuting, affordable housing for employees, affordable housing for students, pedestrian priority, new building standards and building on brownfield sites were considered for SDG 11 (Sustainable Cities and Communities).

In light of this, the paper concentrated on how various universities communicated the SDGs to their internal stakeholders—students, faculty and non-academic staff. It looked into both the channels and the content of these communications. Particularly on the channels, it analyzed university websites and campus-based media, which catered to an internal audience. Table 9.5 identifies and describes six sustainability programs and policies communicated in QU's website. These included commitments against climate change—Climate Action Plan, Climate Coalition, and Sustainability Map. The plans, programs, and initiatives involved waste diversion and food recovery in dining halls, bottled-water-free campus, energy conservation practices, recycling programs, student-led green initiatives, and responsible investing. Aside from these, QU's Accessibility Hub provided information on disability and accessibility issues on campus,

Table 9.5 Sustainability programs and policies featured in Queen's University website

No.	Programs/ policies	Description
1	Global Impact Rankings	For 2021, QU placed first in Canada and fifth in the world in the THE Impact Rankings. This was featured in the website and sustainability report.
2	Sustainable Queen's	Talented researchers, students, and staff engage in a diverse set of sustainability-related activities.
3	Climate Action Plan	In 2010, the university signed the University and College Presidents' Climate Change Statement of Action for Canada, committing the university to engage in activities aimed at reducing greenhouse gas (GHG) emissions and enhancing research and curriculum in the areas of climate change and sustainability.
4	Climate Coalition	In 2019, the university joined the University Climate Change Coalition (UC3), a group of 19 leading North American research institutions conducting collaborative efforts to accelerate local action against climate change.
5	Sustainability Map	The Sustainability Map shows the locations for battery recycling, composting, green roofs, bike racks, and other environmental services and infrastructure at the university.
6	Accessibility Hub	It is a central online resource for accessibility at the university, that aims to elevate inclusion and improve access for everyone on our campus.

including meeting QU's obligations under the Accessibility for Ontarians with Disabilities Act, 2005 (AODA). Sustainable Queen's brought members of the community work together to advance green initiatives, identify and implement new opportunities and create awareness about environmental issues within the university. The Global Impact Rankings is a report regarding the progress of the university vis-à-vis the THE Impact Rankings indicators on the 17 SDGs. The said report was undertaken by the other universities being analyzed in this paper as well.

The USYD website, on the other hand, prominently featured its practices on enabling a sustainable and resilient campus. These included waste and recycling, renewable energy, climate resilient infrastructure, sustainable travel and protecting/improving biodiversity. The university explained it sustainability strategy, which includes a Biodiversity Management Plan that aims to grow and support flora and fauna on campus grounds. It also has the Australasian Campuses Towards Sustainability (ACTS) Green Impact, which encourages staff and students to get together in teams and commit to sustainable practices from April to September. At the UOM website, the university featured its Sustainable Futures Program, which brings together internationally leading research to produce integrated and sustainable solutions to urgent environmental challenges.

The other important channels utilized by these universities to communicate the SDGs to their internal stakeholders were campus-based media. As shown in Table 9.6, there were three USYD campus-based media platforms—Honi Soit, Pulp Media and Sydney University Radio Group (SURG).

Table 9.6 USYD campus-based media platforms

No.	Media	Description
1	Honi Soit	Established in 1929, it is a weekly student newspaper distributed free to all students. It is produced by a team of student editors, who are voted by the student body in Student's Representative Council (SRC) annual elections.
2	Pulp Media	Established in 2016, it is an online student publication—replacement the student magazine BULL. Describing itself as an online platform for student content, it has distinct news reports and entertainment content ideal for social media sharing.
3	SURG	Beginning in August 2011, it is a student-run radio group. It broadcasts five days a week during both semesters of the academic year.

Honi Soit is short for the old French phrase: *Honi soit qui mal y pense* (Shame upon him who thinks evil of it). In 2010, the weekly newspaper launched a website and a Facebook page. In 2014, the Honi Soit mobile app for Android and iOS was developed. Some SDG-related news articles showcased in 2021 on the media platform were second-hand fashion is not the sustainable fashion we need (31 May 2021), the fallacy of neoliberal environmentalism in Australia (23 August 2021), and conservation conversations: the transformation of Taronga Zoo (23 August 2021). Pulp Media is the second student-run publication at the university. In 2021, it featured two SDG-related stories: USYD's $1.666 billion investment portfolio includes millions linked to fossil fuels (8 October 2021), and four ways to support a more sustainable future with your dollars (24 April 2021). The campus radio SURG has three broad labels of its shows: Brekky/Drive (the faces of SURG broadcast team), Specialty (niche shows on a variety of topics), and DJ slot (caters to the strong DJ community at the university).

Aside from student-run media, the universities also utilized other internal communication channels. UOM, for example, has a newsletter that highlights activities across the university including those from non-academic staff. It also has policy blogs, which facilitate communication between the university community, policy audiences, and the wider public. As illustrated in the above discussions, the websites, campus-based media platforms, and other internal channels of these top ranked universities communicated their plans, programs, policies, and commitments on the various SDGs. It likewise facilitated the exchange of opinions on SDG-related issues among internal stakeholders.

Communicating the SDGs: Community Outreach

In the Impact Rankings methodology, university community outreach consisted of direct societal action on each SDG. For SDG 1 (No Poverty), outreach activities consisted of local start-up assistance, programs for basic service access and policies addressing poverty. For SDG 3 (Good Health and Well-being), direct action included collaborations with health institutions, health outreach programs, smoke free policy and shared sports facilities. Taking cue from this, the paper looked at how universities communicated the SDGs to the wider community. The channels explored in this paper comprised of social media, website news and others.

Table 9.7 Number of followers in digital platforms of the top ranked universities (as of 27 October 2021)

Rank	University	Facebook	Instagram	LinkedIn	Twitter	YouTube
1	UOM	220,028	79.2K	394.8K	83.9K	28.2K
2	USYD	436,482	91.2K	358K	85.4K	29.1K
3	RMIT	249,325	45.6K	26.9K	57.8K	26.0K
4	LTU	289,076	28.4K	151K	39.7K	11.7K
5	QU	102,057	48.4K	206.3K	66.1K	4.68K

Table 9.8 Joining date in various social media accounts of the top ranked universities

Rank	University	Facebook	Twitter	YouTube
1	UOM	January 2014	November 2013	September 2008
2	USYD	November 2007	February 2009	March 2007
3	RMIT	December 2007	June 2007	November 2006
4	LTU	March 2008	October 2008	June 2011
5	QU	February 2009	January 2009	February 2009

Table 9.9 Number of tweets, posts and views of various social media accounts of the top ranked universities (as of 27 October 2021)

Rank	University	Instagram (posts)	Twitter (tweets)	YouTube (views)
1	UOM	1363	20.9K	3,769,609
2	USYD	1790	57.8K	7,786,191
3	RMIT	1415	13K	14,953,476
4	LTU	2054	35.2K	2,560,295
5	QU	1101	16.4K	1,380,132

Tables 9.7, 9.8, and 9.9 show the top ranked universities reach, joining date and usage of their social media accounts—Facebook, Instagram, LinkedIn, Twitter, and YouTube. Table 9.7 indicates the number of followers in each type of social media account. From the data, the universities have the greatest number of followers on Facebook and LinkedIn. On the other hand, they have a relatively lower number of followers on YouTube.

Table 9.8 reveals the joining dates of universities for their various social media accounts. Herein, it may be gleaned that these universities started their accounts from the second half of the 2000s. Table 9.9 provides information regarding their usage of their accounts; measured in the number of tweets, posts, and views. One notable revelation was that even with a relatively lower number of followers, the number of views on YouTube universities received was quite significant—reaching up to almost 15 million in the case of RMIT.

In their website news sections, the universities spread various messages on the SDGs. Table 9.10 presents the SDG-related news content found in the UOM website from 16 September to 15 October 2021. There were six news items related to the SDGs discussing sustainable remote working, sustainable travel, energy consumption targets, partnerships for the SDGs, environment and religion and SDG self-assessment report. These contents demonstrated the UOM's commitment and performance toward the SDGs to the wider public.

Table 9.10 Website news content on SDGs at UOM from 16 September to 15 October 2021

Date	News content	Description
12 Oct	New research calls for hybrid working to be more sustainable	The increase in the amount of hybrid working post-pandemic needs to be more sustainable, according to a new study from experts based at UOM and Lancaster University.
12 Oct	University of Manchester commits to tackling UN's Sustainable Development Goals	UOM launched a comprehensive report which highlights how it is to tackle the United Nations Sustainable Development Goals.
11 Oct	Cut European short-haul flights to dramatically reduce emissions according to new research	New data curated by scientists at UOM has found that the main culprit for aviation emissions across the connected continent of Europe is countless short journey flights.
6 Oct	UK can more than halve energy demand by 2050 and improve quality of life	The Centre for Research into Energy Demand Solutions (CREDS) has revealed the vital importance of working to reduce the UK's overall energy demand in order to meet the UK's net-zero target by 2050.
27 Sept	Manchester and Association of Commonwealth Universities collaborate for Sustainable Development Goals	UOM's collaboration with the Association of Commonwealth Universities to drive progress on SDGs.
24 Sept	Event to examine how British Muslims are involved in environmental issues	A free online event to draw attention to how faith in Islam influences the lifestyles of Muslims to care for the environment.

The other media platforms utilized by these universities to spread messages on the SDGs to the general population were videos, podcasts, blogs, and opinion pieces. At USYD, from 16 September to 15 October 2021, Lecturer Dr. Chris Neff has podcasted on SDG-related topics such as vast amounts of polystyrene go to landfill (6 October), Koala genome data (30 September), climate change warning from ancient cities (28 September), research funding to manage water resources (24 September) and the US-EU Methane Pact (21 September). UOM, on the other hand, has the Manchester Policy Blogs, which opened policy conservations between the university, policy audiences, and the wider public. In March 2019, USYD organized an event entitled: The 2030 agenda: Is Australia on track? The panel included UN Foundation Senior Adviser John McArthur.

LTU had utilized podcasts, video recordings, and opinion pieces to reach bigger audiences. One LTU public event was Ideas and Society—a monthly online series of discussions with leading authorities, thinkers and writers. Table 9.11 shows some SDG-related discussions in the said program.

As may be gleaned from the preceding discussions, the top ranked universities have extensively utilized—placing a great amount of resources—in communicating the SDGs to the wider general public. These were

Table 9.11   Select LTU ideas and society events relating to SDGs (2018 to 2021)

Date	Event	Description
15 April 2021	Getting to Zero: Alan Finkel and Tim Flannery	The event discussed the significance of global warming, including the need to reduce greenhouse gas emissions to net zero by 2050.
18 Sept 2019	Climate Change and Australia: Where to Now?	The event brought together frontline fighters across generation to debate on future climate change strategy.
12 June 2019	Feminism, Yes. But, what kind of Feminism?	The event explored the different voices within feminism and the kind of feminism needed today.
19 June 2018	Indigenous Australians: The Promise of Future	The event featured important leaders of indigenous Australians—Noel Pearson and Prof. Megan Davis—to speak about the future of indigenous Australians.
27 Sept 2018	The Climate Change Emergency: What can be done?	During the event, LTU alumnus Tim Flannery and Robyn Eckersley discussed the problems climate change pose and possible solutions.

undertaken through various social media accounts, university website news sections, podcasts, blogs, video recordings, opinion piece, and awareness-building events.

Recommending Performance Metrics for SDG 18

From the findings, the paper has demonstrated that HEIs have allocated resources on communicating the SDGs. HEIs have no other recourse but to invest heavily on communications in order to fulfill their SDG commitments. However, these efforts have been largely unrecognized in the THE Impact Rankings performance metrics, which were developed to monitor progress in fulfilling the UN SDGs. In the hope that the said ranking system would include the work HEIs put into communication in future exercises, the paper has recommended an additional performance metric for communicating the SDGs (SDG 18). Tables 9.12, 9.13, 9.14, and 9.15 illustrated the said recommendations.

Table 9.12 depicts the performance metric on teaching. The metric indicators included the total number of graduates and the number of graduates from communication programs. The paper defined communication program in a broad sense given the various communication-related curricula of universities. Table 9.13 illustrates the performance metric on research. The indicators included the number of publications, number of citations and number of collaborations. Table 9.14 discusses the

Table 9.12 Recommended teaching performance metrics for communicating the SDGs in the THE Impact Rankings

Performance Metric 18.1 Teaching on communicating the SDGs

No.	Indicator	Definition
18.11	Number of graduates	This is the headcount number of graduates at all levels for the year.
18.12	Number of graduates from communication professions	This is the headcount number of graduates at all levels from any communication program (whether communication, media, journalism, film, photography, advertising, public relations, communication design, health communication, communication for development and others) for the year.

Table 9.13 Recommended research performance metrics for communicating the SDGs in the THE Impact Rankings

Performance Metric 18.2 Research on communicating the SDGs

No.	Indicator	Definition
18.21	Number of publications	This indicator looks at the scale of research output from a university around communicating the SDGs.
18.22	Number of citations	This indicator explores the quality of a university's output in the area of communicating the SDGs research using the number of citations received as a metric.
18.21	Number of collaborations	This indicator measures the proportion of a university's academic output where one or more co-authors are associated with a university that is based in another country.

Table 9.14 Recommended stewardship performance metrics for communicating the SDGs in the THE Impact Rankings

Performance Metric 18.3 Stewardships on communicating the SDGs

No.	Indicator	Definition
18.31	Policies on internal communication	This indicator looks at the policies in place regarding internal communications (students, faculty, and non-academic staff) at the university.
18.32	Sustainability content in university website	This indicator explores sustainability content on the university website. Sustainability content may include SDG-related policies, commitments, programs, practices, and initiatives.
18.33	Sustainability content in student-run campus media platforms	This indicator investigates sustainability content on student-run media platforms such as print newspapers, magazines, online newspapers, campus radio, and campus television. Sustainability content may include SDG-related news, features, and opinion pieces.
18.34	Sustainability content in other campus-based media platforms.	This indicator surveys sustainability content on campus-based media platforms such as newsletters, bulletins, notice boards, blogs and others. Sustainability content may include SDG-related news, features, and opinion pieces.

Table 9.15 Recommended community outreach performance metrics for communicating the SDGs in the THE Impact Rankings

Performance Metric 18.4 Community outreach on communicating the SDGs

No.	Indicator	Definition
18.41	Policies on media relations, social media and external communication	This indicator looks at the policies in place regarding external communications (media, government, employers, and wider community) at the university. It also includes policies relating to social media.
18.42	University social media account reach and use	This indicator measures the reach (in terms of following) of the university's social media accounts. It also counts the number of posts/tweets in the said accounts.
18.43	Sustainability content found in university social media accounts	This indicator investigates sustainability content on the social media accounts (Facebook, Instagram, Twitter, LinkedIn, YouTube and others) of the university. Sustainability content may include SDG-related news, features, and opinion pieces.
18.44	Sustainability content found in university website news section	This indicator surveys sustainability content in the news sections of the university website. Sustainability content may include SDG-related news, features, and opinion pieces.
18.45	Sustainability content found in other university channels targeting wider community	This indicator surveys sustainability content in the other university communication channels that target the wider community—blogs, podcasts, video recordings, opinion pieces and others. Sustainability content may include SDG-related news, features, and opinion pieces.

performance metric on stewardships. The indicators consisted of the university policies on internal communication as well as sustainability content in the university website, student-run media, and other campus-based platforms. Table 9.15 focuses on the performance metric on community outreach. The indicators comprised of university policies on media relations, social media, and external communications; social media account reach and use; and sustainability content in social media accounts, website news sections and other channels targeting the wider community.

The recommendations stated should only be taken as an initial attempt at formulating performance metrics on SDG 18: Communicating the SDGs. The indicators were largely based on the top ranked universities, that is, a lot more work needs to be done given the variety of universities operating in various contexts the world over. For example, a study can be undertaken regarding the SDG contributions of academic departments offering Communication for Development (C4D), Development Communication and Health Communication programs. These communication scholars have been greatly contributed to work of the UN and multilateral development agencies. Also, the paper did not recommend any weightage for the different indicators. Be this as it may, the recommendations can serve as basis for discussion regarding future THE Impact Rankings aimed at measuring HEIs' performance in Communicating the SDGs. For if HEIs are given official recognition for Communicating the SDGs, they would definitely place more resources toward these efforts and as a consequence, bring the world closer toward the fulfillment of SDGs.

APPENDIX: COMMUNICATION AND SDG-RELATED BOOKS, BOOK CHAPTERS AND RESEARCH PAPERS (2011 TO 2021) FEATURED IN RMIT WEBSITE

Date	Title	Author/s	Keywords
2021	Pilot trial of a media intervention with journalism students on news reporting of mental illness in the context of violence and crime	Anna Ross Amy Morgan Alexandra Wake Anthony Jorm Nicola Reavley	Crime, Evidence-based practice journalism, Interpersonal violence, Mass media, Media intervention, Mental disorders, Mental health, Psychotic disorders, Schizophrenia.
2021	Blessed be the educated journalist: Reflections on a religious literacy gap in the field of journalism	Enqi Weng Alexandra Wake	Education, Humanities, Journalism Education, Media Representation, Mediatization of Religion, Religious Literacy, Superdiversity
2021	Expanding boundaries in Indigenous news: Guardian Australia, 2018–2020	Alanna Myers Lisa Waller David Nolan Kerry McCallum	Boundary-drawing power, boundaries of journalism, digital media, Guardian Australia, Indigenous News, Open Journalism, Participatory Journalism

(continued)

(continued)

Date	Title	Author/s	Keywords
2021	Local newspapers and coronavirus: conceptualising connections, comparisons and cures	Kristy Hess Lisa Waller	Coronavirus, Local media, Media policy, News business models, Newspapers, Social sphere
2021	Journalism Policy across the Commonwealth: Partial Answers to Public Problems	James Meese	Media policy, Platforms, Australia, Canada, United Kingdom regulation
2021	The Institutional Impacts of Algorithmic Distribution: Facebook and the Australian News Media	Francesco Bailo James Meese Edward Hurcombe	Facebook, Algorithm, Journalism, Distribution, News, Australia
2021	Larrikins, Rebels and Journalistic Freedom in Australia	Josie Vine	Culture, Australasia, Communication, Australasian culture, Media and Communication, Journalism
2020	Portfolio of analytical journalism: Media Freedom in South East Asia	Alexandra Wake	Journalism Studies, Communication Studies
2020	Local journalism in Australia: policy debates	Kristy Hess Lisa Waller	Local journalism, Australian media policy, Local news audiences, ABC charter, Communication Studies
2020	Moral compass: How a small-town newspaper used silence in a hyper-charged controversy	Kristy Hess Lisa Waller	Common good, Community identity, Local journalism, Media and mosques, Media power, Moral disinterestedness, Morality, Silence
2019	Reporting Femicide: A Failure of Latin American Journalism	Antonio Castillo Rojas	Femicide, Journalism, Latin America, Gender violence, Journalism Studies, Communication Studies
2019	A Broader Look at a Student Newspaper under Disruptive Changes	Minh Huynh Nicholas Walsh Scott McDonald	Student newspapers, Digital media, Hybrid approach, Digital transformation
2018	Evolving learning paradigms: Re-setting baselines and collection methods of information and communication technology in education statistics	David Gibson, Tania Broadley Jill Downie Peter Wallet	Evolving Learning Paradigm, ICT, Learner-centered Pedagogies, Teaching and Learning Indicators

(continued)

(continued)

Date	Title	Author/s	Keywords
2018	A new wave of Public Service Journalism in Latin America	Antonio Castillo Rojas	Public Service Journalism, Latin America, Digital News Media, Non-Profit Journalism, Journalism Studies, Communication Studies
2016	Communicating sustainability in the city	Cathy Greenfield	Built Environment, Environment and Sustainability, Global Development, Politics and International Relations, Urban Studies
2016	Introducing a framework for automatically differentiating witness accounts of events from social media	Marie Truelove Maria Vasardani S. Winter	Conference paper, Geospatial information systems, crowdsourcing, Social media, Witness accounts, Supervised machine learning, Dempster-Shafer Theory of Evidence
2014	Building political economic literacy in an unexpected place: Some curriculum suggestions for communication students	Cathy Greenfield	Communication studies, Political economy, Literacy, Market populism, Economics, Governmentality, Political economic literacy, Media, Resource super-profits tax
2014	Filtered smartphone moments: Haunting places	Marsha Berry	Place, Mobile media, Creative practice, Interactive Media
2014	Separating Work and Play: Privacy, Anonymity and the Politics of Interactive Pedagogy in Deploying Facebook in Learning and Teaching	Robert Cover	Social networking, Privacy, Pedagogy, Interactivity, Identity, Communication technology, Digital media studies, Higher education
2014	Slow media creation and the rise of Instagram	Patrick Kelly	Mobile platform, Mechanical reproduction, Mobile video, Personal context, Slow food
2013	Communication for development in sub-Saharan Africa: from orientalism to NGOification	Linje Manyozo	Communication, Development, Orientalism, Colonialism, Africa, NGOs, Information Systems
2013	ICTs and radio in Africa: how the uptake of ICT has influenced the newsroom culture among community radio journalists	Goretti Nassanga Linje Manyozo Claudia Abreu Lopes	Mobile phone, Radio Broadcasting, Computer-mediated Communication, Semiconductor Industry

(continued)

Date	Title	Author/s	Keywords
2012	Models of and approaches to the station management of six African community radio broadcasters	Goretti Nassanga Linje Manyozo Claudia Abreu Lopes	Management committees, community radio, station management, consultation, participation
2012	Crikey, The Australian and the politics of professional status in Australian journalism	Lucy Morieson	Journalists, Professional ethics, Journalism Political aspects, Journalism, Government policy, Journalism Studies, Communication Studies, Communication Technology, Digital Media Studies
2011	Beyond gatekeeping: J-blogging in China	Haiqing Yu	Gatekeeping, Gate-mocking, Gate-poking, Gate-watching, J-blogging

REFERENCES

Bhowmick, J., Selim, S., & Huq, S. (2018). *The role of universities in achieving the sustainable development goals.* CSD-ULAB and ICCCAD Policy Brief. ULAB. http://www.icccad.net/wp-content/uploads/2015/12/Policy-Brief-on-role-of-Universities-in-achieving-SDGs.pdf

De Filippo, D., Benayas, J., Pena, K., & Sanchez, F. (2020). Communication on sustainability in Spanish universities: Analysis of websites, scientific papers and impact in social media. *Sustainability, 12*(19), 8278. https://doi.org/10.3390/su12198278

De la Poza, E., Merello, P., Barbera, A., & Celani, A. (2021). Universities' reporting on SDGs: Using THE impact rankings to model and measure their contribution to sustainability. *Sustainability, 2021*(13), 2038. https://doi.org/10.3390/su13042038

Dobson, F., & Edersheim, K. (2021). *Future directions: International education and the SDGs.* University World News. Higher Education Publishing Limited. https://www.universityworldnews.com/post.php?story=20211022143153986

Dziminska, M., Fijalkowska, J., & Sulkowski, L. (2020). A conceptual model proposal: Universities as culture change agents for sustainable development. *Sustainability, 2020*(12), 4635. https://doi.org/10.3390/su12114635

El-Jardali, F., Ataya, N., & Fadlallah, R. (2018). Changing roles of universities in the era of SDGs: Rising up to the global challenge through institutionalising partnerships with governments and communities. *Health Research and Policy Systems, 16*, 38. https://doi.org/10.1186/s12961-018-0318-9

Lee, P., & Vargas, L. (2020). *Expanding shrinking communication spaces.* Southbound Sdn.

Leicht, A., Heiss, J., & Byun, W. J. (2018). Introduction. In A. Leicht, J. Heiss, & W. J. Byun (Eds.), *Issues and trends in education for sustainable development* (pp. 7–9). UNESCO.

Mulholland, E. (2018). *Communication of sustainable development and the SDGs: Strategies and good practices.* European Sustainable Development Network (ESDN). https://www.esdn.eu/fileadmin/pdf/Workshops/16th_Workshop_2018/16th_ESDN_Workshop_Discussion_Paper_Final.pdf

OECD Development Communication Network. (2016). *Towards a DevCom peer learning hub for SDG communicators.* Organisation for Economic Co-operation and Development (OECD). https://www.oecd.org/dev/pgd/Discussion Note2016.pdf

SDSN. (2015). *Indicators and a monitoring framework for sustainable development goals: Launching data revolution for the SDGs.* Sustainable Development Solutions Network.

Tandon, R., & Chakrabarti, K. (2018). *Partnering with higher education institutions for SDG 17: The role of higher education institutions in multi-stakeholder partnerships.* PRIA Occasional Paper. Participatory Research in Asia (PRIA). https://www.pria.org/uploaded_files/writing_pdf/1527828593_Higher%20education-occasional%20paper-Final.pdf

Traber, M. (2019). *Communication is inscribed in human nature.* Canada. http://wacc-global.live.publishwithagility.com/articles/communication-is-inscribed-in-human-nature

Usher, A., & Savino, M. (2006). *A world of difference: A global survey of university league tables.* Educational Policy Institute. https://higheredstrategy.com/wp-content/uploads/2011/07/World-of-Difference-200602162.pdf

WACC. (2019). *Shrinking civic space and sustainable development. Media Development 2019/2.* Canada. https://waccglobal.org/shrinking-civic-space-and-sustainable-development/

Yusha'u, M. J. (2021). SDG18-The Missing Ventilator: An introduction to the 2030 Agenda for development. In J. Servaes & M. J. Yusha'u (Eds.), *The Palgrave handbook of international communication and sustainable development* (pp. 53–75).

CHAPTER 10

SDG-18 Communication for All: The Tool We Need for Real Development and Social Change

Sol Sanguinetti-Cordero

Abstract The sustainable development goals (SDGs) are an urgent call for action that has been many times relegated to a background position. This is mostly due to the fact that they are not as widely known as being effectively used in decision-making processes at all levels and sectors. What is called the new normal within the COVID pandemic presents us with a key opportunity to explore alternative ways in which the SDGs could be more inclusively applied, and the first step should be to create an SDG-18 in order to foster the realization of each of the 17 SDGs previously agreed upon by the UN, thus promoting development and social change. The technology, knowhow and all the necessary tools we need to have a more developed, inclusive, healthy and sustainable society already exist, SDG-18

S. Sanguinetti-Cordero (✉)
Environment & Technology Institute (ETI), Lima, Peru

CENTRUM Católica Graduate Business School (CCGBS), Pontificia
Universidad Católica del Perú (PUCP), Lima, Peru
e-mail: solsanguinetti@eti-ngo.org

© The Author(s), under exclusive license to Springer Nature   265
Switzerland AG 2023
J. Servaes, M. J. Yusha'u (eds.), *SDG18 Communication for All,*
Volume 1, Sustainable Development Goals Series,
https://doi.org/10.1007/978-3-031-19142-8_10

should be the means through which these reach the people who need them the most. In this paper, we critically analyze and explore what available routes of action already exist and are not being exploited thoroughly, and which could be expeditiously developed or put to use in order to foster a more integrated communication system for development and social change within the SDG framework.

Keywords SDG • Communication • Sustainable development • New normal • Technology

Introduction

With the advent of digital devices at affordable prices, many of us are able to produce immense amounts of data, which is a raw or factual form of information (Merriam-Webster Dictionary [MWD], n.d.). From pictures, to social media posts, to videos and bank statements, the final number of used gigabytes of internet data for 2018 was over 3.1 million (Vuleta, 2021, January 28), and the growth has been so important that the counting has come down to counting data generation by the second by person, these numbers say that every person created on average 1.7 MB of data every second in 2020 (Bulao, 2022, February 6).

We are generating all kinds of information at an unprecedented rate, so much so, that for two decades this phenomenon has been defined as an information glut (Koski, 2000; Voss, 2001). This includes photos and bank statements, as well as scientific knowledge. The latter can be found through different kinds of sources, such as traditional citation indexes, like Web of Science and Scopus which center on specific journals, or academic search engines like Google Scholar with an estimation of with 389 million records for 2019 (Gusenbauer, 2019), and institutional repositories, such as universities' or international organizations'. The World Bank Group is a good example; it has several repositories among which its Data (World Bank [WB], n.d.-a) and Open Knowledge repositories (WB, n.d.-b) are the most widely known.

However, neither data nor information is communication.

Communication takes information, which is contextualized and/or analyzed data, and puts it in a social setting by means of an interchange between parties (MWD, n.d.). Both data and information can exist without socialization, that is not the case for communication which is based on an exchange. This exchange cannot happen on its own; it needs different involved participants. Therefore, communication is a tool, a means through which an interchange of information occurs.

Further to this, communication for development takes that social aspect to the next level by using this process for the benefit of society, thus transforming data or information into an applicable experience. Through communicational means, knowledge, tools, processes, and so on are exchanged between parties with a final objective of positive social change in mind. This tool called communication for development, has a very clear social purpose, and is used for the sustainable development of specific social groups. Most of the time, communication for development initiatives are applied to specific social groups, although there is some mass communication aimed at development.

However, that definition comes with a caveat, because communication for development has many names and many meanings attached to it. From C4D, to Communication for Behavioral Change, and all the other names in between, each stakeholder calls it by a different name according to the use it gives to this tool. And sometimes too many meanings can bring confusion, which is one of the important issues to work upon to facilitate all processes related to communication for development from here forward.

In that framework, and using the abovementioned definition, what we explore in this paper is: how should we proceed with all this information we already have, and keep on getting and producing, to transform it through communication for development into useful knowledge that could be applied for sustainable development, which is clearly embodied in the Sustainable Development Goals (SDGs) (United Nations Department of Economic and Social Affairs [UNDESA], n.d.).

WHAT IS SUSTAINABLE DEVELOPMENT AND WHY DO THE SDGs MATTER?

Oftentimes economic growth is confused with development; they do tend to go together but are not the same thing (United Nations Development Programme [UNDP], 2019, June 24). This tends to happen because the general public, who elect decision makers, is not well informed on development issues. People watch the news on climate change, the pandemic, and other key issues that relate to sustainable development, but in many instances, these issues are not well contextualized. Hence, what "real" information on development reaches the general population?

When the public thinks about sustainable development, we have to foster their understanding to open their perspective to more aspects than just the gross domestic product (GDP) which is always linked to economic growth. We need to inform more and create communicative instances regarding social inclusion, gender equality, and environmental sustainability, among many other key issues encompassed in the SDGs. In sum, we need to think about the people involved in these issues and the manner in which their livelihoods could be improved (UNDP, 2019, June 24).

Thus enter the SDGs fully. These are 17 goals that embody a framework designed for sustainable development worldwide (UNDESA, n.d.). They are guiding principles that contextualize these key development goals in a new and more balanced light, trying to bridge the existing gaps and facing our new challenges, they are the "… shared blueprint for peace and prosperity for people and the planet, now and into the future" (UNDESA, n.d.).

The SDGs are an improvement from what the Millennium Development Goals were (UNDESA, n.d.). As the next step in tackling the sustainable development issues, they aspire to bring real and positive change while factoring the countless challenges we face as a world. This has become more evident today in the midst of the aftermath of COVID-19, how it has affected the most vulnerable countries and their respective populations, and particularly how it is going to be a harder path of recovery for them (Duttagupta & Pazarbasioglu, 2021).

We can view this new reality as a challenge or we could view it as an opportunity for change for the better. What is called the new normal provides us with a unique situation: we could really put the SDGs to good use more than ever, because at the moment more people are thinking about the real challenges. COVID-19 has changed the frame of mind of many people, it has showed humanity at its most vulnerable, and no one wants this to happen again.

In order to use the momentum of the current juncture, we must focus on making the SDGs known to all parties involved, that is the beneficiary population and the decision and policy makers. Because, as people, how can we request better livelihoods if we do not know there is a blueprint for building them? And as decision and policy makers how can we use a tool that we do not know we have? That is the conundrum with the SDGs, they are there, they are well thought of and encompass many crosscutting areas; however, *too few know about them*.

Therefore, we need to make good use of communication and scale it up to an actual implementation of communication for development. That is one of the imperatives to have an actual "SDG 18: Communication for all".

WHAT WE ALREADY HAVE BUT ARE NOT USING TO ITS FULL POTENTIAL

SDGs are being integrated into many areas, though these routes of action are not necessarily being exploited thoroughly. There is a lot of information on the SDGs in institutional libraries, repositories, such as international organizations' (e.g. UN Department of Economic and Social Affairs UNDESA, Economic and Social Commission for Asia and the Pacific ESCAP, United Nations Economic Commission for Latin America and the Caribbean CEPAL, etc.), university repositories, Google Scholar, government research institutions, private sector initiatives ... and we could go on.

However, this information exists in silos, because when trying to access relevant information on sustainable development and replicable linked practices, what tends to happen is that each institution has full access to all of their production within their collections, but in many cases, what becomes public is just a reference to the complete work. Why have the work, but not make it available, particularly, when these are documents that have already been paid for by foreign aid and have proven successful when implemented?

Let us delve on this problem by using the example of the Food and Agriculture Organization of the United Nations (FAO), one of the precursors regarding communication for development, and with many successful initiatives related to it (Balit & Acunzo, 2020). Yet, when we try to access a 1999 document on agricultural extension in Nicaragua, we simply get a title page with downloadable metadata of the document. To observe the example, please follow this link: https://agris.fao.org/agris-search/search.do?recordID=NI2006003834 (FAO, n.d.).

This is also the case of information produced by many public administrations worldwide. In some instances, like my own country, Peru, the information is not even accessible between government institutions, causing administrative setbacks as well as policy ones (Presidencia del Consejo de Ministros [PCM], 2019; Sánchez, 2021, April 21). Therefore, governments, which are usually the main creators and users of public policy (for development) and its related information are not functioning in an interconnected manner, resulting in the duplication of efforts, and the loss of possible synergies.

On the other hand, we have scientific journals. They are custodians and owners of scientific research papers, which for the most part are accessible through complex paid methods (Van Noorden, 2013). Hence, their utility is rendered non-effective as many who need them do not have the funds for the subscription fees, or do not know how to actually pay for them. These scientific research journals do not pay the researchers for their work, they do not pay the peers that review them, and if researchers want to publish in Open Access systems it is the researchers that need to pay to be published. Nonetheless, these journals charge fees, in some cases very high, for accessing these papers. Their business model is effective for their business purpose, but it is not effective for the actual dissemination of the knowledge they possess. This continues to be an ongoing debate among the academic and non-academic communities, on how to find feasible alternatives for fostering the greater good of scientific dissemination with what is already available to just a few (Van Noorden, 2013).

Further to this, we have technologies that enable easier and faster access to information. One of the most accessible technologies we have is data visualization. This could be very useful considering the great amount of information available, because its purpose is to arrange information in visual patterns that are easier to understand than listings, which is usually how data is handled. There are many open-source programs that allow us to visualize data easily and thus apply the findings faster for better decision-making processes (Vílchez-Román et al., 2021). However, the process is somewhat complex, involving several steps, and we would need to have a good technical understanding of computer programs, particularly on information management.

Therefore, although data visualization is something available that could be put to good use, it needs further development for making it more accessible to more people, and particularly for having more user friendly interfaces. Linked with that is the need for better digital literacy as part of school and higher education, and policies related to foster a greater part of the population with access to these digital tools, especially in the Global South.

Additionally, the concept of knowledge as a tool for our improvement is part of our human history and has been evident in different civilizations through the ages. From libraries to universities, knowledge has always been linked with human improvement.

Within the development mainstream, this idea has at least a couple of decades in circulation with initiatives such as Knowledge for Development (World Bank [WB], 1998) among many others. For instance, the knowledge-based economy posited by Steinmueller (2002), delivers benefits from knowledge directly to sustainable development as well as for economic growth.

This connection between knowledge and its application for growth and improvement is also widely used by the private sector. From using data and information to produce a stronger approximation to the projection of their outputs, to supply chain streamlining to marketing strategies, all these initiatives and many more of the same kind, are what now is called "business intelligence" (Liang & Liu, 2018).

Further to this, information technology companies, the biggest and most profitable companies in human history to date, base their growth on how they process and use huge amounts of information to reach almost all strata of society by the mass use of electronic devices and through the use of their applications (Pucihar, A., et al., 2017; Hewage, T. N., et al., 2018). For achieving this, they use a technique that is called data mining, which is part of big data technologies and machine learning.

The possible applications of this technology to gain insight on behavior and project are uncountable; currently it is being applied to many fields, including disease prediction and treatment (Uddin et al., 2019; El Naqa & Murphy, 2015). However, their development and main application continue to be mostly framed within the private sector, from predicting social media reactions, to purchase patterns, to financial and stock markets shifts; its application is still focused on predicting behaviors that will yield revenues.

However, we could and should apply this technology, which will be useful when analyzing enormous amounts of data and information to communication for development, because social stability, healthier communities, better educated children, more sustainable businesses, and so on, also yield revenues, not only to a few companies, but to society in general.

As we have seen, there are many possible sources of information regarding the SDGs out there; however, if you ask any random person about them, chances are they will at best have a superficial idea of what the SDGs are. The information is available but a more in-depth analysis for all is still in its infancy.

To change that we need to work the general public's mindset and behavior, while strengthening the skillset of policy and decision makers in order to actually include the SDGs in any real global agenda.

This can be done, and communication for development would be the ideal tool to carry this out. Therefore, this is one more reason for strengthening communication for development, and the imperative to have "SDG 18: Communication for all" as part of the SDGs.

WHY IS THE POST COVID-19 CONTEXT A PERFECT PLAYGROUND TO CHANGE COMMUNICATION FOR DEVELOPMENT AND PROMOTE SDG-18: COMMUNICATION FOR ALL?

There are amazing success stories related to communication for development. However, when we think of what we are doing with it, we are still working as if we are in the twentieth century. It was during the later part of the last century and the beginning of this century when communication for development was put to use. The United Nations with some of its specialized agencies for communication for development, such as the Food and Agriculture Organization of the United Nations (FAO), and the United Nations Children's Fund (UNICEF), created some great models that we still replicate to date through various international organizations, governments and non-governmental organizations (NGOs).

The audiovisual inclusion into transfer of knowledge that FAO implemented for farming in the developing world is one of such great examples (Balit & Acunzo, 2020). In the 1970s, the revolution caused by handheld video cameras with a medium that did not need processing (such as film did) was applied to initiatives that changed the lives of many farmers in developing countries (Calvelo, 1987; Calvelo, 2001). Then in the early 2000s came the use of digital media, in the form of websites, and even interactive CDs (Sanguinetti, 2021, September 10). But despite this, projects strongly supported by communication for development have dwindled instead of growing and the methods have not evolved much, despite the available technology.

Communication for development still keeps a more passive stand, sending out information via radio programs or even digital platforms, the internet can be passive too. However, who is keeping track of how, when and who consume these communication pieces? What uses do people put this information to? Do they change their behavior? Is the world better off because we tell them to change specific behaviors? And if so, how? Most probably, all these questions could be answered by one single algorithm similar to what is applied to predict sentiment in social media (Yoo et al., 2018).

There are some very interesting initiatives on communication for development seeking more interaction and dialogue, on the use of traditional media like radio, we can see cases where the listeners become the producers, such in the case of the Peruvian NGO, Minga (Durá et al., 2010), on the more technological front we have initiatives like the COVID Behaviors Dashboard from Johns Hopkins University Center for Communication Programs (n.d.). There are very many more; however, if we compare them with the multitude of private initiatives looking for this dialogue with their end customers, the communication for development ones look rather small.

Therefore, the evolution of communication for development has not really kept pace with the evolution of methodologies and available technological tools developed and used by the private sector. It makes sense, an interactive dialogue is much harder to orchestrate, and most of the times uses expensive technology; therefore, these have financially higher stakes.

Nonetheless, with the initially mentioned proliferation of data and information where we could most probably find feasible solutions to current and dire sustainable problems, is it not an imperative that we start finding ways to get up to current trends? Are we doing something for spreading more useful knowledge and giving it to the necessary people?

Part of the call of the SDGs is showcasing to governments and decision makers worldwide where public policies are most needed and where funding should be directed. Currently, there are 17 crosscutting goals for which the call is made for. Communication is not one of them; communication for development with the inclusion of efficient knowledge management as it should be envisioned for the twenty-first century is not even remotely thought about.

Without good use of communication, we just have great amounts of information shelved (physically and digitally) somewhere or trying to ineffectually reach its final users; this is what is currently happening.

In this digital era of too much information, communication for development needs to parse available information into digestible clusters in an understandable language in order to transform the initial information into knowledge. This needs to be directed to policy and decision makers that ultimately need to take the concepts from paper and translate them into a feasible reality (Colby et al., 2008).

To achieve this effectively we need to include communication for development into the call, making "SDG 18: Communication for all", part of the SDGs.

In 2020, the world changed; a pandemic can do that.

People changed the way we view the world, governments changed many of their actions and policies, but perhaps most importantly: business changed how they were able (or not) to do businesses. This is important because, no matter some exceptions, in the majority of cases we live in a free market economy, and businesses are key drivers for our economic and sustainable development.

Since 2015, the SDGs have been out there (UNDESA, n.d.); in some universities and schools; they were already part of the curricula, at least at a cursory level. But they were never really the center piece of how we think about the future or how we plan and strategize for generations to come.

With the COVID-19 pandemic, this can change for the first time.

Now, if we want to teach about businesses for instance, how could we plan and strategize for big and small businesses after COVID-19 without thinking about SDG #3 Good Health and Wellbeing? Can we? Should we?

These questions were not the first thing we thought about when planning for building a bridge, or opening a new store a couple of years ago. Now they are.

And as the poverty gap has widened as a result of COVID-19, the recuperation needs to have a more inclusive view (Duttagupta & Pazarbasioglu, 2021), particularly because the most affected countries are emerging markets and middle-income economies, a classification which includes most of the countries in the world (International Monetary Fund [IMF], 2021). These are the ones that are having the hardest time to bounce back. If we rebuild with more inclusivity, it will allow world markets to prosper, thus fostering consumption and exchange of goods and services, consequently increasing market efficiency, which can promote, if well managed, sustainable development worldwide.

Therefore, this recuperation needs to take place within a framework of communication for development, which in this case is intensely informing decision makers on how to better plan for the future, foreseeing possible similar scenarios, as well as other ones where other SDGs take center stage, such as SDG #11 Sustainable Cities and Communities, or #13 Climate Action (UNDESA, n.d.) just to name two.

Additionally, governments are already spending at a pace not seen since the end of World War II, with a calculated "… 1,600 new social-protection programmes in 2020" (The Economist [TE], 2021, March 04) in order to reactivate their economies. From big economies with stimulus packages such as the United States, or middle-income countries with humbler economic and monetary proposals, the political and social will for reactivation is evident everywhere.

Finally, the rate of technological growth including digitalization evolved at an incredibly fast pace during the pandemic, from remote work alternatives to vaccine development, the world has regained a hope to be better thanks to technology (TE, 2021, January 16, The Times of India [TTI], 2021, September 23). The role of governments is key for the positive continuation of some of these breakthroughs that are not cost-effective for the private sector, but could be useful for sustainable development (Mazzucato, 2013). For this scenario, the policy makers should be better informed with many alternative options, including success cases that can serve as guidance.

What this pandemic leaves behind is the certainty that the unthinkable can happen. That is a strong and valuable lesson that could yield excellent results if put to good use. We could take this as an opportunity to bring more interest, and highlight the importance of the SDGs in general, because this context gives us fertile ground for trying out new things as the paradigms have been altered, hopefully, for the good of all.

To be able to bring all of this center stage, we need communication for development, and have "SDG 18: Communication for all" as part of the global agenda.

CONCLUSIONS AND RECOMMENDATIONS

As we have discussed in this paper, communication can directly help sustainable development by making the related issues evident to the public in general, as well as the involved decision and policy makers. SDGs are a truly amazing initiative; however, few people know about them. With "SDG 18: Communication for all", an SDG fully focused on communicating sustainable development issues this would be more achievable.

SDG-18 could facilitate the allocation of funding into communication initiatives more easily. This in turn will enable that communication and particularly communication for development to be a part of the public policy agendas worldwide, creating a virtuous circle.

If "SDG 18: Communication for all" becomes a reality, it could be the first step to create a specialized agency devoted to communication for development which could harness positive public interest and attention. And since communication for development is crosscutting this issue, it would benefit sustainable development in general. It would be dedicated to communication for development, focusing on sustainable issues and devoted to managing information and transforming it into communication, minus the silos, promoting conversation among organizations and particularly humans.

But to achieve this big goal, we need to start with what we have:

(a) Apply technology to overcome the glut of information

We have clearly identified that much information relating to sustainable development is out there. However, we need to go beyond creating a *body of knowledge* and create a manageable conglomerate of information. Otherwise for the SDGs this will be a key impasse, as the gathered information is simply too much to be manageable.

Physicist John Ziman (1969) was already debating about the path from having some new information (scientific findings), to communicating them to the public, to finally creating public knowledge as a clear necessity in the late 1960s of the last century. His reflections are increasingly relevant with the proliferation of information we currently have; hence, we need to continue building upon his work. Perhaps the most important step is to create a category system that clearly differentiates between data, information, and communication, in order to be able to apply it to communication for development. The definition of the latter also needs to be agreed upon by key international stakeholders at all levels to facilitate the dialogue about it.

The historic moment we currently live in gives us the opportunity to put technology to good use once these categories are defined. After this is achieved, we could seek for more specific technical developments, orient it toward the purpose of parsing information into useful clusters and predicting behaviors.

For this, we already have available technologies at the moment ready for use, as we have discussed previously: data visualization for information clustering and big data, more specifically its machine learning branch, where its rapid identification of predictable patterns is already being applied in many different fields. However, there are also other available technologies that could be applied, albeit with a bit more complexity and investment: Application Programs Interface (API), which allow interoperability between applications and process raw data; these are used in most background processing systems from customer relations to data libraries (Myers & Stylos, 2016), and Artificial Intelligence (AI), as Microsoft Academic was doing when it was still operational (Tay et al., 2021, May 27). Unfortunately, since the technology was developed it is no longer deemed useful for the private sector.

New emerging technologies are probably being created every day. Therefore, we (as communication for development practitioners) need to harness the collaboration of computer scientists to find more specific technological solutions for the systematization and use of information in order to transform what we already have into communication that can become knowledge to be applied and used directly in sustainable development as part of the spear point of this initiative.

And let us not forget that the information that is already created and sealed in institutional repositories needs to be made available to the general public. Information that is just sitting there or that is too expensive to access does no one any good.

(b) Make scientific and SDGs information more accessible

Along with this, we should find a model for making the scientific information more accessible taking into account that timeframes cannot wait when it comes to human lives, particularly when practical usefulness of the subject matter can be directly applied to the improvement of livelihoods and their sustainability.

In this line, we, as stakeholders, need to start finding alternatives outside the box, and in each case, our delimitations will be different. For instance, if we want academic texts to be used by decision makers, these need to be easier to understand, and some "academic rules" need to change. While developing new knowledge in the era of massive information, we cannot be expected to quote from scientific sources only; proliferation of knowledge and easy accessibility to it enable us to apply never before used sources, and that should also be part of the flexibility and adaptability expected from practitioners and academics alike.

Therefore, there will be many sources of information that will have no date, identified as (n.d.) in the citations, because they come directly from platforms, or videos, and so on with no available dates. Therefore, academics must understand that nowadays knowledge has different reliable sources, and be open to change, willing to adapt and evolve, willing to accept that the world is changing at a very rapid pace and that some of the things we were used to will change drastically or simply disappear.

Additionally, we should create Communication for Development Hubs, where specific information related to sustainable development issues could be more easily processed, with a user friendly interface for all level of users. The complete documents (of all types including audiovisual materials) should be available, especially since it is very easy and cost-effective to have them accessible online and thus it could reach parties from all over the globe.

Aligned with this concept, academia should get a more active role within the SDGs framework. It is a necessity that they are part of the curricula taught worldwide and integrated into more cases and projects. If academia makes the SDGs part of the arsenal of future decision makers, they can be better put to use for sustainable development as well as for businesses.

These changes can help bridge the divide between academic research and development practice, making the scientific breakthroughs directly available for on-field needs.

This is a huge task that needs the involvement of many stakeholders, starting with the designation of an 18th SDG. However, it aims to spark a willingness in all of us as communication for development practitioners to find new ways that use technology or revamp some old methods that proved useful to foster positive change through communication and to use communication for development for the improvement of the livelihoods of those that need it the most.

Communication for development can mean a better future for all. Let us focus on that.

References

Balit, S., & Acunzo, M. (2020). A changing world: FAO efforts in communication for rural development. In J. Servaes (Ed.), *Handbook of communication for development and social change*. Springer. https://doi.org/10.1007/978-981-15-2014-3_29

Bulao, J. (2022, February 6). How much data is created every day in 2021? https://techjury.net/blog/how-much-data-is-created-every-day/#gref

Calvelo Ríos, J. M. (1987). Video, nueva herramienta del campo (Video, new field tool). Extracted from: https://repositorio.flacsoandes.edu.ec/bitstream/10469/14968/1/REXTN-Ch21-04-Calvelo.pdf

Calvelo Ríos, J. M. (2001). Desarrollo: comunicación, información y capacitación (Development: Communication, information and training). *Runa Instituto de Investigación en Comunicación para el Desarrollo, 6*.

Colby, D. C., et al. (2008). Research glut and information famine: Making research evidence more useful for policymakers. *Health Affairs, 27*(4), 1177–1182.

Durá, L., Singhal, A., & Elías, E. (2010). Listener as producer: Minga Peru's intercultural radio educative project in the Peruvian Amazon. *Interface of Business and Culture*, 481–502. Extracted from: https://www.researchgate.net/profile/Arvind-Singhal-3/publication/237259534_Listener_as_Producer_Minga_Peru's_Intercultural_Radio_Educative_Project_in_the_Peruvian_Amazon/links/548807c30cf2ef34478ed7b2/Listener-as-Producer-Minga-Perus-Intercultural-Radio-Educative-Project-in-the-Peruvian-Amazon.pdf

Duttagupta, R., & Pazarbasioglu, C. (2021). Miles to go. Extracted from: https://www.imf.org/external/pubs/ft/fandd/2021/06/the-future-of-emerging-markets-duttagupta-and-pazarbasioglu.htm

El Naqa, I., & Murphy, M. J. (2015). What is machine learning? In *Machine learning in radiation oncology* (pp. 3–11). Springer. Extracted from: https://doi.org/10.1007/978-3-319-18305-3_1

Food and Agriculture Organization of the United Nations [FAO]. (n.d.). AGRIS – Metodologia de extension: Proyecto los Maribios [1999]. Extracted from: https://agris.fao.org/agris-search/search.do?recordID=NI2006003834

Gusenbauer, M. (2019). Google Scholar to overshadow them all? Comparing the sizes of 12 academic search engines and bibliographic databases. *Scientometrics, 118*, 177–214. https://doi.org/10.1007/s11192-018-2958-5

Hewage, T. N., et al. (2018). Big data techniques of Google, Amazon, Facebook and Twitter. *Journal of Communification, 13*(2), 94–100.

International Monetary Fund IMF. (2021). Economy groupings. Extracted from: http://www.imf.org/external/datamapper/FMEconGroup.xlsx

Johns Hopkins University Center for Communication Programs [JHUCCP]. (n.d.). COVID behaviors dashboard. Extracted from: https://covidbehaviors.org/

Koski, J. T. (2000). Reflections on information glut and other issues in knowledge productivity. *Futures, 33,* 483–495. https://doi.org/10.1016/S0016-3287(00)00092-6

Liang, T. P., & Liu, Y. H. (2018). Research landscape of business intelligence and big data analytics: A bibliometrics study. *Expert Systems with Applications, 111,* 2–10.

Mazzucato, M. (2013). *The entrepreneurial state: Debunking public vs. private sector myths.* Anthem Press.

Merriam-Webster Dictionary [MWD]. (n.d.). Data. Extracted from: https://www.merriam-webster.com/dictionary/data

MWD. (n.d.). Communication. Extracted from: https://www.merriam-webster.com/dictionary/communication

Myers, B. A., & Stylos, J. (2016). Improving API usability. *Communications of the ACM, 59*(6), 62–69. Extracted from: https://dl.acm.org/doi/pdf/10.1145/2896587

Presidencia del Consejo de Ministros [PCM]. (2019). Estándares de Interoperabilidad de la Plataforma de Interoperabilidad del EstadoResolución de Secretaría de Gobierno Digital N° 002-2019-PCM/SEGDI (Interoperability Standards of the State Interoperability Platform Resolution of the Secretary of Digital Government N° 002-2019-PCM/SEGDI). Extracted from: https://www.peru.gob.pe/normas/docs/estandares_interoperabilidad_pide_segdi.pdf

Pucihar, A., et al. (2017). Use of Facebook and Google Platforms for SMEs Business Model Innovation. 30TH Bled eConference: Digital Transformation–From Connecting Things to Transforming Our Lives, 169.

Sánchez, W. (2021, April 21). GovTech: La transformación de nuestro sector público en un mundo digital (The transformation of our public sector in a digital world). Extracted from: https://desafios.pwc.pe/govtech-la-transformacion-de-nuestro-sector-publico-en-un-mundo-digital/

Sanguinetti, B. (2021, September 10). Personal interview on communication media used in the FAO/GCP/ RLA/114/ITA Communication for Development in Latin America Project.

Steinmueller, W. E. (2002). Knowledgebased economies and information and communication technologies. *International Social Science Journal, 54*(171), 141–153.

Tay, A., Martín-Martín, A., & Hug, S. E. (2021, May 27). Goodbye, Microsoft Academic – Hello, open research infrastructure? Extracted from: https://blogs.lse.ac.uk/impactofsocialsciences/2021/05/27/goodbye-microsoft-academic-hello-open-research-infrastructure/

TE. (2021, March 04). Welfare in the 21st century. How to make a social safety-net for the post-COVID world. Extracted from: https://www.economist.com/leaders/2021/03/06/how-to-make-a-social-safety-net-for-the-post-covid-world

The Economist [TE]. (2021, January 16). The new era of innovation. Why a dawn of technological optimism is breaking. Extracted from: https://www.economist.com/leaders/2021/01/16/why-a-dawn-of-technological-optimism-is-breaking

The Times of India [TTI]. (2021, September 23). Digital revolution triggered by the pandemic a boon, will stay. Extracted from: https://timesofindia.indiatimes.com/city/lucknow/digital-revolution-triggered-by-the-pandemic-a-boon-will-stay/articleshow/86439824.cms

Uddin, S., Khan, A., Hossain, M. E., & Moni, M. A. (2019). Comparing different supervised machine learning algorithms for disease prediction. *BMC Medical Informatics and Decision Making, 19*(1), 1–16. Extracted from: https://doi.org/10.1186/s12911-019-1004-8

United Nations Department of Economic and Social Affairs [UNDESA]. (n.d.). The 17 goals. Extracted from: https://sdgs.un.org/goals

United Nations Development Programmme [UNDP]. (2019, June 24). Human development and the SDGs. http://hdr.undp.org/en/content/human-development-and-sdgs

Van Noorden, R. (2013). Open access: The true cost of science publishing. *Nature, 495*, 426–429. https://doi.org/10.1038/495426a

Vílchez-Román, C., et al. (2021). Applied bibliometrics and information visualization for decision-making processes in higher education institutions. *Library Hi Tech, 39*(1), 263–283. https://doi.org/10.1108/LHT-10-2019-0209

Voss, D. (2001). Scientists weave new-style webs to tame the information glut. *Science, 289*, 2250–2251.

Vuleta, B. (2021, January 28). How much data is created every day? [27 Staggering Stats]. Extracted from: https://seedscientific.com/how-much-data-is-created-every-day/

WB. (n.d.-a). World Bank Open Data. Extracted from: https://data.worldbank.org/

WB. (n.d.-b). World Bank Open Knowledge Repository. Extracted from: https://openknowledge.worldbank.org/

World Bank [WB]. (1998). World Development Report 1998/1999: Knowledge for Development. The World Bank. Extracted from: https://elibrary.worldbank.org/doi/abs/10.1596/978-0-1952-1118-4

Yoo, S., Song, J., & Jeong, O. (2018). Social media contents based sentiment analysis and prediction system. *Expert Systems with Applications, 105*, 102–111.

Ziman, J. M. (1969). Information, communication, knowledge. *Nature, 224*(5217), 318–324.

Conclusion: SDG18—The Soul of An Ambitious Agenda—Communication and the Match Towards Sustainability in the COVID-19 Century

Muhammad Jameel Yusha'u and Jan Servaes

Abstract Communication is the soul of an information society and so also the Sustainable Development Goals (SDGs). Communication for development and social change is about sustainability. Communication can play an important role in each of the SDGs, yet the framers of the 2030 Agenda have missed the opportunity to have a clear role for communication in the global goals. Drawing from examples during the COVID-19 pandemic and debates such as the World Information and Communication order, this chapter proposes that the oversight by UN officials to include a role for communication was caused by what is called "the rat problem." This

M. J. Yusha'u (✉)
Harvard Kennedy School, Cambridge, USA

J. Servaes
KU Leuven, Leuven, Belgium

J. Servaes, M. J. Yusha'u (eds.), *SDG18 Communication for All, Volume 1*, Sustainable Development Goals Series, https://doi.org/10.1007/978-3-031-19142-8_11

chapter concludes by providing strategic recommendations on how to include SDG18—Communication for all in the SDGs.

Keywords Information • Communication • NWICO • UN • SDGs • Sustainability • 2030 Agenda

INTRODUCTION

Every century has a defining moment. This has been evident in history whether it is the expansion of the Roman empire in third century, B.C.E.; the foundation of Christianity in the first century, C.E., or the fall of the Western Roman empire in the fifth century, to the Unification of China in the sixth century, the foundation of Islam in the sixth century, the unification of England in the ninth century, the conquests by Mongols in the thirteenth century, down to European colonization in the sixteenth century, industrial revolution in the eighteenth and nineteenth centuries; or World War II in the twentieth century, there has always been a historical epoch that is remembered at the sprinkle of thought.

Without doubt, the COVID-19 pandemic could be the defining moment of the twenty-first century. The devastating impact of the pandemic would take generations to heal. As of 29th May 2022, more than 6 million deaths have been recorded due to the virus with over 11,387,947,194 doses of vaccines administered so far (Coronavirus Centre, 2022).

While there have been devastating wars such as World War II, in which some inexact estimations had it that about between 35 and 60 million people lost their lives during the war (Britannica, 2022), yet, during World War II there was no total closure of the entire globe. The total closure of the entire world at a point was the exclusive preserve of the COVID-19 pandemic. Despite this monumental challenge, the global economy survived, largely due to the availability of communication and digital infrastructures available the world over (Yusha'u & Servaes, 2021).

This communication and digital infrastructure which has been transforming the global economy, resulting in one of the most rapid social and behavioral changes in human history could not find a seat in the 2030 Agenda for development espoused by the United Nations. This is a major omission which as discussed in several chapters this book seeks to fill.

Communication for development as discussed by several scholars is a major tool in realizing development objectives (Ogan et al., 2009; White, 2004; Pade-Khene et al., 2010; Asiedu, 2012; Melkote & Steeves, 2015; Servaes & Malikhao, 2007; Servaes, 2020).

The chapters in this volume have shown the importance of communication in achieving the SDGs, as summarized below:

- SDGs can be achieved by critically looking at communication rights. The challenge of information poverty must be addressed to achieve sustainable development. It is therefore essential to include SDG18 in the Sustainable Development Goals to ensure that the information and communication deficits in the global goals are adequately addressed.
- The SDGs provide a framework for dialogue among the international community. It is an opportunity that brings together different strands of opinion and interests to work on an agenda that can help humanity to get out of the doldrums of challenges facing human existence. Inter-state actors, journalists, proprietors of social media companies have an opportunity to promote dialogue among the global community with a view to implement the 2030 Agenda for development.
- Achieving the SDGs requires dialogue at regional, national, and international levels. Such dialogue should incorporate the need to understand the variation in cultures, attitudes, and life ambitions. By so doing, the global flow of information could reflect the diversity of interests in the attempt to implement the SDGs.
- The debate about the SDGs can be viewed from different perspectives: from the perspective of development practitioners who would like to see results on the ground, and from an academic perspective where theories can help in providing direction or in explaining complex situations about the SDGs. Extractive capitalism is one of those challenges because it seeks to look at the basic characteristics in understanding the SDGs. On the other hand, can SDGs also be viewed within the context of a post-capitalist horizon? One of the criticisms against the SDGs is that it is elitist or pro-western in nature. What role would communication for development play in this regard to make both practical and theoretical issues make sense as the debate about sustainability continues?

- Still on the theoretical issues, one of the propositions in this volume is the idea of the six forces proposed by Andrea Ricci. The six forces can be summarized as *information overload, defective information directionality, scarce attention, competition, propaganda, and oblivion.* The six forces presented by Andrea Ricci tried to capture the challenges of information society where the amount of data produced is huge, yet retaining information is drastically reduced partly due to information overload. It also highlights the competitive nature of the information society where there is race to capture the available space especially on the web to promote ideas, businesses and interests. This sometimes results in propaganda because users work hard to present a favorable view of their interest. In the words of Andrea Ricci therefore, "The six forces produce a massive *hand break effect* on the information and communication ecosystem: they tend to weaken and compress any piece of crucial intelligence, including key findings that can really help progress and sustainable development." As such, SDG18-Communication for all becomes even more crucial if this hand break effects are to be tackled to ensure the sustainability of the global goals.
- Strategic communication plays a vital role in communication for development. This is even more important because of the challenges faced by women such as domestic violence and other risks they face on a daily basis. Communication is vital if the targets of SDG5 are to be achieved. For civil society and other advocates for social change to help in implementing the 2030 Agenda for development, SDG18 should be considered in the global goals. One of the major criticisms against the SDGs is the issue of elitisms, where closed-door sessions by government officials resulted in proposing the 2030 Agenda (Esser, 2017). If the SDGs are the product of elite consultation, how can the ordinary farmer in Bangladesh, a fisher in Cameroon or truck driver in Oregon understand what the SDGs mean? This is where media literacy becomes inevitable. Media literacy plays an important role in the process of development; therefore, to achieve the SDGs, media literacy should be part and parcel of SDG18.
- Following the devastating impact of COVID19 pandemic, serious attention should be paid to misinformation and fake news. Fake news has the potential to dilute our understanding of the truth without which several SDGs cannot be achieved. Disinformation is harm-

ful to sustainability. Massive awareness would be key to managing or eradicating disinformation.

- Institutions of higher learning are agents of change. From the government officials who meet and decide on the SDGs to the journalists who report on these activities, most of them pass through higher education systems. What role should universities play in communicating the SDGs? Including the contribution of universities in communicating the SDGs is important in changing behavior and educating students and professors alike on the SDGs. Looking at the diversity of the SDGs, one way of helping with implementation is to integrate them in higher education as discussed in our previous book (Yusha'u & Servaes, 2021). The SDGs can be relevant to each discipline whether it is history, journalism, medicine, political science, sociology, or engineering. The best way to capture the interest of future policy makers is to communicate the SDGs when they are at universities as students or tutors.

- One of the challenges of communication for development is that politicians elected into public office may not be aware of development issues. This creates complication in understanding development, and then communicating it in the right way. The COVID-19 pandemic further compounded this challenge. Although some UN agencies such as FAO, UNDP, and so on have tools of communication for development that can be harnessed to advance the call for SDG18-Communication for all, more bottom-up advocacy work is urgently needed (Servaes & Wilkins, 2015; Servaes & Malikhao, 2010; Servaes, 2000).

COMMUNICATION AND SUSTAINABILITY

One of the aims of the SDGs is ensuring sustainability. The idea of sustainable communication calls for an interaction between communication and responsible human interaction with the environment (Godemann & Michelsen, 2011). Communication for sustainability therefore goes beyond sending communication messages from a sender to a receiver. It involves serious dialogue with communities and embraces the tenets of persuasion (Newig et al., 2013).

The premise of formulating the SDGs is to ensure sustainability for people and planet. But human beings by nature do not respond to change without persuasion and engagement. Simple human interactions require persuasive approaches before approaching our desired aims. Politicians work hard to convince the electorates to vote for them. To ensure turnout during election campaigns, various tactics and strategies are employed to convince voters and candidates to cast their votes in a particular way.

In marriage, people do not only work hard to win the heart of their partners, but they go an extra mile to be liked by the relatives of their partners and friends alike. When it is time for admission into tertiary institutions, colleges and universities engage in sensitization programs to convince the best students to join their campuses. The SDGs as a framework for development cannot be different.

To end poverty for instance, the effort should go beyond policy making. The people living in extreme poverty need to be convinced that poverty is not a permanent feature of human existence. It can be temporary. To end hunger, there is need for coalition of all stakeholders to empower local communities to be self-reliant, not to rely on government for handouts, engage in small business, and so on. Sustainability is about endurance and resiliency. This means constant engagement is needed if the social impact on each of the SDGs is to be realized.

THE RAT PROBLEM: BUREAUCRATS, TECHNOCRATS, AND 'POLITICOCRATS'

We would like to argue that part of the problem resulting in the absence of a role for communication in the last two global development frameworks, that is the MDGs and now the SDGs, were caused by what we would call 'the rat problem,' that is the dominance of bureaucrats, technocrats and what we would neologistically call politicocrats' domination of the table where the development agenda is agreed upon. Communication scholars, media practitioners and other communication players are left in the periphery reporting what the trio of the 'rat' triangle ratified. 'The rat problem' refers to the domination of bureaucrats, technocrats, and politicians in determining the global development agenda at the expense of key stakeholders such as communication experts, civil society, and ordinary members of the global community.

Let's take the SDGs for instance. During the debates about the SDGs, several working groups were formulated to ensure robust consultation. The most prominent among these groups was the 27 member high-level panel to advice on the post-2015 development agenda which culminated into the SDGs. The committee was co-chaired by former British Prime Minister David Cameron, former Liberian President, Allen Johnson Sirleaf, and former President of Indonesia, Susilo Bambang Yudhoyono.

The three co-chairs heading the high-level committee was an example of a typical UN way of thinking, where senior government officials always take the lead in matters of global concern. Being politicians, bureaucrats and technocrats, they did exactly what was expected of them. However, the challenge is when given a task, there is the likelihood of an unconscious bias from the professional background of people which influences their approach to assignments. That is where 'the rat problem' sets in. This can be understood much better when the terms of reference of the *High-Level Panel of Eminent Persons on the Post 2015 Agenda* is reviewed. The second term of reference of the panel suggested the following:

> The High-level Panel will consist of 26 Eminent Persons, including representatives of governments, the private sector, academia, civil society and youth, with the appropriate geographical and gender balance. Panelists are members in their personal capacity. (UN, 2012, para 3)

The terms of reference clearly mentioned governments, civil society, youth, private sector, and the academia as part of groups to be represented in the panel. Journalists, media and communication professionals are clearly missing in the terms of reference. So from the onset, the foundation for the omission of the role for communication in the SDGs has been set. Some might argue that the media can fall into the category of civil society or academia. That argument couldn't hold water looking at the role and diversity of communication in each of the SDGs (see the conclusion of Volume II of this book on the role of communication for each SDG).

The picture becomes clearer when the profiles of the rest of the 27 members of the panel of eminent persons are reviewed (See this link for the profiles https://www.un.org/sg/en/management/hlppost2015.shtml). The similarities in the profiles couldn't be more evident. All the members were existing or former government officials, bureaucrats, technocrats, and politicians. Only one member, Tawakel Kerman Karman, the Yemini journalist, human rights activist, and politician who was awarded the 2011 Nobel Peace Prize had a reference to journalism in her profile. Of course, governments have the right to nominate those who would represent them at the highest level of the UN, but a semblance of balance could have seen information and communication ministers in the high-level panel, since it is government officials who call the shots at the UN.

Having government ministers with an understanding of the role of information and communication in society could have drawn the attention of the UN to the role of communication for development. A case to remember was the role played by Mustapha Masmoudi, former Tunisian Minister of Communication in the 1970s. A statement by Masmoudi strengthened the debate about New World Information and Communication Order (NWICO). Masmoudi stated:

> Information plays an important role in international relations both as means of communication between peoples and as an instrument of understanding and knowledge between nations. This role played by information is all the more important and crucial to present-day international relations in that the international community now possesses thanks to new inventions and technological breakthroughs, sophisticated and very rapid means of communications which makes it possible to transmit information almost instantaneously between regions of the globe. (Masmoudi, 1979, p. 172)

It is quite ironic that in the 1970s during the debate at UNESCO, a UN organ, government bureaucrats had a better understanding of the role of information and communication in society compared to the twenty-first century (Masmoudi, 1979). Masmoudi was speaking in the pre-internet and pre-international satellite age. Yet during the debates on the SDGs, we couldn't find such powerful statements that attracted global attention similar to Masmoudi's in the 1970s.

There are at least four issues raised by Masmoudi in his discussion about NWICO in the 1970s that are relevant to the debate about the SDGs today:

- Information as means of communication between people;
- Information as an instrument of understanding and knowledge between people;
- Technological inventions and breakthroughs;
- Instantaneous transmission of information between regions of the globe.

Let us briefly discuss each of these points in an attempt to highlight the monumental oversight of missing a role for communication in the SDGs.

INFORMATION AS MEANS OF COMMUNICATION BETWEEN PEOPLE

The SDGs were products of exchange and debates between representatives of different nations. What makes the SDGs more unique compared to the MDGs were these broader consultations even if they were dominated by bureaucrats, technocrats, and politicians. This dialogue shouldn't have ended with the formulation of the SDGs. It should be a continues process where lessons are learnt and improvements are made until the goals are achieved. We live in a more interdependent world where no country survives on its own strength alone. What is the vehicle for achieving this continues dialogue? It is information and communication. Nearly half of the SDGs, those pertaining to poverty alleviation, ending hunger, provision of healthcare, sound education, gender equality, inequality, partnerships, climate change and peace and strong institutions, require continuous communication between people for them to be achieved.

INFORMATION AS AN INSTRUMENT OF UNDERSTANDING AND KNOWLEDGE BETWEEN PEOPLE

When you look at SDGs pertaining to the growth of the economy such as those on provision of water and sanitation, affordable energy, decent work and economic growth, industry and innovation, sustainable cities, responsible consumption, life below water and life on land, which are nearly another half of the SDGs, the main medium for exchange of knowledge that helps nations to develop the technical know-how to advance their economies is the power of information and communication. China's leapfrogging, India's advancement in technology, and Singapore's or United Arab Emirates' success in trade are products of knowledge sharing and understanding between people and cultures. That is one reason why the proposition by Servaes (2021) to include communication and culture in the SDGs becomes more pertinent.

TECHNOLOGICAL INVENTIONS AND BREAKTHROUGHS

Perhaps the most noticeable change in the twenty-first century is the breakthrough in technological innovation. Mustapha Masmoudi was speaking before the use of email became public. E-commerce as we know it today was non-existent. In the 1970s, there were no smartphones or social media channels like Facebook or Instagram to name but a few. But he could see the relevance of technology as a tool of information and communication in advancing dialogue. As mentioned in the preface of our previous book (Yusha'u & Servaes, 2021), it is nearly impossible to achieve the SDGs without a clear role for the internet. Some of the chapters in volume II of this book have discussed the challenge that technology has posed to the SDGs especially during the COVID-19 pandemic. SDG3 on health suffered a lot of setbacks due to fake news. People utilize various channels provided by social media to spread rumors in order to discourage people from taking the COVID-19 vaccine. So even for the health and wellbeing of society, SDG18-Commmunication for all, deserves a seat in the 2030 Agenda for development.

Instantaneous Transmission of Information Between Regions of the Globe

Finally, there is recognition of instantaneous transmission of information between regions. A critical look at the last two SDGs, SDG16 on peace, justice and strong institutions, and SDG17 on partnerships for the goals: these are the ambitions where instant communication of information could strengthen relationships between people in various regions. It could also scamper progress toward achieving sustainable peace. The role played by the instruments of communication during the COVID-19 pandemic illustrates the importance of instantaneous transmission of information and communication, for example, the use of internet in education, health, tourism and various other sectors that were seen as a luxury prior to the pandemic have now become necessities. Compared to the time when the debates about NWICO where taking place, the advancement in technology is astronomical in the twenty-first century. Communication is the soul of an information society, and so it should be for the SDGs.

Way Forward

We will propose more recommendations in the conclusion of Volume II of these series. To achieve the SDGs and ensure the inclusion of SDG18, the following proposals should be considered:

- Ensure that key players in media, communication, journalism, and digital technology are at the table when reviewing or agreeing on any future goal.
- UN should reflect more diversity by encouraging countries to nominate information and communication ministers to play a major role in debates about international development. The example cited in some of the chapters on public service media illustrates this point.
- To drive momentum, media organizations, universities and civil society organizations should introduce SDG18-Communication for all awards to encourage more debate about the importance of communication for development.
- Academic and professional journalists should publish serious research backed by data on the role of communication in achieving each of the SDGs.
- Encourage policy makers to push for a clear role for communication during debates on the need for SDG18-Communication for all in the UN, meetings of multilateral institutions, national campaigns, and awareness campaigns which target the public at large.

REFERENCES

Asiedu, C. (2012). Information communication technologies for gender and development in Africa: The case for radio and technological blending. *International Communication Gazette, 74*(2), 240–257.

Britannica. (2022). *Killed, wounded, prisoners or missing.* Retrieved May 22, 2022, from https://www.britannica.com/event/World-War-II/Costs-of-the-war

Coronavirus Centre. (2022). *COVID19 dashboard.* Retrieved May 22, 2022, from https://coronavirus.jhu.edu/map.html

Esser, D. (2017). *Sustainable Development Goals: Elite pluralism, not democratic governance.* Retrieved May 28, 2022, from http://www.bos-cbscsr.dk/2017/11/13/sustainable-development-goals-elite-pluralism-not-democratic-governance/

Godemann, J., & Michelsen, G. (2011). Sustainability communication—An introduction. In J. Godemann & G. Michelsen (Eds.), *Sustainability communication.* Springer. https://doi.org/10.1007/978-94-007-1697-1_1

Masmoudi, M. (1979). The new world information order. *Journal of Communication, 29*(2), 172–179. https://doi.org/10.1111/j.1460-2466.1979.tb02960.x

Melkote, R. M., & Steeves, H. L. (2015). *Communication for development. Theory and practice for empowerment and social justice.* Sage.

Newig, J., et al. (2013). Communication regarding sustainability: Conceptual perspectives and exploration of societal subsystems. *Sustainability, 5*(7), 2976–2990.

Ogan, C. L., et al. (2009). Development communication: The state of research in an era of ICTs and globalization. *The International Communication Gazette, 71*(8), 655–670. 1748-0485.

Pade-Khene, C., Palmer, R., & Kavhai, M. (2010). A baseline study of a Dwesa rural community for the Siyakhula Information and Communication Technology for Development project: Understanding the reality on the ground. *Information Development, 26,* 265.

Servaes, J. (2000). Advocacy strategies for development communication. In J. Servaes (Ed.), *Walking on the other side of the information highway. Communication, culture and development in the 21st century* (pp. 103–118). Southbound.

Servaes, J. (2020). *Handbook of communication for development and social change I & II.* Springer.

Servaes, J. (2021). The Sustainable Development Goals: A major reboot or just another acronym? In M. J. Yusha'u & J. Servaes (Eds.), *The Palgrave handbook of international communication and sustainable development.* Palgrave Macmillan. https://doi.org/10.1007/978-3-030-69770-9_2

Servaes, J., & Malikhao, P. (2007). Communication for sustainable development. In FAO (Eds.), *Communication and sustainable development. Selected papers from the 9th UN roundtable on communication for development.* Retrieved November 22, 2020, from http://www.fao.org/3/a-a1476e.pdf

Servaes, J., & Malikhao, P. (2010). Advocacy strategies for health communication. *Public Relations Review, 36*(1), 42–49. https://doi.org/10.1016/j.pubrev.2009.08.017

Servaes, J., & Wilkins, K. (Eds.). (2015), Advocacy and communication for social change, special issue. *Communication Theory, 25*(2), 177–258. http://onlinelibrary.wiley.com/doi/10.1111/comt.2015.25.issue-2/issuetoc

UN. (2012). The High-Level Panel of Eminent Persons on Post 2015 Agenda. Retrieved May 28, 2022, from https://www.un.org/sg/sites/www.un.org.sg/files/documents/management/ToRpost2015.pdf

White, R. A. (2004). Is 'empowerment' the answer? Current theory and research on development communication. *The Gazette: The International Journal for Communication Studies, 66*(1), 7–24.

Yusha'u, M. J., & Servaes, J. (Eds.). (2021). *The Palgrave handbook of international communication and sustainable development.* Palgrave Macmillan.

Index[1]

A

Activism, ix, 49, 150
Advocacy, 4, 36, 40, 43, 48, 53, 73, 124, 154–157, 168, 170, 188, 287
Africa, xii, 12, 131, 184
African development, xi
Asia, 12, 134, 211, 213, 214
Attention, ix, xi, 18, 27, 45, 52, 67, 68, 73, 75, 77, 112, 114–118, 123–125, 131, 133, 137, 151, 153, 155, 159, 166, 201, 209, 211, 224, 276, 286, 290

B

Bureaucrats, 288–291

C

Children, xiii, 12, 52, 76, 182, 271

Civil society, 12, 14, 28n1, 32, 33, 35, 36, 39–41, 43, 45–49, 53, 65, 67, 68, 73, 76, 132, 151, 154–157, 169, 170, 178, 207, 217, 218, 224, 243, 286, 288, 289, 293
Collective action, 150
Commons, viii, 30, 47–49, 62, 64, 69, 71, 74, 77, 87–100, 111, 117, 121, 129, 136, 150, 154–156, 162, 189, 191, 209, 213, 240, 250
Communicating SDGs, x, 6, 238, 240, 243–260, 287
Communication and culture, 5–8, 135, 291
Communication disability, xiii
Communication for All, viii, x–xiii, 2–18, 28, 45–46, 87, 88, 99, 100, 151, 154–157, 168, 170, 178, 194, 200, 201, 217, 224, 225, 244, 266–278

---

[1] Note: Page numbers followed by 'n' refer to notes.

Communication for development (C4D/CfD), x, 5, 16–17, 29, 30, 87n1, 93, 178, 179, 185–194, 219, 243, 260, 267, 269, 271–278, 285–287, 290, 293

Communication for social change (CSC), 29, 92, 100, 153

Communication rights, viii, xiii, 4, 9, 10, 28n1, 42, 47, 87, 154, 285

Competition, ix, 40, 112, 117–118, 123, 125, 128, 130–132, 136, 137, 169, 213, 286

Corporate Social Responsibility (CSR), 63

Covid-19 pandemic, ix, x, xii–xiv, 6, 7, 10–13, 15, 17, 18, 87, 98, 120, 126, 132, 155, 159, 167, 168, 204, 207–209, 211, 216, 220, 222, 268, 272–275, 284, 286, 287, 292

Crisis communications, xiv

D

Debate, xii, 2, 4, 5, 14, 30, 40, 45, 62, 63, 72, 110, 121, 154, 170, 193, 211, 224, 270, 285, 288, 290–293

Digital capitalism, 87–92, 95, 99

Digital communication, 29, 38–40, 50, 53, 74, 88, 90, 166, 223, 244

Digital inclusion, 7, 8

Disinformation, x, xiii, 17, 50, 73, 74, 119, 120, 168, 200–225, 286, 287

E

Ecosystem, 27, 29, 31, 33, 46–48, 50, 110, 113, 118, 121, 132, 134, 155, 286

Education, 7, 8, 11, 14, 32, 36, 37, 44, 50, 52, 71, 77, 87n1, 109, 134, 151, 154, 186, 208, 210, 217, 220, 225, 237, 240, 243, 247, 250, 270, 287, 291, 292

Environment, viii, xii, 8, 9, 32, 47, 51, 65, 73, 74, 98, 112, 117, 118, 124–128, 130, 136, 155, 157, 166, 180, 184, 191, 217, 239, 250, 255, 287

Europe, 10, 67, 93, 96, 213

Extractive capitalism, viii, 87–100, 285

F

Fake news, x, 17, 50, 73, 74, 116, 120, 121, 184, 200, 202, 204, 205, 212, 214, 216, 221, 286, 292

First Nations, xii

G

Gender equality, xiii, xiv, 28, 30, 33–37, 68, 150, 193, 200, 208, 211–212, 244, 247, 268, 291

Global agenda, viii–xi, 62–77, 167, 272, 275

Global and international communication, 65

Global goals, 63, 182, 285, 286

Governance, ix, 14, 18, 29, 31, 32, 38, 40–42, 48, 49, 52, 64, 72, 73, 118, 178, 207, 244, 245

H

Higher education, 11, 238, 241, 270, 287

Higher Education Institutions (HEIs), 237–260

Human rights, 4, 9, 10, 27, 30, 32, 33, 35, 40, 42, 43, 45, 49, 52, 67, 131, 137, 151, 153, 154, 157, 158, 167, 190, 201–203, 207, 210, 289

I

Impact rankings, x, 239, 241–243, 245, 246, 249, 250, 252, 253, 257–260
Indigenous communication, 47
Indigenous rights, 7, 9–10
Inequality, xii, 10–13, 18, 34, 36, 37, 90, 93, 136, 155, 208, 211–214, 244, 291
Infodemic, 17, 207, 209, 219, 220, 222
Information Communication Technology (ICT), 7, 27, 38–41, 63, 98, 211, 244
Information overload, 109, 111–113, 115, 125, 130, 131, 286
Information poverty, viii, 26–57, 154, 179, 185, 244, 285
Innovation, 8, 28, 33, 37–39, 46, 64, 70, 168, 225, 243, 244, 291
Intercultural communication, 64, 68–72, 76
Intersectionality, xiii, xiv
Intimate Partner Violence (IPV), xiv

L

Language communication, 157
Latin America, xii, 11, 46, 71, 89, 94, 135

M

Masmoudi, Mustapha, 290, 291
Media literacy, x, 26, 29, 30, 36, 40, 44, 50, 151, 154, 178–194, 207, 223, 225, 286
Millennium Development Goals (MDGs), xi, 2–5, 9, 11, 288, 291
Multilingual, xiii

N

New World Information and Communication Order (NWICO), 94, 290, 292
North America, 15, 68

P

Peace, 2, 28, 33, 41–44, 110, 178–194, 214, 215, 243, 244, 246, 268, 291, 292
Performance metrics, x, 237–260
Political communication, 72–77, 225
Political Will, 16, 39
Politicians, 27, 63, 117, 121, 184, 207, 211, 213, 220, 287–289, 291
Post-capitalism, 98
Poverty, xiv, 2, 7, 13, 17, 18, 26, 28, 46, 76, 89, 98, 128, 137, 152, 154, 170, 185, 192, 219, 224, 237, 249, 253, 274, 288, 291
Propaganda, ix, 73, 109, 118–121, 125, 126, 128–133, 136, 183, 194, 203, 204, 207, 221, 286
Public opinion, 16, 27, 49, 63, 64, 66, 72–77, 207
Public relations (PR), ix, 100, 150–158, 165–170, 249
Public Service Media (PSM), xii, 40, 44, 293
Public sphère, xiii, 32, 34, 67, 74, 108, 111, 118, 121, 157
Public value, xii
Public Value Scorecard (PVSC), xii

R

The rat problem, 288–290
Regional perspective, xi–xiv

S

Scarce attention, 115–117, 286

Self-determination, 9, 13, 52, 170

Six forces, ix, 110–113, 123, 125, 127–137, 286

Social change, xi, 5, 7, 10, 16, 17, 27, 29–31, 50, 77, 87n1, 88, 96, 98, 99, 152–154, 156, 156n2, 168, 169, 192, 219, 266–278, 286

Social media, ix, x, xiii, 10, 44, 52, 63–65, 67, 68, 70, 74, 75, 77, 110–114, 116, 119–121, 123, 129–130, 158, 159, 166, 169, 183, 188–191, 203, 204, 206, 209–212, 214–217, 221, 222, 245, 253, 254, 257, 259, 266, 271, 273, 285, 292

Social movement, 40, 64, 65, 74, 75, 92, 96, 100, 150, 152, 155, 156, 158, 163, 169, 207

Sovereignty, 113, 117

Strategic communication, ix, xi, 45, 150, 249, 286

Sustainability, xii, 7–9, 27, 33, 63, 67, 68, 71, 72, 75–77, 98, 99, 136, 137, 169, 193, 239, 240, 242, 245, 249, 251, 252, 259, 268, 277, 284–293

Sustainable development, viii, xiii, 4, 7, 9, 11, 13, 14, 27, 28, 30–31, 33, 34, 39, 41, 42, 45, 46, 67, 72, 87n1, 88, 92–98, 100, 134, 136, 151, 153, 154, 157, 193, 201, 208, 217, 223, 225, 237, 239, 240, 243, 244, 267–269, 271, 274–278, 285, 286

Sustainable Development Goals (SDG)
SDG1, 71, 239, 249, 253
SDG2, 17, 71, 239, 246, 249

SDG3, xiii, 17, 71, 132, 168, 208–209, 239, 242, 246, 253, 292

SDG4, 17, 27, 36, 50, 71, 208, 210, 238, 239, 242, 243, 246

SDG5, 17, 27, 28, 33–35, 71, 168, 193, 208, 211–212, 238, 239, 244, 247, 286

SDG6, 17, 71, 239

SDG7, 71, 239

SDG8, 71, 238, 239, 250

SDG9, 27, 28, 33, 37–39, 71, 193, 239, 244

SDG10, 11, 71, 208, 212–214, 239, 247

SDG11, 71, 239, 242, 251

SDG12, 71, 237, 239, 243

SDG13, xiii, 71, 132, 208, 214–215, 239, 243, 247

SDG14, 71, 239

SDG15, 71, 239

SDG16, 6, 12, 27, 28, 33, 41–45, 71, 178, 193, 208, 215, 238, 239, 243, 244, 246, 292

SDG17, 27, 28, 33, 37–39, 71, 193, 239, 242, 244, 292

SDG18, ix–xiv, 13–14, 18, 26–57, 87–92, 150, 168, 178, 179, 182, 191–194, 201, 244, 245, 257–260, 266–278, 284–293

T

Target audiences, 164–165, 169

Technocrats, 132, 288–291

2030 Agenda, ix, 2, 6, 9, 13, 14, 17, 26–28, 37, 41, 52, 87, 88, 151, 153–155, 157, 158, 165–167, 169, 170, 182, 210, 237, 243, 256, 284–286, 292

U

Ukraine, 10–13, 15, 119

United Nations Educational, Scientific, and Cultural Organization (UNESCO), 4, 5, 7, 35, 46, 94, 204, 205, 210, 217, 219, 220, 223, 290

United Nations (UN), xi, 4–7, 11, 15–17, 26, 27, 33, 35, 37, 53, 62, 76, 88–91, 154, 158, 182, 190, 201, 203, 207, 208, 210–214, 216, 237, 239, 242, 256, 257, 260, 272, 284, 287, 289, 290, 293

Universities, x, 6, 11, 134, 218, 237–243, 245–257, 259, 266, 269, 271, 274, 287, 288, 293

University rankings, 236, 242

W

World Health Organization (WHO), 11, 17, 207–209, 220

CPSIA information can be obtained
at www.ICGtesting.com
Printed in the USA
LVHW021807090423
743867LV00005B/920